GUILD & STATE

GUILD_&
STATE

European Political Thought from the
Twelfth Century to the Present

Antony Black

With a new preface, introduction
and conclusion by the author

Transaction Publishers
New Brunswick (U.S.A.) and London (U.K.)

Fourth printing 2009

New material this edition copyright © 2003 by Transaction Publishers, New Brunswick, New Jersey. Originally published in 1984 by Methuen & Co. Ltd.

This book is printed on acid-free paper that meets the American National Standard for Permanence of Paper for Printed Library Materials.

Library of Congress Catalog Number: 2002072678
ISBN: 978-0-7658-0978-0
Printed in the United States of America

Library of Congress Cataloging-in-Publication Data

Black, Antony.
  [Guilds and civil society in European political thought from the twelfth century to the present]
  Guild and state : European political thought from the twelfth century to the present / Antony Black ; with a new preface, introduction, and conclusion by the author, p. cm.
  Originally published: Guilds and civil society in European political thought from the twelfth century to the present. London : Methuen, 1984.
  Includes bibliographical references and index.
  ISBN 0-7658-0978-8 (pbk.: alk. paper)
    1. Corporate state—History. 2. Political science—Europe—History. 3. Guilds—Europe—History. 4. Labor unions—Europe—History. 5. Civil society—Europe—History. I. Title.

JC478 .B43 2003
306'.094'0902—dc21   2002072678

To my Colleagues, at Dundee and Elsewhere, Present and Past

CONTENTS

vii

PREFACE TO THE
TRANSACTION EDITION

This is a history of medieval and modern political thought from the viewpoint of the guild and the values that have been associated with it. It is a history of the idea of the corporate organisation of labour and how it does or does not tie in with theories of the state. I have examined both the writings of philosophers and everyday beliefs.

This is intended for the general reader as well as the specialist, and for the student as well as the professional scholar. It presents new evidence and new interpretations. And I believe the wider public implications are important.

I set out on this work during the 1960s and 1970s partly because, as a convert to Catholicism with a socialist soul, I wanted to uncover an authentic European past that would combine Christian piety with a political praxis based on 'the people' and *their* values. Among other things, it aspired to be a counter-Marxist and counter-secular account of European development. No doubt it was my English public school past that made me renew this agenda of certain nineteenth-century romantics. But I hope the results transcend these origins.

This may also explain in part why, as will become only too obvious, this book at times straddles both the history of ideas and prescriptive political thought. Provided I have not obscured the boundary, I make no apology for this. In the end, this book turns out to be almost a history of 'the third way.'

I am surprised, on revisiting topics after some twenty years, at how much I left unsaid and how many implications of my research I failed to bring out clearly. I am therefore deeply grateful to my friend Cary Nederman for telling me about Transaction Publishers, and to Irving Louis Horowitz of Transaction Publishers for his encouragement in publishing this reissue.

Guilds and Civil Society (as the first edition was called) was published by Methuen; I am grateful to Janice Price for the interest she showed in it. Soon afterwards Methuen became part of Routledge and the book went out of print. Some scholars continued to express interest, or even wanted to buy it, although it had become unobtainable. *Habent sua fata libelli.*

My interest in the history of political thought was inspired by Walter Ullmann, a great man and an amazing teacher. In writing this book I am indebted to James Cameron for reassurance in a moment of disillusion; to Michael Wilks who enthusiastically supported the project; and to my friend Joe Canning who showed me around the medieval jurists. I want to thank those who took the trouble to read and comment on various chapters: John Mundy and Peter King (chs 1-5), Janet Coleman (ch. 3), Joe Canning and Peter Stein (parts of chs 2,4,6), David Luscombe (parts of chs 4,6,7), Quentin Skinner (chs 5,8), Harro Höepfl (chs 9-11), Richard Tuck (chs 10-13), Iain Hampsher-Monk (chs 12-13), William Walker and Chris Whatley (ch. 14), Hans Reiss (chs 16-18), Basil O'Neill (chs 16-17), and Neil Cooper (Appendix). For this reissue, I want to thank Richard Dunphy, Robert von Friedeburg, Chris Storrs, and Jim Tracy for their comments on the Introduction; and Brian Baxter and Nick Hopkins for their comments on the Conclusion. I have not been able to meet all their points and any mistakes that remain are my own.

I would like to thank all those with whom I have discussed these topics over many years, especially Peter Blickle, Mauro Calise, Jonathan Chaplin (who spotted my old-fashioned use of 'civil society': see below, pp. xv-xvi), Gerhard Dilcher, Wolfgang Mager, Cary Nederman, Otto Gerhard Oexle, Diego Quaglioni, Chris Storrs, and Jim Tracy.

It is tragic that, in the era of the European Union, scholars seem more divided by language barriers than 100 years ago. Scholarship is becoming globalised through the wider use of English, but all too often we simply do not read what scholars in our own field are writing in other languages. Let us oppose this appalling trend.

I want to thank my colleagues in the Department of Politics at the University of Dundee, in other departments here, and in many other places. This re-issue is dedicated them. We in our profession are enormously lucky in the sheer comradeship that our work can generate. May we long drink together from the same wells and barrels.

I would like to thank the University Libraries of Dundee, especially the inter-library loans staff, St. Andrews (especially Mr. Hargreaves of the Rare Books section), Edinburgh, and Cambridge; and the Cambridge college libraries of Trinity (especially Mr. Kaye), Gonville and Caius, and St. John's. I am very grateful to the Nuffield Foundation for a research fellowship in 1980-81, which enabled me to range more widely and compose with fewer distractions; and to Ann Aitken, formerly a secretary in our department, who generously helped me with typing.

It is a privilege to be able to revisit one's work, and to revisit in my mind the little garden study where I wrote the first edition. My four older children—Stephen, Thomas, Esther, and Matthew, who played in that garden as I wrote—and now my younger son Christopher have all helped to keep me partly sane.

Style

I have used the author-date system of reference for all secondary works. Primary works are referred to by title (and author when this is not obvious from the context). 'Cit. Bloggs...' indicates that a primary source is quoted in a secondary work by Bloggs. I have listed medieval and renaissance authors by their second names except where there is a strong contrary convention.

INTRODUCTION TO THE
TRANSACTION EDITION

I embarked on this research with the intention of recovering an older, atavistic notion of community, of endorsing its legitimacy by proving its antiquity, and of reintroducing the modern reader to the affective language of Europe's communal heritage. The notion of tightly knit, affective community is notoriously alluring to modern westerners; we tend to associate it with an ideal past, and to see in its restoration a focus for our hopes for a better society. It is an ideal which liberals, socialists, and conservatives can, each in their own way, espouse. Great scholars like Gierke and Michaud-Quantin seemed to point the way. But the spirits of Karl Popper and Quentin Skinner stood impishly at my elbow. The facts of cultural and intellectual history moved at a tangent to the myth that liberal individualism has steadily replaced a strong sense of community. The diverse themes of the present book are the result.

I focused on the guild partly because it seemed especially characteristic of pre-modern Europe, and because it harnessed in a precise way the communal values of brotherhood, friendship, and mutual aid. Though I did not know it at the time, Peter Blickle was at the same time embarking on a study of town and village communities in medieval and early modern Europe. He sees these as forming a distinctive type of direct grass-roots democracy which he calls Kommunalismus (Blickle 2000, 1996), and he believes that this was once far more widespread than we think.

Yet at the same time I became surprised at how early the ideals of individual liberty and security of person and property, maintained by equality under the law (see below, pp. 32-8; Black 2001b), became current and, indeed, were enthusiastically championed. I labelled these the values of 'civil society.' I thought this a convenient term because Hegel had used it to describe a kind of society (*buergerliche Gesellschaft*: civic or civil society) in which individuals cohabit peacefully and lawfully, but primarily in order to be able to pursue their own individual ends (Michael Oakeshott called this *societas*: *On Human Conduct*, ch. 3). I deliberately excluded Hegel's value-judgement to the effect that in this context people are behaving selfishly. Marx interpreted such a society, which translators of Marx tend

xv

to render 'bourgeois society,' as the inevitable concomitant of capitalism, thus greatly emphasising its negative features. But, just as I was writing, civil society was acquiring a new meaning that was in part different, and which it has retained ever since: namely, a range of social bodies for the protection and promotion of people's intellectual, economic, and other interests (Kaviraj and Khilnani 2001). The implication is that such institutions in the nature of modern society are, or ought to be, separate from the political order of the state. In this respect civil society implies something similar to that of sphere sovereignty (below, p. 244). These two senses are connected, however, in that the institutions of civil society in the second sense generally underpin the values of 'civil society' in the first sense.

I have examined the views held about guilds both by their own members and by jurists and philosophers (chs 1-2, 10-11). I have attempted to do the same for their nearest modern equivalents: trade unions and corporations (chs 14, 19). But, right from the twelfth century, I have set this against the contrapuntal values of the free market and bourgeois liberalism (ch. 3). Many social theorists have of course contrasted two such types of society, the one centred on the community, the other on the individual, the clearest example being Tonnies' *Gemeinschaft und Gesellschaft* (*Community and Association* or, in a recent translation, *Civil Society*) (Toennies 1887/2001). Similarly, Ibn Khaldun (1332-1406) contrasted 'primitive' culture (*badawa*) with citied life (*hadara*) on the basis that the former has much stronger 'group feeling (*'asabiyya*)' (Black 2001a, ch. 18).

Previous theorists, however, seldom envisaged that it might be possible, and even desirable, to bring these two types together. This offends modern notions of consistency. Aristotle, however, argued that it is quite reasonable to combine different principles—in his case, democracy and oligarchy—in politics. This is what, in fact, I found happening in many European milieux from the twelfth century onwards. Various combinations of guild-like solidarity with market freedoms were expressed in social and political theory by, for example, Marsiglio and Althusius (both, incidentally, strongly influenced by Aristotle), and later by Hegel and Durkheim.

The argument of this book was primarily that only by considering both these sets of beliefs together—guilds and 'civil society'—can we fully understand the political culture and philosophy of medieval and modern Europe; or estimate the relative historical importance of either strand. In other words, I investigate how far one can use both guild and civil society (in the above sense) as explanatory tools for understanding the genesis of European *political* thought: how far ideas about political organisation and its purposes *either* sprang from *or* replicated these values. This was perhaps not as clear as it should have been in the first edition: hence the change of title.

It has become fashionable to see the development of 'modern political theory,' and even of 'the modern state,' as being almost synonymous with the development of liberal individualism, both in the sense of the individual's practical emancipation from feudal or collective ties and in the sense of the ideology of individual rights. This view may be traced back to (at least) the Enlightenment; it has recently received new support and wider diffusion through the work of Quentin Skinner and others (Brett 1997, Tierney 1997, Skinner 1998, Hamilton-Bleakley 2002). One example is the quite disproportionate attention given to John Locke—important though he undoubtedly was—in current historiography (see Black 1997b). It is, moreover, often asserted that it was precisely this liberal individualism which differentiated Europe from other cultures.

I argue that guilds and cities, and the corporate values associated with them, were also an integral part of the formation of early-modern European states, and of their legitimation. They were, furthermore, the first and original basis for the theory and practice of popular democratic government in Europe. In Athens and Rome a somewhat similar function was perhaps performed by the 'tribes.' One thing that distinguished medieval from ancient democracy was, therefore, the role of labour organisations in the polity. Indeed, if we compare Europe with other pre-modern civilisations generally, the *political* role of guilds was, to my knowledge, peculiar to Europe. It too should therefore be included in any explanation of European difference.

It was the widespread diffusion of guilds, and also of village and town communes, and the participation of craft-guilds in city government, which, alongside the development of markets and the freedoms associated with these, facilitated a decisive move away from feudalism. The individual achieved his liberty in and through his incorporation into guild and civic structures; this gave Europe its first post-feudal states. On the other hand, cities continued to assert seigneurial rights over the countryside.

Guilds and cities were part of a wider corporate culture. The Church adopted the Roman-law collegium and transformed it by applying to it the early-Christian norms of election and consent (Black 1997a). In Latin Christendom, from the eleventh century onwards, there was a blossoming of corporate bodies, such as cathedral and monastic chapters (including the college of cardinals) and the new orders of friars. Superiors were elected, major decisions required consent by the chapter, church properties were collectively owned and administered (Tierney 1955, Black 1979).

Smaller towns and villages established themselves as oath-bound *communia* in many parts of Europe, with their own courts, elected officials, and general assemblies of, at least, well-established householders. Such communities administered collective assets such as streets and bakeries, oversaw crop rotation, and settled minor economic disputes. Parishes, sometimes organised as confraternities, played an important role (Bossy 1985, Genicot 1990).

Medieval Latin Christendom was, broadly speaking, communitarian without being collectivist (Nederman 1992). In religious terms, individual choice was the ultimate key to salvation (as in Islamdom). The way a theologian such as Thomas Aquinas defined the relationship between individual and society reflects fairly accurately this synthesis between guild and civil society (Gilby 1958:241-56, Black 1988:599-601).

Blickle, as we have seen, has identified the political culture of these smaller towns and villages as 'communalism' (not to be confused with communalism in today's sense of separate religious or ethnic groupings in society). His model is at times too essentialist and idealised: it disregards local variations and internal strife (Schilling 1988 and 1992, Scribner 1994, Friedeburg 2001). It suggests more ideological coherence than there actually was. Critics of Blickle also point out that these 'communes' (not of course to be likened to modern groups of that name, such as the Paris Commune of 1870-71) often ruled over neighbouring localities and treated their inhabitants as feudal subjects (Brady 1978, Scott 1986). In general, they argue, one should not assimilate this communal mentality to the republican values associated with the Renaissance and the English Civil War (Pocock 1975, Viroli 1992).

But the issue here is perhaps more complex than either Blickle or his critics have so far allowed. In early Renaissance Italy the terms *commune* and *respublica* were used interchangeably to describe a self-governing city (Bruckner 1977, Najemy 1982). Very often the same political entities (self-governing towns), procedures (oligarchic or democratic), and values (the common good, liberty) were simply being expressed in different languages (Black 1992:4-12), depending on whether the writer was a town clerk, a jurist, a 'humanist' trained in neo-classical (i.e. Ciceronian) Latin, or a 'scholastic' versed in the arts curriculum and Aristotle. It may even have depended on whether he was using the vernacular or Latin. Bartolus made a heroic attempt to bridge the gap between Aristotle and Roman law (below, pp. 83-4)—but he was a genius.

Our perception of all this is skewed because after the Reformation neo-classical Latin became the dominant mode for expressing republican ideas (for example, Clemens Jaeger, below, pp. 114-20). Renaissance literati tended to ignore small towns and villages, either because these were culturally alien to their largely aristocratic or big-business milieux, or because such modest entities did not fit into their romantic neo-Roman paradigm.

Nor was early-modern republicanism necessarily more democratic than medieval communalism. Many neo-classical republicans preferred government 'by the best' to 'by the many.' The fact that city-states and communal regions (such as the Grisons in Switzerland) ruled over feudal subjects may not make them fundamentally different from ancient Athens, modern England, Netherlands, or the USA. Rights have continued to be applied selectively even after being proclaimed 'universal.' Rome stands out because it extended citizenship—legal, not political—to outsiders. Blickle may have overstated his case, but he has at least drawn attention to phenomena which others have overlooked.

The connection between guild and polity was especially pronounced in the medieval cities. We consider first the mentality of the inhabitants of towns (chs 4-5). Medieval political philosophy, on the other hand, laid much greater emphasis on the values of civil society (ch. 6). This must qualify the conventional view of 'the Middle Ages' as a predominantly communitarian culture: it depends where you look. Marsiglio, however, welded the two themes together in a novel and extraordinary way (ch. 7).

The canon and civil lawyers meanwhile developed principles for the government of corporations that can now be seen as the first statement of direct, participatory democracy (Tierney 1955 and 1982). This 'corporation theory' was applied to the church as a whole in support of the authority of general councils over the pope. The conciliar movement (1378-1449) was the first 'parliamentarian' episode in European history; for a moment it looked as if constitutionalism and representative government might become the norm (Black 1970, 1979). Civil society, on the other hand, made triumphal progress during the Renaissance (ch. 8). The values of guild and commune renewed their strength in the Reformation (ch. 9). The conventional view of the Reformation as libertarian and individualist obviously needs qualification (Blickle 1985/1992, Brady 1998).

A true philosophy of guilds eventually emerged in Bodin and Althusius (ch. 11). The two strands of guild and civil society—each of which straddled the economy as well as the polity—throw light on the foundations of modern political theory. State and nation were conceptualised not only, as Pocock and Skinner have rightly emphasised, in terms of neo-classical humanism, but also in terms of corporate, sometimes explicitly guild, values, and—to extend C.B. Macpherson's argument—in terms of the values of market exchange, which, however, seem to bind together as well as to differentiate participants (chs 12-13). Moreover, we discover that the theory of a social contract that defines and limits the role of political authority was first developed in the corporation theory of the jurists. They applied it in particular to the mercantile *societas* (partnership), and then by analogy to the state (ch. 12 below, Black 1993). Rousseau's theory of the social contract theory may be seen as an attempt to make civic corporatism the vehicle for individual liberty—the Swiss and south-German model.

Meanwhile, during the seventeenth and eighteenth centuries, French society and government became permeated by 'an extraordinary variety' of corporations, from craft guilds to professional *collèges* (Revel 1987:226-31). According to one observer (writing in 1776, perhaps influenced by Rousseau), these communities

> can be considered as small republics, uniquely occupied with the general interest of all the members who compose them; and, if it is true that the general interest is made up of the sum of the interests of each particular individual, it is equally true that each member, in working for his truly personal advantage (*utilite*), necessarily, without even wishing it, works for the truly general advantage of the whole community (cit. Revel 1987:228).

This applied republican language to the corporations themselves; it expressed the notion of the 'hidden hand' usually associated with Adam Smith (whose *Wealth of Nations* was also published in 1776). The French monarchy gave corporations privileges in return for long-term credit; indeed it came to rely on 'corporate structures and monopolies to finance the state' (Bossenga 1991: 5-7; Andress 1999:35). This alliance between corporations and absolute monarchy vindicated Bodin's view of the role of *corps et collèges* within a sovereign state (below, pp. 130-31).

Guild values of brotherhood, and the corporate protection of producers, were taken up in the nineteenth century among early trade unions (ch. 14), and by advocates of 'co-operation' or co-operative socialism (ch. 15). The most dramatic development of guild ideals, however, was undertaken by the Romantics, and then by Hegel, Gierke, and Tönnies. While liberal values dominated French and British political thought, communal ones shaped the perception of association, corporation, and nation-state in Germany (chs 16-18). The most articulate exposition ever undertaken of the community of labour was in the modern corporatist movement, itself influenced by the Romantic movement and Hegel. Durkheim, the most outstanding exponent of the moral community of labour in this school, gave it a quasi-scientific basis in sociology (ch. 19).

The European tradition of communal self-government was transported across the Atlantic with the first English settlers. This was due very largely to the Congregationalist ethos of the religious emigres; their notions of socio-political authority were a lightly secularised version of the covenant between God and the people of (new) Israel (Miller 1939, Black 1997a). The first North American towns were also transplanting the European tradition of municipal self-government (Fiske 1899; see below, pp. 150-51), underpinned by the value of fraternity (McWilliams 1973).

A serious omission from the first edition was a more specific destiny of the corporation in North America, and in the USA today. As Lustig puts it, 'a corporation came to America aboard the Mayflower' and many of the colonies—the future states of the Union—'began their existence as corporations' (Lustig 1982:46). Mauro Calise is charting, in greater subtlety and depth than I can suggest here, the institutional continuity between the medieval corporation of the European guild and city and the modern multinational corporation in America. As he puts it, 'modern American corporations (are) the descendants of their European ancestor' (Calise 1994:33); 'the development of the modern corporation as the master institution of American life' is 'an evolution of the medieval pattern of corporate authority, a pattern of pluralism and diffusion of political power' (Calise 2002:2).

In general, twentieth-century democratic countries obviously maintain elements of the medieval commune in the role given to local communities as an integral part in the polity, especially in federal states. Attempts are being made to introduce a similar element throughout the European Union by encouraging the devolution of power to the lowest practicable level, in accordance with the principle of subsidiarity (Norr and Oppermann 1997, Blickle et al. 2002).

Recent communitarian critiques of liberal democracy (Sandel 1998, Nederman 1992) could find some support in the argument of this book (although some of them use the liberal story of Western political development as part of their argument: Nisbet 1953). Above all, those engaged in current political debates might like to note that liberal individualism developed for the most part out of communal milieux; and that at least some political philosophers saw the two as complementary rather than mutually exclusive.

The intellectual phenomena and strategies of sentiment highlighted in this book throw up questions about the origins of European difference, and about the development of modernity, capitalism, individualism, and the modern state. First, let us recall the need for a comparative study of history. It ought never to be forgotten that all attempts to find causal connections between the modern state or modern political thought and what went before, are largely intuitive until one can corroborate them by finding that, in other histories, like causes produced like effects, or their absence produced different effects. Alas, scholarship has 'progressed' beyond the point where one scholar, even a Max Weber, could undertake such a task on his or her own. Even Peter Blickle blanched before the prospect; his third volume, which was to deal with Communalism outside Europe, will never be written. The routinisation and competitive ethos of scholarship (promoted in Britain by the government's 'research assessment exercise') do not encourage genuine collaboration among scholars.

The scholarly world has not so far produced a comparative study of the role and influence of guilds in different civilisations. This would have made it easier to estimate their importance in the development of Europe (Black 1996).

At a cursory glance one may say that in China, India, and the Arabo-Islamic world, and especially in the Ottoman Empire (Inalcik 1973:150-62), guilds, or something like them, flourished. In the Ottoman Empire, reforming bureaucrats even proposed a kind of corporatist programme: the empire will only revive, some said, if people stick to the age-old ideal (of Indo-Iranian origin, in fact) of the four-fold division of society into the learned, warriors, merchants, cultivators. Unlike in Europe (and of course India), it was implied that these four 'pillars of society' were equal in value and status. As well as stability, what was needed above all was reciprocity between these; the needs of cultivators were stressed (Black 2001a:262-5). The widespread diffusion of craft-guilds cannot, therefore, in itself be part of an explanation for the rise of the modern polity or of capitalism. European guilds were, however, unique in their *constitutional* structure, their legal personality, and their formal incorporation into civic polities. Like cities themselves and parliaments, they had formal constitutions, established procedures, could issue regulations, and their members were formally equal in decision-making rights.

On the other hand, it does look as if the early development of the values of 'civil society' differentiated Europe from other cultures. These values were not found in anything like the same frequency in any other pre-modern culture. In the Muslim world, for example, craft production and long-distance trade, which had once flourished earlier than in Europe, went into stagnation or decline, and this may partly have been brought about by the development of 'military patronage states' (Hodgson 1974 iii:25-7) in response to the Mongol invasions of the thirteenth century. From about that time, merchants who accumulated wealth seem to have been more subject to arbitrary confiscations by the sultan or other representatives of the military-agricultural complex than they were in Europe.

Was there in Europe, partly as a result of the guild ethos and its legitimation, greater self-esteem among skilled manual workers? Were craft skills accorded greater social esteem in society at large? In the Arabo-Islamic world one has the impression that military and religious personnel determined the social tone to a much greater degree. Crucially perhaps, in the late-medieval and renaissance cities and city-states of Italy, Germania, and the Netherlands, a mercantile aristocracy or haute bourgeoisie became dominant and acquired political control. Some of these, and many of the artists and lawyers they employed, were guild members. (The products of guildsmen often amounted to works of art, but not only in Europe).

There is another way in which guilds and guild-like groups may have played a part in the transition to a modern society, polity, and economy. The small face-to-face group plays a unique role in human life and action. This was, after all, the social setting in which humans evolved; in terms of self-esteem and social psychology it is probably next in importance after the family. Olson argued rather convincingly that, in cost-benefit terms, the 'logic of collective action' differs fundamentally between the small and large group: for the rational maximizer, participation in small-group activities pays off, whereas in large-group activities it does not (1965:2,33,62). Hence small groups do not depend so much on coercion as large ones but can rely on 'the voluntary self-interested action of the members' (34). It has been suggested that in most enterprises, including many businesses, key decisions tend to be shared between very small groups of, say, three to four people at the top; the same is often observed in governments.

Now one of the crucial differences between tribal clan society and modern civil society and the modern state is the social scale: in the latter face-to-face relationships become progressively less important. As a small face-to-face group, the guild perpetuated some of the characteristics of primitive tribal human association. Such groups may have, therefore, eased the transition from the close personal bonds of clan and tribe to the dispersed and impersonal relationships of modern society and the state. To be sure, this would require stronger ties than we find in a 'voluntary association' today: guilds were bound together by mutual oaths (Prodi 1992:199-214) and employed severe sanctions. In Durkheimian language, then, such groups could have provided a vital link between the segmental and the organic forms of society. This role of small groups seems largely to have escaped the notice of moral political theorists of all schools. Of course the everlasting question is whether such groups confer advantages or disadvantages on *non-members* (see Olson 1982).

It is true that guilds declined, at least in England, well before the industrial revolution. But the view that guilds in general obstructed economic growth (Olson 1982) has recently been challenged (Munro 1999, Epstein 2000). It has also been argued that 'the corporate character of urban government was one of the necessary preconditions for the emergence of long-term debt' (James Tracy, personal communication; and see Tracy forthcoming). Besides, in seventeenth- and eighteenth-century England the guilds' organisational traditions were to some extent taken over by religious sects such as the Congregationalists and Quakers. These too were face-to-face groups, operating partly on meritocratic principles and according to members' estimates of each other's personal qualities; they too empowered members through general meetings (Troeltsch ii 726).

Neither Marx nor Weber attached much explanatory significance to this peculiarly rich communal mix. The one social theorist who *did* ascribe historic importance to guilds was Otto Gierke (Black 1990, Oechsle 1988). For him they were important partly as a Germanic substratum in a rapidly Romanising society, but also because they along with other groups embodied the fundamental human value of *Genossenschaft* (fellowship-comradeship as well as just association).

But perhaps the most important factor when considering European difference was precisely the legacy of the incorporated and internally democratic small group (the collegium of Roman and canon law), to which we have referred above. For this was taken over by capitalists and served as the basis for the joint-stock company and the public limited company—corporate bodies with legal personality, approved by common law, whose constitutions provide for elected office-bearers and annual general meetings (below, pp. 151-2, Black 1993). It was surely these bodies that made possible the investment strategies which, from the East Indies to New England, precipitated the take-off of capitalism, by providing a secure legal basis on which men with money and talent could pool their resources. The corporation was a wonderfully flexible instrument for any kind of joint enterprise (as a business colleague in a voluntary organisation once pointed out to me). Corporations seem, therefore, to have been crucial both for the organisation of labour and for the investment of capital; they underpinned the upper as well as the lower end of the political economy.

Thus, if Weber's *Protestant Ethic* (Weber 1904-5/1930) suggests one explanation for the rise of modern industrial society in terms of personal motivation, the corporation suggests an explanation in terms of microsocial organisation. Indeed, one must remember (since it is so often overlooked) that before there was a Protestant ethic, there was a Christian ethic and a Roman-republican ethic; both enjoined scrupulous adherence to worldly duties for the sake of personal salvation, and/or one's public image. (This is obvious in Dante's *Inferno*.) Duty in this context meant, most obviously, public service or devotion to the common good—service of one's community, religious, political, or both. Exactly the same kind of sentiment was found in early Islam; for example, a Caliph was reminded that he should devote every waking hour to the welfare of the community because he was going to be judged strictly for this (Black 2001a:25). Weber's argument survives this criticism of anticipation, however, in that neither medieval Christianity nor republicanism promoted worldly asceticism in the sense he gave it.

In general, however, both laid down patterns of behaviour that encouraged (among other things) the careful calculation of long-term economic gain to be achieved by unremitting hard work. More obviously, they promoted behaviour friendly to the development of the *state* as a community in which all were united spiritually as well as for material ends (like stones in a house, as Girolami put it: below, p. 78, Black 1988:596-7). The state (*respublica*, commonwealth) was the vehicle of a common good to which all were obliged to contribute on religious-ethical grounds. Lasting honour and true glory are to be found in its service, said both pseudo-Aquinas and Leonardo Bruni (Black 1988: 605-6). In fact the idea that the pursuit of private interest serendipitously promotes the public weal was enunciated for politics before it was for economics. Of course political stability was then as now a prerequisite for economic growth.

Alongside the motivated individual-family entrepreneur, another characteristic crucial for understanding European difference was precisely that *combination* of guild and civil society, identified above as central to European political culture. Here were combined, on the one hand, market freedom, security of property rights, enforceable contracts, and, on the other, security of person, property, *and employment* for artisans, to be achieved through their own collective structures. This was a new social order. It was helped by the independence gained for religious organisations from feudal nobles during the Investiture Controversy (below, pp. 62-3). Thus the military-agricultural complex (which European historians reify as 'feudalism' [Reynolds 1994] and which existed in all contemporary civilisations but without some of the specific features attributed to feudalism) was fractured. Independent cities developed in the cracks. At precisely the same time the European economy began to take off. This new order found expression in the concepts of *universitas* and *civitas* that are discussed below.

All of these questions obviously need much more examination. To invoke comparison once more, we find neither internally self-governing nor independent *cities* in other major civilisations of this period. Nor do we find the *combination* of the strategies of guild and civil society elsewhere.

It seemed best to leave methodology to the Appendix, in the belief that people prefer to sample the pudding before reading the recipe. A few remarks must, however, be made at the outset. Objectivity is notoriously difficult in the history of ideas. The subject matter of this book is laden with moral overtones; few if any of the sources studied were morally or politically uncommitted. But I have attempted to be objective and empirical in assessing evidence, describing viewpoints, and drawing conclusions. It was through testing contrary hypotheses that the twin emphases of this work emerged. I have been sufficiently excited by the beauty of the sources positively to enjoy the shock of discovering that the truth was unpredictable. It is difficult to study any great thinker without falling under the spell of his writings; but I dare to hope that even here I have been impartial, if that is possible, in my affections. I reserve the right, nevertheless, at the end to draw a moral out of the story, distinct from the story itself. The reader will be inclined to draw his or her own moral anyway, and it is perhaps as well that they should know mine, and that I should state explicitly what I have almost certainly occasionally implied by tone of voice. Weber was right that one cannot exclude a kind of moral judgement from one's choice of theme: in the human sciences scholars will choose topics they find 'culturally significant.' Nor can one alter the tone of one's voice. The best way is to try sincerely to appreciate different viewpoints.

'Political thought' here covers everything from popular culture (*mentalité*) to scholastic philosophy. I distinguish between ethos (the spontaneous convictions of everyday life), ideology (the *ad hoc* presentation of a case—political advocacy), and philosophy (the systematic, rational examination of political norms): clearly, there are many overlaps (see Appendix). Since Gierke, it seems to me that not enough attention has been paid to this, except for the *Annales* school, which focused on popular *mentalités*. One needs always to ask whether there were similarities or differences between ideas held in various sections of society, and especially between those held in the population at large and among various elites, including the learned elite. These may or may not vary more than one presupposes, but let us at least examine the question. The more one does so, it seems, the less one is inclined to generalise about 'medieval' political thought, or about any period or culture.

In Europe (in intellectual history the relevant cultural entity is more often Europe than individual nations) the Romanization of high culture from around 1050 led to divergence between popular and elite political conceptions. This was Gierke's historical insight—and dogma. There is more truth in it than is often recognised. There appear to have been similar divergences in all literate cultures (Bulliet 1994). This was doubtless the price of intellectual development. The two drifted further apart during the Renaissance, then came together during the Reformation. They diverged once more during the Enlightenment; again, one may say, the price of progress. One of the ideals of the Romantic movement was of course to bridge the gulf.

There were many interactions between high and popular culture. In pre-modern times, the visual arts and drama tended to close the gap, much as fiction can do in the modern world. Popular culture did not (pace Gierke and Marx) set itself up as an alternative to elite culture. Working-class writers, whether in Germany during the Reformation or Britain during the industrial revolution, were quick to absorb high culture and to adopt its language.

PART I

FROM 1050 TO
THE REFORMATION

In the first part, we shall consider the development of guilds in general and of craft-guilds in particular (ch.1), and the ethos enshrined in them, together with learned writings about them, which are virtually confined to the great medieval jurists (ch.2). Then we shall consider the emergence of an opposite set of values focused upon personal liberty and market exchange (ch.3). From then on, we shall be chiefly concerned with ideas about political institutions and structures in so far as these appear to reflect the influence of one or the other of these patterns of thought. This will take us, first, to the early urban communes, to the development of civic life and some kind of civic culture in Europe (ch.4); then to the craft 'revolutions' of the later Middle Ages, and the ideology of the more developed cities and city-states (ch.5). Secondly, it takes us into scholastic and juristic ideas about civic communities and, to a limited extent, states in general (ch.6): Marsiglio emerges here as a unique example of a kind of 'corporatist' philosophy in the medieval world (ch.7). In the Renaissance, Bruni applied the ideas of civil society to the state and Machiavelli replaced communal concepts with republican *virtu* (ch.8). The Reformation reawoke communal stirrings in Germany and produced the first articulation of the guild-town ethos (ch.9).

1

THE GUILD: HISTORY

To most of us today the term 'guild' suggests either a professional organization (the Writers' Guild, for example), or the craft-guilds of medieval Europe. But guild in the Germanic languages (more often, in this context, spelled 'gild') originally meant 'fraternities of young warriors practising the cult of heroes' (Le Bras 1940–1, 316n.), and then any group bound together by ties of rite and friendship, offering mutual support to its members upon payment of their entry fee (*geld*). In its first known use, some time before AD 450, the word *gilda* signified a sacrificial meal. This was accompanied by religious libation and the cult of the dead. The sacred banquet, signifying social solidarity, was, and remained throughout medieval times, 'an essential mark of all guilds' (Coornaert 1947, 31; Wilda 1831, 29ff.), which were sometimes actually known as *convivia*.

Although *de facto* the craft-guild became to a considerable extent hereditary, guilds in general differed from the caste, which in India functioned partly as a craft group (Lambert 1891, 15–16), on account of the voluntary nature of the bond, which rested not on hereditary status but on the mutual oath, on artificial rather than blood fraternity. The early social guild formed one basis for the later craft-guild, an evolution which may (using Durkheim's language) be described as the development of 'segments' into 'organs' of society: that is, groups originally general and identical in function gradually assumed specialized and differentiated roles in particular branches of economic life. They were indeed the cells of a new kind of society.

Although social groups of this kind have probably had a wider variety of functions, greater diffusion, and a more continuous and varied history in medieval and modern Europe than elsewhere, they are by no means peculiar to Germanic culture. In several tribal societies, young men form distinct groups. Male drinking clubs played an important role in ancient Greece. The Roman *collegia* (also called *corpora, sodalitia*), which included social clubs, burial societies and cultic groups, went back 'earlier than recorded history', being mentioned in the Twelve Tables as an imitation of a Greek model (Duff 1938, 103). All such groups were artificial families which differentiated themselves, like the natural family, from the outside world. They have their own special ethos. Sometimes they have played a part in specifying the moral obligations of their members and even, like peer groups, in forming their members' moral consciousness. The modern world too is shot through with such groups. The typical modern private association is more specialized and less tightly-knit, without the same serious and permanent obligations of 'brotherhood' and 'friendship'. Regiments, schools and a variety of 'old-boy networks' bind people together as select groups with a common interest and ethos. Such groups operate, for good or ill, as a counterbalance to the modern state with its legal impartiality and meritocratic criteria. The phenomenon of peer-groups and gangs even suggests a general human tendency to form groups of this kind.

The development of political clubs in the late Roman Republic led to a general suppression of colleges under the consulate of Cicero, and again by Caesar. Augustus stabilized their position as friendly societies for religious purposes, burial and other forms of mutual aid; a distinction now emerged between 'licit' and 'illicit' colleges (Duff 1938, 107–8). To this dates back the juristic and political tradition according to which such guilds are subject to the common law and to government, require a special licence and may be dissolved by the state, and should be excluded from politics (Duff 1938, 110–11, 117).

During the Germanic settlement of northern and western Europe, from the fifth to the tenth centuries, the guilds played an especially important role as a form of social organization not dependent on blood ties but sacred in character, providing security as 'artificial families' (Le Bras 1940–1, 362–3; Michaud-Quantin 1970, 180). Known as gildonia, confratriae or convivia, they were at first most common in lower Germania, Frisia and the Low Countries (Coornaert 1947, 28). They were mutual support groups, an alternative to feudal relations in an age of acute instability when something more than family bonds was required. If their primary religious function was service of the dead, their primary moral ethos was summed up in the oath enjoining 'an obligation of mutual aid' (Bloch 1961, 420). Their members were not necessarily of equal social status, and they might include women (Coornaert 1947, 37; Wilda 1831, 33–4); but within the group the oath was taken not to a single leader or lord but to each other. Their functions were now extended to all kinds of mutual protection: burial funds, support for poor members or dependents of deceased members, an insurance service in case of fire or shipwreck (Coornaert 1947, 37–40; Michaud-Quantin 1970, 182–5; Wilda 1831, 119ff., 125ff). Their ties were expressed as 'brotherhood' and 'friendship': guilds were confratriae, their members confratres, forming an amicitia (Coornaert 1947, 34; Wilda 1831, 124). These ties extended to mutual needs arising from social as well as natural causes: guildsmen must support one another in their quarrels and vendettas, and protect each other from outsiders, even if they have committed a crime (Wilda 1831, 124–9, 138). 'For friendship as well as for

4

vengeance we shall remain united, come what may', said the London guild ordinances of the tenth century (Bloch 1961, 420). Guilds settled disputes among their own members, exercising over them a kind of jurisdiction (Coornaert 1947, 34; Wilda 1831, 136–7). The ties contracted in the guild acquired a sacred character from the mutual oath; it was a clearly-defined relationship with specific rights and duties.

These social guilds provoked the opposition of lords and bishops, of the Lombard kings and Carolingian emperors: they were accused of orgiastic rites, drunkenness and lasciviousness. Their rites were suspect to the church, their secrecy to lay rulers too. They made claims, quasi-legal in character, which were bound to stand in the way of feudal lordship and any would-be state. The mutual oath made them appear dangerous; as Cicero and Caesar had banned the Roman *collegia* as politically subversive, so medieval rulers from time to time charged guilds with the crime of sworn conspiracy (*coniuratio*) (Michaud-Quantin 1970, 229–30; Wilda 1831, 39–40). As time went on the term *coniuratio*, an accurate enough description of the guilds, became less pejorative in some contexts, being applied without disfavour to some early urban communes.

During the Dark Ages guilds were gradually Christianized. This obviously affected their religious character; yet in this and other matters their functions were transformed rather than radically altered. Prayers were offered for the departed; guilds adopted patron saints. Since so little is known about the moral language of the pre-Christian guilds, it is difficult to know whether what now emerged as the central guild values – brotherhood, friendship, mutual aid – derived from Christian or Germanic origin. Whatever was the case, these were from now on the essential components of guild moral sentiment. On the other hand, the private execution of justice was forbidden by higher authority and on the whole dwindled in importance.

Many guilds called themselves 'confraternities', as did other groups formed under ecclesiastical influence for pious and charitable purposes, which also had a guild-like organization. Some of these performed charitable work in local society outside their own ranks; some extended to the whole local population (Duparc 1975). Since, on the one hand, such 'grass-roots' organizations of clergy and laymen – in some ways akin to South American 'basic ecclesial communities' today – had previously been frowned upon by the church, and, on the other hand, Germanic guilds had previously confined mutual aid to small groups, this may be seen as a fusion of the Christian ideals of the universal brotherhood of believers and of charity to all men, with the Germanic institution of the guild; or, as an expression of the one through the other (cf. Le Bras 1940–1, esp. 324; Michaud-Quantin 1970, 129ff.). Throughout the Middle Ages, and often beyond, many villages contained one or more such confraternities, sometimes embracing the whole parish community; their basic principle, says Le Bras, was 'spiritual mutuality' (1940–1, 314). This was a territorialization of the guild, a process which contributed not a little to the communal movement in town and countryside during the eleventh and twelfth centuries. Like the original guilds, their activities focused upon the communal feast, usually once a year, at which food was distributed to the poor (Duparc 1975; Heers 1973, 322–3, 326). They might include a wide diversity of social ranks and a high proportion of women (Heers, 1973, 328).

The other new development at the end of the Dark Ages was the use of the guild organization by merchants. As Coornaert points out, the Dark Age guild was peculiarly suited to the needs of merchants: mutual aid and insurance against natural or human hazards provided the social instruments by which both long-distance merchants and the local trading community could operate in a period of instability (1947, 45, 50–3). Sometimes, however, 'merchant guild' referred simply to the trading element in a local community, particularly in a fiscal context; not all members were necessarily professional merchants.

The first known medieval European craft-guilds appeared around 1100 in Italy, the Rhineland and the Low Countries, and they proceeded to spread very quickly over western Europe. It has been suggested that their formal appearance was a rationalization of an already existing practice (Mickwitz 1936, 233; cf. Coornaert 1947, 209). The origin of their existence and of their organization has been disputed and remains obscure (Thrupp 1963, 233). Were they a continuation, or perhaps revival, of the craft colleges of the Roman Empire, or were they a specialization of the Germanic social guild? Mickwitz argues the former as most probable for Italy, and suggests that the practice may even have been borrowed from Constantinople (1936, 166–235). In any case, the degree of continuity is unclear; the Lombard kingdom set up a coiners' guild in the seventh century (to control the money supply?). Coornaert stresses continuity with the Germanic social guilds in view of shared features: the mutual oath, insurance against sickness, poverty and death, ceremonial drinking and communal feasting. This seems highly probable for northern Europe, where many craft-guilds called themselves 'fraternities' from the start; indeed, a similar evolution may well have taken place in the early Roman Republic. In the later twelfth and thirteenth centuries some craft-guilds arose as splinter groups of small retailer-craftsmen out of the all-embracing merchant guild, dominated now by big merchants (Martines 1980, 47). On the other hand, the term 'gild' was less often used of crafts, which in official documents tended to be called *arte*, *métier*, *Zunft*. Craft-guilds seem to have spoken less often of 'mutual aid' than either social guilds or territorial fraternities and communes. Another possibility, particularly in view of the widespread appearance of craft-guilds in other artisan cultures, is that this was a more or less natural and spontaneous response to the needs of manual workers, or a social expression of handicraft production itself (as Unwin (1904) suggests: cf. Martines 1980, 47). But the form of organization (see pp. 23–4), and much of the ethos, appear to have been carried over from the social guilds which were already so widespread in northern Europe. This could be described as a process of secularization (see pp. 63–4). That a living tradition of cultic association was at hand may help explain the relatively sudden diffusion of craft-guilds in the twelfth century, and their peculiar prominence in European culture; that it was being secularized may explain the steady adoption of more practical, less affective language.

Analogous institutions certainly existed among merchants and craftsmen in other parts of the world, for example in China, Japan, India, and in medieval and modern Islam (Klein 1967, 164–8; Weber 1958, 83–4, 87–8). Hobsbawm suggests that artisan guilds are 'a type of organization which appears to be quite universal wherever and whenever there are pre-industrial cities' (1971, 108, 111). In ancient Rome, numerous trades had their own colleges, but from Augustus onwards these functioned only in specified trades under state licence (Duff 1938, 109ff., 126, 148, 150–1). The European crafts seem, in general, to be characterized by a greater degree of independence, at least in the Middle Ages; they functioned in every artisan calling, and, like the European economy itself, underwent a process of continuous development. There may even, as we shall see, be some continuity with the modern labour union under industrial capitalism, which may be seen as a response to needs in some ways analogous to those experienced in the early Middle Ages. Likewise, some trade unions evolved out of friendly societies and manifested the same qualities of brotherhood and mutual support, in short moral ties (see pp. 175–6). There are further similarities with the evolution of the medieval crafts both in cases where trade unions have in their turn become powerful and monopolistic, and in cases where they have become integrated into the governmental process in a system which has been called 'liberal corporatism'.

Were craft-guilds set up by the authorities (lord or town council) or on the initiative of their own members? Again, there would appear to be considerable variety over Europe: there are cases of crafts agitating for corporate recognition and also of towns determining the number of permitted craft associations, usually in collusion with the larger merchants and the more powerful crafts themselves.

In the craft-guild, the 'mystery' of craftsmanship is joined with the dynamic of the pressure group; skill and endurance, on which life and progress depend, are powered by a specific social bond. Craft-guilds varied enormously, not only in the trades or crafts pursued, but in size, social status and the wealth of their members. Although in many cases they

7

developed out of groups of a social and religious character, they were primarily characterized by a concern for economic and above all artisan-manufacturing interests and policies. They were formed specifically to oversee and to regulate the activities of all practitioners of a given craft in the region controlled by the town. While recent scholarship has tended to play down their social and religious affiliations, it seems clear that they in fact combined juridical, political, religious and social aspirations, but that the economic motive of establishing corporate monopoly was primary; it was this which specifically brought together all those engaged in a single craft (Mickwitz 1936, 156–62). The economic policy of the merchant guilds and early towns was aimed at maximizing the volume of trade and the consequent benefits to the town and its own merchants: all goods passing nearby must go through the town, tolls must be paid, a certain amount of handling must fall to local men, and so on. The craft-guilds, on the other hand, were concerned with maintaining a steady volume of business for their members. Their chief aims were a satisfactory standard of workmanship and a fair price for its products (Rörig 1967, 150–1; Thrupp 1963, 254), and the restriction of 'the number of apprentices a master might keep, the hours he might work and the tools he could use' (Hibbert 1963, 214). There was thus a mixture of public spirit and self-interest in craft-guild policies. These were particularly entangled over prices. Guilds were 'concerned that a good product should be sold at a fair price' (Rörig 1967, 151), but the line between protecting producers and exploiting consumers was obviously fine. Coornaert sees a transition from social to economic priorities, and a move away from social solidarity to mere collective self-interest within the group, around the end of the thirteenth century. This would approximately coincide with the saturation point reached by the medieval economy. About the same time Hibbert (1963) sees a change from liberal policies to protectionism and over-regulation in the towns themselves.

One of the chief attractions of the medieval crafts for some modern observers was their attempt to safeguard the small independent producer. On the other hand, there were, then as now, allegations of price-fixing by a restricted group, of 'monopoly'. Recent scholarship, at least on the later Middle Ages, has emphasized the self-interested nature of the guild, *vis-à-vis* both customers and workers lower down the scale. 'The guilds, once seen as associations of equals embodying the principles of urban freedom, are now usually regarded as privileged corporations of promoters of monopoly' (Brady 1978a, 15). Heers believes that later-medieval crafts consistently raised prices and kept them high (1973, 225–6). Doubtless it depends where one looks, and above all whether one is speaking of the earlier or later Middle Ages. Thrupp, for example, maintains that 'direct evidence of price policies in a local industry, or of their success, is rare' and that 'evidence that points to restrictive policies ... is seldom conclusive' (1963, 263). Similarly, the supervision of training through the apprentice system both maintained standards ('the secret economies or improvements effected by individuals would if possible be passed on and would become guild property' (Thrupp 1963, 274)), and provided cheap labour, as guilds sought to keep down the wages of unskilled labourers, usually employed in small numbers (Heers 1973, 275; Thrupp 1963, 257, 264). It was partly to co-ordinate policy on apprenticeship and wages that craft-guilds of the same trade in different cities sometimes entered into agreements with each other (Gierke 1868, 383; Klein 1967, 185; Rörig 1967, 160; Thrupp 1963, 257). On the other hand, masons involved in building major churches – the *crème de la crème* of craft-guildsmen – met from time to time on a more or less international basis to discuss all kinds of craft questions, and a central European meeting at Regensburg in 1459, which included journeymen as well as masters, stipulated that no one should be taught for money (Harvey 1950, 21).

Craft-guilds aimed typically to secure continuity of work and income for their members, 'a burgher livelihood' (Rörig 1967, 151), and to maintain the fixed number of small independent producing masters in each craft. To this end they sought to limit competition. While most guilds 'took for granted a certain spread in the scale of operations', so that masters might employ 'at least five times the amount of workshop help', the general aim was to prevent the expansion of one man's business at the expense of others. It was here that the idea of equality came into play. Thrupp points out that this 'referred to independence, not to absolute equality of income', and that 'they far preferred independence in a small slow-moving business to the prospect of working under the direction of great merchant entrepreneurs in a thriving export trade'. They pursued 'extreme caution' rather than profit (Thrupp 1963, 272–5, 279). Thus the typical craft-guild was pitted against, on one side, unskilled labourers and would-be newcomers to the trade, and, on the other, the large-scale enterprise of capitalistic entrepreneurs and the putting-out system (Weber 1958, 187).

Workers lower down the economic and social scale formed their own organizations, from the early fourteenth century onwards, in opposition to the artisan élites. These were similar to craft-guilds in aim and structure, but were usually denied formal recognition as workers' associations, though they often maintained corporate status as religious confraternities. Sometimes there was division within the craft itself between masters and others, especially day-labourers (journeymen), who were known as the yeomanry, *compagnons*, *Geselle*. In other cases, the restricted entry to the craft, often confined to masters' sons, gave rise to 'a class of unqualified workers not admitted to the full rights of the guild' as well as of ordinary manual labourers (Heers 1973, 397; Unwin 1904, 10). As Martines puts it, 'the dividing line cut between those who employed labour and those who hired

9

themselves out; those who had tools, working premises ... and those who had little other than their labour' (1980, 186). Such groups were the driving force behind urban revolts in Italy during the later fourteenth century, demanding, as the crafts had earlier, less tax, a fairer distribution of wealth and the right to form guilds (Martines 1980, 180ff.). From about 1400 workers in France unable to form legitimate guilds created *compagnonnages*, often of itinerant labourers, replicating therein the guild structure of their masters, sometimes with their own peculiar ritual and ideology (Coornaert 1966; Heers 1973, 282–3). Some have survived till today and may be classed as a third species of the professional guild genus, distinct from merchant and craft-guilds. City governments regularly proscribed such groups as 'conspiracies' (Brucker 1977, 312–3; *Fonti* i 114–5; Heers 1973, 278–9). The struggle for guild rights continued into the sixteenth century; at the time of the Reformation urban workers were involved in widespread unrest.

The craft-guilds have been subject to widely different interpretations and assessments. From the Enlightenment onwards, modern political economists have generally regarded them as imposing irrational fetters upon free enterprise and free trade, as self-interested groups opposed to the interests of the consumer and of society at large. Others who, especially after the Romantic movement, have questioned the beneficence of market forces, have seen them as agents of social solidarity and economic morality. Marx, characteristically, combined these two assessments: the opposition between guildsmen and journeymen was a specific phase in pre-capitalist class struggle, the masters constituting an exploiting class. On the other hand, the guild system recognized the human value of labour and had to be abolished before labour could be treated as a mere commodity, and before capitalism could fully develop (1976, 284–5, 423, 439, 479–80; 1977, 370–1). Among more recent historians, Coornaert emphasizes the guilds' specifically social functions, 'their essential aim was to sacralize the cohesion of their members'; but from the thirteenth century their internal bonds became juridical rather than affective (1947, 52–5, 217–23).

On the one hand, they promoted sound workmanship, ensured security and a fair return for the producer and were concerned with the welfare of all guild members. They helped produce a cadre of skilled manual workers, whose discipline and self-esteem as craftsmen were no negligible factor in the development of European manufacture and technology (cf. Unwin 1938, 4–5). On the other hand, they became increasingly restrictive in membership, struggled to maintain fixed and rather low wages for apprentices and journeymen, and opposed the interests of unskilled, non-guild labourers.

Despite parallels in the ancient world and non-European civilizations, it would appear that social guilds, merchant-guilds and above all craft-guilds, were more widespread and significant in medieval and early modern Europe than elsewhere. Not only did they permeate all branches of the handicraft economy in the towns (though not in the countryside), but parish confraternities and merchant guilds formed the first cells of many village and urban communes; craft-guilds were frequently incorporated into the structure of urban government. The phenomenon of guilds was certainly one very important factor which differentiated medieval Europe from other societies which (in other respects) were at a similar level of economic development. In particular we may note that 'guild membership and servile status were, in general, incompatible' (Martines 1980, 46). Modern capitalism and socialism grew directly out of a milieu in which guilds were the cells of commercial and industrial life, one dominant mode of socio-economic organization. While it is difficult to judge how much weight to attach to this factor, it has been suggested that 'the Western gild, in its various forms and in its subsequent developments, has been one of the main instruments of what we call progress, the progress which distinguishes the West from the East' (Unwin 1938, 4–5).

It thus seems appropriate to use the guild as a tool with which to prise open the chambers and tracts of European political consciousness and theory; to see what the landscape looks like from this vantage point (cf. Unwin 1938, 13–14). How did guilds affect European social sentiment and political theory? To what extent did they provide, as the family obviously did, an analogue or prototype for the polity? But first we must further consider the ethos of the craft-guilds and contemporary opinions about them.

2

THE GUILD: ETHOS AND DOCTRINE

What can we know about the ethos or mentality of medieval guilds? We have already summarized the moral temper of the early *general* guilds: brotherhood, friendship and mutual aid among guild members – obligations incurred by mutual oath and confined to the fellowship of the small group. Now we must consider in more detail the mentality of the *craft*-guilds of the high Middle Ages. Here our main sources are statutes and other official documents produced by guilds and city authorities. Secondly, how were craft-guilds regarded by outsiders, and in particular by the more articulate spokesmen of society? References to guilds are not very common in medieval literature, and theoretical discussion of them is confined, with few exceptions, to the Roman law jurists. Three principal spheres of thought may be distinguished: what the guild was held to exist for, what made it a legitimate corporation, and its internal procedural (constitutional) principles. Together, these will tell us something about what kind of association the guild was held to be. It will be instructive to compare the views held by guild members and jurists upon each of these topics in turn.

As we have already seen, scholarly opinion has moved a long way from the romantic view of guilds as agencies of social solidarity and craft honour. We are not, however, concerned here with the actual behaviour of guilds – which is what has chiefly given rise to this revision of opinion – but with what guildsmen and others actually thought about these bodies. There is no recent synthesis of popular and juristic opinion on this subject; the evidence must therefore be presented in detail before our questions can be answered.

It is necessary to re-assess the views of eminent late nineteenth-century historians, in particular Gierke and Durkheim, about the medieval guild mentality, even though their views on how guilds actually behaved in public life have already been superseded. How do their interpretations, none the less, relate to the *perceptions* that guildsmen and their contemporaries had of such corporate groupings of producers? Gierke thought the medieval craft-guild morally significant in four ways. First, it took its place 'between family and state' as a distinctive type of social entity; like family and state it 'embraced the whole man', was 'for its members a miniature commonwealth (*Gemeinwesen in Kleinen*)' and 'united its members with one another like brothers' (1868, 359, 383, 387). Secondly, it imposed moral standards upon its members, both in that it 'made the colleagues have, in relation to one another, an earnest brotherly love for duty', and by means of coercive control through its 'moral polity' (Gierke 1868, 387). Thirdly, the morality of the *Zunft* combined both 'rights and duties' (Gierke 1868, 383). Fourthly, it embraced its members in a legal 'collective personality' (1868, 405). Durkheim believed that medieval guilds were a historical example of the kind of occupational group which provides for its members a *milieu moral*, in which 'professional ethics' could develop without state coercion on the basis of moral standards engendered within the group itself (see p.229). Lastly, Gierke held that, on the question of how a guild became a legitimate corporation, the guilds saw themselves as self-authorizing associations in the Germanic legal tradition, but the jurists held that they only became legitimate by superior fiat, in accordance with late Roman legal tradition. This view also requires careful scrutiny.

Certain names given to the early craft-guilds indicate a special conception of social solidarity, and also a degree of continuity with the earlier guild tradition of brotherhood, friendship and mutual aid. There were numerous regional variations. The most common would appear to be those indicating brotherhood (*fraternitas, confraternitas, bruderschaft, frairie, fraternity, brotherhood*); others indicated fellowship or comradeship (*communio, consortium, compagnie, company*); others simple union (*innunge, unio*) (for these and all references to craft-guild names, see Coornaert 1947, 50; Gierke 1868, 359–60; Heers 1973, 222; Leeson 1979, 26; Michaud-Quantin 1970, 149, 165; Mickwitz 1936, 233; Planitz 1954, 298–9). All these were terms of social bonding. They signified the belief that a specific relationship existed among fellow-members. But they were also moral terms, defining how members ought to behave towards one another, brotherhood or fellowship being one important purpose of the guild. These values were endorsed at all levels of medieval Christian society. Friendship, analysed and eulogized by Cicero, was a cultured ideal. Guilds adopted ideals such as friendship in a limited, practical, down-to-earth sense: certain people had agreed to support one another in specific ways; it entailed clearly defined obligations. Le Roy Ladurie finds friendship in this sense, though not in the form of a guild, among the shepherds and villagers of the French Pyrenees, some of whom had a 'highly developed sense of friendship ... a fraternity not based on ties of blood'. He sagely observes that in such a context 'it is hard to distinguish between emotional impulse and the pressures of work' (1980, 125–9). One should not, as Gierke did, read into these terms a romantic idea of group personality; nevertheless, there was a blend of idealism and dour practicality, such as one finds in early trade union slogans. In the later Middle Ages, when guild documents are more plentiful, they are mainly concerned with details of organization and policy, and contain little that one could call moral language.

Membership of a craft-guild was important both psychologically and practically. One incurred serious and enduring obligations and benefits, affecting one's self-perception and moral identity (Michaud-Quantin 1964a). It gave one a position in society. It enabled one to ply a trade, and so crucially affected one's economic status. Sometimes even political rights depended on guild membership. Membership was sealed by the collective oath, the essential mark of the medieval association (Michaud-Quantin 1970, 130–1, 135) – much as promise or contract lay at the core of modern political, and sometimes moral, theory. Yet there was joviality too. Guilds held regular drinking sessions and feasts, at which merriment was combined with a certain solemnity: 'they shall drink their guild' (*potabunt gildam suam*). Membership was no transient or purely contractual relationship, but rather 'eternal brotherhood' (*Codex diplomaticus Lubecensis* vii 731, used by a seafarers' brotherhood established in 1401). This aspect was perhaps faintly echoed by the jurists' *universitas non moritur* (an association never dies). With this comradely ethos went a 'high rate of intermarriage and occupational heredity' (Thrupp 1963, 249, 265), the pursuit of purely economic interests, and the operation of the closed shop (*Zunftzwang*).

The jurists had a very different conception of guild membership. This was because they assimilated the craft-guild to the *collegium* of late Roman law, and because they were primarily concerned with its legal aspects and the effects upon outsiders. They ignored the mutual oath (Michaud-Quantin 1970, 234). Innocent IV (d.1254) defined the craft 'college' as 'voluntary and not necessary' so that 'even those who are of the same profession or business, whether more or fewer than those who have already entered the college, are not compelled to enter it. And those who have entered may leave it' (on *Decretals* 5.31.14). Bartolus asserted that you may 'freely enter and leave' what he too called 'voluntary colleges' (on *Digest* 47.22.4). Butrio (d.1408), on the other hand, added 'unless perhaps the statutes say the contrary, namely that one may not leave, or that anyone exercising such a craft must enter, because then he would be compelled' (on *Decretals* 5.31.14, fol.83v–84r).

Another focus of the guilds' moral language was the practice and product of the craft itself. This is reflected in a whole series of names for craft-guilds, which in the later documents probably outnumber terms of social solidarity: *opus, opificium, artificium, craft, mystery, arte, métier, hantwerk*. Together with mutual aid, the 'honour' of the craft defined the purpose for which guilds existed. There was a sense of pride in the '*misterium artis*', in the special technique and skill known only to oneself and one's colleagues, and in the excellence of the finished article. Artefacts must be 'loyal' (Thrupp 1963, 264). To be a skilled craftsman was to occupy and fulfil a recognized role, an *officium* (lit. duty), with its own dignity. In this way professions began to acquire something of the status of 'vocations' (Mundy 1973, 34–5).

14

This concept of a publicly recognized duty is conveyed by a further set of names: *officium, Amt, ministerium.* The term *officium* is especially common in civic and juristic documents. The guild craftsman took pride in the honour or good name accorded to men doing an honest job well (cf. Thrupp 1963, 264). This surely was one origin of the much-derided 'solid burgher'. One was admitted as a full guild-master by producing one's 'masterpiece'; guild inspectors insisted on a high standard of workmanship. Thus 'in guild documents of the thirteenth century ... concern for the quality of the goods is particularly stressed as being the main purpose of the guilds' (Rörig 1967, 150). On the other hand, the idea that there is something intrinsically virtuous in *hard work* was no part of the guild mentality; and the idea of the highly motivated, self-made individual as an asset to the commonwealth, which one occasionally finds in Renaissance authors (Skinner 1978, i 74), was directly opposed to the guilds' aim to limit output to what all could achieve. Perhaps the notion of the intrinsic worth of manual labour and of the manual labourer came across to the widest audience through Luther's teaching on callings.

The craftsmen's self-esteem had to face the opposition of chivalric and feudal attitudes, fortified in due course by the intellectualist heritage of classical antiquity. In an epistolary textbook written *c.* 1276, out of six social categories, 'honest and rich merchants' come fifth while the sixth includes 'those exercising every artisan skill (*artis mechanice ... professores*), especially in sordid jobs, such as tanners, furriers ... shoe-makers ... iron-workers ... sculptors ... painters', alongside 'everyone of servile status, rustics' (Rockinger 447–50, cf.727–8). Craftsmen are no better than serfs.

On the other hand, the craftsman had allies in theology. Jesus was, after all, a carpenter's son and (it was to be presumed) apprentice. St Paul made tents and taught that the humblest and dirtiest jobs were high in God's eyes. All this gave the craftsman and even the peasant a dignity, at least in his own eyes. Moral theologians began to regard manual work as no longer a penalty for sin, but a positive means to salvation (Le Goff 1964, 52–6; 1977, 97ff.). Productive human work was given cosmic significance: beside God and nature stood 'man the craftsman (*homo artifex*), imitating nature' (Chenu 1968, 40–1). Aristotle had assigned to the manual skills a necessary, although strictly subordinate, place in the polis, and political philosophers were prepared to recognize that artisans were essential to a satisfactory civil life (Ptolemy of Lucca bk iv, ch.ii; Remigio de'Girolami p.129 and in Davis 1960, 666, 669). Aquinas explained how natural man, unlike animals, could meet his needs only 'by some industry'; nature gave him 'reason and hands' but he had to use these creatively to get food and clothing (*Summa Theologiae* Ia IIae q.95 a.l resp.). There was continuity between these scholastic attitudes and the Renaissance cult of 'business' (*negotium*) and the active life, of *homo faber* (man the creative worker: lit.

man the smith) (Skinner 1978, 92, 109; Trinkaus 1970, i 282). Nevertheless, philosophers and moralists always ranked manual below mental skills;
in the building trade the architect was of much higher status and received a
far greater income than the skilled mason (Harvey 1950, 42ff.). In juristic
discussions of occupational groups which might form colleges, manual
crafts are always listed last, sometimes, one has the impression, almost as an
afterthought; Innocent IV, nevertheless, placed them in the category of
'praiseworthy profession' (on *Decretals* 1.38.7, fol.71r).

By the 'honour and interests of the craft' (*Fonti* ii 1; Najemy 1979, 65n.)
was meant in particular legitimate remuneration and the pursuit of
legitimate producers' interests. This was further related to the guilds' special
conception of *justice*: the duty to produce work of a certain standard and
the right to secure employment. The chief means to this was the restriction
on craft entry. Rules stipulating maximum hours and so on comprised a
large part of guild regulations, and it was with the enforcement of such
rules, together with the maintenance of standards, that guild courts were
primarily concerned. The main purpose of the corporate legal rights claimed
by guilds was to ensure a secure livelihood. In this way their sense of justice
led to belief in approximate equality of output and of the returns due to all
craft members; their main opponent here was the merchant-capitalist (often
himself member of a guild) who, by employing more men and working them
harder, undercut their price and ruined their livelihood.

Justice was one feature of the guilds' moral universe to which the jurists
did pay sympathetic attention. They made considerable use of it, probably
more so than the guilds themselves, as the rationale for the guilds' corporate
status. Here, the jurists had difficulty in reconciling Roman law with
contemporary reality. According to the *Digest*, craft workers could only
form a college by permission of senate or emperor, with the exception of
tax-farmers, miners of gold, silver and salt, bakers and shippers, to whom
such permission was expressly granted in *Digest* 3.4.1 pr.; severe penalties
were prescribed for 'illicit colleges' (*Digest* 47.22.2, 3). Medieval jurists got
round this in various ways. The part of their argument which concerns us
here was initiated by Bassianus in the late twelfth century: every 'assembly'
(*congregatio*) is permissible 'which exists for preserving for each one his
justice' (*pro conservanda cuique sua justitia*) (cit. Michaud-Quantin 1970,
221). This sweeping moral criterion radically strengthened the crafts' case
for corporate legitimacy. It was accepted by the late twelfth-century
canonist Hugolinus ('to speak more generally, every assembly may be called
licit which exists for preserving its justice': cit. Gierke 1881, 208), and a
little later by Accursius' standard Gloss on the *Digest* (gl.*Aliorum ad Digest*
3.4.1). Innocent IV reiterated Bassianus more exactly: provided there are at
least three members, corporate status follows automatically if the aim is 'to
preserve *for each* his justice' (on *Decretals* 1.31.3, fol.63r). Elsewhere he

16

was a little more explicit: craftsmen may 'set up a college, providing they do so for some just cause, for example to defend their own and others' justice, to prevent fraud in their profession and for similar reasons' (on *Decretals* 5.31.14). *Justitia* in this context may just as well be translated 'rights', and the language of Bassianus and Innocent indicates that they had in mind individual as well as corporate rights (*cuique*: to each). In his eulogy of the Florentine constitution (1403–4), the humanist Leonardo Bruni, who had a legal training, described how 'power of enquiry and judgment among its own men is given to certain colleges', in order that 'each person' may find it 'easier to pursue what is his due/right (*ius suum consequi*)' (*Eulogy* 260). Other equally eminent jurists, however, such as Hostiensis (d.1271) and Baldus (d.1400), juxtaposed pursuit of justice and grant by superior authority as *alternative* criteria for determining corporate legitimacy, leaving the reader to decide which one to apply (Hostiensis, *De Syndicis* fol.104r; Baldus on *Digest* 3.4.1); while Bartolus made no reference to justice in this context (on *Digest* 3.4.1, 34.5.20, 47.22.4).

Although jurists had experience of collegiate life in universities and notaries' guilds, what they said did not necessarily reflect the moral sentiments of craft-guildsmen themselves. Pursuit of justice was doubtless only one reason why craftsmen believed themselves entitled to have guilds. Nevertheless, the language of Bassianus, who introduced the concept of justice here, has a contemporary ring, and he may possibly have been reproducing a contemporary guild argument; if so, it suggests that guilds had some notion of their and their members' 'rights'. In any case, it is important to note that pursuit of justice was the only moral meaning which jurists – or any learned men – saw in the craft-guilds.

The criterion of justice might of course be invoked against crafts by those who wished to show that they were invading the 'rights' of others. Hostiensis said that guilds' legal rights were to be understood 'without prejudice to their lord (sc. the town lord) if they have one' (on *Decretals* 1.31.3, fol.147r). City governments were generally concerned to safeguard consumers' interests, which led them sometimes to restrict guild regulations, sometimes to dissolve a recalcitrant guild. The rules made by crafts were usually subject to revision by the civic authorities. Jurists insisted that craft rules must operate within limits set by the 'common law' (i.e. Roman law as interpreted by the Gloss: Stein 1973), for example Belleperche (question 453), and that they must respect natural justice. Thus Bartolus was careful to state that, while craft-guilds in general may 'make statutes ... on matters pertaining to their craft', they may not 'make an agreement that a job begun by one man may not be finished by someone else' (on *Digest* 47.22.4). He even challenged the right of craft-guilds to limit the number of practitioners of a given trade: they may not make 'a law by which another is prejudiced, as for instance if they make a law that only certain persons and no others can exercise that craft' (on *Digest* 47.22.4). St Antonino of Florence (1389–1459), quoting Guilelmus de Cuneo on the right of a corporate group to renounce obligations entered into by collective oath, drew examples from the obligations of butchers, shoemakers and other craftsmen to the general public, as determining whether or not the guild oath could be renounced (*Summa Theologica* pt 2, tit.10, ch.6: vol.ii, p.1094).

In this context, we may return to the question of the guilds' corporate legitimacy, which made up the bulk of juristic discussion of the crafts. Here we enter the complex world of 'corporation theory', which played such a vital part in medieval legal thought and practice. What makes a group into a legal corporation? Who can create and dissolve corporations? What powers do present rulers and members have over the corporation's assets? What kind of entity is the corporation? We are here concerned chiefly with the first two questions, and in particular with the different answers implied by Roman and Germanic legal tradition, the former asserting the authority of the prince, the latter the self-authorizing rights of the customary group.

Guilds needed recognition as 'colleges' or corporate legal bodies both for 'security in the handling and disposition of funds' (Thrupp 1963, 252), and in order to establish their position as traders' or producers' monopolies. Recognition of the guilds' economic status was a matter for the city council or lord. As crafts sprang up in one city after another during the twelfth and thirteenth centuries, their position was usually established by mutual agreement with the town authorities. The guild was allotted a prescribed role in the city's economic life, often designated specifically as a duty or office (*officium*). To begin with, it was usual to allow each trade or craft to form its own guild. As time went on, the number of permitted craft-guilds tended to become fixed; this operated particularly to the detriment of lower-grade workers in the cloth industry. Thus the moral or legal right to form a guild was a matter of great practical importance; it was also an area in which (as Gierke emphasized) the old Germanic tradition was faced with restrictions deriving from Roman law.

The attitude of city authorities was most permissive during the economic expansion of the twelfth and thirteenth centuries. In granting the Magdeburg shoemakers the right to elect their own 'magistracy', the archbishop stated his desire that 'liberty be the mother of our action' and that 'the guilds (*officia*) of our city, large or small, should each exist in their dignity according to their integral right (*in suo honore secundum ius integrum*)' (Keutgen 354). It was, for him, a matter of 'freedom' and 'right'. The Basle authorities, on the other hand, in licensing a shoemakers' guild in 1268, merely observed that 'nearly every kind of men in our city who exercise mechanical arts, commonly called handworkers (*Handwerkluete*)' already have a guild (cit. Wilda 1831, 308).

In Germanic custom, the guild was formed by the spontaneous will of its members, not unlike the company (*comitatus*, *Genossenschaft*) (Schlesinger 1975). Late Roman law, as we have seen, severely restricted the right to form colleges to a few groups listed in *Digest* 3.4.1 pr. and such others as emperor or senate might allow. Licit colleges might 'after the example of the public body (*rei publicae*) have common goods, a common chest' and a representative to conduct common business (*Digest* 3.4.1). Ecclesiastical law provided a go-between: for, while 'the crime of sworn association and conspiracy, which the Greeks call brotherhood (*fratria*)' had been condemned by a canon of the Council of Chalcedon which was put into the *Decretum* (C.11. 12), the eleventh-century reform movement had given cathedral chapters new powers, particularly in the election of bishops. The principle of functional differentiation among formal equals according to vocation, with different groups dedicated to specific callings, was embedded in Christian thought and monastic practice. Both chapters and monasteries had an established position in the church, which was further developed in the twelfth and thirteenth centuries at the very time when the craft-guilds were expanding. The *Decretals* gave chapters considerable scope over against bishops (*Decretals* 3.10 and 11), and canonists developed a generous doctrine of 'the rights of communities (*universitates*)' (Gillet 1927, 95–7; Michaud-Quantin 1970, 84–90). This may help explain why church authorities and canon lawyers tended to be rather more sympathetic to the claims of guilds than their secular counterparts.

Jurists reiterated the *Digest*'s strictures on colleges but at the same time they expanded the grounds on which craft-guilds might be permitted without superior consent. Despite what Gierke says (1881, 369, 437, 439), they thus went some way towards accommodating Germanic tradition. First, some Glossators argued that the list of trades in which workers could form colleges (*Digest* 3.4.1 pr.) was not *exclusive* but *indicative*: all craft-guilds in similar professions were authorized as falling within the formal requirements of the law. *Digest* 3.4.1 pr. and other passages referring to specific trades (*Digest* 47.22.4 and 50.6.6) were, implausibly but advantageously, treated as general 'enabling' acts (Gierke 1881, 206–9; Gillet 1927, 70–1). Craft-guilds generally were said to be legalized 'by the law', that is by these parts of Roman law, and so required no further superior approval in order to qualify as legitimate corporate bodies.

This view received authoritative support from the church, when Innocent III, in a judicial verdict which was included in the *Decretals* (1.38.7), told the Paris scholars that their right to legal representation through a proctor – a mark of corporate status – was ensured by common law (*de iure communi hoc facere valeatis*), and did not require his approval, though he willingly added it. This accorded with a view gaining currency among canonists, that heads of ecclesiastical colleges, including bishops, received their jurisdiction at least in part from their election by the college. In such cases, Hostiensis explained, 'the law gives ordinary jurisdiction', and he went on to draw the analogy: 'bodies or colleges of any craft or partnership (*societatis*) or business are permitted and approved *by the law*' (on *Decretals* 1.31.3, fols 146v–147r). An even stronger supporter of the rights of craft-guilds was Hostiensis' teacher, Sinibaldo de' Fieschi, later Pope Innocent IV. This is surprising, because Innocent took a more monarchical view of ecclesiastical colleges (Tierney 1955, 107–8), for which he has gone down in history as an absolutist. But Innocent drew a sharp distinction between ecclesiastical and secular 'communities' (*universitates*). A church, it is true, cannot legislate without the bishop's consent; 'but about other communities it may reasonably be said that they can make statutes concerning their own affairs' (on *Decretals* 1.2.8, fol.2v). He was particularly keen to apply this to craft-guilds. The general rule, he says, is that rulers elected by communities acquire jurisdiction when the superior confirms the appointment. But, while cities may acquire corporate status, and so elect their own rulers, through the tacit consent of a superior, crafts '*need no privilege or consent of a superior for them to be colleges approved by the law* [see *Digest* 3.4.1]; all their members, or the greater part, if they wish, can set up a judge for themselves and exercise the other rights of an association (*iura universitatis*)' (on *Decretals* 1.31.3, fol.63r). He added that there should probably only be one college per craft in each city, and that crafts from different cities should not amalgamate.

Among later civilians, Bartolus too said that 'colleges of many persons performing one craft in one city or place are approved by common law' (on *Digest* 47.22.4 and 3.4.1). Paulus de Castro (d.1441) pressed the point: 'those elected by a community comprising an approved college, thereupon acquire jurisdiction or its exercise by the authority of that law [on *Codex* 3.13.7] *without further confirmation by a superior*' (on *Codex* 3.13.3). Among later canonists, Butrio, Zabarella and Tudeschi all agreed that craft colleges were authorized 'by the law' (on *Decretals* 5.31.14). Tudeschi (d.1445) was most explicit: scholars and others 'exercising some permitted profession, such as clothiers, shoemakers, tanners and the like ... are granted leave by common law to come together ... to set up a college or community, and elect a ruler for themselves.' He took pains to reconcile this with the Roman law's general prohibition of colleges by saying that two kinds of college are exempt from this: cities, which are permitted 'by the law of nations' and craft colleges 'such as bakers, barbers and the like', which are permitted 'by the positive law' (on *Decretals* 5.31.14). According to this argument, therefore, *the Roman or universal law was itself the legitimizing agency*. It was a remarkable step towards the principle of free association, and deserves recognition as a milestone in western liberal thought.

Another argument for the automatic legitimacy of craft-guilds was, as we have seen, that they pursued justice. Two further arguments were put forward by Innocent: their members pursue a 'praiseworthy profession' (on *Decretals* 1.38.7, fol.71v), and 'they have much to do together' (on *Decretals* 5.31.14, fol.217r). Bartolus made the latter into a general principle: 'all who have much to do and handle together may form a college approved by common law' (on *Digest* 47.22.4). Antonius de Butrio (d.1408) agreed with Innocent that the law authorizes those who come together 'for their craft' (on *Decretals* 5.31.14), and Zabarella said it authorized 'those who conduct a licit craft' (on *Decretals* 5.31.14). Tudeschi too said that the law permitted craftsmen of all kinds to form colleges 'so that they may meet together by reason of the licit profession they ply' (on *Decretals* 5.31.14). But, reflecting the current views of established guilds, he confined this to qualified masters: 'the apprentices (*discipuli*) of furriers or other craftsmen' may not form colleges, precisely because 'these do not need to come together to conduct business, because it is all done by their masters'. This does not apply to students of law and liberal arts because they have common expenses and may be lodging together (on *Decretals* 1.38.7).

This was still far short of the Germanic tradition, and of the contemporary view common among craftsmen, that the corporate status of the guild derives from the consent or will of its members. But, contrary to what Gierke maintains, some jurists did go this far, and so brought Roman and canon jurisprudence into line with Germanic custom and contemporary reality. There is a hint of it in Accursius' standard Gloss: listing ways in which a magistrate may acquire jurisdiction, he mentions 'consent by a town community, but he must be confirmed by the provincial governor' and then 'consent by a group exercising the same profession' *tout court* (gl. *Lex ad Digest* 2.1.6). But it was Innocent IV who took the plunge. He gave three ways in which those engaged in a craft might form a corporation:

[1] It seems that men in any profession (such as grammar), or business (such as food suppliers), or office (such as bakers), can come together and set up their own ruler or syndic and a common chest *by their own authority if they wish*; provided they enter partnership or form a college for some cause. [2] Some, however, say that in colleges of persons [sc. the above] they are always confirmed by a superior, just as in [territorial] colleges.... [3] It also seems that, even without a ruler or syndic, chest and formal agreement, they can *set up a college by their own authority, or their will alone* (provided it is explicit), so long as they do so for some just cause. ... All the above colleges, which are formed for good purposes and do not proceed to evil, we say are authorized by [*Digest* 47.22.1].

(on *Decretals* 5.31.14)

While Innocent leaves the student to choose between these alternatives, he had elsewhere explicitly rejected the second (on *Decretals* 1.31.3, see p. 20).

The first came closest to what he had said on *Decretals* 1.31.3, except that there he was speaking primarily of legitimation by the law itself – with which, it is true, he also concludes here. The third option meets objections by allowing tradesmen to set up an *informal* college; but this would have legal disadvantages. While Innocent remained open-minded, he at least gave the members' will as a possible authorization.

This reference to the 'authority' or 'will' of the group was a profound theoretical innovation. Taken as a whole, the passage suggests that if the guild is to be considered authorized by a human agency rather than the law, Innocent prefers the group itself to any superior. He wrote this at the very time when craft-guilds were multiplying all over Europe, and on the eve of their rise to political power within certain cities. Seen in that context, and compared with what other jurists were saying, it looks like an expression of definite support for craft-guilds. In this respect, it may be contrasted with Bartolus' more famous justification of the already established autonomy of city-states. In the circumstances, Innocent appears to have moved towards the liberal and democratic option of freedom of association and self-legitimation. All in all, his commentaries provided a *Magna Carta* for the guilds.

The radicalism of Innocent's views is further attested by the fact that no other jurist seems to have accepted or even mentioned them until the early fifteenth century, by which time guilds were very well established. Then Tudeschi and Paulus de Castro, canonist and civilian, both acknowledged that Innocent, together with Bartolus, had dealt authoritatively and exhaustively with 'the question of colleges' (Tudeschi on *Decretals* 1.38.7; Castro on *Digest* 3.4.1 and on *Codex* 3.13.3). Butrio refers to the opinion that for corporate status 'their mere will, tacit or expressed, suffices, provided they [form the college] for an honest and just cause, permitted by law', but appears not to have accepted this (on *Decretals* 5.31.14). Castro informs us that people in general regard jurisdiction as coming from the community, but that doctors of law think superior confirmation necessary: he himself implies a preference for legitimation by the law, but *via* the college:

> It is therefore clear that rulers of colleges or crafts have jurisdiction, for which that law [*Codex* 3.13.7] is always cited. But who gives them jurisdiction? Commonly it is said that it is given by the association (*universitate*), and that therefore its members possess jurisdiction. It could, however, be said that it is given by the law, through the mediation of election by the college (*mediante electione ipsius collegii*).... The doctors seem to hold that confirmation by a superior is required, of which I have stated the contrary [sc. on *Codex* 3.13.3].   (on *Codex* 3.13.7)

Lastly, craft-guilds could be legitimized without superior approval by classifying them as 'pious colleges' formed 'for the sake of religion', since blanket permission was given for such colleges in *Digest* 47.22.1. As we have seen, some craft-guilds called themselves 'confraternities', and in the later Middle Ages craftsmen or labourers forbidden to form guilds organized themselves as religious or charitable associations. All jurists accepted the corporate legitimacy of religious confraternities. Both Bartolus and Baldus argued that they were legitimated 'by the law/by common law/ by the law itself (*a lege/de iure communi/ipso iure*)' (Bartolus on *Digest* 34.5.20 and on *Digest* 47.22.1; Baldus on *Codex* 1.2.1, fol.10v/a). Bartolus, whose reservations about craft-guilds have already been noted, was careful to add that 'they must not on this pretext deal with matters relating to the city government and the like; and if they do so, they should be punished' (on *Digest* 47.22.1). Baldus, on the other hand, reported sympathetically the opinion that those prevented from forming a guild might organize themselves as a confraternity: 'the armourers, who cannot make an assembly for their own affairs, make one by going to Santa Maria del Monte, and [Butrigario] says that, since they do so for the service of God, it is permitted for them by the law itself to assemble' (on *Codex* 1.2.2, fol.10v/a).

There would appear, therefore, to be truth in Le Bras's statement that the jurists 'legitimized and strengthened the unity of the guilds'; but when he goes on to say that they 'reduced the obstacles in the way of the working bodies on whom depended the organization of labour and the levels of prices' (1963, 574), one must make a distinction. The jurists were perfectly prepared to accept craft-guilds as legitimate colleges, and went to great lengths to circumvent the technical difficulties posed by Roman law. But we should not confuse this with thinking that they thereby sanctioned the guilds' economic privileges. These are seldom explicitly discussed, and here one cannot take silence for consent. For both Innocent and Bartolus, who came to be recognized as the main authorities on this question, affirmed one's right freely to enter and to leave such 'voluntary' colleges (see p.14); Bartolus explicitly invalidated any regulation by which 'only certain persons and no others can exercise that craft' (p.18). They were thus clearly opposed to craft-guild 'monopoly', both on the ground that this infringed the rights of others, and because individual craftsmen must be free to join the guild or not – both significant signposts as to the direction in which European values were developing.

We turn now to the internal constitution of the guild: what were its *procedural* values? The guild being, in its origin at least, a voluntary group in the sense that one opted into it, and existing for fairly specific, well-defined and generally agreed purposes, the concept and exercise of ruling authority in the political sense was virtually absent. The old Germanic guilds were artificial families but without father/mother figures. The formation of a guild was the act of its members, and, in the case of craft-guilds, the economic rights acquired by membership were of such fundamental importance to each individual that the principle of unanimity dominated guild decision-making, at least in the early stages. For example, foreign products may not be sold in the city 'except with the agreement of all those who are participants in the right which is called the union' (*nisi cum omnium eorum voluntate qui iuri illo, quod inninge appellatur, participes existunt*) (Keutgen 354). Similarly, in Germanic law family property was at the disposal not of the head but of all adult males; unanimity was also becoming a requirement for certain acts regarding the disposition of property belonging to ecclesiastical colleges (Gillet 1927, 134ff.).

Guild officials had two main functions: the administration of the common fund and, in the case of the crafts, the enforcement of guild regulations; from early times they were called 'judges' or 'the magistracy'. The early Germanic guilds elected their officials, and the craft-guilds argued and fought for their right to elect their own judges, instead of having them appointed by town council or lord, as they very often were to begin with. In this context the terms 'by common consent/counsel' were used (Keutgen 354–5), as they were in ecclesiastical elections. The town authorities, however, usually retained the power to ratify the election. This and other guild business was transacted in general meetings of guild members, held at least once a year, known as *plaids* or *Morgensprache* (Coornaert 1947, 209–11). These were ceremonial and festive occasions. The guild statutes, often drawn up by a select number of 'honest' guildsmen, went before the assembly, which also dealt with admission of new members. These statutes, though commonly described as having been made by the guild itself (Gierke 1868, 380–1), were also subject to ratification by the town authorities (Calasso 1954, 433; Loesch 184–5; Planitz 1954, 292). All other guild business was usually conducted by its officials, although their measures were subject to approval by the assembly. In a time of crisis, however, the assembly became an occasion for debate on policy, and for this purpose majority voting replaced strict unanimity (Calasso 1954, 433; Planitz 1954, 292; Weider 1931, 105–9, 130–9, 252ff.; Wilda 1831, 118). While the overall setting varied from time to time and from place to place, election and consent emerge as procedural principles embedded in the guild ethos. Here there was a close parallel with the early town communes and with ecclesiastical developments following the Gregorian reform.

The jurists devoted little attention to the constitution of craft-guilds as such; the closest they came was in their general formulations of procedural principles for associations (*universitates*), a category embracing cities, villages and, for canonists, ecclesiastical colleges. They assumed that policy, and in particular legislation, was a matter for the whole membership, though this might be represented by a select council, especially in the case of towns. Their main concern was with the technical procedures for decision-making within the council or group; and it is fair to assume that they applied to guilds what they said of associations generally, namely that all must be summoned, two-thirds must be assembled, and a majority of those present decide (see p.61).

On one point they were more specific: the election of the guild judge or ruler. In their language, he was assimilated to the syndic or *actor* of the Roman law association (*Digest* 3.4.1); and they took it for granted that, just as such an association could appoint its own legal proctor, so the ruler or judge was elected by the guild, though he might still be subject to confirmation by the town authorities. In other words, they bowed to current practice. Jacques de Révigny (d.1296), however, who held that only colleges explicitly approved by a superior had the right to elect a judge, deplored the way in which 'that law [sc. *Codex* 3.13.7] is cited all day to show that those from any profession can elect a superior for themselves' (on *Codex* 3.13.7). Cino da Pistoia (1270–*c*.1336), on the other hand, sided with custom: although the law does not explicitly mention the *election* of professional judges 'this is how custom is interpreted' (on *Codex* 3.13.7, fol.147r).

Finally, jurists discussed the craft-guilds' legislative and judicial competence. This was connected with their status as corporations. The general view was that they might legislate and judge in matters related to the trade or craft; this followed from the principle that any corporation (*universitas*) 'can make rules about its own affairs'. The main question was the relation of guild courts to the city authorities. Bartolus formulated the proposition that 'it seems that one should say that licit and approved colleges can make statutes on matters over which they have jurisdication and which relate to their own members' (on *Digest* 1.1.9, n.6). As so often with Bartolus, this was an analytical statement. His pupil Baldus said, with particular reference to the powerful cloth guild, that they may even make statutes contrary to city laws, provided these strictly concern 'the affairs of the craft or profession'. To the objection that different laws within the same city produce 'odious diversities full of very sad results', he replied that guild statutes on craft matters 'do not harm anyone but themselves and their heirs' (on *Digest* 1.1.9, fol.13v/b): statutes of merchant and craft-guilds do not need civic ratification because 'they are confirmed by the common law' (*De Constituto* fol.105v; *De Statutis* fol.91r/b). To merchants Baldus was yet more generous: the rules they make for the transaction of business, for example specifying the conditions under which a contract is valid, are to be upheld by secular and church courts. Again, the reason is that these derive their authority not from the merchants themselves, but from the common law (*De Constituto* fol.105v). Castro also denied that craft-guild statutes require superior confirmation (on *Codex* 3.13.7); while Giason del Maino (1435–1519) said that confirmation of merchants' statutes 'by the people or prince . . . is not essential or necessary' (on *Digest* 1.9.9, n.38, fol.16v/b). We can see that there was a tendency, as time went on, to give powerful and established guilds wider legislative powers.

On the question of judicial competence, *Codex* 3.13.7 said that craftsmen were subject to special judges in public as well as private suits. This was taken to justify the competence of guild courts not only in disputes between members of the same guild, but also in cases brought by outsiders on a matter relating to the trade, in support of which Cino and Bartolus cited custom (on *Codex* 3.13.7), and in suits brought by the guild itself against one of its members. In the thirteenth century, some jurists gave an outside plaintiff the choice between guild and city courts (Hostiensis on *Decretals* 1.31.3, fol.146v–147r; Innocent IV on *Decretals* 1.31.3, fol.63r – citing custom; Révigny on *Codex* 3.13.7, fol.142r). But Cino said that anyone with a trade complaint against a merchant *must* go to the guild court, because 'custom is interpreted in this way, we can do nothing else' (on *Codex* 3.13.7, n.4, fol.147r). Baldus assigned cases between the guild and one of its members to the guild judge, who may also hear cases between a craftsman and an outsider if they relate to the craft; but not otherwise, 'because they are not subject to him altogether, but only by reason of the ministry or profession' (*De Statutis* fol.91r/b). But he insists that both craft colleges and individual craftsmen may also be sued before the city court (*sub potestate*), because this 'is called the superior not only of the crafts (*artium*) but of the craftsmen (*artificum*)' (on *Codex* 3.13.7). While there was no discussion of the appellate powers of city courts, Bartolus had remarked that 'colleges are subject to the secular judges' (on *Digest* 47.22.1), and Baldus appears particularly concerned to uphold the position of the city courts. Castro, however, once again favoured the guilds when he added that the craft judge retains jurisdiction even over members who have left the guild (on *Codex* 3.13.7, fol.132v).

We may now summarize our findings, and compare them with the views held by Gierke and Durkheim on the moral attributes and general self-image of the medieval craft-guilds. In the first place, it is clear that up to a point the craft-guilds did, for the most part, provide a *milieu moral for their members*. They were indeed, and felt themselves to be, obliged to give each other 'mutual aid' as 'brothers' or 'friends'. Here, however, it should be stressed, particularly apropos Durkheim's desire to revive a form of guild in the modern world, that these attitudes derived from a fusion between a long tradition of mutual association in Germanic culture and the Christian ethic. Mutuality was perhaps stronger in the early Germanic general-purpose protection guilds than it was in the urban crafts, certainly after about 1300.

Craft-guildsmen did have a strong sense of the 'honour' of their trade;

they believed in and enforced standards of craftsmanship. They believed that their organizations promoted 'justice'. They believed that guild officials were strictly accountable and that decisions within the guild should be made, so far as possible, by general consent. All these beliefs certainly made up a distinctive moral ethos. But of course to say that guilds fostered specific beliefs about right and wrong is not to say that they fostered a morality we should wish to emulate. The obligations of the technical guild concept of fraternity extended only to fellow-members; outsiders did not count. To put it less harshly, their success as *milieux morales* depended entirely on the degree to which producer and consumer interests were compatible. The corporate self-interest practised by medieval guilds clearly undermines the historical credibility of Durkheim's argument.

It is probably true that guilds played a more important part in the life and consciousness of more people in the European Middle Ages than in any other culture or period; their moral influence was considerable. Corporations played a more important role in urban and ecclesiastical life, organization and government than at any later time. Ties within the guild were deeper and more extensive than in private associations today. Guild membership was a serious matter for those who belonged; the sentiment of brotherly membership was often strong; loyalty to one's craft might rival or outweigh loyalty to the state. It would, therefore, be true to say that in many instances guild authority rivalled or complemented state authority. The best modern analogies are probably churches and trade unions. As time went on, either the civic authorities gave the guilds a distinct but subordinate jurisdiction, or the guilds themselves became part of the civic government. Among theorists, some jurists allowed them more autonomy than others; the Aristotelian scholastics and the humanists, with a few significant exceptions, sided with the city or state and concentrated attention upon man as citizen.

Gierke exaggerated when he said that guilds 'embraced the whole man'. At no point, it would seem, did they outweigh family ties which, craft-guild membership usually being hereditary, were actually incorporated in the guild system. The contrast between medieval and modern *practice* should not be exaggerated. While modern political theory, like that of the Middle Ages and Renaissance, with few exceptions supports state authority over any guild-like group, modern practice is more variable. Business corporations and trade unions can play a role not unlike that of the medieval guild. For some people, their moral authority sometimes outweighs that of the state. Business corporations and trade unions do not have their own courts, but they are inclined to regard the legal system as not quite applicable to them in 'craft matters'. Perhaps, not unlike the family, when guild-type groups appear to be in decline they are simply changing shape. Far more often than is commonly supposed, intermediate groups of one kind or

27

another exist between individual (or family) and state. Whether people's interests or individual liberty are thereby promoted or frustrated is a matter of opinion, and depends to a great extent upon circumstances.

In speaking of the guild's 'collective personality', Gierke meant not only that the guild was a legal presonality in the modern sense, but also that guildsmen thought of their personal rights and duties as somehow embedded in and issuing from the group. Gierke raises further problems because he saw the craft-guilds as the supreme medieval realization of the Germanic 'idea of comradeship' (*Genossenschaft*): guildsmen were willing and free members of an invisible unity.

> The guild (*Zunft*) was thus an association resting upon a freely willed union or a spontaneous comradeship (*gewilkürte Genossenschaft*) ... [it was] a unity in peace and justice, a comradeship in law.... The fellowship (*Genossenschaft*) was, in its external as in its internal relations, in public as in private law, a collective group-person (*Gesammtpersön-lichkeit*). Just as, in the city, the communal entity (*Gemeinwesen*) as such stood above the inhabitants, citizens and council as the supreme legal personality, so was the guild as such, as an invisible unity living in the totality of the guild-colleagues, raised to the status of a true right-subject, for which the visible totality or assembly was only the body and the guild officials only the organs.　　　　　(Gierke 1868, 359, 396, 405–6)

This supposedly popular and widespread conception of the guild as comrade group and collective person was the basis for all Gierke's subsequent criticism of medieval jurisprudence and political philosophy which, throughout the third and fourth volumes of *Das deutsche Genossenschaftsrecht*, he tirelessly blamed for having failed to grasp the essence of this Germanic conception, on account of the influence of Roman ideas.

Gierke's analysis is not borne out by the evidence. His model is essentially based on his own strong imagination, reinforcing a popular nineteenth-century myth still alive today of a good, old, warm, cohesive society, located in a fictitious past. Every time sufficient evidence becomes available, this past has to be pushed farther back until, no doubt, one reaches the impenetrable forests of Tacitus' *Germania*. The medieval guildsmen personified guilds in so far as they made them the subjects of sentences, just as people generally do with all kinds of groups; the difference between this and Gierke's model is the same as the difference between saying 'oaks grow' and animism.

It is true that moral meaning was attached to the guild, but not in any collectivist sense. Guilds were valued in a special way as objects of personal loyalty, much as people today value the union, firm, school, club or regiment; this is the truth behind Gierke's myth. Given the variety of craft-guilds, such attitudes would be likely to vary widely, depending on whether one is speaking of upper Germany or northern Italy, and depending on a multiplicity of individual situations. For some the guild was a sacred social bond, for others a means to a livelihood.

It is very surprising, given the social and economic importance of guilds, that so little attention was paid to them by social and political writers. References to craft-guilds are hard to find, outside the jurists, in medieval works on philosophy, politics and theology. There are passing mentions in book iv of Albert the Great's *Commentary on Aristotle's Politics* (somewhat exaggerated by Martin 1951, 41). Ptolemy of Lucca included 'crafts and guilds' (*artes et officia*) alongside 'households and families' as 'distinct grades among the citizens' (bk iv, ch iv). It is amazing that an institution so widespread in society and so characteristic of the times should have been so neglected. Even the jurists only discussed their moral and social meaning in the context of justice. Even after the rediscovery of Aristotle might have made philosophers aware of the moral significance of specific types of association, hardly anyone conceptualized the guild in the way Plato and Aristotle had conceptualized the polis. The guild was accorded virtually no status in the scale of human values; nowhere was it argued that it is good for people to belong to guilds. The silence is deafening.

One reason for this was probably that the intellectual space was occupied by other types of association. It was partly occupied by social concepts taken over from antiquity, such as *civitas* and *imperium*; here, once again, one senses a truth lurking behind Gierke's speculation about the conflict between Germanic and Roman ideas. The rediscovery of Aristotle and the Italian Renaissance, by reinforcing the ascendancy of classical models, made appreciation of craft-guilds more unlikely. Perhaps, however, the most important alternative was the church, both as an international community and as a local spiritual bond; since guilds and confraternities had a religious element, part of their spiritual meaning for people may have been expressed in liturgy. But Gierke's explanation falls down when we look at nation, kingdom and other forms of principality. For these were native 'Germanic' institutions which came to play an increasingly prominent part in learned political discourse as well as in popular imagination. Both jurists and philosophers adapted the Greco-Roman heritage to contemporary realities far more than Gierke's thesis allows.

A second possible explanation is that of Marx: philosophy and jurisprudence were essentially designed to support the ideology of a ruling class, in this case the feudal nobility, and, in some areas, merchant capitalists. This might explain why kingdom and nation were discussed, but not craft-guilds. There is more truth in this explanation than historians of political thought tend to admit. More often than not, both Aristotle and Cicero were used in such a way as to be compatible with courtly, chivalric and, in the cities, merchant-oligarch opinion. It was not difficult to find in them arguments for 'aristocratic' government; Aristotle was sometimes made more 'monarchical' than he really was. A great deal of civic and Renaissance political thought was commissioned by or written for princes or merchant-oligarchs. But this explanation fails on two points. Craft-guilds did in fact, in many late medieval cities, become part of the establishment. Secondly, there was an enormous volume of radical social criticism vigorously directed against the 'ruling class' in the form of exploiting nobles, merchants and clergy, and against current economic practices such as usury. This was not only the product of fringe groups and eccentric satirists, but of popular preachers and respected theologians. But none of these seems to have shown much interest in craft-guilds.

There is a third explanation, compatible with Marxism but more in line with the 'philosophical history' of Adam Smith and, above all, of Hegel and Oakeshott. This is that there was, within medieval urban society itself, a tendency that ran counter to the corporate organization and mentality of guild life, which may best be characterized by Hegel's own term 'civil society'. This was a set of practices and beliefs centred upon a market economy, social mobility, individual self-determination and private property. It formed much of what was then and is still called 'freedom'. When thinkers discussed and conceptualized city or state, they tended very often, and as time passed increasingly, to do so in terms related to these values rather than to guild values. This trend was at once economic, social and intellectual.

A fourth possible explanation must not be entirely overlooked. This is quite simply that systematic political philosophy is an extremely rare phenomenon in the history of human cultures. We should not, therefore, be surprised if Europe in this period produced no Aristotle. If we compare this situation with our own, we find that such a widespread and important institution as the trade union is rarely mentioned in works of literature and has received relatively little attention from social philosophers. Guilds, or something like them, are of great importance in most societies; but that they were not and are not very deeply analysed or evaluated should not, given the propensity of the human mind to concentrate upon some objects to the exclusion of others, altogether surprise us.

By way of contrast, we shall see how much the moral language and social ideology of the city and city-state had in common with the guild mentality. It was here that the ideals of mutual aid and consent really made their mark. But it was to a large extent in the guilds that fraternity, consent and the like were imprinted upon the minds of town-dwellers. The political class of early towns was often defined by membership of a merchant fraternity. When crafts rose to power they brought with them a fresh influx of guild assumptions. City governments were for much of the time run by men whose political socialization had taken place within guilds; the notaries' guild at Florence provides a well-documented example (Martines 1968, 53; Najemy 1979, 58). Thus the towns provided the intermediary through which guild ideals did in fact become part of the political language and formed part of the political aspirations of large sectors of the European population. Guilds were thus one of the several models upon which modern 'democracy' was fashioned. In particular, they were a seedbed of fraternity as a political belief.

3

CIVIL SOCIETY

It will be helpful at this point to consider an alternative set of values to those generally found in the guild milieu. These may be called liberal or bourgeois values; I shall use the term 'civil society' throughout this book to refer to the complex of ideas and practices described in this chapter. As soon as one starts looking at guild or communal ideas in the Middle Ages, one cannot fail to be impressed by the widespread incidence of this alternative. Briefly, the values of civil society comprise, first, personal security in the sense of freedom from the arbitrary passions of others, and freedom from domination in general. This involves freedom (or security) of the person from violence, and of private property from arbitrary seizure. But these, it would appear, can only be maintained if legal process is credibly and successfully enforced as an alternative to physical force, in settlement of disagreements, and in redressing wrongs committed by violence. This leads to the notion of legal rights (whether or not so called), both in the sense of the right to sue in court on equal terms with anyone else – legal equality – and in the sense of claims, for example to property, recognized and upheld by the law. This complex of ideas was present in medieval Europe, at least from the thirteenth century, notably but not exclusively in towns. It played a formative part (as will be seen later) in political thought, sometimes alongside guild ideas, sometimes in place of them. Civil society overlaps with the concept of exchange, which also connotes equality of status between parties. To describe this complex of ideas, I have used 'civil society' in preference to other available shorthands (such as 'liberal values' or 'bourgeois ideology'), because it is not much used today and therefore has a more neutral connotation. It does, however, have the slight disadvantage that it was used from the later Middle Ages to the nineteenth century to mean, approximately, political association (which we today call 'the state'). It also acquired a specialized meaning in Hegel as a society in which people peacefully pursue their own ends (*bürgerliche Gesellschaft*: see p.203); and again in Marx (from whom it has often been translated back into English as 'bourgeois society'), as meaning that, and also the ethos and institutions favourable to capitalism (since Marx called Xenophon an exponent of civil society, the concept was not closely tied to the capitalist epoch). But, in the great majority of cases, this earlier usage was sufficiently non-specific to allow (it is hoped) the term to be used here in the sense outlined, without confusion. No specific parallel is intended with the usage of Locke, Adam Smith, Hegel or Marx.

We have to deal with two kinds of overlapping phenomena: socio-economic development, and *mentalités*, or ideas. Whether either was the 'cause' of the other seems a philosophical, not a historical question; for neither the available evidence nor the kind of evidence that could be available can decide the question. Since, however, not dissimilar economic phenomena (in the sense of raw materials, density of population, technical skill, capital and the like), in other historical situations, appear to have failed to produce the same results – continuous economic development, liberal policies and capitalism – it would seem that social institutions, such as credit, towns and guilds, and also the available ideas, must be included among the essential and not merely contingent historical causes.

From the late eleventh to the early fourteenth century, Europe experienced economic development on an impressive scale: the population expanded, commerce and handicraft industry developed in volume and technique, capital was accumulated, and there was widespread improvement in living standards. By about 1270, it is possible to speak of mercantile capitalism in northern Italy and Flanders (Heers 1973, 217). Whether or not there was economic decline or stagnation in the later Middle Ages, and despite decline in population due to plague, these achievements were permanent and provided a basis for the industrial revolution of modern times. All this was accompanied by distinctive social phenomena: development of credit and partnership, of merchant- and craft-guilds, of towns and markets, increased social mobility and connubial freedom, chiefly but not exclusively for males. Alan Macfarlane has found in England, from as early as the thirteenth century, affluence and a relatively wide distribution of wealth, the willingness and legal capacity to dispose of all forms of property, including land, by sale or will, the nuclear family, and ownership of family property by the head of the household – these last making for social mobility, easier exchange of goods and capital accumulation: it was 'an open, mobile, market-oriented ... nation' (1978, 163). It is interesting to note, by way of parallel, that in 1249 the Peace of Christburg, drawn up between the native Prussians and the Teutonic Knights by a papal legate, stipulated that the Prussians be given freedom to buy and sell to whomever they wished, freedom to sell land, to dispose by will of property including land, and to marry or enter religion: their wives may not be bought, sold or inherited (Philippi 159–61). These characteristics could also be found, in varying degrees, in many cities all over Europe, increasingly from the twelfth century. House land could be bought and sold freely (Harding 1980, 427; Werveke 1963, 19–21). Those who moved into towns and became legal town residents were free to contract a marriage, enter a partnership and make a will without seigneurial consent (Mitteis 1975, 211). Nuclear families were common in some towns, though not in others (Brady 1978a, 39–40). One of the objects of the urban revolutions of the thirteenth and fourteenth centuries was to achieve conditions under which 'all could buy and sell freely' (Hibbert 1963, 204). In this way many acquired liberty of person. Towns, moreover, provided special facilities for the exchange of commodities, the right to hold a market being one of the first ambitions of the urban movement from the late eleventh century. They protected local commerce and manufacture; craft guilds were an urban phenomenon. A world was developing which was, in important respects although by no means entirely, withdrawn from feudal ties, a world in which personal independence could certainly be more easily achieved.

This was reflected in legal practice, urban constitutions and ideology. To secure these advantages was one of the aims of the corporate 'customs, rights, liberties' which numerous towns clamoured for and acquired from the eleventh century onwards (cf. Harding 1980, esp. p.442). The transition from servile to burgher status was summed up in the famous German proverb 'city air makes you free after a year and a day' (Planitz 1954, 99, 118), that being the usual requirement under town law. As a fourteenth-century Saxon town law treatise said:

> If any man has resided free for a year and a day in a town under town law without challenge, he will the more easily retain liberty, for himself and his relatives ... no one can reduce him to servitude ... all who dwell in a town are subject to one law of the freed (*uno libertorum jure*).
>
> (*Sächsische Weichbildrecht* 66, 70)

Aquinas, whose parents had attempted to inveigle him into marriage, generalized to the effect that 'servants are not obliged to obey their lords, nor children their parents, in contracting marriage, maintaining virginity or any such matter' (*Summa Theologiae* IIa IIae q.104 a.5).

Legally secure ownership of his own property was inherent both in the burgher's view of his own status and in the orderly pattern of commerce and industry, upon which towns for the most part subsisted. The first alliance between Lübeck and Hamburg (1210) included the clause

> that our right (*ius*) should also be your right and vice versa, so that [your] townsmen, with their goods which they have brought into the city without seizure, should in every respect enjoy that peace and security which our townsmen with their goods are recognized as having.
>
> (cit. Gierke 1868, 461n.)

The cities which joined the Rhineland league in 1254 declared as one of their aims: 'that not only the greater among us should enjoy this common defence, but that all the lesser with the greater, clerics secular and religious

... laymen and Jews, should rejoice in this protection (*tuitio*)' (Keutgen 80). At its next meeting in October 1254 the league defined its aim as 'the common utility equally for rich and poor ... to the benefit of the poor and the greater ... laymen and Jews' (Keutgen 81). Just as the craft-guilds aimed to provide a secure environment for artisan production, so towns aimed to provide a secure environment for trade in general and to minimize its risks. The very idea of economic rationality, corresponding to the rationalizing trend in all branches of learning (Bolgar 1958, 157ff.), can perhaps be detected in the Rhineland league's lament that 'the innocent are oppressed without reckoning of thought (*sine calculo rationis*)' (Keutgen 80; cf. Weber 1958, 223).

The second part of the *Decalogue*, which dominated medieval legal and social thought as it dominated ethics generally, forbade crimes against person and property, and so provided the mould in which civil society and respect for individuals might be cast. The ideal of personal liberty, and of property rights, was a consequence of looking at those commandments from the viewpoint of the recipient. Again, medieval scholars and legal practitioners inherited from the *Digest* the notion of human society as an arena of relatively free-floating relationships, in which people were involved in buying, selling, contracting, marrying and entering partnerships. The Roman civil law, as well as giving the head of the family greater control over family property than did Germanic law (Stein and Shand 1974, 115–16), comprised a system regulating relations between persons and in respect of property in such a way as to make individual ownership secure and transferable by defined legal procedures, and so to make property relations in general predictable and property itself subject to rational exploitation. 'Law for the Romans is a boundary enclosing and protecting an area which it does not occupy, and which is therefore free' (Tellenbach 1940, 15). Ownership, exchange and partnership are part of the law of nations, practices common to mankind (*Digest* 1.1.5; *Institutes* 1.2.2). Aquinas proceeded to speak of 'just purchases, sales and suchlike, without which men cannot live together' as 'derived from the law of nature' (*Summa Theologiae* Ia IIae q.95 a.4).

The idea that what belongs to a person, 'propriety' as Locke would call it, cannot be snatched from him without undermining the social bond itself, was already contained in Cicero's *On Duties* (*De Officiis* III.v.21), probably the second most widely read book in medieval and Renaissance Europe. The first duty of rulers is to see that 'each keeps his own'; they must on no account attempt economic redistribution or 'equality of goods ... than which what could be more noxious?' (II.xxi.73; II.xxiv.85). Mutual trust can only exist in a society where debts have to be paid (II.xxiv.84). In the study of the Bible, law and the liberal arts, men could find plenty of moral matter conducive to the values of civil society.

35

The notion of property *rights* appears first to have been formulated in the twelfth and thirteenth centuries by the civil law Glossators, who saw possession (*dominium*) as a right (*ius*), and introduced the notion of absolute individual ownership (*ius in re*) which 'one may claim against all men' and which is 'transferable by an act of their possessor' (Tuck 1979, 13–16, developing Villey). This became common doctrine (Calasso 1957, 170n.; Gierke 1881, 442). Aquinas defended individual possession as 'necessary for human life' because it ensured the orderly and peaceful conduct of affairs and made men careful and industrious (*Summa Theologiae* IIa IIae q.66 a.2 concl.). John of Paris (*c.* 1300) produced a theory of property rights so radical that it has been compared to Locke's (Coleman, forthcoming).

Alongside this concern for property arose a conception of privacy. Legal rights guarantee domestic security, that freedom from fear of arbitrary seizure within one's own house which is still very much a mark of the 'western' polity. Not only for the Englishman was his house his castle; an old German proverb ran in the same vein (Blecher 1975, 285), and a fourteenth-century canonist said that 'everyone is called king in his own house' (cit. Calasso 1957, 171; cf. Viterbo ch.1). Ockham called this the human right of 'vindicating one's claim to one's house if one is illegitimately driven from it and also of defending it if anyone tries to despoil one of it' (cit. Lagarde 1946, 204n.; cf. Le Roy Ladurie 1980, 24ff.). To the modern western reader there is already a suggestion of suburbia and privet hedges.

The legitimacy of commerce, in the strict sense of buying and selling, was taken for granted. Even serfs could sell their surplus; in the fifteenth century Brandolinus referred to trade (*commercia*) as something which 'is everyone's due by right' (*unicuique iure debetur*) (116). To be a professional merchant was another matter; but, although aristocratic feudal society disdained merchants and peasants suspected them, the mercantile profession, which was the nerve of urban life, was entirely acceptable among townspeople. Bolgar believes that familiarity with ancient Rome enabled the merchant to acquire 'public esteem': the Romans 'had been men aware of wealth and its importance, men who had devoted much of their attention to the wise use and the prudent making of money, men in whom the progressive Italian merchants could see their own prototype' (1958, 137). Moralists had nothing against men who served the community by transporting and distributing goods; the merchant was accorded his own skill (*peritia*) and industry (*industria*) (Michaud-Quantin 1964b, 39; Mundy 1973, 176). The accumulation of wealth, however, was widely regarded as a sign of greed and extortion; consequently many successful merchants spent their gains on lavish public projects. During the later Renaissance wealth was sometimes explicitly extolled as contributing to the public weal (Skinner 1978, i 74), while the profession of commerce came in for contempt (Martines 1980, 423).

It is worth noticing how the idea of contract, which was later embodied in a political theory peculiarly suited to the values of civil society, was already acquiring a special status in the Middle Ages. Contractual relations were one thing the feudal world and the world of commerce had in common. Mutual trust that contracts will be honoured, bills paid and goods delivered was a prerequisite for the development of trade. The Roman law jurists were the first to introduce contract into political theory. Bartolus held the emperor to be bound by pacts concluded with cities, because pacts belong to the immutable law of nations (on *Codex* 1.14.4; cf. Baldus on same; and Ullmann 1967, 83n.). Some held that a prince's contract is actionable (Andreas ab Exea, *De Pactis* fol.17r; R. W. and A. J. Carlyle 1936, 153ff.).

In the case of the mercantile partnership (*societas*) (cf. Baldwin 1970, i 288–90), contract was the constitutive element in the association. According to the *Digest*, a partnership was something one 'entered into' or 'contracted' (*Digest* 17.2.5; cf. Buckland 1963, 506–7). Medieval jurists distinguished the partnership from the college by saying that the former existed for business and profit; as Hostiensis put it, 'a partnership is contracted (*societas contrahitur*) for more favourable profit and richer gain' (*De Syndicis* fol.104r; Evans 1979, 39; cf. Michaud-Quantin 1970, 67). The principle of equality in the sharing of profit was held to be inherent in the nature of the contract of partnership. In the first juristic monograph *On Partnerships*, Angelus de Periglis stated that 'the person contributing the money must be repaid a sum equal to what he put in, and the person contributing the labour must be paid a sum equal to the value of his labour, and whatever surplus remains must be divided between the two parties equally' (O'Brien 1920, 209). St Antonino of Florence (d.1459) said that 'it is in the nature of the contract of partnership that the parties be equal, having regard to the amount invested in the partnership' (*de natura contractus societatis sit, quod partes sint aequales, habito respectu ad quotam in societatem positam*) (*De Usuris* fol.85v/b n.72). Similarly, Christophorus Porcius said that 'in case of doubt, loss and gain are equally shared in a partnership, because the partnership has a bond of fraternity ... and therefore in it equality is desirable' (fol.151r). In one of the earliest formulations of social-contract theory the partnership was used as a direct analogy for the polity (see p.85).

A distinctive tone of behaviour was coming to be identified as civil, urbane, polite. *The Shepherd's Eye* (*Oculus Pastoralis, c.*1220) advised a town ruler to behave 'with conspicuous urbanity', to avoid saying anything that was not 'urbane' (107–8); in turn he must urge the citizens to live 'by urban moeurs' (*moribus urbanis*), that is keep the peace and give no offence 'to those greater than, equal to or lesser than' themselves (97). Ptolemy of Lucca said that 'political rule', which is specially suited to cities, should be 'gentle' (*suave*) and conducted 'with a certain civility' (bk ii, ch.8). *Civilitas*, originally meaning legal citizenship, was coming to connote a civilized way of life that was or ought to be found in cities (cf. Machiavelli, *Discourses* I, ch.lv, 205). In contrast to feudal or rustic *moeurs*, it meant treating people as formal equals, a readiness to be nice to one's neighbour, the friendly greeting of the shopkeeper, *Gemütlichkeit* between people who do business together but have little else in common. In general, we may say that civil society institutionalizes the encounter between strangers; it provides a framework within which the development of closer, *gemeinschaftlich* relationships is not expected. The city itself supported this through its shared facilities and the promotion of trade; it was a place where different localities and points of view might rub shoulders and intermingle, and so a 'civilization' be born.

Liberty of person and property were as often as not formulated in terms of security, which in this context meant much the same thing. Security or liberty of person was seen to depend upon the possibility of defending oneself by law, that is upon the capacity to sue in court, under impartial laws and judges. One of the earliest statements of urban political thought (*c.*1250) started with a definition of the specific character of cities, which emphasized security of person from arbitrary violence, ensured by the right to a fair trial.

> A city is called the liberty of citizens or the immunity of inhabitants ... for that reason walls were built to provide help for the inhabitants.... 'City' means 'you dwell safe from violence' (*Civitas, id est 'Ci(tra) vi(m) (habi)tas'*). For residence is without violence, because the ruler of the city will protect the lowlier men lest they suffer injury from the more powerful, since 'we cannot be equal with those more powerful' (*Digest* 4.7.3). Again, 'no one must be unjustly treated on account of the power of his adversary ...' (*Digest* 1.1.19). Again, since the home (*domus*) is for each person a most secure refuge and shelter, no one should be taken therefrom against their will; nor is it reasonable that anyone in a town should be compelled by violent fear and so on (*Digest* 2.4.18 and 2.4.21). Again [the city] is truly called a place of immunity, because its inhabitants are guarded by its walls and towers and protected in it from their enemies and foes.   (John of Viterbo ch.1)

The author went on to paraphrase Cicero: 'cities were invented ... so that each might hold onto his own, and no one should be anxious for the safety of his goods' (ch.3, pp.218–19; cf. Cicero, *De Officiis* II.xxi.73). Similarly, Rolandinus of Padua's *Chronicle* (1262) said: 'it is believed to be an act of the supreme divine providence that governments have been established in cities, so that acts of violence might be repressed ... and rights (*iura*) preserved unharmed' (56).

Brunetto Latini (whose *Treasury*, written in the 1260s in the Languedoc dialect, has been called the 'first encyclopedia to be written for learned laymen ... as burghers': Martines 1980, 156) explained the origin of cities in very similar terms, combining Augustinian, Ciceronian and Aristotelian formulae adapted to the contemporary scene:

> For since people first began to increase and multiply, and the sin of the first man took root in his lineage, and times pressed hard so that people coveted their neighbours' possessions – some in their arrogance subjected the weaker to the yoke of slavery – it came in the end to the point where those who wanted to live by their own law and escape the force of evil-doers grouped themselves together in one place and under one government. Thence they began to build houses and establish towns (*viles*) and fortresses, and enclose them with walls and ditches. Thence they began to establish customs and law and rights (*drois*) which should be common to all the burghers (*borgois*) of the town. (391)

The town rescues men from seigneurial oppression. Similarly, the Peace of Christburg (1249) insisted that Roman Christians have the right to sue in ecclesiastical and secular courts. It concluded a list of 'civil rights', enabling people to do just those things which typify civil society, by saying that the conquered Prussians were 'legal persons' (*legitimae personae*) and must be granted 'all manner of personal liberty' (*libertatem omnimodam personalem*) (Philippi 161). Writing a century later, William of Ockham stated that, in general terms, ownership is contingent upon the right to plead in court (*ius fori*) (Lagarde 1946, 204–5).

The same basic idea was expressed in somewhat more modern terminology by the humanists. Salutati, chancellor of Florence, defined liberty (1380) in terms of Roman citizenship: it means 'to live by right (*iure*) and to obey laws to which all are subject ... to follow laws which treat everyone with the most just reckoning of equality' (*Invectivum* 30–2). Leonardo Bruni boasted of Florence (1403–4): 'no one here can suffer injustice, nor can anyone lose his property against his will. Judgments and magistrates are prepared; the way to court and the supreme tribunal lie open. Pleas against every condition of men are completely free in this city' (*Eulogy* 262). After he had succeeded Salutati as chancellor, he declared (1428), 'we fear no one as lord ... we are released from the fear of men'; 'true liberty' is to live where 'there is no fear of force or injury to anyone, where there is legal equality (*paritatem juris*) among the citizens' (Strozzi speech 230–1). Aeneas Sylvius Piccolomini, writing in the mid-fifteenth century, used the same criteria to contrast the cities of Italy, where 'the citizens, save for the few who lead the rest, are treated as slaves, since they cannot use their goods as they please, nor say what they wish', with those of Germany, where 'no one is deprived of his own goods, each one's liberty is intact, the magistrates

39

harm none but the harmful' (*Germania* bk ii, ch.xxiv, p.62). Machiavelli believed that most people desire to be free not in order to rule but in order to 'live in greater security'. 'The advantages that result to the mass of the people from a free government' are 'to be able freely to enjoy one's own without apprehension, to have nothing to fear for the honour of one's wife and daughters or for himself'. Such things 'are not appreciated by anyone whilst he is in enjoyment of them' (*Discourses* I, chs iv–v, 16, trans. Detmold).

Equality before the law and the rule of law were political ideals to which civil society gave rise (some kind of equality being implicit in exchange). In this respect Locke's concept of 'equal laws' is a direct descendant of medieval thought. Yet all this had been said before.

Since, therefore, law is the bond of civil society (*civilis societatis*), and justice is equality under the law (*ius autem legis aequale*), by what right can a partnership of citizens (*societas civium*) be justly maintained unless there is equality of status among the citizens (*cum par non sit condicio civium*)? For, while it is undesirable to equalize wealth, and everyone cannot have the same talents, legal rights (*iura*) at least should be equal among citizens of the same commonwealth.

(Cicero, *De Republica* I.xxxii.49)

Cicero here encapsulated the ideals of liberal society: *equality*, not of wealth or talent, but of legal and political rights. Europe was to hear more of this 'equality of conditions'.

Yet, at least in town law and ideology, none of this led to a theory of rights or liberty as due to men in general. Townsmen did not extend their privileges to rural subjects. Pocock's remarks about the absence of 'particularity' in medieval thought (1975, 9ff.) seem here, alas, peculiarly inapposite.

These priorities were by no means an exclusively urban concern. One of the most common ways of distinguishing between just and tyrannical government was to say that under the former the ruler ruled according to law, under the latter he ruled arbitrarily. Aquinas said that under tyranny 'there will be no security, but everything will be uncertain, since there is departure from *ius*, and nothing can be held safe that is placed in the will or lust of another' (*On Princely Government* I, ch.3, p.16). Rule by law is here seen as the basis for predictable social relations and personal autonomy. Machiavelli thought that, in kingdoms as well as city-states, people put security first, so that if the prince refrains from breaking the laws and imposing arbitrary taxes, his subjects will be content and 'live in tranquillity' (*Discourses* I, ch.xvi; *Prince* ch.3). Far from being an 'ideology' of a possessing 'class', these sentiments seem to have percolated in all directions in medieval and Renaissance society.

One reason why the idea of personal liberty as something inherently desirable and valuable became so very widespread was that it was sanctioned, and indeed partly inspired, by both Germanic and Christian tradition, as well as having a respectable classical pedigree. Every people in history has desired freedom in the collective sense, to live in their own way, according to their own customs. But the notion of individual self-determination as a goal does not seem to be so widespread, and has certainly not become such a dominant theme in social, legal and political thought, in other cultures. In Frankish and Teutonic society, the freedom or *franchisia* of members of the warrior aristocracy (Harding 1980, 427) was a mark not only of social status but of individual prowess. In feudal times, nobles could quote Sallust to the effect that 'every good man loses freedom only with his life' (Tellenbach 1940, 18). Cicero had said that 'nothing is sweeter' than liberty (*De Republica* I.xxxi.47). Stoic philosophy, reflected in Roman law, taught that freedom had been part of the original condition of mankind 'in nature' (A. J. Carlyle 1941, 4–7); the *Digest* defined freedom as 'the natural capacity (*facultas*) for each one to do as he pleases, unless constrained by force or law' (*Digest* 1.5.4; *Institutes* 1.3.1) – a definition widely quoted, for example by Bracton (vol.ii, p.28). In late Roman and patristic thought, freedom was extolled as the distinguishing mark of the civilized man as opposed to the barbarian (R. W. and A. J. Carlyle 1903, 113ff.; Tellenbach 1940, 2ff.).

But it was perhaps Christianity which revolutionized people's consciousness in this matter (see pp.82–4). For its teaching was precisely that, whereas the ancient Jews had been liberated from Egypt as a people, Christ had liberated mankind individually as well as collectively. Salvation was a personal passage from death to life, solemnized by baptism, and it was expressed, notably by St Paul, in terms of *liberation* from sin. This meant that the Christian was pre-eminently and above all else a free person. Of course all this could be given a strictly internal, non-legal meaning; but this might begin to seem unnatural, and certainly the biblical language of liberation could assist anyone, who desired freedom in a more external sense, to articulate himself and to present his demands in what were, given the cultural ethos and dominant doctrine, convincing terms. It was in the name of 'the liberty of the sons of God', and because all men are equal unless subject to sin, which makes any man whatever his social status a slave, that civil liberties were extended to the converted Prussians (Philippi 159–61). Free choice was the gift of God to man; although virtue or sanctity was the ultimate goal, this could not (as John of Salisbury put it) 'be perfectly achieved without liberty, and the loss of liberty shows that perfect virtue is lacking' (*Policraticus* VII, ch.25: vol.ii, p.217).

The inherent dignity of the individual, whatever his social or economic status, was clearly implied in parts of the Bible. Recent scholarship has increasingly recognized the existence in the Middle Ages of an individualism, in the sense of a tendency for individuals to differentiate themselves from the social group (Harvey 1950, 38, 49; Le Roy Ladurie 1980, chs 6–7; Macfarlane 1978, 196–9). As Aquinas said, while all men share a single final goal, 'it happens that men proceed to their intended goal in different ways, as shown by the very diversity of human studies and actions' (*On Princely Government* I, ch.1, p.2; cf. *Summa Theologiae* I q.96 a.3). Religious practice, moreover, embraced wide diversities and some eccentricities. Outward behaviour was probably less regulated and conformist in medieval Europe than it has been since. A recent interpretation ascribes the Renaissance 'ascent of "the individual"'' to 'the course of urban economic relations' (Martines 1980, 108; cf. Seigel 1966, 28–9); here urban experience and upper-class literary perceptions converged (Morris 1972, 65ff.). On the other hand, the individual might sharpen his self-image, and advance his claims, through membership of a group of his own choosing or with which he felt a definite bond – such as a guild.

It was perhaps this combination of forces – ideas from different sources, social traditions and practical circumstances – which made liberty such a commanding ideal in European culture. It was championed both in the Ciceronian ideology of the Renaissance, and in the Pauline ideology of the Reformation. A humanist like Mirandola could add an existentialist touch: man, unlike any other creature, has no specific nature but can 'be what he wants to be' (104–5). Aristotle, on the other hand, was quoted in support of the introduction of slavery into the New World (Skinner 1978, ii 142). In fact, in parts of Italy and throughout central and eastern Europe, serfdom was revived at the end of the Middle Ages, and in Russia in the eighteenth century (Martines 1980, 228; Slicher van Bath 1977, 114ff.).

From all this emerge the contours of what is fashionably called today 'negative liberty' or 'freedom from ... ', but what might more usefully be called private or personal liberty. Berlin's distinction between 'negative' and 'positive' liberty merely indicates the boundary between what happens to be taken for granted in certain 'western' countries at the moment, and what requires 'affirmative action'. For people in medieval Europe, and in many other periods and cultures, freedom to possess, buy, sell, dispose by will, choose one's spouse and profession definitely enlarged one's sphere of action.

It is a fair indication that what we have called 'civil society' was becoming well established by about the end of the thirteenth century that reactions against it, which have lasted to this day, also began at that time. The emergence of a market economy, increased use of money, the creation and diffusion of wealth and luxury, the extension of private ownership, domesticity, and a variety of life-styles – all these provoked reactions in the name of poverty, economic equality or communism (Cohn 1957). Such revolts comprise a sporadic counter-history of medieval and modern Europe. Their continuity is indirect testimony that their target remained basically unchanged. The correlation which we have suggested between property, security of person, legal equality, individual diversity and the like, is mirrored in counter-schemes for redistribution of wealth, the abolition of private ownership, greater social conformity and a tightly-knit, warm, charismatic community, *Gemeinschaft* or fraternity. 'Collectivism' has, from the fourteenth century onwards, provided the counter-culture to civil society, to which it poses a constantly unsettling threat.

One may say that, throughout the Middle Ages, the Renaissance and beyond, liberty in a legal, social or political context practically always *included* the postulates of civil society as outlined here, which may be summarized as individual liberty. But liberty also had a communal and corporate meaning. It was used to define the claim of rural and urban communities to territorial immunity from baronial jurisdiction (Harding 1980, 427, 442), just as 'freedom of the church' meant, to the eleventh-century reformers, ecclesiastical immunity and self-government. In civic politics, liberty meant the city's internal autonomy, particularly in jurisdiction and economic affairs, but not usually excluding subjection to the ultimate authority of king or emperor, who was the guardian of communal liberties, ruling over free subjects. The corporate liberty of the town or village was indeed coterminous with the individual liberties of its members (cf. Harding 1980, 442).

We may identify the central ideal of civil society as personal independence, and its central imperative as respect for persons. The ideas discussed here were the soil out of which grew the political ideology of liberty and equality. They, above all else, comprise the ideals of 'western', 'liberal' or 'capitalist' society and determine its particular notion of 'democracy'.

4

THE ETHOS OF THE EARLY
TOWNS (COMMUNES) UP TO 1250

The values of guild and civil society flowed like red and white corpuscles in the bloodstream of medieval and Renaissance political thought. Their diffusion coincided with the development of self-governing towns, parliaments and the 'common law' tradition; it is related to the whole question of the distinctive development of European political culture. In our pursuit of guild ideas, we must now turn to the early communes of 1050–1250. What kind of communities did their members perceive them to be? How did they regard and define the new bonds of civic association? What were their procedural (constitutional) values? Was the civic ethos of this period a Roman, Germanic or Christian product? These enquiries lead to our main point: how were the values of guild and civil society reflected in the communes? It may be argued, *inter alia*, that in their economic protectionism and in the kind of community their members perceived them to be, towns and guilds were groups of a markedly similar type.

The early communes did not establish themselves and conduct their policy according to a clearly stated programme. But that does not mean that they were not acting upon principles of some kind. Clearly, cities, merchant- and craft-guilds could not develop without certain economic opportunities: plentiful raw materials, reasonably peaceful conditions for commerce, a growing population, technical improvements in agriculture, and the like. Yet social techniques involving exchange, credit and the organization of labour had to be learnt, borrowed and transmitted. Material circumstances *enabled* development to occur; but some appropriate mental attitudes were a *sine qua non* for the successful exploitation of those material conditions. Since the European level of economic achievement in the eleventh century has been reached in other cultures and times, it alone cannot explain why this particular society now went in a particular direction. In order to discover the political sentiment of the early communes, one has to look for thought patterns implied by their actual policies and by the language they used (see pp.244–5). From documents produced within the town milieu and from the jurists, there emerges a discernible political language, which gives us an impression of how these townspeople were conceptualizing their political world.

A distinctive and clearly-defined notion of community developed during the take-off period of the urban movement, and was applied indifferently to towns of all sizes, to villages and to guilds. Popular and official opinion in towns appears to have regarded such a community as by its very existence having a moral right to corporate status, to juridical personality, to the ownership of collective property, and also a moral right to elect its own rulers and govern its internal affairs. This was part of the secret behind the rapid spread of the word *universitas* to describe such groups.

Oath-bound civic communities (*coniurationes*) appeared along the Rhine in the 1070s, and 'communes' ruled by 'consuls' appeared in Italy by at least the 1080s. In the late eleventh and early twelfth centuries, the communal movement spread rapidly through northern France and the Low Countries. During the twelfth century, internally autonomous cities became a regular feature of the European landscape from the Baltic to Provence. They varied in size from the great Italian and Flemish cities to the very numerous small towns of Germania. Towns varied in type between those concentrating upon long-distance commerce, such as Venice, Lübeck and Genoa, those producing for export, especially of cloth (Florence, Cologne, the Low Countries) and metal (upper Germania, including Augsburg), and finally the great majority of smaller towns producing for and trading with their local region. The town population included great merchant-capitalists, small retailers, independent craftsmen, and dependent workers; cloth and metal workers, producers of luxury goods, and those engaged in the myriad everyday crafts, from bakers to shoemakers. It included rentiers living off profits from commerce and land (Hibbert 1963, 159; Waley 1969, 22, 34), those engaged in service industries from barbers to innkeepers, and considerable numbers of clergy.

The typical medieval town has been described as 'a commune living, under the shelter of its surrounding fortifications, on trade and industry' (Pirenne, cit. Werveke 1963, 25). This defined its political destiny: 'the town constitutions were new phenomena, a response to profound changes of an economic and social nature' (Werveke 1963, 25). The urban communes attempted to suppress lawless nobles, private jurisdiction and the vendetta (Bloch 1961, 417). This is not to say that they were created by a new 'bourgeois class'; in many cases they were the work of local nobility (Heers 1974, 122–3, 265). But trade and industry were vital links between town and merchant- or craft-guild.

Internally, city governments undertook a very wide range of activities: there was 'constant intervention by the commune in every aspect of social and economic activity' (Waley 1969, 93). Security required a citizen army – only in Italy did mercenary armies become common, probably for technical reasons (Jones 1965, 89n.) – police, law courts and a criminal code.

Revenue was raised by direct and indirect taxation, sometimes by state debt or forced loans (Martines 1980, 240–9; Planitz 1954, 118); large cities minted their own currency. Commercial freedom and security required supervision of trade routes, negotiation with outside powers, and complex procedures for civil jurisdiction. All this gave rise to the improvisation of new organs of government, which tended to become increasingly complex as adjustments were constantly being made for the interplay of sectional interests: new offices were created beside old ones, a new council was superimposed on the old, there were overlapping jurisdictions of commune, *popolo*, guild and family. There was a constant flow of legislation, and relatively frequent changes to the constitution.

The towns' dependence on industry and trade led to a volume of economic legislation aimed at removing obstacles to commerce, increasing its volume, concentrating it in a particular town, controlling prices and sometimes fixing wages and interest rates (Hibbert 1963, 159–65, 202; Waley 1969, 95). Attempts were made to control the supply and export of raw materials. The dependence of town on country led to grain policies. Some towns played an even more direct role by providing granaries, breweries, mills or factories (Schneider 1954; Spandrel 1968, 56–7). Private life was subject to city legislation on such matters as dowries and wills (Waley 1969, 100), while civic public life was planned to a high degree. The building of churches and the town hall, sometimes the planning of a whole new town, was undertaken by town councils, whose concern for public grandeur, visual display and artistic patronage has left plenty of visible evidence, whether homely, solid, quaint or magnificent (Mumford 1966, 344–51; Rörig 1967, 171–3; Waley 1969, 147–63).

Yet it is the volume of social legislation, control and provision that most strikes the modern observer, inviting perhaps comparison with modern welfare socialism. Not only streets and hygiene but also morals were a public concern (Becker 1967, 227–8; Rörig 1967, 177; Waley 1969, 99–100); here Savonarola stood firmly in the medieval tradition. Hospitals, almshouses and old people's homes were either sponsored or run by town governments; poverty was an area of widespread civic concern (Feine 1950, 347–9; Mumford 1966, 309, 348). According to Rörig 'the town was more concerned than the church' in social welfare (1967, 177), though it was usually church bodies or lay confraternities that did the job. Some Italian communes employed 'a sort of "medical officer of health"' (Waley 1969, 101); while 'in Hamburg, Vienna and Augsburg the brothels were under municipal protection' (Mumford 1966, 324). Municipal schools, answering the need of merchants and town authorities for literacy, accounting skills and legal proficiency, were common in Germany and Italy (Feine 1950, 349–51; Rörig 1967, 177; Waley 1969, 101). The universities of Bologna, Cologne, Erfurt and Basle were civic foundations (Rörig 1967, 138; cf.

Andreas 1943, 428ff.). This social concern was to a considerable degree informed by Christian teaching (cf. Mundy 1973, 183). Yet here too, as in the whole programme of economic protectionism, the guild ethos of mutual aid, mutual protection and insurance was also at work. When at Berwick the town formed itself into a guild of all the citizens (1249), it took over functions previously performed by the guilds, such as poor relief and burial (Coornaert 1947, 211; Wilda 1831, 147ff., 376ff.).

Cities tended to develop a unique ecclesiastical and even spiritual complexion. City governments concerned themselves with the administration of church property and buildings, and with clerical appointments. The main city church with its vast internal space might, like San Marco at Venice, be considered to belong 'more to the Commune than to the bishop' (Lane 1973, 98): 'the ideal was still that ... the entire population could find room in the cathedral' (Waley 1969, 158). There were clashes with the church hierarchy over clerical immunity, taxation and jurisdiction. Yet numerous clergy, especially the friars, played an integral part in town life, while town governments frequently concerned themselves with church reform. New religious orders like the Friars, Beguines and Brethren of the Common Life, developed charitable work and a spirituality peculiarly suited to the towns; a bond, evident in guild chapels, communal festivals, patrician patronage and the adoption of a patron saint, developed between civic and ecclesiastical life (Holmes 1973, 114–18; Rörig 1967, 130).

In the early towns, political authority centred upon the full members of the original commune, sworn association or guild, and their descendants; in large Italian cities these numbered more than 800 (Waley 1969, 106–8). In Italy, the general assembly of such full citizens was consulted on matters of legislation and war and peace; in Germania, where the assembly was usually smaller, it also dealt with taxation, military matters and the admission of new citizens (Planitz 1954, 116–19) – this last a distinct parallel with the guild. The general assembly was called, in Italy, *concilium maius* (greater council), *arenga*, *parlamentum*, *adunantia generalis*; in Germania, *universitas civium* or *cives*; in France, *plaids généraux, placita*. On the other hand, *all* adult male town residents were expected to swear obedience to the laws, allegiance to the rulers and fidelity to treaties or alliances contracted with other states (Waley 1969, 32, 39, 61–2).

A small committee with judicial and executive powers managed daily business. These were called *rectores* (rulers) and, in Italy and Provence, *consules*; in northern Europe – Germania, the Low Countries, France and England – *scabini, échevins, Schöffen, jurati* (jurymen or judicial elders), and also *iudices, magistratus, magistri civium*. In Italy these were from the start elected by the commune. In Germania and elsewhere, rulers were frequently, at first, appointed by the town lord, then later more often elected by citizens and confirmed in office by the lord or king. By the mid-thirteenth century the more powerful German and Flemish cities were electing their own rulers (Feenstra 1954; Gilissen 1954).

During and after the twelfth century, in both Italy and northern Europe, a city council, usually of twelve or twenty-four members elected by the full citizens, took over most of the functions of the general assembly and some of those of the earlier 'rulers' or 'consuls'. This was known in Italy as *consilium minus* (lesser council) or *consilium, senatus, credenza* (Waley 1969, 62), in northern Europe as the council (*concilium civitatis, Rat, conseil*). Although its formal position remained advisory, in practice it dealt with all major matters, including legislation, and became the focus of political power (Planitz 1954, 297–9, 310–12; Waley 1969, 62–5). Italian cities developed a complex system of interlocking advisory and judicial panels, drawn from militia leaders, craft-guilds and other sections of the community (Martines 1980, 30–2; Waley 1969, 107–8). Both council members and other leading citizens who participated in this way were styled *maiores et meliores, meliores et sapientiores* (the wiser and better), *savi, prud' hommes, optimi civitatis, nobiliores civium, discretiores, prudentissimi civitatis, viri honesti, viri honorabiles* (Planitz 1954, 102, 109–21, 266; Planitz 95). In German cities, and in Italian cities which escaped the rise of despotism, the council remained the centre of government, to which later on craft-guilds clamoured for admission.

From the start towns established their own courts and made their own laws. This activity rested upon a clear though implicit belief about the community's legal functions, a belief which was based partly on their notion of justice, partly on their notion of self-authenticating community. Already in the early towns the rule of law, a prerequisite of civil society, was widely adopted as a constitutional principle. This was partly because the town judge was often appointed by the lord, and townsmen were therefore keen to insist that he give sentence according to their own laws. The charter granted to Freiburg-im-Breisgau in 1120 stated: 'If any quarrel or disagreement arises among my citizens, it shall be decided not according to my judgment (*arbitrium*) or that of their ruler, but it will be judicially investigated in the light of custom and the legitimate right (*legitimo iure*) of all merchants' (Planitz 55). Regensburg's law code, ratified by the lord in 1207, stated: 'If within the city [the magistrate] gives commands for anything to be done, this must only be in accordance with the city laws (*civilia instituta*) and by the consent of the townsmen' (Planitz 76, 140). (Goslar decreed that a noble might not appeal against the city courts, though a citizen might: Michaud-Quantin 1970, 260.) The Italian treatise called *The Shepherd's Eye* (*Oculus Pastoralis, c.* 1220) was particularly indignant about rulers who said 'I will so, let will stand for reason': Justice protests that she cannot ignore the popular clamour against illegality 'unless I should wish to dissolve the machinery of the world'. Rulers must at all costs abide by the laws (*leges*) of Rome, municipal statutes or rights (*iura*) which the 'people's consistency' (*populi cohaerentia*) makes for itself, and 'the approved customs of localities' (125–6).

The early town community went under a number of names: *civitas*, *commune*, *communitas*, *universitas civium/burgensium*, *urbani*, *burgensis populus*, *universi cives*, and the vernacular *commune* (French and Italian), *Gemeinde*, *burgh*. The vernacular term *commune* was from the start widespread in northern France, the Low Countries and Provence; from the mid-twelfth century it was used in Italy of the town in its legal capacity. By the late twelfth century the equivalent term *Gemeinde* (community) was current in Germania (Michaud-Quantin 1970, 147, 154–5 and cf. 149, 159–60). *Commune* was used as a rallying cry by early towns in defence of their liberties: 'no word ever evoked more passionate emotions' (Bloch 1961, 354). These terms, not without religious connotation, were used in asserting claims to common property such as meadows, forest and commons. They designated sworn fellowship in pursuit of common aims in the Germanic tradition; they had been similarly used in the early eleventh-century peace movement. Both *commune* and the cognate term *communitas* were used of citizens banding together in revolt against a local feudatory. But in Flanders and northern France *communitas* 'designated to an increasing extent not the whole body of citizens, but the lesser townsmen as opposed to the patriciate' (Werveke 1963, 36).

Universitas civium came into use in Germania from the mid-twelfth century (Gierke 1873, 593–4; Michaud-Quantin 1970, 51; Planitz 1954, 115, 118, 296–7, 338); it was also used in Catalonia, and in Italy of smaller towns (Michaud-Quantin 1970, 47, 50). *Universitas* sometimes served simply as the Latin for the French or Italian *commune* and the German *Gemeinde*; in formal documents the abstract collective noun tended to be preferred to *universi cives* (Michaud-Quantin 1970, 18). It may have been particularly current in Germania because it suggested less self-assertion against the Empire, but nevertheless evoked the unity of qualified male residents incorporated into the civic body. In Roman law *universitas* meant a private corporation such as the town (*municipium*) or guild (*collegium*); in the Middle Ages it was used as a generic term covering guilds, chapters, cities, kingdoms and the Empire itself (Gierke 1881, 198ff.) Thus the distinction between sovereign and non-sovereign corporate bodies was blurred. But although 'sovereignty' in the modern sense was not implied in the towns' claim to be *universitates*, they did, as Gierke puts it, regard themselves as self-contained bodies which already had within them the 'kernel' of public 'commonweal' and of 'state' (Gierke 1881, 192–202).

The Roman law meaning of *universitas* as a group with legal and property rights (Duff 1938, 35ff.) was also brought into play from the start. The jurists came to use it as their principal term for the town community, perhaps again because it left imperial sovereignty intact. By the fourteenth century *universitas* without the suffix *civium* meant town (Rockinger 450). In its general meaning as a legally recognized association, *universitas* 'spread throughout Christendom' in the period 1190 to 1220 (Gierke 1881, 277–8; Michaud-Quantin 1970, 48, 57), which coincided both with the rise of the *popolo* (see pp.66–8) and with the development of jurisprudence. Mundy finds a correlation between the use of this term and the adoption of a more popular constitution at Toulouse (1954, 362–5). It was frequently used when one spoke of the consent of citizens – *consensus universitatis* – implying a corporate act by the assembled burghers. It was the term chosen by Marsiglio to express the agent of legislative power. It implied legal personality, but there is no reason to follow Gierke (1873, 593–4) in thinking it implied collective consciousness in any further sense.

There was implicit in the word *universitas* as it was now being used, and in its vernacular equivalents *commune* and *Gemeinde*, the concept of all members, the commonalty, as together forming the community, so that when it was asserted that the *universitas* owned something, e.g. pasture and forest, what this meant was that everyone had a share in it and could use it (cf. Duff 1938, 79). For instance, an Innsbruck law of 1239 decreed 'that use of the common pasture (*pascuarum communio*), which is called "the commons (*gemeinde*)", be offered equally to the community of rich and poor' (Planitz 100). While equal access to communal assets seems to have been inherent in membership of the commune, no equality of personal property was implied, unless perhaps in a case of spoil, as when the Worms fishermen's statute of 1106 stipulated that fish confiscated from fishermen operating outside the guild 'be divided equally among the townspeople' (Keutgen 351).

The most immediate and widespread purpose of the claim to be *universitas* was to assert the town community's right to possess corporate property, vindicate such possession in court, appoint a legal representative and plead in court. These aspirations were common also to villages and guilds. In Germanic law towns and villages possessed by customary right pasture (*Allmende*), heaths, forests, fishing rights and water supply, all of which provided individual inhabitants with usufructuary rights essential to their livelihood. With the growth of towns, the question of the community's right to possess and administer streets, markets, almshouses, the town hall and communal mills also assumed importance. One reason why *universitas* became a generic term for organized groups was that it enabled them to avail themselves of the legal rights specified in *Digest* 3.4.1 (see p.19).

Following Roman usage, these corporate legal and property rights of towns were summed up as 'to have corporate association' (*habere universitatem, avoir corps et commune*) (Maitland 1957; Michaud-Quantin 1964a, 3; cf. Duff 1938, 141, 151–2). This claim was established by a considerable number of dependent and quasi-independent towns, and even villages, both in feudal monarchies and in the Empire. The patchwork arrangement of feudal lordships and monarchies could accommodate new bodies with powers of internal jurisdiction; the corporate collection of taxes and the raising of militias by towns was widely sanctioned and even encouraged by overlords, so long as their own superior authority was recognized (Hibbert 1963, 191–3; Werveke 1963, 26–30). Towns secured charters of liberties, the right to hold markets, raise taxes, police themselves, elect officials, and exercise certain powers of internal jurisdiction. Property rights were usually recognized on the basis of custom. All this was at stake in the conflict between Frederick I and the Lombard cities, which claimed customary rights 'in pastures, fishing, mills, ovens, banks, food markets and houses built on public streets' (cit. Pacaut 1963, 83).

The jurists rationalized the situation in two stages. First, they were prepared to recognize the corporate property of towns as falling into the category of *bona universitatis* (goods belonging to a private association). Individuals might use pastures and mills but these belonged to the town; they remained town property even if all the townsmen perished (Gierke 1881, 375–6; cf. Michaud-Quantin 1970, 286–90; Tierney 1955, 118). Secondly, they were sometimes prepared to go further and say that town property belonged to the town as *bona publica* (public property) – a first step towards recognizing the town itself as a *respublica* or quasi-state. This position was argued from custom: for example, the early thirteenth-century Glossator Roffredus replied to the objection based on *Digest* 50.16.15 (which stated that 'it is an abuse of language to call a city's property "public", because only those things that belong to the Roman people are public') by simply saying 'however, public they are called' (q.28). All this has been seen as an attempt to render in Roman terms the Germanic system of ownership, the *gesammte Hand*, in which all adult males of the agnatic group jointly controlled the family property (Gillet 1927, 64–7).

Recognition as *universitas* meant that a group could vindicate its corporate possession of property, which it had traditionally treated as common to its members, and also that it could claim other judicial and administrative functions traditionally carried out at the village or communal level. Here again Roffredus is interesting both in his assumptions and in his forthright and far-reaching appeal to custom. He argued that, in general, a village may 'have *universitas*' – and therefore own property – for three reasons: (1) city property is called public; (2) its streets are commonly called 'village (*vicinales*) streets'; and (3) 'even if written law is lacking, custom nevertheless upholds the power of the law; for all villages and burghs which have anything also have corporate status and elect judges (*potestates*), so that custom, especially when universal, may be recognized as legal right (*pro iure servetur consuetudo*)' (q.28). This development in juristic thought culminated in the statement by Accursius in what became the standard gloss on Roman law, that 'the assembly of any city, village or burgh' can 'have corporate status' (*corpus habere*) (on *Digest* 3.4.1).

The belief in the right of the towns themselves to undertake legislative and judicial responsibilities appears principally to have been based upon their perception of themselves as self-authenticating communities in the Germanic and especially the guild tradition. Town laws were made not only for but by townsmen, they were 'what the city has decreed' (cit. Planitz 1954, 501). The town was here acting in its corporate capacity as *commune*, *universitas*, *Gemeinde*, so that one could speak of 'the will of the city' (cit. Gierke 1873, 822). Although the respective roles of general assembly and city council were often only vaguely alluded to in official documents of the early period, it was understood that legislation was to be transacted 'by common consent'. This notion of law as the product of popular will was not, however, peculiarly Germanic: it was mentioned by Cicero (*De Republica* I.69) and in the *Digest* (1.3.32).

Concerning the legislative power of cities, the jurists were once again the first to attempt formal and general theoretical statements, and to work out the cities' position in the official political order. They suggested that a city or people might make laws in virtue of its being a corporate community (*universitas*). The Gloss spoke of rule-making as a power normally held by an *universitas* (Calasso 1957, 91; Michaud-Quantin 1970, 248, 282). Yet, as a matter of fact, there was nothing in the ancient code to say that an *universitas* might make rules. The jurists were apparently using this term to describe actual contemporary communities of the Germanic genre, of which both town and guild were instances; they were endorsing contemporary practices as 'the right of community' (*ius universitatis*). In another context, however, the Digest did appear to give 'the people' a kind of law-making power:

> For since the laws themselves bind us only because they are accepted by the judgment of the people, those things which the people approved without any writing also deservedly bound all: for what does it matter whether the people declares its will in a formal decision (*suffragio*) or by things and acts themselves?
>
> (*Digest* 1.3.32; cf. 1.3.35; cf. Dawson 1968, 128ff.)

It went on to say that laws could be repealed 'by the tacit consent of all, through disuse' (*Digest* 1.3.32). These texts were applied to the cities (Calasso 1957, 94).

Towns claimed, in most cases successfully, that they were legitimate corporate communities, with the right to plead in court and hold property, and in some cases, chiefly in Italy and Germany, the right to make and apply their own laws. These claims sprang directly from the notion of the town as a sworn association or *commune* which, exactly like the guild, was authorized for its members by their mutual oath and consent. The conflict between this burgher outlook and seigneurial or royal jurisdiction was resolved in a wide variety of ways, ranging from incorporation of towns into large states (England, France, Castile, Aragon) to their complete *de facto* independence in northern and central Italy. Even the Italian cities – which, at the Peace of Constance (1183), won imperial recognition of their right to make and apply their own laws, elect consuls and raise taxes – based their claims not on a classical notion of the *polis* but on custom (Pacaut 1963).

Counsel, consent and election were the procedural values most commonly invoked in the early towns. Things were done 'with common counsel and consent': *urbanorum communi consilio, consensu urbanorum, consensu et consilio civium, laude communi, communi civium favore* (Planitz 1954, 101–2; Planitz 76, 100). Both John of Viterbo (*c.* 1250) and Brunetto Latini (1260s) described in remarkably similar terms the process of consultation in the greater council, in event of crisis or war.

> If the matter requires it, [the *podesta* should] take counsel more widely again and again, and afterwards hold a *generale consilium* of the knights and foot soldiers of the city and of wise men, of captains and consuls of the knights, judges and bankers, and of the heads of the craft-guilds (*priorum artium*) ... so that, when the common will of all has been sought out and agreed (*perquisita et concordata communi voluntate omnium*), he may proceed the more safely.
>
> (Viterbo ch.132, p.270; cf. Latini bk III, ch.87, p.408)

These are classic descriptions of decision-making by the city qua *commune*, by general consent in accordance with 'the common will of all'.

The election of rulers or judges was considered an expression of the principle of consent. Early thirteenth-century German city charters gave townsmen 'the power of electing the magistracy by their own will (*ex arbitrio suo*)'; 'let no judge be elected without the consent and counsel of the citizens' (Planitz 76, 100). The Roman law jurists accepted the right of the community (*universitas*) to elect its ruler or judge (Accursius gl. 'facere possunt' *ad Digest* 3.4.15; Roffredus q.28); but they added that as a general rule he must be 'confirmed by the governor of the province' (Accursius in Michaud-Quantin 1970, 252 and cf. 271ff.).

Where did this idea of community and these procedural values come from? The answer will tell us something about what differentiated western political thought from that of other cultures. In terms of *sources*, there are three possibilities: ancient Rome, Germanic lore and Christianity. In Roman law cities were private groups subject to the 'Roman people' in the person of the emperor (*Digest* 50.16.15–16; Duff 1938, 62–3). On the other hand, despite the predominantly monarcho-imperial doctrine of the *Corpus* of Roman law, the *Digest*, as an attempted synthesis of the entire legal tradition of Rome, contained civic and republican survivals (e.g. *Digest* 1.1.9 and 11). *Digest* 1.2.2 contained a *résumé* of Roman republican history, detailing the divisions between patriciate and plebs which led to *plebis scita* (commoners' decrees) acquiring the status of law, the establishment of the authority of the senate because it was 'difficult for the *plebs* to assemble', and the election of consuls who had 'supreme legal power' (*summum ius*) but could not execute a Roman citizen 'without an order from the people'. Cicero, whose *De Officiis* (*On Duties*) was widely read and admired (Bolgar 1958, 124–5, 197–8), clearly stated the natural sociability of man: 'the bond of human community and association ... is reason and speech, which ... reconcile men to one another and join them in a kind of natural partnership (*naturali quadam societate*)' (I.xvi; cf. III.v). Commonwealths and cities are founded so that men may hold onto what is their own (II.xxi); Cicero had also described the first cause of the commonwealth (*res publica*) itself as 'a kind of natural coming-together (*congregatio*) of men' (*De Republica* I.xxv). While only fragments of his *Republic*, which discussed constitutional questions in much greater detail (I. 41–4, 56, 69), were known, definitions of the *respublica* as a 'thing of the people' (*res populi*) and of a people as 'a group of many persons brought into partnership by an agreed notion of right and community of interest' (I. xxv) had been transmitted through Augustine. (Virgil too afforded glimpses of civic patriotism.) Such ideas would be familiar to educated men in the eleventh and twelfth centuries (Bolgar 1958, 142, 423). Their relevance to the urban movement could have been that they legitimized precisely what was happening: men spontaneously congregating to live under law and protect their interests and property (cf. R.W. and A. J. Carlyle 1903, 212; Michaud-Quantin 1970, 111n.).

As for evidence of Roman influence, the term *civitas* was from the start particularly common in northern Italy (Michaud-Quantin 1970, 114); it was used in Germania from the twelfth century (Planitz 1954, 101). *Civitas* suggested the independent status to which northern cities from the first aspired. City rulers were known as *consules* or *consulatus* in Italy and Provence; in Italy the city council was sometimes called *senatus*. Clearly, Italian cities tended to adopt ancient Roman language (avoiding *plebs*). Though the language of the *Digest* was also used, its meaning was often crucially adapted. It has been argued that Rome, and Cicero in particular, offered the twelfth-century Italian cities a political 'paradigm' of the kind usually associated with 'civic humanism' around 1400, involving 'the practice of civic virtue ... urbanity ... [and] the possibilities of a culture based on the city-state' (Bolgar 1958, 138; cf. 134–40). When political thought was articulated in the thirteenth century, Cicero and the *Digest* appear on every page. It is certainly remarkable that in Europe as a whole the communes developed in 'an epoch when classical studies [were] on the whole zealously pursued, and antiquity [was] looked upon with favour' (Bolgar 1958, 183).

The communes contained several features found in early Germanic tribal society. First, there was the idea of the popular assembly, 'which every free and law-worthy member of the group had a duty to attend', as the forum of jurisdiction (Dawson 1960, 35). Such assemblies persisted throughout the Dark Ages in parts of France and Germany: free men served as judge-cum-jury (*scabini*) at sessions which others might also be required to attend (Bloch 1961, 268, 368–70). Outside Italy, the first town rulers were generally called *scabini* (*échevins, Schöffen*).

The idea of law which appears in the early towns of northern Europe was to a considerable extent Germanic. While in late Roman and ecclesiastical thought law was the application of transcendent norms, in Germanic tradition legal rules 'came from no lawgiver or other external source. They were known to all law-worthy men, as an inseparable part of common group experience' (Dawson 1960, 35). They expressed 'the community's sense of justice' (Kern 1939, 70–3, 153), and could be conceived as a quasi-contractual *ewa* or *pactum* which was 'tied to the life of the group' (Calasso 1954, 124–5). The idea of law as custom, agreement and will comes out in town documents. Some words for urban law included the notion of will: *Burkoer, Wilkoer, eininge et kure* (Planitz 1954, 341). A town is said to have been given (by the lord) 'free will (*arbitrium*), which in common speech is called *wilkore*' to make 'commoners' decrees (*plebiscita*), which in common speech are called *kuiren*' (Planitz 1954, 340–2, 371, 502). A fourteenth-century Saxon treatise on town law spoke of 'the civil or municipal law, which men of one city or market have concluded among themselves (*concluserunt inter se*), maintaining it according to their own judgment (*arbitrium*) and ancient custom' (*Sächsische Weichbildrecht* 65). Indeed, we may note that the idea of law as *will* eventually became the basis for a new philosophy of law in those very thinkers who broke with the classical and Christian heritage, notably Marsiglio and Hobbes. It provided one ingredient for the theory of social contract, and was the original kernel of the recently dominant theory of legal positivism.

Voluntary association and conditional allegiance had characterized the warrior bands of the type known as *comitatus* (*companionage, Genossen-schaft*) (Schlesinger 1975, 69–75). But voluntary association and the oath among equals for mutual aid were to be found pre-eminently, and with greatest historical continuity, among the guilds. In several respects, the early town and village communes appear to have developed from within the guild tradition. In some north-western towns, the merchant-guild took the initiative in providing the nucleus of the town membership, organization, government and legal code (Planitz 1954, 75–9; Wilda 1831, 143ff.). At Cologne the managing committee of the merchant-guild, elected by the merchants, became the first town government. In several places the merchant law (*ius mercatorum, antiqua consuetudo negotiandi*) formed the basis for civic codes (Planitz 1954, 100, 332–3).

Further, at least by the fourteenth century, a surprisingly high proportion of villages in the French Alps and the Auvergne had all-embracing village confraternities (Duparc 1975). These were not, however, solely an expression of Germanic culture, for they had a strong Christian element. Their basic function was an annual common meal and distribution of food, which was known as 'faire la confrairie'. Some confraternities owned pasture or a mill. These appear to have been a territorial species of guild fraternity: 'to a certain extent they were mutual aid societies; at the beginning they represented the entire community of inhabitants' (Duparc 1975, 347). The striking thing is that they were often 'identical with the commune, being nothing but the parish or communal administration.... One might thus argue that the confraternities of the Holy Spirit appear to have been the original organization of the rural communities' (Duparc 1975, 347). Duparc suspects that this practice may have been fairly widespread in several parts of Europe. There is a possibility that some towns developed in a similar way (cf. Unwin 1938, 8).

Such a supposition would certainly fit in with some early communal practices and sentiments which provide further analogies between town and guild. First, there was the mutual oath, taken as between equals and entailing mutual aid: Bloch contrasts the communal with the feudal oath in that it 'united equals ... substituting for the promise of obedience, paid for by protection, the promise of mutual aid' (1961, 355). In Italy and the rest of Europe the mutual or collective oath signalled the arrival of the commune (Michaud-Quantin 1970, 235–6; Planitz 1954, 102–11, 251–2; Weber 1958, 104–5, 108). Bloch describes its importance: 'Hitherto [the burgesses] had been only isolated individuals: henceforth they had a collective being. It was the sworn association thus created to which in France was given the literal name of *commune*' (1961, 354). Planitz says of German cities: 'the oath-comradeship (*Eidgenossenschaft*) was a sworn brotherhood in the German legal tradition. It obliged all companions to mutual brotherly fealty' (1954, 111; cf. Gierke 1868, 332; Weber 1958, 138). According to Michaud-Quantin, 'this "municipalization" of the oath ... is the basis upon which the urban collectivity constitutes itself and upon which the members' consciousness thereof develops' (1970, 235–6). In many towns, the communal oath was renewed annually or at regular intervals. In Italy it tended to become an oath 'of loyalty to the commune: [the new citizen] was to obey its statutes and officers, to attend meetings and give counsel ... to perform military service ...to pay his taxes' (Waley 1969, 106). In

56

Germany, where the *Schwörtag* (oath-day) remained one occasion when the whole adult male population assembled (Gierke 1868, 268; Michaud-Quantin 1970, 235–6; Weber 1958, 108–10), it more often remained an oath of mutual aid, 'of faith and friendship binding each man to his neighbour', in the words of a late medieval document from oligarchical Nuremberg (cit. Strauss 1966, 71). Such oath-taking was a solemn event prescribing moral conduct. While on the one hand fealty and trustworthiness were paramount values in Germanic and feudal society (Kern 1939, 65, 87), the communal oath also acquired sacred value from the Christian theology of the promise and covenant, especially in its sacramental role of pledging individuals to God and one another.

As for language and sentiment, we find that in England a town was sometimes styled *communis gilda* (Michaud-Quantin 1970, 165). The guild ideas of brotherhood, friendship and mutual aid were widely invoked. A twelfth-century French commune stated that

> certain of us, not wishing to destroy but to fulfil the law, have elected to be governed by a common oath-association (*ad sui regimen communem coniurationem elegerunt*), so that each one if need be may sustain his neighbour as his brother (*proximum quasi fratrem*).
> (cit. Michaud-Quantin 1970, 130)

In 1188 the inhabitants of Aire-in-Artois declared that

> all belonging to the friendship of the town have agreed by faith and sacrament [or oath] that each will help the other as his brother in anything useful and honest (*omnes autem ad amicitiam pertinentes villae per fidem et sacramentum firmaverunt quod unus subveniat alteri tamquam fratri in utili et honesto*).
> (cit. Wilda 1831, 148)

The term friendship (*amicitia*) was often used of the commune itself (Bloch 1961, 417; Coornaert 1947, 237; Wilda 1831, 255); communal law was occasionally called 'the law of friendship' (Wilda 1831, 149). *The Shepherd's Eye* (c. 1220) once praises friendship, and once blames it as inducing judicial bias (*Oculus Pastoralis* 107, 128) – a fair reflection of the ambivalent role of the guild ethic in politics.

One consequence of adopting the guild view of political organization was that internal discord was rendered the more unreasonable, as contradicting in a most flagrant way the principle of guild friendship. One response of political writers to urban conflict was to invoke the wider values of love and charity, which appealed to the same instinct as friendship but were more universal in scope. *The Shepherd's Eye* strongly advised the *podesta* to show love towards, and avoid giving offence to, all ranks in society, 'the greater, the middling, and the lesser' (*Oculus Pastoralis* 95, 97). Government, it said, is sustained by 'justice in the ruler, reverence in the subjects, love in both' (*Oculus Pastoralis 95*).

But, when the guild ethic was adopted by territorial communities, a crucial transmutation took place. It came increasingly to be insisted that the mutual obligation among members referred (only) to whatever is 'useful and honest' (or honourable: *utile et honestum*; e.g. Planitz 1954, 498; Planitz 93; Wilda 1831, 148 – the phrase also occurs in the first mutual-defence treaty of the Swiss cantons, 1291: Lasserre 20). Towards outsiders, villages and towns maintained the same posture as guilds: members are fully involved in their quarrels and alliances ('he who does not fight with us is no citizen': Goslar, cit. Gierke 1868, 329). But, internally, the commitment of man to man is delimited or diluted by moral principle and the subjection to common laws.

In the thirteenth century, some fully developed towns undertook to reconstitute themselves as a guild: this occurred at Berwick in 1248–9 and again in 1284 (Coornaert 1947, 29, 220; Wilda 1831, 255, 376ff.) and at Florence and Padua in 1293 (Najemy 1979, 58–9; Waley 1969, 200). The object was to remove dissension, including dissension between guilds. At Berwick, all 'particular guilds' were declared abolished, and a single 'guild of the townsmen' (*gilda burgensium*) was established in order to achieve 'firm and sincere love in relation to one another' by creating 'one partnership (*societas*), firm and friendly'. At Florence, citizens were required to swear that they would not enter into any other pact or association 'other than this present partnership and company, oath-group and general union (*presentem societatem et compagniam, sacramentum et unionem universalem*) among all the crafts themselves'. This guild of the whole city was styled 'a good and pure and faithful partnership and company', and at Padua 'a single body, society, brotherhood or league'.

There was constant interaction between craft-guilds and the town. In cities where they achieved political power, the crafts' own organization often formed part of the new city constitution; on the other hand, craft-guilds not infrequently used the pattern of city government as a model when reforming their own constitutions. The jurists, we may notice, habitually treated towns and craft-guilds as sub-species of the same genus of corporate organization (*universitas* or *collegium*: e.g. Accursius gl. *Aliorum ad Digest* 3.4.1).

Lastly, Christian doctrine ascribed value to social life in general, and to the fellowship (*communio*) of Christians in particular. In the Trinity, God himself lives a community life. Corporate life is not a mere means to salvation but part of the goal of love. Believers are united at the deepest level in *homonoia, unanimitas, concordia, con-sensus* (Grossi 1958; cf. Rom. 12: 4–8). In the *Metalogicon* (1159), John of Salisbury joined Cicero's notion of human society, and civic community in particular, as the product of nature and speech, to the Christian ideal of a communal beatitude:

> Grace fertilizes nature ... all are born with a love of good, under the impetus of natural desire. ... But, since any beatitude untouched by fellowship (communio) – whatever beatitude might be outside society (societas) – cannot even be imagined, therefore whoever impugns [reason and eloquence] which are able to connect and strengthen the just bond of human association (which is as it were the single unique fraternity of the sons of nature), he would seem to obstruct the path by which all achieve felicity. ... Thus, for a firmer clasping bond and the protection of charity, the creator-Trinity, the one and true God, arranged the parts of the universe (universitatis) in such a way that each thing should require the aid of something else and that one should supply what the other lacked, since they are all members of one another. ... This is that sweet and fruitful mingling of reason and speech, which has given birth to so many fine cities, brought together and allied so many kingdoms, united so many peoples and conquered them with charity ... [without eloquence] cities themselves will seem more like sheepfolds than companies of men allied by some bond of society, so that, through the sharing of duties and friendly interchange with each other, they live by the same law (ut participatione officiorum et amica invicem vicissitudine eodem iure vivant). ... What sharing (communicatio) of wills can there be without verbal exchange? Our opponent, therefore, by his ignorant and wicked attack on the study of rhetoric, is attacking not one or a few but all cities (urbes) at once and the whole political life.　　　(Salisbury 6–8)

This could be read as a paradigmatic statement of guild and civic belief: the ideals of love and mutual aid are set at the centre of the cosmos and of human society. Civic life is here conceived – well before the recovery of Aristotle or the 'civic Renaissance' – as an integral stage to beatitude. In fact, however, John of Salisbury's starting point here was not the contemporary urban movement; he may not even have had this in mind at all. The passage is an abstract speculation about human nature. In his political treatise, the *Policraticus*, written about the same time, there is little mention of cities and none of guilds. One can perhaps discount altogether any mutual influence between John of Salisbury and contemporary associations. What this passage shows is that, in northern Europe, philosophy and communal sentiment were running along parallel lines. These did not meet, but both were partially inspired by Christianity.

The idea of the church as a brotherhood found institutional expression not only in the universal episcopate but in local confraternities. That it was capable of such local realization probably assisted the communal movement (Michaud-Quantin 1970, 342). The Christian conception of community flowed over onto practical economic life. Ever since St Benedict, western

59

monasticism emphasized the community, and a vigorous monastic revival centred on the Franco-German borderland coincided with the rise of the communes. Natural human sociability was a commonplace among the learned in the twelfth century, when the term *socialitas* (socialness) was coined (Michaud-Quantin 1970, 65; Post 1964, 530). Thus it is not surprising that religion quickly entered the everyday language of the Italian communes (Lane 1973, 91; Waley 1969, 147). Ullmann's view of the authoritarian impact of medieval Christianity (1961, 32ff., 57ff.) must surely be treated with reserve.

In the Romano-Christian tradition as it entered the Middle Ages, the purpose of government was the enforcement of natural justice, conceived as an eternal, absolute norm enshrined in scripture and philosophy. Society was a product of human sociability, an extension of friendship in diluted form. Coercive law was essential to restrain criminals, make peaceful social life possible, and protect those bent on the honourable pursuits of piety, learning and industry. Government had a special duty to care for those without natural helpers (orphans and widows). Society is one body in which there is a natural division of labour, different members fulfilling different functions for rewards which vary in earthly value, but whose proportion of heavenly rewards may be quite different. Such amicable, corporate notions predisposed twelfth-century European man to be willing to adopt, and perhaps positively to seek out, corporatist, associational solutions to the problems posed by his environment. They were taken out of the common treasury of inherited ideas because they coincided with the aspirations of the towns and other associations, on account of what Weber called 'elective affinities'.

The procedural principles of counsel, consent and election derived from both ecclesiastical and Germanic sources, which it is often impossible to disentangle. Early Christian texts prescribed election of bishops by clergy with the laity consenting; in Benedictine tradition, abbots were elected by their community for life. Episcopal election was being vigorously revived in the eleventh century (cf. Moulin 1953). But the parallel with guild officials was much closer, since they were elected from the community at large with a limited, usually annual tenure, like the early town rulers, and had rather similar functions. In some village confraternities, the officials (known as priors, proctors, rectors or syndics) were 'elected by the brethren every year in general assemblies, or selected by the syndics and councillors of the community' (Duparc 1975, 345). Election of town officials was sometimes the prerogative of the merchant-guild or a similarly privileged fraternity. In 1258 the citizens of Cologne could confront their archbishop with the claim that the 'judges and officials' who held jurisdiction from him 'by a custom observed of old are elected by the fraternity which is called *Rigerzegeit*' (Keutgen 167). It would appear, then, that the principle of election *could* be derived from Christian, Germanic and Roman sources, and in general one must suppose a combination of these influences, although the Roman would have been confined to Italy. But the most *immediate* precedent for the practice of election, and for the manner in which towns practised it, was the guild.

The Germanic judicial assembly and the *comitatus* would appear to provide the closest parallels and the most immediately available precedents for the practice of consulting a general assembly of citizens. Here too the guild may have been an important model in people's minds: when Berwick constituted itself as a guild, it was stipulated that henceforth the whole town should, like the former guilds which were being amalgamated into it, assemble regularly in *placita* (Coornaert 1947, 211; Wilda 1831, 147ff., 376ff.). The idea of general citizen participation in important decisions owed something to the prototype of the guild and village confraternity, for which regular general assemblies were the common current practice. But the general principle of consent probably owed its ascendancy to a combination of ecclesiastical and Germanic influences.

One procedural principle, majority voting, was derived solely from Roman and ecclesiastical sources; which of these was more important has been disputed (Michaud-Quantin 1970, 273; Moulin 1953, 112). Decision-making by a simple majority was adopted very early in some towns: in 1143 the Genoese council affirmed that 'what the greater part of the court (*curiae*) has done, is regarded as if all had done it' (cit. Moulin 1953, 112) – this also hints at the idea of collective responsibility. On this question, the jurists made their one substantive contribution to civic constitutions. Following *Codex* 10.32.2, the Glossators stated that, for a valid decision in councils or assemblies, all must be summoned, two-thirds must attend, and a majority of these must consent (Gierke 1881, 218–22; Michaud-Quantin 1970, 273). Italian cities soon adopted the practice of a two-thirds quorum and decision by a majority of those present (Waley 1969, 63–4), which implies Roman law influence.

What we have found so far is a mixture of Roman, Germanic and Christian influences. In Italy, Roman and Germanic influences would appear to have been of about equal weight; in the rest of Europe, the Germanic far outweighed the Roman. It would seem that urban political sentiment and policy was inspired by a conviction that the town was a community in the Germanic genre, analogous to the guild: a group formed by the will of the members and thereby legally valid. That conviction appears also to have lain at the root of attempts, from the thirteenth century, to democratize the commune; craft-guild supremacy (*governo largo*) constituted, as was often claimed, a return to the first principles of the commune. There was no other available precedent for decision-making by the people as a whole. This Germanic model runs as a *leitmotiv* through

61

subsequent democratic tradition in Europe: here Gierke's central insight is valid. This is not to say that Germanic political culture was superior or even distinctive; only that it happens to lie at the root of this particular tradition.

The ideals of civil society – which derived principally from Roman and Christian sources – were more likely to lead to indirect democracy, with the emphasis on accountability, so as to ensure that the conditions of fair exchange are not tampered with. Here popular participation meant consultation, understood as a procedural value based upon justice. This would lead away from a guild outlook towards a republican state. Much, perhaps all, popular and successful European democracy, both direct and representative, can best be explained historically in terms of the guild on the one hand and civil society on the other. Classical ideals sometimes inspired leaders and intellectuals, but never the masses.

But, while Germanic tradition may go far towards explaining the ethos of the communal movement, it does not explain why it occurred when it did; nor does it explain the growth of civil society. True, Europe was now relatively peaceful and economic opportunities abounded; but similar circumstances have not produced the same *kind* of city elsewhere. If we ask what, from the later eleventh to the early thirteenth centuries, differentiated European culture, we can pinpoint a phenomenon which in fact also had prodigious effects upon other aspects of life: changes which 'cluster around a redrawing of the boundaries between the sacred and the profane', associated in particular with the Investiture Controversy. Peter Brown seems to have put his finger on the crucial point:

> A release of energy and creativity analogous to a process of nuclear fission stemmed from the disengagement of the two spheres of the sacred and the profane. ... Gifted men could find leisure, incentive and personal resources to tackle more strictly delimited tasks. The laity also, though technically made inferior to the clergy, came to enjoy the freedom that came from a vast unpretentiousness.... Throughout society, the disengagement of the sacred from the profane opened up a whole middle distance of conflicting opportunities for the deployment of talent.
>
> (1982, 305–6)

The development of towns coincided exactly with the great crisis in the Roman universalist heritage and the ecclesiastical polity – the Investiture Controversy. This began as an attempt to 'free' the clergy from lay appointment and investiture; it developed into a radical reappraisal of the relationship between church and state, and of the nature of political authority (Robinson 1978, ch.4; Ullmann 1955, 262ff.). The issue of imperially appointed aristocratic bishops was most sharply contested in the Rhineland and northern Italy; that is, precisely where communes were claiming the 'liberty' of territorial immunity and conditional allegiance

(Mitteis 1975, 213ff.; Planitz 1954, 98–9). 'Liberty of the church' (*libertas ecclesiae*) and communal liberty were related parts of the same movement for corporate self-determination (Buttner 1973; Keller 1973). The church reformers' emphasis on the duties of kings, limited fealty, righteous government – popularized in propaganda warfare – was reflected in the actions of the communes. They challenged sacred monarchy and ended up by partially secularizing politics (Tellenbach 1940, 183–5). Like the church, towns claimed to be champions of justice as a universal norm: 'the justice of the city' (*oppidi iustitia, civilis iustitia, urbanorum iustitia*) (Planitz 58, 61) was, by implication, superior to feudal law. 'The consuls . . . shall not judge according to the law of the province called *Landreht*, but according to truth and the following statutes of the city' (Strasbourg law code, 1214: Planitz 77).

Brown's notion of the 'disengagement' of the sacred and profane (which is a development of Weber's thesis on rationalization in European culture) seems to fit the facts of the communal movement very well. It explains why it happened when it did, and it also explains the rise of civil society. It may help also to explain why constitutionalist principles were first elaborated by the twelfth- and thirteenth-century canonists (Tierney 1982), and widely practised in some medieval states, but later taken up and implemented principally in Protestant nations. It is akin to the modern theologians' notion of 'secularization' as a process implicit in Christianity, which always had a tendency to view politics, law and human authority as contingent.

> Secularization . . . is the legitimate consequence of the impact of biblical faith on history. . . . The rise of natural science, of democratic political institutions, and of cultural pluralism – all developments we normally associate with Western culture – can scarcely be understood without the original impetus of the Bible.   (Cox 1965, 31, summarizing Gogarten)

The history of the first Christian millennium, and that of eastern Christianity thereafter, however, show that this was not an inevitable development. That secularization occurred in western Europe from the eleventh century may perhaps be ascribed to the peculiar history of the western church, focusing upon the Investiture Controversy, and to the fluidity of conditions and multiplicity of political units, due to the absence of effective empire. Yet it was made possible in the first place by the Christian notion of the relativity of human laws to true human needs ('the Sabbath is not made for man'), and by the fact that Christianity, unlike Judaism and Islam, did not include precise social, economic and political rules. It was due in the last analysis to the doctrine of grace.

There was a datum of doctrinal belief, but over wide areas of human life it was non-specific. Thus law and politics could be thought out afresh to meet new contingencies in the light of a few very general principles; even the moral commands of the *Decalogue* were ultimately reduced – in the Gospels themselves – to the *mandatum* of love. The Sermon on the Mount could not be mistaken for a new legal code. Thus, for example, legitimation of interest upon capital did not have to await the Reformers' attack on ecclesiastical ordinances: the scholastics already subsumed usury under theft and the common good, to say that, where there was risk, profit was not usurious. Christianity was a destabilizing and an enabling factor.

But, as with the Gospels themselves, all this did not simply push back the boundaries of the sacred, but rather re-defined the whole relationship between God and the human world. It was not that political institutions, including communes and guilds, were made purely secular; rather, new institutions to meet new needs could claim the same kind of divine sanction, one that was always contingent upon their being perceived to promote human welfare. The shake-up in the sacred–profane connection led to a new cross-fertilization between the two spheres. Thus it was that guilds, villages and towns could be seen as institutions of love and friendship. Sacred value inhered nowhere and could therefore flow back, in diffuse form, anywhere; even marriage was not quite immune, as both dispensations and the development of erotic poetry indicate.

Theology and the church were not, of course, secularized in the same way. Rational argument was applicable to them, but they could not be 'cashed' in terms other than their own. Thence came the problem of medieval ecclesiology (and the peculiar flavour of much Catholic philosophy then and since) – as Ockham most fully demonstrated. Popes could err and be deposed: the papacy was sacred. This maintenance of the idea of the church, which was ultimately discarded at the Reformation, also predetermined what a city or commune could never be.

The precise value of this thesis for understanding guilds, towns and civil society is that it explains how members of guilds and communes came to regard these groups as agencies of brotherhood and love, as manifestations of the heavenly rather than the earthly City. The very terms *commune* and *communitas* were cognate with *communio* (Michaud-Quantin 1970, 157ff.). Like the bishops of the tenth-century peace movement, townsmen campaigned against the vendetta; town laws were 'holy institutions' (Bloch 1961, 414–17 at 417), and the town itself was ' a community of peace' (Michaud-Quantin 1970, 149). *Universitas*, on the other hand, was precisely a low-key, middle-ground concept, without pretensions but highly serviceable. The communal movement itself was, for former serfs, a kind of Exodus – the type-case of the 'desacralization of politics' (Cox 1965, 38–9). Further, this thesis explains why an archbishop could support craft-guilds in the name of 'liberty' and why Innocent IV became their sponsor in jurisprudence. Craft-guilds themselves were a secularized form of the earlier Germanic guild; that was why the Reformation could not hurt them.

Civil society, on the other hand, was the beneficiary of the enhanced value now ascribed to the individual: the sacred was becoming identified with the human, personality was beginning to be seen as the only human entity with absolute value (Morris 1972). As Brown again has it, whereas previously the supernatural had been 'the depository of the objectified values of the group', it now 'came to be regarded as the preserve *par excellence* of ... intensely personal feeling' (1982, 323–5). The crucial point about both guilds and communes was that here *individuation and association went hand in hand* (cf. Bynum 1980). One achieved liberty *by belonging to* this kind of group. Citizens, merchants and artisans pursued their own individual goals by banding together under oath. *Pace* both Gierke and Michaud-Quantin (1970, 47, 57, 149, 341), the evidence does not tell us that medieval communes and guilds had a particularly holistic or collectivist mentality. People apostrophized groups only in the sense that they made 'the city' etc. the subject of sentences, and spoke of 'the will/consent/spirit of the city', much as we today talk about nations, states and parties. Emphasis upon the group as a real whole separate from the individuals composing it was – with the one exception of the church, personified as Christ's body – a modern Romantic invention (see ch.16).

5

GUILD POLITIES AND URBAN IDEOLOGY, 1250–1550

During the later Middle Ages the relation between town and guild took a new form as craft-guilds developed political ambitions and acquired an overtly political role in a number of towns. This symbiosis marked a distinctive phase in guild history. Here we are concerned with the question: how was the guild town, and guild participation in city government, conceptualized by townsmen themselves and the civic authorities? First, we must briefly consider the political rise of the crafts.

In the thirteenth and fourteenth centuries craft-guilds assumed political power in a great number of towns. The original communes had developed into oligarchies dominated by a patriciate of leading families, usually with a mixture of landed and commercial wealth. Power had gravitated from the general assembly to the small council. Both newly enriched merchants and (in large cities) the urban proletariat had an interest in political change. But the core of this new 'people' (*popolo*) or 'community' (*Gemeinde*) was generally the artisans with their ready-made guild organization. In towns and cities all over Europe both guild and neighbourhood provided a means of popular organization which in Italy from the later twelfth century was already developing into a 'commune within a commune' (Planitz 1954, 325–7; Waley 1969, 185–90).

From the early thirteenth century these groups began to take over political control of the cities, first in Italy and then in northern Europe. They were helped by family rivalries within the patriciate; their leaders were often scions of old families, or new merchants seeking a political voice (Heers 1974, 120–30). Sometimes, notably in the great textile centres of Flanders, the movement generated considerable violence. Family and class divisions were intensified, and power see-sawed from one group to another. By 1300 central and northern Italy was dotted with guild republics, of which Perugia is an outstanding example (Blanshei 1976, 7ff.). After the battle of Courtrai (1302), guild government developed in Flemish cities, and, from about 1327 onwards, in Germany, especially the south and west (Dollinger 1955, 388ff.). The craft-guilds' political successes were most marked in smaller towns, reflecting their economic ascendancy, and in areas where towns were relatively independent of seigneurial or royal power (northern and central Italy, southern and western Germany, and, during the fourteenth century, Flanders). In larger cities, their power was usually short-lived, or else the new regime was effectively run by leading merchants and bankers, on whom the economy of such towns depended, often through their own 'great guilds' (Maschke 1959). Florence was a clear instance of this (Brucker 1977, 14, 39–53). Where the guilds established a political role, this was very often, particularly in Germany, by means of power-sharing between guilds and patriciate, represented in new and old councils respectively, often laid down by formal constitutional treaty. Where craft-guilds were prevented from establishing political power – in great cities like Florence, Cologne and Liège – there were repeated attempts to reverse this iron law of oligarchy; sporadic risings took place during the later Middle Ages, with brief periods of craft-guild ascendancy.

Political success affected the guilds themselves. It became usual for allied trades to federate into a fixed number of political guilds, and for political power to become dependent upon membership in one of these; it was possible, however, for wealthy non-tradesmen to enrol. This strengthened the guilds' monopolistic position (*Zunftzwang* or closed shop: Planitz 1954, 329–30). Increasingly, guilds were becoming privileged groups, albeit with a relatively broad membership; so they remained in the German guild towns until the nineteenth century (Walker 1971, esp. ch.3).

The effect of all this on civic policy varied according to the degree of control achieved by the guilds. The whole movement was inspired by diverse goals. All non-patricians opposed the economic, fiscal and juridical privileges of the old élite, and aimed at legal equality and the suppression of magnate lawlessness (especially in Italy, where this problem was acute because landed gentry played a greater part in civic life). In this respect, the changes in urban government were geared to the values of civil society, so that continuity may be discerned between the medieval guild risings and 'bourgeois revolutions' of more modern times (cf. Harding 1980, 442). Bologna liberated the serfs of the *contado* in 1256. But, beyond that, the great merchants (who in larger cities dominated certain guilds) generally desired more liberal economic policies, which might also be attractive to newcomers – conditions under which 'all might buy and sell freely' (Hibbert 1963, 204–6; Rörig 1967, 89ff.). Unincorporated workers at the bottom of the social scale wanted better pay and working conditions, and the right to form guilds. But artisans wanted to impose their own form of guild protectionism on the town. Generally speaking, these last were again most successful in the smaller towns. Here, 'successful craft revolutions ... typically ... led to a victory for the *petits bourgeois* and their policy': the rise of the guilds led to 'a shift in outlook, interest and policy' involving local protectionism and careful regulation of production in the interest of the small craftsman. The regime was 'typically monopolistic, xenophobic and exclusive', with 'intense, detailed and effective control of economic affairs' (Hibbert 1963, 181, 185, 209–15, 220).

These, then, were among the reasons why the fourteenth and fifteenth centuries witnessed a wide variety of civic regimes – despotic (mainly in Italy), oligarchical and democratic (in the guild sense). Where they achieved a degree of power, the guilds left their mark on the cities' form of government, economic policy and political ethos. In such cases, the spirit of the guilds influenced both the nature and the range of activities undertaken by city governments. It left traces in everyday political language and sentiment. In some ways, the corporate polity aspired to by medieval popular movements in towns stands in direct contrast to modern 'western' notions of democracy, which are to such a large extent based upon the idea of competition and the interests of citizens as consumers. Yet later echoes of the guild outlook may be found in mercantilism and socialism.

The political rise of the crafts and the ensuing constitutional upheavals more or less coincided with the rediscovery of Aristotle and the development of a quasi-Aristotelian political philosophy, which could have been relevant to what was going on in the cities. Italians like John of Viterbo (writing *c.* 1250), Brunetto Latini (1260s) and Egidio Romano (1277–9) were the first to write systematically about city government. The two latter, writing for audiences north of the Alps, did something to transmit the precocious civic consciousness of Italy to north-western Europe at the very time when cities of that region too were being engulfed by the political movement of the guilds. But it is unlikely that they had any impact outside academic circles. The ideas northern townsmen took from Italy (cf. Lentze 1933, 23–4, 28–9, 50–4) were transmitted by other forms of traffic. Further, from about the mid-fourteenth century, Renaissance humanism was adding a new dimension to political discourse in Italy (Kristeller 1961; Skinner 1978, i 71ff.). But the Ciceronian ethos of the new culture was friendly neither to the guilds themselves nor to artisans as political participants. Not till the sixteenth century did humanism spread to northern Europe, where its impact was, from this point of view, somewhat different.

In this period when guilds were winning a greater share of political power in many towns, formal expressions of urban ethos and ideology changed less than one might have expected. The idea of the city as a corporate community capable of expressing a unified will remained an essential feature of civic sentiment and public relations exercises. The document amalgamating the Berwick guilds into a single guild of the whole town stated that the 'many bodies' (sc. the separate guilds) desired that 'union and a united will (*unica voluntas*) be achieved ... with all members looking to one head' (cit. Wilda 1831, 376). A late thirteenth-century diplomatic phrase-book recommended the use of terms like 'unanimity of counsel', 'with unanimity, fellowship and concord', 'the impregnable unanimity of the citizens' (Rockinger 450). In Germany particularly, political sentiment continued to focus upon the old ideas of the city as community (*universitas*, *Gemeinde*, *commune*), of friendship, communal unity and honour. In Italy too the terms *commune* and *universitas* continued to be used interchangeably with *civitas*; sometimes, however, *universitas* was used more specifically to mean the ancient constitution with its broadly-based citizen assembly, in contrast to the oligarchy of the small council (Albertini 1955, 124, 127–8). One reason for this continuity with the earlier communal ethos was the general belief in the organic unity of society. A more pressing one was the need to promote communal harmony against familial and factional conflict. It might be a rhetorical device, it might be sincerely believed in: it was the subject of appeals by both new and old governments.

A distinction between 'rich and poor' burghers was often explicitly recognized in official documents. But it was insisted that the town community transcended such divisions. German city documents frequently speak in this way when alluding to the sharing of power between patriciate and guilds in old and new councils. A sworn agreement between patriciate and guilds at Strasbourg in 1334 (significantly reversing the usual order) referred to 'the community (*gemeinde*), poor and rich ... common justice for the poor and the rich' (*Chroniken* ix 932). Similarly, a new power-sharing constitution at Augsburg (1340) was introduced with the phrase, 'We, the community (*gemainde*), rich and poor ... we all generally (*gemainlich*) with the many people, rich and poor'; and the regime finally established there in 1368 wrote to other guild cities as, 'We, the citizens generally, rich and poor, of the city of Augsburg' (*Chroniken* iv 129, 135; cf. Ennen 424). Similar phrases were used in Italy, for instance during the Ciompi revolution at Florence (1378) by an artisan advocating such power-sharing (Brucker 1977, 47; cf. Waley 1969, 218–19).

Traditional guild and communal ideals of corporate friendship, brotherhood and love were invoked for similar purposes. Friendship was the term preferred in Germany, where it reflected a deeply and widely held sentiment about the kind of community a town was. The new guild regime at Augsburg (1368) stated that, having observed that guild rule (*Zunft*) brings 'honour and good friendship, peace and good order', they too had opted for it 'in a common, loving and friendly way with a united council and the good will of rich and poor' (*Chroniken* iv 135; cf. 129, 142–3). At Nuremberg, where the patriciate remained in power, friendship was also invoked as a civic value (*Chroniken* i 136, 145). Tengler's *Mirror of Laymen* (1509) described cities as places where there is 'more peace, civic and communal friendship (*bürgerliche und gemeine freundschaft*) among the inhabitants' (cit. Gierke 1881, 665). Frescoes at Siena proclaimed that a city was held together by the virtue of charity among its citizens (Rubinstein 1958, 185).

At Florence in 1427, Stefano Porcari, as *Capitano del popolo*, urged citizens to see their *Repubblica* as a unity held together by love, in quasi-religious language. Men are incorporated into the republic by their solidary nature 'and to provide for each other's mutual needs (*comodita l'una dell' altro*) ... We long to preserve such a divine being, in whose life we live, and to direct towards it our energies, love, loyalty, concord, truth and our soul, as loving the universal good most of all' (Porcari 38; cf. Baron 1966, 434–5). This was a rare anticipation of the later romantic idea of community. On another occasion, Florentines were urged to treat each other 'as brothers not as vassals, so that unity will be achieved' (cit. Brucker 1977, 310n.; cf. 304–7 and Skinner 1978, i 89). In the revolt of 1378, the new ruling group attempted to ensure that its members put loyalty to the commune above any faction, by forming a *consorteria*: its members pledged 'one with another, in life and in death' (cit. Brucker 1977, 44).

Ideals of peace and the common good filled a similar need as counterbalances to the centrifugal forces of guild, family, party or class. For these could appeal to their own 'corporate' values; such alternative loyalties might, by driving opponents into exile, make property insecure and undermine the very goals of civil society. In search for a peaceful solution, Italian city-states tended increasingly to submit to absolute rule by a lord or tightly-knit oligarchy. Devotion to 'the common good' (*bonum commune*) or 'the good of the commune' (*bonum Communis*) was seen as a way of transcending factionalism without recourse to tyranny (Rubinstein 1958, esp. 185). Peace was extolled as the common *desideratum* of rich and poor; but it could only be attained if 'laws are observed' by all (Waley 1969, 218–19). Similarly in Germany, standard phrases for use by city secretaries included 'desist from civil discord by loving peace and concord', 'abomination of lawsuits, quarrels, dissensions, seditions, contentions' (Rockinger 450). Everywhere, the ideal of the common good might also be employed as an ideological defence of consumer interests against guild monopoly.

> Consumer defence ... gave scope to ... ideals of commonweal, to church teaching on fair prices and neighbourly dealing.... There was constant insistence that economic laws should be 'for the public good', for 'the good and profit of the whole community'. (Hibbert 1963, 161, 172)

The Stoic juxtaposition of *utile et honestum* (the useful and the honest or honourable) featured often in town documents (Keutgen 354–5; Planitz 1954, 498; Planitz 93; Wilda 1831, 148). This was also a statement of sound commercial practice, as in Dundee's motto, *prudentia cum candore*. Combined with the concept of mutual aid, it appeared in the first treaty of the Swiss cantons (1291): 'Honesty is upheld and public utility is assured when a quiet and peaceful condition is duly established ... each community (*universitas*: sc. canton) has promised to help the others with all its power

70

and effort ... and to come to their aid in every eventuality' (Lasserre 20).

Over and against all this, official documents and spokesmen inevitably acknowledged the existence of sub-groups within the city. Internal opposition to a regime was never acceptable; but under certain circumstances, dissent in the form of discussion of policy in the councils, involving some criticism of prevailing government policy, was permissible. It was sometimes commended as a means of healing disunity and achieving the truth (Brucker 1977, 47, 306–7; Rubinstein 1968, 457–60; Witt 1971, 191). Only guilds were spoken of – in guild towns, that is, or during periods of guild rule elsewhere – in terms implying, or even enthusiastically endorsing, their legitimacy as corporate groups within the whole. Italian civic parties were never sanctioned in this way (Peters 1977). Family was recognized, overtly, as a basis of authority only in those Italian cities where despotism was established. The guilds in question might be the traditional crafts, or the political guilds (amalgamations of allied trades) specially formed for communal participation. Such a guild was called *Zunft* in Germany, where *zünftlich* government emerged as a distinctive and – to its supporters – friendly and co-operative type of regime. Often such guilds were denominated as the 'members' of the city (e.g. the Flemish *lede*). Proponents of popular guild government at Florence in 1343 claimed that it was right and proper for that city to be 'ruled through the crafts and craftsmen' (cit. Najemy 1979, 61n.); while in 1380, the renowned Florentine chancellor Salutati, defending the Ciompi regime against its exiled opponents, accused the latter of planning 'to wipe out the most honourable colleges of the crafts of our city, through which (after God's grace) we are what we are, and without which there is no doubt that the name of the Florentines would disappear from the face of the earth' (cit. Najemy 1979, 66–7). In Germany, generally speaking, popular government (in the sense of a broader distribution of political power) was referred to simply as *Zunft*. Cities adopting it spontaneously spoke of its rectitude in religious terms: the new guild regime at Augsburg (1368) intended 'with God's help to ordain and establish all things in the best, safest and most Christian way' (*Chroniken* iv 135).

Further, in Germany the 'commonalty' (*Gemeinheit*) of all householders sometimes emerges as a legitimate political category, distinct from the traditional patriciate on the one hand, and the 'brotherhood' of the guilds on the other (*Chroniken* xxiv cixff.). After the rising at Cologne in 1396, the new constitution (later effectively controlled by great merchants) began, 'We, all the crafts (*ampte*) and street associations (*gasselgesellschaften*), together with the whole community (*gemeinde*).... We, the community, poor and rich in common (*gemeinde, gemeinlichen arm und rich*) of all and each of the crafts and street associations' (*Chroniken* xiv cliv; cf. Ennen 424). Perhaps the best example is a constitutional agreement signed at

71

Brunswick (1445) between the (old) council, the guilds and all house-holders:

> We, the council . . . and we the masters [sc. of the various guilds named] and the common guild brothers of all the aforesaid *gilden*, and we the householders of the commonalty (*hovetlude der menheit*) and the whole commonalty in all five districts have legally agreed by mutual treaty and for the benefit of the whole to help each other with all our might to withstand all those who might conspire against the council, the guilds and the whole manhood of the city of Brunswick.
>
> (Altmann and Bernheim 452–6)

The recognition of sub-groups was thus combined with insistence upon the 'whole'.

This more class-orientated notion of community was most marked in Italy, where the term *popolo* was appropriated by non-patricians and became identical in meaning with the formerly excluded middle and lower classes. Oligarchical opponents referred to these as *plebs*. During the thirteenth century, in cities such as Florence and Perugia, the organization of the *popolo* was merged with, or wholly superseded, that of the old commune. Thereafter, 'Long live the *popolo* and the guilds' became a slogan of opponents of the new oligarchy (Brucker 1977, 16). Similarly, at Mainz, the guilds themselves, as distinct from the traditional city council, were called 'the community' (*gemeinde*) (*Chroniken* xviii 72ff.).

On the whole, however, guilds, especially in Italy, received very much less attention in public debate and official documents than their political role and importance warranted. (They were hardly ever mentioned in academic discussions of popular government: see ch.6.) This was probably due to juristic and humanist prejudice against political guilds, which in Roman times had been suppressed by, among others, Cicero himself, and which were abominated in Roman law. It could also be due to social prejudice among the upper classes and the learned against artisans and small men: manual workers were too stupid to govern (cf. Gilbert 1968, 500; Najemy 1979, 61n., 68). In such a cultural ethos, humbler folk and artisans might understandably prefer the appellation of 'citizens' or 'the people', just as great merchants liked to equate themselves with the *optimates* of Rome. Nevertheless, on one occasion the great humanist Salutati, writing as chancellor of Florence, explicitly defended their political status.

> What could be sweeter, more joyful, more pleasing than that the welfare of your city should reside in the hands of merchants and artisans? For they naturally love liberty, since they are liable to be more heavily oppressed by the pangs of servitude. They desire tranquillity, in which alone they can usefully perform the crafts they are devoted to. They love and cherish equity (*equabilitatem*), not wishing to be dependent upon

their ancestors' glory or blood nobility, and not being borne up by a mass of relatives or clientele. In other words, this is the type of citizen which, in every state ruled by the people (*populari re publica*), pursues justice ... and does not glory in domination but rules and holds public office by giving way to each other in turn. ... How fortunate are republics governed by such people! (cit. Witt 1969a, 454–5)

Here artisan and merchant political participation is seen as functionally beneficial in humanist republican terms, on account of their social background. Savonarola and his supporters seldom explicitly assigned a political role to *artifici*, though they were among the chief beneficiaries of the programme of extended participation (*governo largo*) undertaken at Florence in 1494–8 (cf. Weinstein 1970, 156). One advocate of *governo largo*, however, Salamonio, in a public speech delivered in 1499, attacked the view that trade and manual work make men unfit to govern; against Plato and Cicero he quoted Hesiod and Solon, who wisely perceived that 'honour nourishes the crafts' (*Speeches* 100–1).

It is remarkable that this age of guild polities produced no corporatist ideology. True, principles deriving from the juristic theory of corporations, such as 'let what concerns all be approved by all', were applied to civic government (cf. Najemy 1979, 56ff.); and guilds were mentioned in public documents as component parts of some states. But all this was far too implicit for one to be able to say that such constitutions were 'firmly grounded in the principles of corporatism' (Najemy 1979, 56). Political guilds had to be mentioned because they were there; guild regimes claimed to be decent and Christian. But there was no sign of any recognition of a natural or *de jure* place for guilds in the polity. Possibly, another reason for this was that political guilds were sometimes vehicles for other forces, whether of democratization or of new oligarchy, and were sometimes a means of sectional economic advantage.

The most explicit ideological formulation of popular movements and a wider franchise was in terms of liberty and equality: this, however, was largely confined to Italy. All European communes gloried in their corporate 'liberties'; but *libertas* in a more general sense had, from the twelfth century, been a special characteristic of Italian civic aspirations (Skinner 1978, i 6ff.; Witt 1971, esp. 175). This was a less qualified claim to external autonomy, and it became in due course an internal constitutional ideal as well, meaning elective government under the laws, not dominated by any specifiable group or individual. Its usage is best recorded at Florence, where the ejection of the old patriciate by an alliance of great merchants and *populares* was followed by long periods of, in effect, merchant–capitalist government. Liberty thus has two meanings: first, the Guelf ideal of independent cities, which around 1400 Florence was championing against Milan, although she herself readily subjugated hostile cities ('Let the Pisans be urged to liberty: and if they will not, let provision be made for the defence of liberty': a 'Rousseauistic' statement of 1392, cit. Herde 1973, 219n.; cf. Baron 1966, 470 n.19). Secondly, it meant *governo largo*, the extension of political rights to the middle classes, that is the guilds among others. As such it became, at Florence and elsewhere, a slogan of popular dissent and revolt against magnates or mercantile oligarchy. '*Liberta, popolo e Guelfo*' were invoked in public documents during periods of popular guild rule, and by advocates of the wider franchise (Herde 1973, 183n.; Witt 1971, 190). Revolt in Bologna (1376) was heralded by 'Long live the people and liberty' (cit. Witt 1971, 176). When Lucca ousted its oligarchy (1369), the new regime, having debated whether to adopt rule '*a comune*' (allowing magnates as well as *populares* to hold office) or '*a popolo*' (excluding the former), decided for a government '*in liberta e a popolo*' (Meek 1978, 182–3). '*Popolo e liberta*' was again a slogan in the Savonarolan uprising of 1494 (Skinner 1978, i 143).

A leader of the pro-popular revolt at Florence in 1527 declared that 'liberty is nothing other than equality among the citizens' (cit. Albertini 1955, 127). Equality in this context meant fiscal fairness, open access to the law courts for all burghers, and the eligibility of all full citizens for political office. It too was widely advocated by popular opponents of oligarchy in fourteenth- and fifteenth-century Florence (Brucker 1977, 45; Rubinstein 1968, 451, 455, 461).

It must be remembered, however, that (if the present analysis is correct) both liberty and equality were ideals of civil society. Their ideological role in Italian popular movements was partly due to the relatively wide penetration of Ciceronian humanist values, which was probably one reason why it was at Florence that burgher aspirations were most articulately developed into a political ideology (Holmes 1973). The new language of Renaissance humanism did not significantly affect the substance of political beliefs, which continued to be grounded 'in communal political traditions rather than in humanist writings' (Rubinstein 1968, 460). The traditional ideals of sworn association and the assembly of armed citizens provided the model and inspiration for popular government: the revival of Latin culture provided new conceptual tools to articulate and justify this.

This accounts in part for the differences that now emerged in the expression of burgher, popular-guild beliefs in Italy and in Germany. In Italy, city-states achieved wider dominance than elsewhere, but they were also more prone to factionalism and despotism (*Signoria*). In Germany, the only other region of self-governing cities in the later Middle Ages, conflict between patriciate and guilds was more often resolved by power-sharing based upon compromise. Several Italian critics noted that German cities enjoyed greater harmony and more popular participation: and these features were to survive much longer in the German guild polities than elsewhere. Thus the differing ideological emphases also reflected somewhat different political realities.

6

GUILD AND CIVIL SOCIETY
IN MEDIEVAL POLITICAL
PHILOSOPHY

To what extent did men of learning – scholastics and jurists – conceptualize or legitimize the *civitas* and its government either on the basis of guild concepts and values, or in terms of civil society? While the values of civil society entered into medieval philosophy at all levels (national as well as provincial), guild values were principally referred to in the context of the *civitas* (city, city-state or simply state). To answer that question, therefore, we must consider the notion of *civitas*, which relates back to that of the commune.

Just as there was, surprisingly, no philosophy of the guild in the Middle Ages, so too there was no philosophy of the city as such. One would have expected the revival of Aristotle to provide the means by which cities' fiscal, jurisdictional and legislative claims might be justified philosophically, to kindle some notion of the human and moral value of the *civitas*, and perhaps of other associations. But, with some exceptions, Aristotle's *polis* was taken to mean not city-state in the literal sense but political society in general. Far from revolutionizing the conception of the city-state, Aristotelians most commonly used their master to justify and extend the authority of whatever secular political order already existed. This was partly because the word *civitas*, by which *polis* was translated, was already currently used to mean political society in a generic sense, as well as city-state in the literal sense. Aristotelians tended to shift without warning from one level of meaning to another. Rather than using Aristotle to develop a notion of either guild or city as morally significant collectivities, there was from the start a tendency loosely to combine Aristotelian with Ciceronian terms, and to use the former too to ascribe value to the city because it made possible burgher freedom and the rule of law, that is to underwrite the values of civil society.

Thomas Aquinas (1224–74), in transmitting Aristotle to contemporary theologians and those in positions of political power, continued to employ the term *civitas*, with its Aristotelian qualities, largely in the abstract sense, so that it can often best be translated 'state'. He did not regard the city or city-state as generically superior to other kinds of state. When he reproduced Aristotle's argument that, whereas family and village enable men to live, the *polis* enables them to live well, he did not contrast family with city but 'domestic association' with 'civil association' (*multitudo civilis*). He did, none the less, go on to say that the latter is superior in two ways: because 'in the *civitas* there are many crafts', and 'in moral matters' (ed. d'Entrèves 190). Similarly, Ptolemy of Lucca said that 'the community of the *civitas* is essential for the necessities of life', because clothing, housing, medicine and the whole variety of skills 'without which man cannot live decently' are most easily obtainable in a city, with its 'many crafts and craftsmen'; and also that the *civitas* provides special opportunities for moral and intellectual growth (bk iv, chs 2–3). But on the whole scholastics, while they emphasized the importance of a civic environment for moral growth, did not see the *civitas* itself as a transmitter of moral values in the manner of Aristotle. In their thought, as in the practical politics of the Investiture Controversy and its aftermath, church–state dualism worked in favour of individual liberty, of a private sector of morality. The state had moral goals, but not of its own making, and there was a wide range of moral activity outside its purview (cf. Gilby 1958, 214ff.). This was inherent in Christian belief; it also meshed well with the values of civil society. Obey the general precepts of morality and the law, and you are free to be yourself, to do your own thing: so the Europeanized Aristotle would emerge in Locke.

Scholastics did not see the craft-guild as a morally significant community. They did, on the other hand, give political meaning to the values of friendship and mutual aid, and related the latter to the division of labour. This did not of course mean that they were consciously applying guild values to the state, because friendship and mutual aid were embedded in Stoic–Christian thought, while the idea of division of labour, which from now on was increasingly emphasized in European thought, if it did not occur to them spontaneously, was suggested by the organic analogy and by Aristotle. But, granted this, there was here at least a parallel with guild values. The *civitas* had moral significance both because it implemented justice through its law and punishments, and also because it was a community of friendship and love (cf. Ptolemy of Lucca bk iv, chs 2–3; Buridan I q.4, pp.16–17). But this politicization of guild values changed their meaning: it was no longer 'brotherhood' in the sense of a commitment to specified persons come what may, but rather a readiness to be friendly to others just because they are one's fellow-citizens. It was a social relationship under the rule of law; law now defines the commitment of citizens to one another. But some degree of fellow-feeling was necessary to make these looser relationships tick. In other words, the values of both civil society and guild are brought into play.

Aquinas stated, in general terms, the relationship between social life, mutual aid and division of labour:

> It is natural to man that he live in partnership (*societate*) with many. . . . It is therefore necessary, if man is to live in an association (*multitudine*), that one should be helped by another, and that different people should be occupied in discovering different things through reason (*diversi diversis inveniendis per rationem occuparentur*).
> (*On Princely Government* I, ch.1, pp.2–4; cf. Girolami, *Benefit of Peace*, 129)

In the north-west, Henry of Ghent (writing in 1279) said that the 'disposition of the *civitas*' – envisaged by Plato as the highest natural condition of man – was

> the appropriate condition for men living in civil partnership and community (*societate et communitate civili*); since that disposition could not exist unless bound together by the deepest friendship, by which each person is regarded by each other as another self (*quilibet reputaretur a quolibet alter ipse*), and by the deepest charity, in which each of them loves the other as himself, and by the highest benevolence, by which each wills for the other what he wills for himself.   (cit. Lagarde 1958, 178)

This was the first appropriation by a north-western European of the classical notion of the *polis*. It already points to the direction in which Hegel was to take the concept of the state, as the embodiment of moral mutuality (cf. Godfrey of Fontaines: Lagarde 1943b, 90). Similarly, Francesc Eiximines, a late fourteenth-century Catalan jurist (in a work dedicated to the city of Valencia), based civic community on brotherly mutual aid: 'The community of the city is firm and strong when one aids another, just as a good brother readily aids his brother. . . . The basis of the commonwealth (*la cosa publica*) is union, charity and the sincere attachment of men's hearts' (40, 58; cf. Maravall 1966, 165).

The scholastics, then, interpreted Aristotle's doctrine of the *polis* as the product of nature, to mean that men have a general tendency to *communicatio*. In the moral sphere, they interpreted man's political nature not as meaning that men, to be good, have to practice virtues in a public or civic context (as later humanists would have it), but as meaning that the good life necessarily involves friendship, fraternity and mutual aid. This was a reinterpretation of Aristotle in the light of Christian values. It was also, in effect, an application of the guild ethic to the polity. Lagarde believes that this was their conscious intention: theologians, he says, were 'directly influenced by the corporative order of the towns', and there was a 'deep connection' between corporate politics and 'the political doctrines of the Aristotelian–Thomist school' (1958, 311, 320–1). It is always difficult to determine the exact relation of the somewhat abstract formulae of men like Aquinas to contemporary phenomena. Apart from Marsiglio there is no explicit discussion of any political role for the guilds. It seems most reasonable to conclude that what we have here is, once again, a parallel between philosophy and popular consciousness, stemming from shared Christian values.

Scholastics were at least as much, and in the case of Aquinas even more, inclined to apply to the state the values of civil society: personal liberty, the rule of law and fiscal impartiality. Aquinas distinguished between authority (*prelatio*) (or lordship: *dominium*) over slaves and over subjects; this also served as his distinction between illegitimate and legitimate government, because subjects, as persons in their own right, *could* expect to be governed for their own common good.

> Authority which aims at the subjects' utility does not remove their liberty; therefore it is not improper that those who have been made sons of God by the Holy Spirit should be under such authority.
> (*Commentary on the Sentences* bk II, dist.44, q.2, a.2 ad 1: ed. d'Entrèves 184)

> A community of free persons has a different purpose to one of slaves. For the free person exists for his own sake (*sui causa est*); but the slave is one whose being belongs to another. If therefore a community of free persons is directed by its ruler to the common good, that will be a right and just government, suitable for free persons.
> (*On Princely Government* bk I, ch.1, p.6)

> Lordship ... in one sense is the opposite of servitude. ... In another sense it means, in a general way, any kind of relationship to a subject: and so he whose duty it is to govern and direct free persons may also be called a lord. ... In the second sense [but not the first], men could have been lords over each other in the state of innocence. ... Someone is lord over another as free person when he directs the subject to his own good (*proprium bonum*), or to the common good.
> (*Summa Theologiae* I q.92 a.2 resp.: ed. d'Entrèves 104)

In this significant contribution to the concept of liberty, the cutting-edge of Aquinas' argument is liberty in the personal or legal sense, not liberty to participate in government. It is the formal, almost Kantian criterion of whether free men could rationally consent to a regime and its actions, which ultimately governs Aquinas' profound understanding of political legitimacy. These statements were not inspired by the civic movement but rather by the whole temper of medieval Germanic Christianity, perhaps by Christianity *tout court*. But they demonstrate the underlying agreement between the civic emphasis on liberty as a value and practical right, and the general medieval moralists' view. Ptolemy defined political rule as involving a degree of popular government, but the feature which he most stressed was the rule of law. Political rule is 'a distinct manner of ruling, because [ruling must be done] according to the form of communal or princely laws, to which the ruler is bound'. It is found 'when a region, province, *civitas* or burgh is ruled by one or many according to its own statutes, as happens in the regions of Italy' (bk ii, ch.viii).

> Political rulers are bound by laws and cannot proceed beyond them in pursuit of justice ... they dare not make any innovation outside the written laws. ... One must consider also that in all regions, whether Germania, Scythia [sc. Russia] or Gaul, *civitates* live politically, the power of king or emperor, who is bound by definite laws, being circumscribed.
> (bk iv, ch.i)

The values of civil society were also invoked apropos peace and the common good as end-values for the state. Aquinas said:

> Laws can be unjust ... either in their purpose, as when a president imposes burdensome laws on his subjects, not for their common utility but rather for his own cupidity or glory ... or in their form, as when burdens are unequally distributed among the community, even though they are aimed at the common good.
> (*Summa Theologiae* Ia IIae q.96 a.4 resp.; cf. Godfrey of Fontaines in Lagarde 1958, 195–7)

This probably referred, among other things, to unfair taxation, which we have seen to be a standard complaint among townsmen; such 'tyranny' or 'greed' strikes at the root of respect for persons and property.

Thus it seems that, contrary to what is often thought, when scholastics discussed cities or 'the political life', they focused upon civil society rather than corporate values. This was partly because they had little acquaintance with the world or mentality of the ordinary townsman, guildsman or craftsman. But the values of civil society appear also to have appealed to them more strongly in their own right than did the values of guild or town commune. They were sanctioned by Christian and Stoic philosophy. They left room for the 'liberty of the church' and the unimpeded pursuit of things spiritual. They could be aspired to be everybody.

Jurists can only be said to have discussed guilds from a philosophical angle inasmuch as they discussed the nature of corporations (*collegia, universitates*) in general. This category embraced guilds as well as cities and numerous other bodies: but in these general discussions they hardly ever referred explicitly to guilds; the examples usually given were city, cathedral chapter or university (Canning 1980; Feenstra 1956; Gierke 1881, 279–80; Gillet 1927, 160; see esp. Bartolus on *Digest* 48.19.16(10), fol.200r/a).

It would appear, therefore, that medieval learning put relatively little value on any of the institutions under discussion, whether city, *universitas* or guild. Moral value was ascribed to the kingdom and, by Aristotelians, to the *civitas* or state in the abstract. But neither scholastics nor jurists seem to have regarded membership of popular associations or even of cities as morally advantageous; here, as Gierke intimates, they did not always reflect ordinary opinion. In this respect, there was perhaps never a true rebirth of the ancient ideal of the *polis*.

The institutions to which medieval learning did ascribe a moral, indeed a cosmic, function were of a different kind. First, there were the unique and universal institutions of church and empire. Secondly, there was the law, in all its many manifestations. Law, rather than any particular type of society or state, was the categorical moral authority for the Middle Ages ('the point where life and logic meet', as Maitland said). It was through law that supreme moral values (eternal, revealed or natural) were transmitted to human society and realized in the everyday life of man's present experience. This outlook had of course a classical parentage in the Stoic theory of natural law, which underlay the late Roman philosophy of law, magnificently summarized in the opening sections of the *Digest*. It went back to the conceptual change wrought in the fourth century BC, when the values of the *polis* (which Plato saw as culminating in 'righteousness/*dikaiosune*') gave way to the universal value of justice as the supreme norm that ought to govern men's allegiance and will in any kind of state. The great scandal of Machiavelli was that he subjected justice to the state.

Justice was a solid point of reference; it was the inherent principle of a harmonious universe. There was a correspondingly rich vocabulary of law: *ius, lex, statutum, consuetudo, conventio, constitutio, pactum, ius commune* and so on. Associations were legitimate in so far as they pursued justice, it was said, or, alternatively, in so far as they could be subsumed under a category sanctioned by the law of nations, Roman law or custom. They were validated 'by the law'. Law was a political actor; it did things and created institutions: 'law makes the king', as Bracton put it.

Medieval thinkers explored in depth the relationship between transcendent and actual law; medieval lawyers attempted to apply the universal and eternal principles of justice to the minutiae of government, adjudication and daily transactions. Here, there was indeed 'particularity' in medieval thought (*pace* Pocock 1975, 53–4, 75–8). Once one sees the all-pervasive moral value ascribed to the law, one can no longer accuse medieval thought of abstraction or other-worldliness. The importance of this in the present context is that it is law and the rule of law which make possible those transactions that comprise civil society.

Finally, how were popular government and the political role of guilds regarded by scholastics and jurists? We have noted that urban revolutions occurred about the time of the rediscovery of Aristotle. One's first reaction is how little they had to say on the subject: both Aristotle's nuanced discussion of *oligarchia, demokratia* and *politeia* (moderate *demokratia,* tempered with oligarchy and the rule of law) – in which he so brilliantly intermingles moral, analytical and empirical questions – and the actual constitutional upheavals in towns evoked little academic interest. (From this and much that follows Marsiglio – see ch.7 – must be excepted.) This was partly because scholastics were principally concerned with abstract questions and universal truths, such as which is the best form of government (monarchy, was the usual answer). Also, outside Italy, they paid more attention to royal and seigneurial government than to civic politics. Political questions were not the jurists' primary concern, a fact lamented by Bartolus. What scholastics did have to say was largely couched in classical idiom and related to Aristotle's typology of regimes. There was virtually no development of Germanic concepts like *Gemeinde* (community); classical values and categories were grafted onto the native stem. Participation by guilds in government was not mentioned, let alone legitimized, by a single scholastic or jurist, including Marsiglio.

But scholastics did learn from Aristotle that, while one form of government may be the best in ideal terms, others may also be just and therefore legitimate: this was a fruitful step in view of the actual diversity of regimes in towns and of types of political units generally. Popular government was conceptualized in two ways: first, as *demokratia* in Aristotle's sense of rule by the majority in their own interest. By this they may have meant those contemporary regimes in which magnates were excluded from power or discriminated against by the new *popolo.* This *demokratia* was usually denounced as unjust because self-interested (Aquinas, *On the Politics* 139, *On Princely Government* 6–8; Egidio Romano bk iii, pt 2, ch.2, fol.269r). But even Aquinas was prepared to admit that 'popular power' (*potentatus populi*) was less perverse than oligarchy (*On Princely Government* 6): scholastics tended to regard wealth as the last thing that could legitimate political authority. Canon John Hocsem of Liège (1297–1348: Feenstra 1963, 487–8, 506) thought that the difference between oligarchy and *democratia* was that in the former 'the rich seek honour to excess', whereas in the latter 'the people irrationally always seek ... equality *simpliciter*'. *Democratia* means rule by the many without 'discipline', as 'is clear from examples today wherever the *populus* is sovereign', for instance at Liège between 1312 and 1326 when 'the *populus* itself alone, as it were, held sovereignty' (Hocsem 17–18). Hocsem implied that it is in practice no worse than monarchy, since 'all kings of the earth today are, briefly, tyrants' (17). Bartolus too regarded self-interested majority rule as the least bad of the perverse regimes, since 'inasmuch as [the rulers] are the majority, it has some savour of the nature of the common good' (*On City Government* 93).

Among scholastics, the most favourable to *democratia* was Albert the Great (1206–80); German by birth, he spent most of his life at Cologne, where he frequently acted as a mediator between the city and the prince-archbishop (Martin 1951, 40). His support for *democratia* probably derived from his apostolic sympathy with the poor, certainly from a belief in human equality. (*Pace* Martin 1951, 39ff., I can find no trace of support for *political* guilds.) Albert does not explicitly refer to rule by the lower classes; since he cites 'cities of Lombardy such as Genoa' he can hardly have had that in mind. What he meant was rule 'for the benefit of the poor', which might mean social welfare rather than exclusion of upper-class interests from the common good. In any case, he equated *democratia* with *politia*, and legitimated it as 'popular polity' and 'the sovereignty of free and equal men' (*On the Politics* 238, 344–5). Rule by men of wealth, on the contrary, 'is not true polity but a sort of corruption' (*Commentary on the Sentences* 807–8). The *populus* prefer law to princely decree. Under the democratic principle of 'what the majority decide is ... just', 'natural right (*iustum naturale*) is maintained, according to which nature made all men equal. ... Thus, just as nature engendered them as equals, so they are equal *vis-à-vis* governmental office (*equaliter se habeant ad dignitatem in principatu*)' (*On the Politics* 563). Albert shows that political equality as understood by the urban middle and lower classes accorded with a scholastic view of natural justice. It was out of this fusion of Athenian and Stoic–Christian principles that the modern European philosophical ideals of citizenship and democracy were born.

Bartolus regarded *regimen ad populum* (rule by the people) as the best kind of government for small cities like Perugia (*On City Government* 87–9). By this he meant rule by a 'middle-class' majority. In Italy government *a popolo* generally meant exclusion of the patriciate, which Bartolus sanctioned if they are 'so powerful that they oppress the rest'; he also excluded 'the lowest' (*vilissimis*) (*On City Government* 89). Like Albert, he equated this regime with Aristotle's *policratia* (moderate *demokratia*). Not only is it intrinsically good, but it had been 'greatly commended' by the emperor Charles IV and 'seems to be a constitution laid down by God rather than men' (*On City Government* 88–9).

Popular government in the more traditional, less revolutionary sense, with the balance of power residing in the assembly of full citizens rather than in the small council, was more favourably regarded. It was called rule by the community (*multitudo*: the liberal arts and theological equivalent of *universitas*): this may be taken as referring either to communal government in the original sense (prior to the development of oligarchy) or to power-sharing between patriciate and guilds. This was assimilated to Aristotle's *politeia* (a mixture of oligarchy and *demokratia*) and thus rendered

83

legitimate. Egidio Romano said that 'in the cities of Italy the many as a whole people (*multi, ut totus populus*) generally rule', and that, if 'the aim is the common good of the poor, the middling and the rich, and of all according to their position', such a constitution 'is right and fair' (*equalis*) and may be called 'popular government' (*gubernationem populi*) (bk iii, pt 2, ch.2, fols 268v–269r; cf. Aquinas, *On the Politics* 139, *On Princely Government* 6–8 and ch.4; Ptolemy of Lucca bk iv, chs i–ii, viii; Jean Versor, d.1485, bk iii, fol.43v). This Italian 'myth' represented exactly what a great many guilds and townsmen in north-western Europe were at this very time trying to achieve. In fact Hocsem of Liège regarded mixed government as both desirable and inevitable: 'thus we see among us at present that one bishop and the few rich are equally sovereign with the populace' (17–18). The city as *universitas, commune, Gemeinde* was thus far more readily endorsed by scholastics than was the more revolutionary form of popular government.

As regards political guilds, therefore, Gierke's hypothesis of a gulf between popular consciousness and learned doctrine again seems valid. Most people participated in public affairs through guilds and similar associations. But philosophers saw social personality only in terms of family and state, domesticity and formal politics. A whole range of actual socio-political life vanishes into the air whenever we look at a work of political theory. Was this gulf a price paid for the classical heritage?

On the other hand, certain constitutional ideas and procedures were taken over from juristic corporation theory and applied to city government, or even to government in general. Participatory consent is an outstanding example. Writing of ecclesiastical colleges, Hostiensis (d.1271) had said that, if consent were given by 'each in his own room' or by 'one person today, another tomorrow, or one person in one place, another somewhere else', they might give different opinions to those they would have given collectively in public: 'he who consents in his room could dissent in the chapter' (cit. Gierke 1881, 313–14; cf. Gillet 1927, 134–5). Bartolus applied this to the city or 'people': it is not sufficient if 'all of the people consent separately in their houses. ... In matters pertaining to all corporately (*ut universos*), the simultaneous consent of all (*simul omnium consensus*) is required' (on *Digest* 1.1.9, n.18). This reveals an element of participatory democracy in corporation theory and practice (see also Aquinas, *On Princely Government* ch.4). It anticipates in legal terms (to prevent personal pressure, and avoid reneging on commitments) Rousseau's notion of the categorical difference between private and public decision-making.

Similarly, Mario Salamonio (*c*.1450–1532: cf. d'Addio 1954; Skinner 1978, i 148–52 and ii 131–4) introduced a revolutionary conception of the relation between law and the prince for all kinds of government, by invoking the analogy between the state (*civitas*) and mercantile partnership (*societas*: cf. *Digest* 17.2.1 and 5; Cicero, *De Republica* I.xxxii.49). In his dialogue *On Sovereignty*, a philosopher forces a jurist to concede that, just as a partnership is entered into by, and essentially based upon, contractual agreements (*pactiones*) equally binding upon all partners, so too contracts are constitutive of the state ('the means by which the state is arranged and preserved'). Laws are contractual in nature; the ruler is a contractual partner in the state; and, if he breaks the laws, the state is dissolved – 'inequality of conditions breaks up a partnership' (28–31).

This was a remarkable anticipation of later contractual theory. It is of particular interest here because it indicates a connection between, on the one hand, government by law plus legal equality – values emerging from civil society – and, on the other hand, the mercantile partnership, which was one of the prime social instruments for the expansion of commerce and development of commercial capitalism. Indeed, the actual term 'civil society' was now becoming a common designation for a civilized political community. Salamonio's argument suggests that people's day-to-day experience of life in small groups could affect the way they conceptualized political relationships. In the same way, Juan de Segovia, a conciliar constitutionalist, had applied the model of the *collegium* (university, chapter, guild) to the church as a whole (Black 1979, 162ff.). The model of the small group was used to support the rule of law, or indeed popular sovereignty, against monarchical theory.

7

MARSIGLIO OF PADUA: A PHILOSOPHY OF THE CORPORATE STATE

Marsiglio of Padua (1275/80–1342) requires separate treatment on account of his genius, and because, more than any other medieval or Renaissance writer, he worked out a systematic philosophical basis for the city-state and for a quasi-popular mode of civic government, taking matters back to the first principles of human existence. In system and originality, in the thoroughness, depth and precision of his argument, he surpassed all his contemporaries (except, as always, Ockham); one does not find another such earth-shaking yet well-tuned civil philosophy until Hobbes, who in fact shared much of Marsiglio's outlook. He set aside the Greco-Roman and the patristic-ecclesiastical mentality, and was thus able to forge closer links between political philosophy and contemporary civic experience.

Just as Marsiglio broke with scholastic – and indeed classical – tradition in other ways, so he was the only medieval thinker to take seriously the role played by corporate organization in contemporary city-states. He placed functional groups at the centre of his theory of the state; the idea of the community as a totality, made up of diverse 'parts' or 'members' in the form of vocational groups, is built into the very structure of his political model. Perhaps no other thinker has ever made such a fundamental connection between occupation and citizenship. He put them on the same ontological plane, since both take their origin from man's natural dispositions and needs.

The son of a Paduan university notary, Marsiglio studied liberal arts and medicine; he was elected *rector* of Paris University in 1312 (a three-month post). Returning to Italy, he was active in pro-imperialist politics, and may have served Cangrande, despot of Verona. From 1320 onwards he practised medicine. His masterpiece, *The Defender of the Peace*, finished at Paris in January 1324, was composed on behalf of Ludwig of Bavaria (the imperial claimant in conflict with Pope John XXII), to whom it was dedicated. Several of its theses were declared heretical, Marsiglio was excommunicated and took refuge with Ludwig. He joined in the would-be emperor's Italian campaign of 1327–8, which culminated in the deposition of John XXII and the election of an anti-pope. Both actions appear to have been performed in a manner suggested by Marsiglio's writings; he was briefly made spiritual vicar for Rome. After the collapse of the Italian venture, Marsiglio remained at Munich till his death (Gewirth 1951, 20–3; E. Lewis 1954, i 69–71; Sullivan 1896–7, 594–5).

The Defender of the Peace is divided into three *dictiones* (discourses), the last of which is a brief summary and conclusion. In *Dictio* I, Marsiglio examined the basic principles of political association and worked out their detailed constitutional implications; in *Dictio* II, he used scriptural exegesis and textual criticism, along with the theses of *Dictio* I, to refute the claims of the papacy, in particular over secular affairs but to a large extent in the religious sphere as well. He proceeded to set out a constitutional model for the church, in which the emperor and secular rulers played a leading organizational role, while pope, bishops and clergy were confined to pastoral and sacramental functions – much as they are today, in fact. Even doctrinal questions were to be settled by a general council, organized by the secular rulers and conducted under their gaze.

The purpose of the work as a whole has been disputed. Was it meant as an examination both of political structures and of church organization? Or was the first part merely meant to provide a basis for the second? In other words, how seriously did Marsiglio intend the position worked out in *Dictio* I – which is what concerns us here – to be taken on its own account? It is perfectly true that many of the propositions established in *Dictio* I point towards the conclusions of *Dictio* II. Certainly, Marsiglio's contemporaries and succeeding generations regarded him almost exclusively as a religious and ecclesiastical controversialist. *The Defender* was popular among early Protestants, being translated into German and, in 1535, English (p.xl). But it is perfectly possible that this contemporary understanding of Marsiglio overlooked aspects of his thought which he himself considered important (as also happened with Machiavelli). The carefully elaborated argument of *Dictio* I certainly reads as if it were meant seriously. This would then be an instance of political philosophy being conceived in the womb of religious controversy.

The actual message of *Dictio* I has also been much disputed. Some hold that it was chiefly about the empire. Marsiglio's argument, they believe, was essentially abstract: he used the theory of the origin of authority in the people as a means to establish the self-sufficient and absolute status of imperial authority *in relation to the church*: 'the *populus*, which is said to transfer its *imperium* to the prince, is that abstraction, the State itself . . . it is essentially a theory of monarchy' (Wilks 1972, 284–5, 292; Quillet 1970, 18). Gewirth, on the contrary, believes that Marsiglio's knowledge of civic government at Padua made 'by far the more profound contribution' to *The*

Defender, providing 'the particular circumstances which were the main sources in Marsiglio's experience of the general doctrine set forth in the *Defensor Pacis*' (1951, 23). Gewirth maintains that 'popular sovereignty ... is the central thesis of Marsiglio's entire political philosophy' (1951, 167, 253). This view is supported by Rubinstein, who has examined the roots of Marsiglio's political language in the civic culture of Italy, and concludes that Marsiglio was indeed talking about the problems of the city-state, whatever else he may also have had in mind (1965, 44, 46–9, 68, 70, 74; cf. Skinner 1978, i 61ff.). Moreover, in chapter ii (of *Dictio* I) Marsiglio briefly disposed of the kingdom (*regnum*) by saying that it differs from the *civitas* in size only; it is therefore understood that what he had to say about the *civitas* applied no less to the *regnum*, but that *civitas* is the general category of political association. We may reasonably conclude that, although by *civitas* he did not mean only the city-state, the city-state is nevertheless the type-case of what he also referred to as 'civil communities' (*communitates civiles*) (p.7).

Having in mind the ecclesiastical argument that was to follow, he constantly referred to the area of life, activity and organization which is 'civil' – 'civil governments' (*civilia regimina*) (p.1), 'civilization' (*civilitas*) (p.3), 'civil happiness' (*civilis felicitas*) (p.6) – namely the arena in which men achieve 'the sufficient life' (p.12). Law and legislation are concerned with 'the political or civil actions of men' (*Dictio* I.x, p.37); they determine 'civil justice' and prescribe 'civil judgments' (I.xi, p.40). Marsiglio defined this civil area principally in distinction from the ecclesiastical, which concerns the after-life.

Chapters iii–vii deal with 'what the *civitas* in itself is and what it is for'. The *civitas* is defined as the community in which men live *civiliter* and 'well', with leisure to pursue 'liberal tasks' (*opera liberalia*) and to exercise the 'practical and speculative virtues of the soul' (I.iv, p.12). This is the 'sufficient life' which 'all men, not deprived or otherwise naturally impeded, desire' (p.12). Elaborating in his own way upon Aristotle, he said that the sufficient life requires both diversity of skills (*artes*) and a means of regulating disputes, because man 'is born naked and unarmed' and is subject to 'contrary actions and passions' (p.13).

The need for a diversity of skills gives rise to a variety of functional 'parts' (*partes*) in the *civitas*, an idea which Marsiglio took over from Aristotle. Aristotle had analysed the *polis* in terms of its constituent parts, each of which performed a distinct function in the life of the whole. He classified these parts in three different ways: household and villages (*Politics* I; cf. *The Defender* I.iii), the individual citizens (III), and occupations – farmers, craftsmen, soldiers, men of wealth, priests and judges (VII.7.4, 1328b). It was this last classification which Marsiglio adopted here. He proceeded to expound their significance and role in chapters v–vii, before going on to examine the specifically governmental aspects of the *civitas* in chapters viii–ix. To judge from their place in Marsiglio's argument, therefore, such 'parts' play a fundamental role in the underlying structure of the *civitas*, more fundamental than they do in Aristotle.

Marsiglio, then, saw the *civitas* as essentially composed of separate 'parts', each of which is necessary to the sufficient life. He called them *officia* (lit. duties, ministries) and spoke of men as having natural inclinations towards certain 'crafts' (*artes*) – both terms currently used of craft-guilds. Marsiglio was of course using these terms in a wider sense, to include all occupations necessary to civil life (farmers, etc.). He did, however, make a point of saying that 'the *genus* of craftsmen' (*mechanicarum*) was introduced in order to 'control the actions and passions of our body [so that they are not affected] by the external elements and their impact'; it includes 'makers of cloth, cordwainers, shoemakers and all aspects of the building trade', as well as painters, doctors and architects (I.v, p.17). The 'material cause' of these 'offices or parts of the state' is *nature itself*:

> The specific substance (*materia propria*) of the different offices, according to which the offices refer to conditions of the soul (*nominant habitus animae*), is men, disposed (*inclinati*) from their conception or birth to different arts or disciplines. ... The material causes of the offices of the *civitas* ... are men, conditioned by arts and disciplines of different classes and types (*habituati per artes et disciplinas diversorum generum et specierum*), from which different orders or parts are established in the *civitas* to achieve the satisfactions (*propter finales sufficientias*) produced by the arts and disciplines of these men.   (I.vii, pp.26–7)

The 'formal causes of the offices', their 'moving or creative causes' (*moventes causae seu factivae*) are to be found in 'the minds and wills of men', their natural desire or disposition for different pursuits (p.27). Not only the *civitas* or state itself, then, but also its parts are the product of nature and of the innate dispositions of men.

It is quite clear that Marsiglio's conception of the *civitas* is, at its very basis, corporatist (cf. Gewirth 1951, 199). The whole civic community is 'the multitude or people of all the *colleges* of the polity or civil order (*omnium collegiorum politiae seu civilitatis ... multitudo sive populus*)' (I.xiii, p.57). His conception was broadly similar to that expressed by a Florentine decree of 1293, which referred to the 'crafts and craftsmen' as the 'parts of the city' (cit. Najemy 1979, 59n.). Marsiglio's corporatism, however, was purely metaphysical. When it came to law and government, he did not envisage the six parts as functioning separately, or maintaining their distinct identities at the political level. Rather, he returned to the concept of the citizen, and affirmed the completely unitary nature of 'the corporation of citizens'. Indeed the six parts are dependent, for their recognition and organization as parts, upon 'the human legislator': this is 'the efficient cause, according to which there are parts in the city' (I.v, p.27), and 'the ruling part', under the authority of the legislator, 'determines the other offices or parts of the *civitas*' (I.xv, pp.68ff.). Marsiglio was, therefore, no corporatist in the political or constitutional sense; in this respect he too rejected contemporary practice. This was partly because his overriding aim was the unity of the state. It would, therefore, still be possible to argue that Marsiglio's 'corporatism' was motivated by his desire to isolate and subordinate 'the priestly part'; even so, the way he achieved that goal sets him apart from other medieval thinkers.

Marsiglio next proceeded to discuss that 'part' of the state whose special function is the execution of the laws, namely the 'ruling part' (*pars principans*) (chs viii–ix, xiv–xviii). His chief purpose was to assert the advantages of elective over hereditary rule (chs ix, xv-xvi), and to argue that the imperative need for unity in the judicial and administrative system can be met by collegiate magistracies (ch.xvii). In other words, he was arguing against the development of absolute hereditary rule, or despotism (Rubinstein 1965, 63, 70–1).

Having dealt with the 'parts' of the *civitas*, Marsiglio turned in chapter x to the regulation of disputes through law, which in chapter iv he had intimated to be the other essential feature of the state. Law, whether statute or custom, is the form or guiding principle of the judicial and executive officials (*forma principantis*: I.x, p.37); Marsiglio argued with great care that judgments must be made in accordance with the laws (ch. xi). It is, therefore, the framing of the laws which is, as Bodin was to say, the supreme act of authority in the state, and it is in defining the legislature (*legislator*) that Marsiglio came closest to giving us his definition of what we would call the sovereign.

> Let us say, in accordance with the truth, and the counsel of Aristotle (*Politics* III.6), that the legislature or the first and proper effective cause of law is the people or corporation of citizens (*populum seu civium universitatem*), or its weightier part (*valentiorem partem*), according to the election or will of the citizens in the general assembly by explicit vote (*per suam electionem seu voluntatem . . . per sermonem expressam*); when these prescribe or define something to be done or avoided, with regard to civil human actions, under threat of penalty. . . . With regard to the composition of the weightier part, both the quantity and the quality of persons in the community for which laws are to be made should be considered. This [act of legislation] may either be done by the aforesaid corporation of citizens or its weightier part directly through themselves, or it may be entrusted to some person or persons, who are not and cannot be the legislature *simpliciter*, but only for a certain purpose and duration, according to the authority of the first legislature. (I.xii, p.49)

What did Marsiglio mean by 'the corporation of citizens', 'the weightier part', and those others to whom legislation may be conditionally entrusted? Given the language and content of the passage, it is immediately reminiscent of current alternative methods of legislation practised in Italian cities (cf. Rubinstein 1965, 47ff.). It is certainly possible that Marsiglio was constructing a single universal model applicable to all states – a typically abstract scholastic procedure. Yet it is difficult to see why, if Marsiglio was primarily – and not only as an afterthought – concerned with imperial authority and the like (cf. Wilks 1972, 179), he went about things in such a very roundabout manner. It seems most reasonable to hold that Marsiglio meant the passage to be understood in the way in which, given the historical context, it was most likely to be understood.

Taking this crucial passage in this way, we can see that it had an immediate bearing upon the contemporary question of civic constitutions; indeed it comprised a unique formulation of the principles of the commune. The three alternatives offered – legislation by the whole citizen body, by its weightier part, or by a specially and conditionally deputed person or persons – corresponded to the alternatives currently available in Italian cities. The way in which the alternatives are formulated leaves us in no doubt that Marsiglio, while accepting the validity of each method, was especially concerned to safeguard the traditional principle of *the sovereignty of the commune as a whole*. He did so by insisting that the council must be explicitly elected, and, what is more striking, by affirming the merely provisional character of legislation enacted by a *Signoria*. The legislative authority of the corporation of citizens is placed first, as if to suggest an underlying norm, of which the other methods are legitimate variations. It is as if he were saying that government by the many, the few and the one is equally legitimate, but that the last two are in principle variations of the first.

This was a revolution in scholastic political theory, and it was a direct expression of the communal tradition. It was made possible by Marsiglio's carefully argued distinction between legislature and executive, which also had roots in communal civic practice going back over two centuries. The 'ruling', that is, judicial and executive organ, may be monarchical or oligarchical, but this in no way affects the fundamental distribution of authority, since the ruling part is subordinated to the whole citizen body by its being elected and open to correction or deposition (ch.xv; cf. pp.52–3). Ultimate political authority is not located in any government, but in the law, which is made by the corporation of citizens or some agent responsible to it. Had Marsiglio been proposing this merely as *one possible* arrangement, it would not have been new. But he stated that this was not merely a custom or a convenient practice, but 'the truth'. It was the inescapable logical conclusion from the syllogistic reasoning which made up the structure of

Dictio I. The reasons given for this in chapters xii and xiii refer back to the requirements of human nature which underlie the *civitas* itself: the decisions of the *universitas civium* are sure to be sound, because most men desire the sufficient life, and so on (I.xii, pp.51–3; I.xiii, pp.55, 57). Such arguments make no sense unless applied to the corporation of citizens in the literal sense, to consent given in person by the united citizens.

Marsiglio did not derive this doctrine from Aristotle. True, he refers us to a passage in which Aristotle argued that the best constitution for *most* states is moderate democracy (*Politics* III.6.4, 1281b). For Aristotle, this was a prudent generalization, based largely on observation; whereas Marsiglio's doctrine takes the form of a general proposition derived from the intrinsic nature of man and the *civitas*, a 'truth' based on deductive reason. Aristotle, accordingly, is cited only as supporting evidence (*consilium*). Marsiglio's central argument about legislative authority was a typically scholastic piece of abstract logical deduction; what Aristotle had cautiously recommended, Marsiglio presented as a necessary truth.

Here, for the first and only time, the dominant ideology of the medieval city as *universitas, commune, Gemeinde* was expounded as a philosophical absolute. This was surely why Marsiglio used the traditional term 'corporation of citizens' (*universitas civium*) (see pp.49–52): he placed the old burgher view, that what counts legally and politically is one's status *as a burgher*, at the centre of political philosophy. He thus attempted to throw the whole weight of philosophy behind the idea of the city as community, taken beyond the realm of custom and founded on the dynamic of the human will.

The manner in which Marsiglio ascribed legislative sovereignty to the *universitas civium* implied, furthermore, that both upper and lower classes were to be subsumed in the corporate legislature. In discussing the 'parts' of the city, Marsiglio had recognized the existence of two distinct classes when he said that the 'priestly, judicial and consultative' functions (*officia*) make up 'the honourable element' (or 'the nobility: *honorabilitas*'), while 'agriculture, craft (*artificium*) and soldiering' are only parts of the city 'in a broad sense' (*largè*); 'and the whole of these [latter] are called "common"' (or the commons: *vulgaris*) (I.v, p.15). This suggests that he was adopting a patrician attitude. But, in discussing the legislature, Marsiglio stated that, when Aristotle argues for the collectively superior wisdom of the many,

> he means that the people or the community (*multitudo*) of all the colleges of the polity or civil order, taken together, is greater and therefore its judgment is more secure, than the judgment of any part taken separately; whether that part be the common people (*vulgus*) ... such as farmers, craftsmen and the like, or the [imperial] guard (*praetorium*) ... or the nobility (*honorabilitas*), that is the college of aristocrats (*optimatum*).
> (I.xiii, p.57; cf. Gewirth 1951, 176, 180–1)

This endorsed the current claim of *popolo* and guilds to a place in the legislative body. Equally clearly Marsiglio was not endorsing, as Bartolus later did, popular government in the class sense and the exclusion of magnates. It would appear, rather, that he was advocating the acceptance of craft-guilds and new men into city assemblies beside the patriciate. By arguing that the whole community will make better decisions than the few wise, Marsiglio departed from the dominant platonic view that political authority belongs to those superior in intellect (cf. Gewirth 1951, 205). He was proclaiming the right of the non-learned manual craftsman to participation in the key legislative decisions of the *civitas*.

Marsiglio further reflected the social and political consciousness of medieval townsmen by combining collectivist with individualist arguments in support of his proposition that the whole people or its weightier part must be the primary legislature. The townsman saw the civic community as the necessary basis for his private status as a free person, pursuing individual interests under the shield of corporate rights and liberties. So too Marsiglio argued, on the one hand, that the *universitas civium* or its weightier part will make the best laws because 'when the whole corporation of citizens is directed towards something with its intellect and sympathy, the truth of that object is judged more certainly and its common utility weighed more carefully'. He also, on the other hand, argued that 'no one harms himself knowingly' – relating back to the hypothetical nature of man – and that 'that law is better observed by each citizen, which each appears to have imposed on himself' (I.xii, p.51; I.xiii, p.57). The two strands are fused in the argument that laws thus made will be good because 'all men desire the sufficient life and shun its opposite', and because 'in most instances nature does not err or fail' (I.xiii, p.55). The impression one sometimes has that the individualist element is uppermost in Marsiglio is, however, countered by his emphasis on the 'parts' of the *civitas*.

Marsiglio's accord with the ethos of the commune is again apparent in the way he combined the ideas of guild and of civil society. He suggested a caritative and guild-like notion of human community: 'individual brothers and, still more, colleges and communities are bound, both by the affection of charity above and by the bond or law of human society, to aid each other to attain [the benefits of peace]' (I.i, pp.3–4). At first sight, however, the ethos of civil society is more dominant. The principal driving force of Marsiglio's *civitas* was not so much men's sociability as their desire for 'the satisfactory life', in which they have material sufficiency and security and can 'live well, having leisure for liberal tasks, such as the practice of the virtues of the active and speculative soul' (I.iv, p.12). Marsiglio's notion of law has a distinct flavour of civil society. It is based upon concern for security: law, for him, is not primarily an expression of natural justice, but a means to resolve or repress those 'contentions and quarrels' which 'arise among men thus assembled' (I.iv, p.13). While, to be perfect, a law must also be just, the essential character of law is that 'its observance is made dependent upon a coercive command, distributing penalty or reward in the present life' (I.x, pp.38–9). Marsiglio's principal motive may have been to undermine the clergy's claim to review legislation in the light of their own moral standards. Nevertheless, the doctrine that the basic purpose of law is not to make men good nor to model society upon absolute values, but to ensure civil tranquillity (cf. Gewirth 1951, 207), meant that security, without which peaceful exchange is impossible, was made the focal point of law; and law itself is the basis of the state.

The ideas of guild and civil society are, however, brought together in Marsiglio's concluding definition of the 'active or productive cause of tranquillity'. This is

> the mutual intercourse of the citizens, their communication to one another of their works, their mutual aid and assistance, and in general the ability to perform their own private and communal [common] tasks, unimpeded from outside, and their participation in communal [common] benefits and burdens in a measure appropriate to each (*civium conversatio mutua, et communicatio ipsorum invicem suorum operum, mutuumque auxilium atque iuvamentum, generaliterque suorum propriorum operum et communium exercendi ab extrinseco non impedita potestas, participatio quoque communium commodorum et onerum secundum convenientem unicuique mensuram*).
>
> (I.xix, pp.100–1; cf. Althusius, pp.133–5 below)

Here at last we find fully conceptualized the idea of a single society based at once upon mutual aid, particularly through the exercise of different crafts – the guild notion – and upon the exchange of goods – the notion of civil society. This stands out as a unique statement by a medieval theorist of how these twin strands could be interwoven, and made interdependent, as they actually were in the life of medieval towns. It was a formal articulation of the ideals of the medieval commune.

Marsiglio wrote with the concise elegance of a framer of constitutions, subsuming particular contingencies and possible variants under general propositions. In his 'corporatism' and in his notion of the *universitas civium* (corporation of citizens) as embracing both patriciate and craftsmen, he laid out a theoretical model remarkably similar to the programme being pursued at this time in cities of Germany and north-western Europe. Like no other scholastic, except perhaps Albert the Great, he seems to have been able to align the reflections of Aristotle with the perceptions of the medieval burgher. He bridged the gap between high learning and ordinary life. It was perhaps his adoption of a radical stance towards the clergy that led him to break the mould of received intellectual and clerical culture. In both his idealism and his earthy humour, he would have been instinctively attuned to his fascinating contemporary, the Pyrenean shepherd Pierre Maury (Le Roy Ladurie 1980, 120–35).

Yet it is impossible to detect any Marsilian influence upon contemporary civic politics, and it is unlikely there was any. Twenty manuscripts of The Defender in the original Latin are known. (During the fourteenth century a canon of Liège possessed a copy, from which another canon of that city made a copy in 1416.) But so far as is known such manuscripts belonged only to learned churchmen, especially Franciscans, who were most likely to be concerned with Marsiglio's ecclesiastical message, and who seldom had direct influence on civic politics (Marsiglio, ed. Previté-Orton pp.xxiv– xxxiv; Sullivan 1905, 294–5). The only medieval vernacular translations were Italian (1363) and French (some time before then) (Sullivan 1896–7, 598). The Defender achieved wide circulation only during the Reformation, when its ecclesiastical implications were in everyone's minds, and then it was translated into both German and English (Marsiglio, ed. Previté-Orton, p.xl). The limited circulation of the Latin version and of the French and Italian translations (of which only single copies are known), and the absence of a medieval German translation, show beyond reasonable doubt that it could not have been known among leaders of popular movements in cities and could have had no influence on townsmen. The scholastics in general portrayed civic and guild life with as much clarity as an astronomer observing the moon through a magnifying glass. Marsiglio, on the contrary, was evidently in close contact with the constitutional and ideological phenomena with which he was dealing. Yet here too philosophy and ordinary life were, in actual fact, moving on different planes (cf. Sullivan 1896–7, 61). What we have in The Defender is a conceptualization of dynamic trends in contemporary popular consciousness which made no impact whatever on the movements concerned – an awkward fact for a political theorist.

8

THE ITALIAN HUMANISTS: CIVIL SOCIETY AND THE REPUBLIC

The Renaissance sculpted a large part of the modern political value system. To what extent and in what ways did the humanists articulate the values of guild and civil society? What moral status did they assign to them? As with the scholastics and jurists, it is in relation to their conceptions of the city or city-state, and of popular government within the city, that these matters were dealt with.

The nature of the changes wrought in political consciousness and philosophy by the Florentine 'civic humanists', and by the generation of Machiavelli, has to be re-assessed in the light of what has already been established concerning the values of guild and commune, and those of civil society. The points already made here reinforce the view of those who argue that Baron (1966) exaggerated the originality of the Florentine world view around 1400 (Herde 1973; Seigel 1966). Skinner (1978, i) has indeed rightly argued that political liberty was advocated in much the same sense from the twelfth to the fifteenth centuries. Yet, despite his justly celebrated emphasis on historical context (1969), he pays little attention to the peculiar economic and social milieu of Italian republicanism, and so at times fails to grasp exactly what 'liberty' meant, could mean, or was intended to mean.

The exaltation of legal and political equality among citizens, and of personal liberty, were direct extensions of the longstanding ideology of civil society. As with other aspects of Christian humanism, there was continuity with the 'renaissance' of the twelfth century. There was also continuity with well-established burgher aspirations, both economic and political. Furthermore, the humanists continued to conceptualize and legitimize the sovereign rights of the *civitas* not, for the most part, as a general principle of right, but as the historical prerogative of certain privileged cities, based upon customary right (cf. Baron 1966, 387ff.). Finally, they continued the trend of medieval philosophy by largely ignoring the guild and its values. Their principal innovations, on the other hand, were related to their philosophy of man. Liberty was advocated as a function of human personality. Political participation, and the procedural values that went with it, were given a new basis in the Machiavellian idea of *virtu*.

96

In the first place, the guild never featured in renaissance political thought, either as a significant social entity or as an integral component of the polity. Nor, outside public documents and speeches (see pp.71–2), was political participation by merchants or craftsmen as such discussed. Occasionally, they expressed approval of the admission of 'men of middling fortune' (*mediae sortis*) to government (Bruni, cit. Baron 1966, 427–8, 559–60), or of a mixed government which included 'men of every sort' (*ex omni genere*) (Patrizi, *Republic* fol.8v). Even Giannotti, one of the most 'democratic' of the later Florentine theorists, never considered admitting *popolari* 'who practice the most base crafts to make a living' to political citizenship (Pocock 1975, 278). Such virtual silence may indicate a certain myopia, but more probably disapproval based on their class position and classical training.

The conceptualization of the state in terms of the guild ethic of love, friendship and mutual aid was also very rare. Francesco Patrizi of Siena (1413–91), in his *On the Kingdom*, gave 'social or civil friendship' (*socialis seu civilis amicitia*) a prominent role in the moral structure of the state. This is, he said, the most diffuse and least noble form of friendship; reaching out to many persons, it is based at first on advantage (*utilitas*), but it may 'as days go by through use and custom become more abundant (*accumulatior*), until advantage is mostly set aside and gracious benevolence and friendship remain' (bk VIII, tit.xii, fol.497v). This gives rise to patriotism, defined as mutual benevolence among people whose common tie is inhabitancy of the same land; their affection for each other is mediated by their affection for their country and its ways. By sharing a market-place and other civic facilities, citizens can achieve 'a wonderful charity', 'a common friendship' among themselves.

> To be under the same sky, breathe in the same air, feed upon the same fruits and nourishment of the earth, drink the same water; to be instructed by the same teachers, hear and speak the same language, become used to the same crafts (*artibus*) and studies ... to be governed by the same laws ... to observe the same religion – all this is a great bond of benevolence. Also, citizens have many things in common among themselves, such as temples, markets, theatres, colonnades and several other things which have been established for the common use of all, and which link the citizens together in a kind of wonderful charity. This is that common friendship, which, as Cicero says, if it were taken away from the life of men, it would be as if the sun were torn from the sky. From this comes that abundance of friends ... when we associate ourselves with a great number of citizens in festivities, in vernacular speech, in the delight of shared customs and in the sweetness of life, and pour upon them that kindliness which we can bestow without any inconvenience to ourselves. He who lacks this common benevolence would appear to be living in

solitude a life full of snares and fear.   (bk VIII, tit.x, fols 492v–493r)

Here patriotism is conceived as love and friendship based on locality and *moeurs* – an anticipation of Hegel. But, as with earlier statements of friendship as a political value, this was an expression not so much of a specifically guild-related idea as of a Ciceronian virtue. Once again, learned and guild concepts of friendship ran on parallel lines without being directly related to each other.

Rather, humanists celebrated the city-state and popular government in terms of their capacity to realize liberty and equality. Here humanist thought was at one with the spirit of civic officialdom (see pp.73–4); for in Italy humanists moved in the same circles as city rulers and were often employed by them. Liberty was of course a central Renaissance value. The humanist treatment of equality has received less attention (Pocock seems a trifle puzzled by it: 1975, 208–10, 226–7). Liberty in the 'public' sense of political self-determination, both by the sovereign city-state and by the participating individual, has been the focus of recent study (Pocock 1975, 66ff.; Skinner 1978, i 71ff.). In fact, however, the humanists would seem to have attached at least as much importance to liberty in the personal sense of legal freedom etc. (see pp.38–41; cf. Hexter 1979, 297–300). While only those employed by or favourable to sovereign republics like Florence extolled *political* liberty, and indeed sometimes argued that the two aspects were interdependent, all humanists extolled personal liberty and social mobility. Again, the ideal of equality before the law, the *isonomia* beloved of the Athenians, was already widespread. Both this and personal liberty were regarded as attainable under different forms of government. Further, far from there being any tension between liberty and equality in these particular senses, the two were seen as almost coterminous and certainly interdependent: free persons need fair courts.

In advocating personal liberty and legal equality, the humanists were not, as has been implied (Baron 1966, 418ff.; cf. Pocock 1975, 99), innovating but rather conceptualizing certain traditional values of the *commune* and *popolo* in new language. They did not invoke guild values; it was, rather, the merits of civil society that drew their attention and excited their admiration. This was probably due to Cicero, but it may also have been because their audience consisted largely of nobles and merchants rather than craftsmen. The old burgher ideal was being expressed in Ciceronian idiom. The notion of the city-state as a free, trading polity of property owners remained an assumption around which humanist reflections on civic liberty and equality invariably revolved.

This is especially evident in Leonardo Bruni of Arezzo (1369–1444), an outstanding classical scholar who, like many humanists, served both the papacy (1405–15) and Florence, where he spent most of his life in the practice of rhetoric, eventually becoming chancellor in 1427 (Baron 1966,

245–53; Rubinstein 1968, 446–55). He completed a translation of Aristotle's *Politics* into humanist Latin in 1435. In his essays on the constitution and *moeurs* of Florence, composed between 1403 and 1439, he recaptured the surge and leap of Cicero's prose, without altogether sacrificing, as Cicero sometimes did, brevity, simplicity and precision, Latin virtues which one finds, *pace* humanist propaganda, in Bartolus – whose sentences cannot be paraphrased without being expanded – and in parts of the *Digest*. The distinction of Bruni's style often conceals the unoriginality of what he was actually saying.

Bruni held up for admiration, not city-states in general, but a particular form of government (which he described sometimes as mixed, sometimes as popular) in a particular city-state, Florence, because it realized justice, liberty and legal equality. In his *Eulogy of the City of Florence*, written in 1403–4 (Skinner 1978, i 78–9), Bruni described the Florentine constitution as mixed government in the Polybian sense, that is with monarchical, aristocratic and popular elements. As with Cicero, the few – magistracy or senate – are given a central role (259–60). This constitution is laudable because it realizes justice (*ius*) and liberty: all our institutions, he said, are directed 'at these two joined together' (259). Similarly, Salutati had described 'the bridle of liberty' as 'living by right (*ius*) and obeying the laws' (*Invectivum* 32). The rule of law in public and private affairs, says Bruni, ensures liberty: 'the magistrates are set up for the sake of justice ... lest the power of any person should surpass that of the laws in the city' (259). Through popular consultation, 'liberty flourishes and justice is most sacredly observed in the city, because against the opinion of so many men nothing can be obtained by the whim of one or another individual'. Since magistrates are accountable when they leave office, 'in every aspect the people and liberty are dominant' (260).

It is clear that all of these ideals, which Baron saw as part of the new 'civic humanism', were in fact a reflection of an existing popular and official ideology, a pure expression of the ideals of civil society which had grown up in the early towns. That Bruni was celebrating this tradition, and also that in 1403–4, despite his allusion to mixed government, he conceived the Florentine regime as government *a popolo* in the 'class' sense, is evident from his justification of discriminatory laws against magnates, in a passage which otherwise is almost pure Cicero:

When the more powerful, relying on their own resources, were seen to harm and despise the weak, the state (*res publica*) itself took up the cases of those with less power, and defended their property and persons with greater punishment. It was considered reasonable that the unequal condition of men should lead to unequal punishment, and it was thought prudent and just that he who was in greater need should receive more assistance. Thus out of different classes (*ordinibus*), a certain balance

(*aequabilitas*) was created, as the greater were defended by their power, the lesser by the state, and both by the fear of punishment.
(262; cf. Salutati in Witt 1969b, 215; and Cicero, *De Officiis* II.xli; *Digest* 1.1.19 and 4.7.3)

The law itself may be used as an instrument to redress social inequalities, not by equalizing wealth but by ensuring personal *security*. Bruni was praising Florence's constitution and laws because they eliminated magnate lawlessness and *feudal* superiority.

In his description of the Florentine constitution composed for the emperor Sigismund (1413), Bruni identified it as 'popular (*popularis*) ... the third form of government which we referred to above as legitimate ... a form called *democratia* by the Greeks, but by us a popular regime (*popularis status*)' (cit. Rubinstein 1968, 447n.). Here he was describing Florence in terms used by Egidio to describe Italian cities in general (see p. 84), and by Bartolus to describe the constitution suitable for small cities. Like Egidio, Bruni here only asserted that this was *one* of the three legitimate forms of government; there was no implication that this might be offensive to an emperor. But in the funeral speech for Nanno Strozzi, given in 1428 just after he had become chancellor, Bruni went a crucial step further. The alleged merits of rule by one or the few, he now said, are based on fiction; in reality the one and the few are not necessarily virtuous: 'so the popular form of governing a republic remains the *only* legitimate one' (231). Bruni thus appears as the first European theorist to claim legitimacy for the popular form of government alone. Again, he appears to have had in mind popular rule in the class sense. On the other hand, he valued such a constitution precisely because it had those merits which others had earlier ascribed to cities in general: 'we dread no one as lord (*dominum*). ... This is true liberty, this is the equity (*aequitas*) of the city, to fear force from no one, injury from no one' (230–1; cf. pp.38–9 above). What was new about Bruni's values was the enthusiasm with which he monopolized them on behalf of a particular city.

Finally, in his *Constitution of the Florentines*, written (originally in Greek) in 1439, after he had completed his translation of the *Politics*, Bruni declared that 'the republic of the Florentines ... is rule neither wholly by the aristocrats (*optimates*) nor by the people, but mixed from both forms' (cit. Baron 1966, 427–8, 559–60; cf. Rubinstein 1968, 445). It was now mixed government in the Aristotelian sense of oligarchy with democracy; like both Aristotle and Bartolus, he mentioned the importance of 'men of middling fortune' in this context. But, realistically enough in view of the development of Medici rule, he added that the popular element had gradually waned; now the people can only approve or reject proposals put to them by the *optimates*; the regime 'inclines towards the aristocrats and the more wealthy, but not towards the excessively powerful' (cit. Baron 1966, 427–8,

559–60). It was indeed by manipulating the organs of communal government (which scholastics had often characterized as 'mixed government') that the Medici secured their ascendancy at Florence. But this was neither despotism nor a new feudalism because the ideals of civil society – personal liberty and equality under the law – were still operative.

Baron claims that Bruni and other 'civic humanists' were the first modern thinkers to develop the explicit connection made by Cicero between liberty and 'republican' government (Baron 1966, intro. and p.422; cf. Skinner 1978, i 155ff.; Witt 1971, 198). (Cicero had said, for example, that 'liberty has no domicile in any *civitas* except where the power of the people is supreme': *De Republica* I.xlvii.) The concept of 'republicanism' is perhaps a little anachronistic. What was at stake was, rather, 'popular government' in the traditional Italian sense of government *a popolo* to the exclusion of magnates. Bruni was able to portray Florence, where political management lay increasingly in the hands of a mercantile 'familial' oligarchy, as a popular or mixed republic precisely because, at Florence, the original patrician regime had excluded even the great merchants, who had consequently joined forces with the *popolo*. As a Florentine document of 1390 put it, 'we are a popular city (*popularis civitas*), devoted only to commerce' (cit. Baron 1966, 28, 470). And, once again, Bruni was not being particularly original. Townsmen had long since instinctively perceived that political power was necessary to the maintenance of personal rights. The whole political movement of the *popolo* and guilds, in both Italy and northern Europe, had developed around the perception that liberty for economic enterprise and corporate organization, and judicial and fiscal equality, were to be achieved by the appropriation of political power by the guilds. In popular and official thought at Florence, Lucca and elsewhere, an explicit connection had already been made between liberty and popular rule (Meek 1978, 181; Rubinstein 1968, 448–9; cf. Guenée 1971, 316). Bruni was perhaps the first modern theorist to expound this connection as a necessary one, but here once again he was a devout disciple of Cicero.

Bruni also saw a necessary connection between popular government and equality, in the sense of both equality before the law and equality of access to political office. Florence is praised for providing 'equality ... of law for the citizens among themselves, equality of entry into government (*paritatem reipublicae ineundae*)' (Strozzi speech 231). This again was an old *popolo* and guild demand; it had been endorsed by Albert the Great. Where Bruni did break new ground was in his argument that equality of political access is desirable because it stimulates virtuous activity among the citizens.

It is built into the nature of men that, when the way to greatness and honours lies open, they more easily raise themselves up, but, when it is closed, they sit back in inertia.   (cit. Baron 1966, 424, 558n.)

[at Florence] the hope of attaining honour and office, of raising oneself up, is equal for all, so long as one has industry, talent and a proven, solid way of life. Our city requires virtue and probity in the citizen. Whoever has these, she thinks sufficiently qualified for governing the republic.

(Strozzi speech 230–1)

That this argument carried a hint of the later 'Protestant ethic' of hard work and earthly reward, of the idea of 'incentive', is, in view of what has been said about Bruni, no coincidence. That the idea of equality of opportunity was first articulated in the political rather than the economic sphere was probably due to Cicero's ideal of the self-made man (*hominem per se notum*) in politics, and to the fact that politics was the area of practical activity in which the articulate and learned most aspired to excel. A little later, Brandolinus (1440–97) boasted that Italian civic liberty and republican government promote international freedom of trade and an enterprising commercial and industrial spirit:

Our citizens enter into commerce and partnerships freely with all nations, open up the whole world for their own gain, and come to the aid of all men with their industry and skills (*industria ... artibus*); and all nations from everywhere flow together into our cities as into markets common to all peoples (*communia gentium emporia*).   (123–4, cf.116)

According to Bruni, the Florentine constitution is *popularis* precisely because it puts men on an equal footing before law and state, and because it throws office open to all. Political equality is presented as an expression of justice and as coterminous with liberty: 'We have a form of governing the republic that is directed most of all towards the liberty and equality of all the citizens; this, because it is most equal (*aequalissima*) in all respects, is called the popular form' (Strozzi speech 230–1).

It seems clear that Bruni was holding up for admiration popular government of a very special kind. The emphasis lies less on the assembly, less even on popular consent and election, and much more on fairness raised to the political level, meaning *equality of access to political office* and fair assessment of candidates – *carrière ouverte aux talents*. Not only have we lost sight of the guilds, we have also – and Bruni was trained as a lawyer – lost sight of the *universitas*. The ideal that all citizens together determine the course of the polity, or have power of veto on major issues, has given way to the ideal that all may apply for governmental posts. The Ciceronian perspective has now completely displaced the Germanic. Popular rule doesn't mean that all or many actually do participate, but that they have the *opportunity* to. It is noticeable how little Bruni has to say about the 'many'; there is no reference to Aristotle's notion of their collective wisdom. Indeed this may be called an *individualist* defence of popular rule.

What counts for Bruni is the supremacy of law, the openness of the political system, and the fact that there are safeguards against 'domination' by one or few: Bruni's insights were borrowed from Cicero but applied with fresh force and conviction. *He presents us with the first type-case of the application of the norms of civil society to the state*, and that is why his ideas have attracted scholars in the Lockeian tradition. This is indeed a foreshadowing of what the twentieth century has come to know as 'western/liberal/modern democracy' and 'the open society': participation is strictly instrumental, and no value whatever adheres to the collectivity.

Perhaps, if we look at him in this way, Bruni emerges as somewhat less fanciful in his musings on the Florentine constitution than at first appears. As Rubinstein shows (1968, 452–3), he glossed over disagreeable aspects of the regime, such as fiscal inequity. But his conceptual perspective was peculiarly suited to a political situation dominated by a mercantile oligarchy, since the political norms he advocated, such as equal opportunity and an element of competition among individuals, could co-exist with economic and social inequalities. The point upon which rich and poor in such a society could unite was opposition to feudal privilege, servitude (in the city), and despotism. In this way, Bruni expressed one of the strongest aspirations of citizens throughout the Middle Ages, the desire for personal independence, fair play and wide horizons: his political rhetoric was quintessentially urban, bourgeois, civil.

Personal liberty and legal equality remained stock humanist themes throughout and beyond the fifteenth century. Piccolomini admired the German cities' practice of sharing power between patriciate and commons because it removes the cause of class strife so prevalent in Italy: whereas in Italy citizens are subjected 'to the most base *plebs*', in German cities both classes 'live together under equal *ius* [justice/law]' (*Second Description of Basle* 202). Patrizi argued that 'equality among the citizens renders political association (*societatem civilem*) stable ... equality among citizens breeds concord ... so that they live together under equal *ius*' (*Republic* ch.5, fol.9r; ch.6, fol.10v). These values were taken for granted by the generation of Machiavelli. Salamonio combined the prudential argument that 'inequality of conditions disrupts society', with the moral and metaphysical argument that 'the *civitas* is an association of like persons (*de similibus societas*)' and that 'nature or God from the beginning created all men equal': the state should 'recognize equality of status (*la parita de conditioni*)' (*On Sovereignty* 16, 31; *Speeches* 96–7). Machiavelli himself restated the link between personal liberty and popular government. If, he said, one cannot have mixed government and has to choose between rule by the upper classes and rule by the people, the latter is preferable because, whereas magnates have 'a great desire to dominate', the people 'have only the wish not to be dominated ... the demands of free peoples are rarely opposed to their liberty ... [because] these demands are generally inspired by oppressions, experienced or feared' (*Discourses* I, chs iv–v). Under both republican and princely government, such personal liberty is desirable, attainable and, from the ruler's viewpoint, advisable. The rule of law and personal liberty, that is 'freedom from other men's ascendancy' so that 'a man might enjoy his own under the law' (Pocock 1975, 232) formed an undercurrent in Guicciardini's theory of virtuous civic participation. Whereas Guicciardini thought these things attainable under aristocratic rule (Pocock 1975, 225ff.), Giannotti took up Machiavelli's point in favour of popular government: whereas 'the few desire to command ... that *liberta* which the many desire to preserve – that condition in which each enjoys his own under the law – is close to being the common good itself' (Pocock 1975, 310; cf. Salamonio, *Speeches* 100–2). Clearly, the ideal of participatory citizenship presupposed the personal freedom of the citizens.

Machiavelli took the argument for equality into the social and economic sphere, thus anticipating Rousseau (see pp. 161–2). With the experience of Medici rule clearly in mind, he argued that social equality was the key to the success of the Swiss and German cities in maintaining uncorrupted 'the political life' (*il vivere politico*) (*Discourses* I, ch.lv, 205). The Swiss communities, he said, are opposed to any form of social inequality: 'in their country there are not different classes (*non e dell'una specie ne della altra*), and therefore, without any distinctions among men except for *magistrati*, they have true liberty (*una libera liberta*)' (*German Affairs* 488–9). Both the Swiss and some German cities are able 'to maintain among themselves true equality (*una pari equalita*)', because they do not allow any citizen 'to live like a *gentiluomo*' and are 'most hostile to lords and landed gentry living in their province' (*Discourses* II, ch.xix, 272–3; cf. *Discourses* I, ch.lv, 204–5 and Pocock 1975, 208–10, 226–7). Machiavelli emerges as a champion, in his own way, of the values of civil society projected into the political orbit, in the tradition first articulated by John of Viterbo (see p.38). It is difficult to say whether they lay closer to his heart than communal *virtu*; but they did provide an element of prescriptive continuity between *The Prince* and *The Discourses*.

Several humanists, therefore, based the legal and political structure of cities under popular government upon considerations of both prudence and morality, by invoking the norms of civil society which, unlike those of the guild, enjoyed widespread support and admiration among the intellectual classes. Instead of conceptualizing the city as a specific form of human society, to be admired either because it enshrined certain values or as the supreme expression of human nature, the humanists, even more than the scholastics, tended to conceptualize and attach value to a particular mode of living, transacting affairs, behaving towards one's fellow-men and governing a state. This they called 'civil', 'urbane', 'political'. Egidio Romano had referred to 'civil life' (*vita civilis*) in which one lived 'as a man' (fol.7v).

Bruni's highest praise of the Florentines was that they were outstandingly 'industrious, liberal ... affable, and above all urbane' (*Eulogy* 263; cf. Bolgar 1958, 137–8).

'Civil presidency' (*civilis presidentia*), like the scholastics' 'political rule', meant government of free men by their equals, 'by which one is set over those of the same kind as oneself (*similibus genere*) and over free men' (Acciaiuoli fols245v–246r), in contrast to feudal *dominium*, manorial estate management and despotism. Machiavelli distinguished *ordine civile* from *ordine assoluto* by saying that, although *ordine civile* was also ruled by one man, he was a private citizen who had attained power through 'astuteness and good fortune' (*una astuzia fortunata*) (*Prince* 32–4) – not unlike a modern party leader or city boss. All this formed an integral part of *vivere/reggimento/governo civile* (Pocock 1975, 118). While *vivere civile* 'became a technical term for a broadly based civic constitution' (Pocock 1975, 57) and was equated with *vivere populare*, it referred to a way of life as well as a form of government. One may infer that popular government was only thought desirable on the understanding that it sustained the values of civil society.

But the norms of civil society transcended the city-state. The corresponding social entity might indeed be a *civitas*, but it might just as well be *societas civilis*, the state in general, the 'civic' factor becoming adjectival. And in fact northern humanists, while maintaining the emphasis on liberty and equality, abandoned the connection with either city-state or popular government. Erasmus, in a treatise for the future emperor Charles v, distinguished a true king from a tyrant because 'he delights in the liberty of his subjects' and rules 'as a good *paterfamilias*'.

> He stands foremost yet is of the same class (*eiusdem generis*), ruling as a man over men, as free over the free. ... Nature begat all men free. ... Consider that it is not appropriate for a Christian to usurp lordship (*dominium*) over Christians ... for whom Christ ... has won a common liberty.   (*Education of a Christian Ruler* 527, 574, 578)

From the later fifteenth century onwards, several European monarchies were equally, or better, able to satisfy the demands of civil society than the city-states, on account of their size and their effective guarantee of law and order: the progress of civil society belongs from now on to the history of larger states. Yet by this very fact they always contained within them seeds that had already once given rise to aspirations for political liberty and political equality.

This concentration upon the values of civil society left intermediate groups, intellectually, in the background (cf. Gierke 1900, 99–100). Thanks to the growing influence of Renaissance ideals in Europe during the succeeding centuries, learned political thought focused upon the state and the individual as the two chief agents in the political spectrum, as to a considerable extent it still does today.

In their appreciation of the ontological meaning of the commune, of the city-state as a human enterprise, Machiavelli and his generation were profound innovators, when compared to their medieval and even, to some extent, their classical forebears. This topic has been most skilfully excavated by Gilbert (1965) and Pocock (1975). Discarding the idea that one should strive to realize the ideals of Stoicism or Christianity in politics, they argued that men should realize their potential for heroic excellence (*virtu*) by participating in the perilous and delicate endeavour of establishing the republic in a hostile environment dominated by corruption and despotism. Politics became an intricate skill; might must be met with might and guile with guile, in order that adverse conditions might yield the best possible state. The key concept is *virtu*, meaning both political craft exercised under adverse conditions with precarious results, and participation in government as intrinsic to the development of the individual. By accentuating this latter aspect, Pocock implicitly linked this endeavour to the political ideals of the 1960s and of Hannah Arendt (cf. Pocock 1975, 550). The aim of such a state would not be 'the good life' so much as security, the aggrandizement of the republic, and the political virtue of citizens proudly and adventurously dedicated to their common goal. Rome and Venice were the models. Pocock calls this a new 'paradigm' (1971, chs 1, 8; cf. Kuhn 1963; Seigel 1966). He argues that this 'Machiavellian moment' acted as a catalyst transforming political consciousness during the English Revolution, and generating the Jeffersonian strand in American republicanism.

Once again, however, the exact nature of their innovation requires re-assessment in the light of what has been said about the existing tradition of guild and commune. Pocock's thesis compelled him to demonstrate a radical discontinuity with medieval tradition (1975, chs 1–2); the model of medieval thought which he presents in order to establish his case significant-ly overlooks the entire medieval tradition of guild, commune and corpor-ation. Skinner, on the contrary, has lucidly expounded the considerable continuity in Italy between the medieval communal tradition, its legitima-tion by medieval scholastics and jurists, and the political thought of the Renaissance in both its earlier and later phases (1978, i chs 1–4, 6). He focuses upon the ideal of liberty in the sense of both external sovereignty and popular participation. He thus connects Baron's 'civic humanism' and Pocock's participatory *virtu*, but sets both these movements – centred upon Bruni and Machiavelli respectively – in the much wider context of the whole development of city-republics in Italy.

If we look at the way in which popular government was expounded and defended at Florence in the period 1494–1528, we find, in fact, that what had changed was not the substance of participants' desires, but the way some of them perceived and argued for their goals. Those who advocated the restoration of the more or less sovereign power of the popular assembly, as it had existed, and was perceived to have existed, before the rise of the oligarchical city council – in other words traditional communal government in which the balance of power would revert to the full citizens (*beneficiati*) (Pocock 1975, 291; Skinner, 1978, i 144, 148, 159–60) – had goals very similar to those of the original communes and earlier guild risings. Indeed some, including Savonarola, still conceived their desideratum as rule by the *universitas* or *commune* (Weinstein 1970, 297ff.). (Giannotti characterized this as a kind of mixed government, but with its fulcrum in the popular assembly: 4–6, 10–11; cf. Pocock 1975, 308ff.) This was perfectly reasonable, since the traditions of the tribal assembly, the adventurers' *comitatus*, the early Germanic guild, the *commune* and the craft-guild pointed towards general participation by members in public affairs (see pp. 24, 47, 55, 61–2).

On the other hand, some of the arguments used to support this 'return to first principles' (*ridurre ai principi*) (Pocock 1975, 205, 358–9) were radically new. First, there was much more emphasis on the specific conditions required for its successful operation (Baron 1966, 169ff.; Pocock 1975, 184–5; Skinner 1978, i 164–7). Secondly, Machiavelli produced an entirely new conception of mixed government. His peculiar sense of the relation between the possible and the good led him to adapt the ideal of mixed government to the problem which lay at the very core of Italian civic politics: class conflict between magnates and *popolo*.

> Those who blame the quarrels of the senate and people of Rome condemn that which was the very origin of liberty; and all the laws that are favourable to liberty result from the opposition of these parties to each other.
>
> (*Discourses* I, ch.iv, trans. Detmold, pp.101–2; cf. Pocock's skilful discussion: 1975, 196–8, 272–3)

Stability with liberty may be achieved by tension between the upper and lower classes. This lesson from Roman history was peculiarly appropriate to Italy. At the same time it was, for an Italian, a novel and rather extraordinary suggestion. For the very assumption of corporate politics had always been the *unity* of the people, which required a unified government: thus Guelfs and Ghibellines, magnates and *popolo*, rival families, had consistently attempted to gain control of the state for themselves, where-upon it was common practice to exile one's opponents. In other words, there was no conception of the legitimacy of factions or parties (Peters 1977, 129–31). German cities had been more successful here, often sharing power between patriciate and guilds. But Machiavelli, while observing that in Germania 'diversity of life-style' and 'disunity between the communes and the princes' had facilitated the growth of free cities (*Discourses* II, ch.xix, 272; *German Affairs* 488), did not mention northern experience in this context. His insight would have required a revolution in Italian civic sentiment; yet it was perhaps the one sure alternative to despotism as a way of stabilizing the Renaissance civic polity.

As a theoretical observation, it was profoundly original. It contained the new perception that liberty could be attained despite and even through disunity, and that stability could exist amid the conflict of interests. Diversity is no longer absorbed in a higher existential unity, as in medieval thought, but rather liberty is fragilely erected upon inherent class conflict. It had the simplicity of Adam Smith's theory that the rational pursuit of personal gain engenders wealth, of which it was an anticipation in the political sphere. Once again, the principles of civil society were being applied to politics: not only self-advancement, but competition and a kind of cold tolerance (it is implied) are politically functional. This provided one element of a 'modern' view of politics and the state which would focus upon conflict and the need to contain it, and placed little if any value on the collectivity, relegating the value of 'fraternity' to private life.

Finally, there was the new stress upon *virtu* (Pocock 1975, 76, 78, 152–4; cf. Skinner 1978, i 175–86). According to Machiavelli, Guicciardini and others, men can only become virtuous, excellent, heroic, by taking part with their fellow-citizens in the determination of public policy; states can only avoid corruption if they have such men as participating citizens. Aristotle, although he thought men could not be courageous, prudent or just without suitable opportunities, which public life might provide, held that truly good men 'would not need to take part in the government of their community; the good life does not require such participation' (Mulgan 1977, 6–7). These Florentines gave a historical and social analysis of how corruption was to be avoided, and presented a new ideal of human excellence as self-determination and strength of will. They tied participation to the interests of the individual as a human being rather than to corporation membership. Machiavelli, though he idealized the Swiss cantons, was the theorist who did most to undermine the principles upon which such political groups were based, replacing the medieval idea of corporate membership with the Renaissance idea of man as citizen. (The medieval notion appears to have lasted longest where it came closest to direct democracy – in the Swiss mountains: Barber 1974, esp. 94, 99–102.) Participatory *virtu*, then, replaced corporate membership, and also the guild ethic of mutuality. One might say that they inhabited the same 'ideological space'. Self-government was given a new spiritual importance; it was made the fulcrum of morality. It was a more demanding ideal.

This was accompanied by a new idea of the state (*citta, civitas*) as fully self-determining or sovereign (*signore*). For the first time, the case for sovereignty in the modern sense was given an existential basis in the human predicament. This propelled the city-state, previously the guardian of corporate privileges and trading rights, into a new orbit beyond the gravitational tug of princely or imperial overlordship. The nature of the argument meant that such sovereignty depended logically upon some degree of popular participation. The transition from corporation to state was complete.

The idea of participation as *virtu* had the strength of being based upon a universal predicate of the human personality. Yet the Machiavellian argument was peculiarly nationalist, and especially appropriate for an expansionist and mercantile imperialist state, such as Florence, England or the USA. Machiavellian *virtu*, like the capitalist ethic, works only so long as it is not universalized: if everyone tries to maximize their gain, if all states spiritedly promote their own glory, we enter a black hole. The weakness of Machiavellian *virtu* is that, by glorifying self-assertion, it undermines the principles upon which society and, as seems likely, the very existence of the human species depend. Brotherhood and mutuality are easily mocked but not so easily replaced. In any case, the influence of the Machiavellian conception of citizenship should not be exaggerated. Even today, it would appear that the popular and official ideology of 'modern/western' democracy remains largely medieval Germanic: consent and election, not participation, stand out as its chief procedural values (cf. Pateman 1970, chs 1–2).

9

GUILD AND CITY IN THE GERMAN REFORMATION

The effect of the Reformation upon social and political thought has long been discussed and debated. Did the idea of the community of believers pave the way for democracy? Did the doctrine of resignation cede ground to absolutism? Did the emphasis on personal faith give rise to a general belief in liberty? Did 'worldly asceticism' promote capitalism? The question which concerns us here, however, is a somewhat different one: namely, the relation between the Reformation and the guild tradition – a subject which has not received a great deal of attention. For, at least in its early stages, the Reformation seems to have had a special affiliation with the guild ethos, especially in Germany. This topic is closely related to the question of the Reformation and civic tradition in Germany, which has occupied scholars' attention, particularly since Berndt Möller's pioneering work (1972) first appeared in 1955. Möller argued that in some respects the Reformers' teaching evoked a return to first principles among townsmen, stimulating restoration and reinvigoration of communal values and practices. It was, moreover, in post-Reformation Germany that the guild-orientated ethos of the 'home town' (Walker 1971) developed. What part, then, did guild values play in the Reformation, and how did the Reformation in turn affect those values?

On the one hand, Luther and Calvin objected to the closed brotherhood of the confraternities as contrary to true Christian charity, which must be forgiving and universal in scope (Nelson 1969, ch.2; Trinkaus 1970, i 309). Craft-guilds themselves, nevertheless, emerged from the Reformation unscathed, a sign perhaps that theologians could accept them as no longer having any properly spiritual pretensions. On the other hand, Luther's attack upon the clergy as a separate, superior caste, his conception of all Christians as 'truly of the spiritual estate', of priests as elected officials, of the radical equality and dignity of each and every vocation, his elevation of manual work to the same spiritual status as lecturing, governing or administering sacraments, above all perhaps his profound and touching notion of the Christian community of love and brotherhood – so often overlooked in accounts of his 'political thought' – all this was an application to the church of principles latent in guilds and communes. It was what the medieval townsman and artisan had been faintly aware of in his various strivings at self-expression, but it was something he had not previously grasped so clearly: it was what he had been waiting to hear, a recognition of his value as what he was. The elevation of the laity by Protestantism in all its forms was surely one key to the enthusiasm which met the Reformation in the cities (cf. Möller 1972, 71–2). The idea of the equal dignity of every profession in the eyes of God, and that the meanest, most workaday labour is a godly calling, was obviously a tremendous boost to the 'honour' of craft. For Luther every form of human activity, so long as it contributes to the welfare of the community and is not immoral, is of equal standing and supremely worthy in the eyes of God. The artisan and journeyman were thus given a revolutionary assurance of their worth as what they were, a recognition of their standing in the highest court (cf. Ozment 1975, 61–7; Troeltsch 1931, 561, 609–11). In Luther, at last, artisans and farmers are placed alongside princes and lords as equal members of the 'spiritual estate' (Skinner 1978, ii 11). This was a profound revolution in thought: it overturned not just medieval values, but those of classical antiquity and the Renaissance too. Some were even prepared to place manual work *above* leisured mandarin pursuits. Bucer saw 'the most Christian stations and occupations' as not the priesthood and politics but 'farming, raising cattle and the handicraft trades' (*De Regno Christi* II.49, Ozment 1975, 66); Eberlin held that no calling should be considered more honourable than agriculture (Ozment 1975, 97ff.). This theme appears in most early Protestant tracts.

The very fact that the great majority of German cities initially showed such enthusiasm for the Reformation is itself significant. What is more, contrary to the earlier view that the adoption of Protestantism by cities was usually the work of city magistrates, Möller showed that it was frequently – especially in the South and West – the result of pressure from below, to which city authorities time and again wisely yielded (Möller 1972; Ozment 1975, 122–3). And it was especially among the *artisans* that Protestantism made many of its most ardent first converts – printers, miners, textile and metal workers, and so on (Möller 1972, 60–5; Ozment 1975, 123–4).

> A broad spectrum of lower and middle strata burghers appears to have been the majority group within the first Protestant congregations.... The rank and file of first generation Protestant clergy ... came mainly from families of craftsmen and artisans ... they were recruited from among schoolteachers, sextons, typesetters, printers, and clothmakers.
> (Ozment 1975, 123; Dickens 1974, 160, 184)

In Saxony, miners formed 'the first specific social group that could be called a Lutheran majority'; Joachim Slüter's first congregation in Rostock 'consisted of master artisans, journeymen and harbour workers'; while 'members of the gardeners' guild were prominent within Martin Bucer's first congregation' (Möller 1972, 60–5; Ozment 1975, 124). The situation was to some extent similar in France (Imbart de la Tour n.d., 254ff.; Ozment 1975, 12–13). And 'of the 2,247 Genevan refugees who listed their professions between 1555 and 1560, two-thirds were textile workers, craftsmen, metal workers, and goldsmiths' (Ozment 1975, 124).

In the next place, Möller argued that 'the Reformation gave the imperial cities a new awareness of their original communal foundations' (1972, 69). Its success was partly due to the fact that it touched upon and re-awoke the first principles of civic association, namely fellowship and equality. Zwingli, Bucer and Calvin each in their own way assimilated the community of the church to that of the city; continuity with medieval notions of urban community was especially marked in Zwingli and Bucer, who worked out 'a theology stamped with civic values' (Brady 1978a, 12–13, 294; Möller 1972, 76, 79–82; Oberman 1981, 276, 294; Ozment 1975, 6–7). The religious change was sometimes effected by a procedure akin to the customary collective oath of civic allegiance (cf. pp.56–7 above). In some places, all this was accompanied also by a renewed movement towards craft-guild supremacy in town government (Friedrichs 1978, 52–4; Ozment 1975, 11, 124).

Many of the early adherents of Protestantism looked for a reform of political, social and economic life. Thus, 'in many places citizens demanded simultaneously from their council a Protestant preacher, suppression of tax payments to the church, and greater participation in city government' (Möller 1972, 55). The spiritual enfranchisement of the common man was taken to have social and political implications. This was most of all the case in southern Germany, but in some northern cities also the first Protestants formed committees to 'speak in the name of the entire citizenry', and secured wider participation in internal and foreign policy (Ozment 1975, 122–3).

In the sphere of social welfare, the early civic Reformers breathed new life into the earlier guild and communal tradition. The town authorities were to extend their charitable functions and their concern for public morality, partly by taking over duties previously belonging to clergy and religious orders. Luther himself, in 1523, suggested that in general care of the poor and sick be supervised by boards of 'guardians' elected by parishioners (Koenigsberger and Mosse 1968, 131, 136). In towns which followed Zwingli or Bucer, citizens 'worked with particular energy to perfect and consolidate the spiritual and moral life of the ecclesiastical and urban communities, to renovate public charity, public instruction and civil discipline' (Möller 1972, 92, 68). The radical constitution proposed by Geismayr for the Tyrol advocated state homes for the sick and aged, and public ownership of the mines (151).

Lastly, the ideal of both personal and civic liberty featured in some early Protestant programmes. According to the *Twelve Articles of the Peasants* (1525, probably written by a Memmingen furrier: Möller 1972, 55–6), release from the bondage of serfdom was a universal right of Christians (art. 3). The *Reformation of the Emperor Frederick III* (c. 1523) stated that:

> All free, imperial and royal cities and other communes and communities in the Holy Roman Empire of the German nation shall be granted, each and all, their just rights and proper government, without regard to their ancient privileges, customs or ranks, but in accordance with the principles of Christian freedom.   (104–5)

There was a spirit and ethos in the early Reformation which appears to have been in many ways a profound, though indirect and oblique, expression of some of the ideals which had lain at the basis of the old urban and guild movements: in particular a strong sense of spiritual community and of the radical equality of all believers. For Luther, the Church was a *Gemeine* (community) (Hoepfl 1982, 25). Of the two long-standing procedural values of both guild and commune – election and consent – the Reformers, particularly Bucer and Calvin, emphasized the former but not the latter (Baron 1939, 37–8; Hoepfl 1982, 51; McNeill 1949, 160, 165). The idea of the spiritual *Gemeinde* or *universitas* of believers is emphasized time and again in early Protestant tracts. Later smothered in official Lutheranism and Calvinism, it was kept alive most of all in the sects descending from the radical Reformation; eventually, mediated by Pietism, it re-surfaced in a secularized form in the Romantics.

The earlier guild values of brotherhood and friendship played a prominent part in the ethical language of the early Reformation. Social and political relationships are to be based upon brotherhood and friendship (e.g. Eberlin cit. Ozment 1975, 103). Bucer, in particular, described the church as 'the most perfect, most friendly and most faithful brotherhood, community and union' (cit. Möller 1972, 81). Love was the central principle of his 'community ethic' (Möller 1972, 81–2). The Reformers took such values primarily from the Bible; but, as we shall see, they could also retain something of their guild and communal meaning.

One may also ask whether there was not at least some relationship between the Protestant covenanted community and the traditional oath of mutual aid. In the early days, the Reformation was adopted in some cities by means of a renewal of the communal oath, by which each burgher pledged himself and his goods to the city. One such oath reproduced exactly the spirit of the old guild formulae: 'We in common citizenship will sacrifice our body and blood for the word of God' (Möller 1972, 64–5: Strasbourg 1524; cf. Dickens 1974, 188). Calvin, child of the Renaissance and trained in Roman law, cannot compare with the first civic Reformers as an exponent of fraternity and community spirit. Yet the Calvinist notion of the Church as a community founded by covenant, a covenant to be explicitly renewed among believers, while based above all on biblical ideas of the covenant between God and his people, was also in effect establishing as a theological principle a common social and constitutional practice of medieval guilds and towns. For Calvin, a church is formed by 'a group of godly men' meeting together 'formally to reaffirm their contractual relationship with God':

> The outcome in practice was the peculiarly Calvinist concept of the covenanting community, the prototype of which was established in 1537, when all the citizens of Geneva were asked to swear an oath binding them to abide by the ten commandments.
>
> (Skinner 1978, ii 236; cf. Hoepfl 1982, 65–6)

This bore striking resemblance to the earlier formation of sworn associations (see pp.55–7). In attempting to apply an Old Testament phenomenon to sixteenth-century Geneva, Calvin may in part have had recourse to the idea of a group of people spontaneously creating a new and profound social bond among themselves by means of a communal oath. The fundamental difference was that the substance of the promise – obedience to the Decalogue – was not an outcome of popular agreement but the public affirmation of an absolute and universal norm.

One minor author from the milieu of the urban Reformation, Clemens Jäger of Augsburg (c. 1500–61), shows in particular how Protestant and guild values might interact. Jäger, a shoemaker by trade, became secretary of his guild and then a city councillor. In 1540 he abandoned shoemaking to become city archivist (Chroniken xxxiv 3ff.; Dirr 1910; Roth 1926 and 1927). Partly self-educated, Jäger's talent was recognized by the eminent Peutinger, who, uncharacteristically, agreed to give this craftsman some classical training (Roth 1926, 13). Jäger proceeded to compile a series of histories of Augsburg and its guilds (Dirr 1910, 3). In his chronicle of the dominant Weavers' Guild, Der erbern zunft von Webern herkomen Cronica und jahrbuch, written in 1544–5, he gave an extended account of the 1368 revolution which had established guild rule at Augsburg. Into this he inserted a rhetorical and historical defence of the principles of guild rule in cities (Chroniken xxxiv 78–139). His overt advocacy of guild government is unique not only in sixteenth-century Protestant humanism but in premodern political thought as a whole.

At the time Jäger was writing, Augsburg had a relatively open guild government and was engaged on the Protestant side in the Schmalkaldic war (cf. Dickens 1974, 185–6; Dirr 1910, 4). Jäger's tone of Protestant spirituality and his quaint and fanciful comparisons with the ancient world are eloquent testimony of how the Reformation and Renaissance helped to articulate guild and burgher sentiment in Germany. That he was born and bred in craft and guild enhances the value of the work as an expression of artisan-burgher sentiment, albeit laced with 'humanistic trifles' (Dirr 1910, 7).

But there is a nasty surprise. In 1547 the Schmalkaldic League was defeated and Charles V entered Augsburg in triumph; the following year guild rule was abolished and Augsburg reverted to patrician government. Jäger, who had for some time been under the patronage of Hans Jakob Fugger, now agreed to write in favour of the new regime (Roth 1926, 38, 44–5). Following a brief restoration of the Protestant guild party in 1552, he composed in 1555 a strongly partisan historical treatise, in response to propaganda by the now exiled guild leaders. He praised 'the honourable ancient Geschlechter [patriciate]', condemned the 1368 revolution as mob usurpation, accused the guild regime of gross misconduct, and welcomed its abolition as a just punishment (Dirr 1910, 19-22). As Dirr puts it, the discovery of Jäger's authorship of this last treatise 'is absolutely astonishing', but 'however strange it may seem, it is a fact' (1910, 22).

This example of the power of patronage and of tenuous adherence to constitutional principles has precedents in fifteenth-century Italian humanism, and also in the conciliar controversy (Black 1979, 115). It bears out the observation that 'a swordsmith educated in the humanist vein was not thereby fashioned into a humanist swordsmith' (Martines 1980, 263). Above all, it shows how easily civic issues could be subordinated to religious considerations and princely interests. But this does not necessarily invalidate Jäger's earlier work as a genuine expression of guild values: the sentimental eulogy of guild rule he wrote in 1544–5 bears the stamp of conviction.

Before examining Jäger's thought, we must briefly consider the place of civic values in early German humanism. The northern Renaissance was orientated towards moral and social reform and, especially in Germany, national revival. Just as Luther's Reformation kindled feelings of pan-German solidarity and of a national vocation to preach the pure Gospel so long tarnished by Rome, so too German humanists extolled the unique liberty of the early Germans, and embarked on the study of national history. The two movements went together: Gebuyler wrote his Libertas Germaniae in 1519, Rhenanus his commentary on Tacitus' Germania in 1520 (Andreas 1943, 555ff., 567f.; Bolgar 1958, 118–19; Joachimsen 1910). In contrast to the French, English and Spanish humanists, the Germans, like their Italian predecessors, generally inhabited an urban rather than a courtly milieu and were employed in civic government: Sebastian Brant was syndic and city secretary at Strasbourg, and Conrad Peutinger was city secretary at Augsburg (Bolgar 1958, 303–4; Rupprich 1935, 9ff.). The humanists exercised particular influence in Germany through educational reforms carried out in cities under Protestant auspices during the early Reformation (Andreas 1943, 429ff.). German humanists also had a tendency to form their own kind of quasi-guild, the literary society, sometimes based on a city like the *sodalitas Augustana* at Augsburg, sometimes on a region like the *sodalitas literaria Rhenana* and the *sodalitas Danubiana*.

Not only did German literary scholars frequently lend their support to the religious Reformation (Spitz 1963), they also joined forces with it in opening the way for systematic reflection upon contemporary city government: this combined movement of thought culminated in Althusius. The early humanist contribution was chiefly in the field of urban historiography (Andreas 1943, 402) and in descriptive analyses, such as Christoph Scheuerl's letter on the constitution of Nuremberg, addressed to Staupitz (Luther's superior) in 1516 (Rupprich 1935, 25–6; Strauss 1966, 58–68). Skinner suggests that it is 'appropriate to regard the political theory of the northern Renaissance essentially as an extension and consolidation of a range of arguments originally discussed in *quattrocento* Italy' (1978, ii 244, 201); although perhaps 'their basic demand ... not so much for a reformation of institutions, but rather for a change of heart' (Skinner 1978, ii 28) may be related to their sympathy with Luther rather than Machiavelli. On the whole, it would appear that the early German humanists were, like their Italian predecessors, unwilling to ascribe any intrinsic value to the city itself, still less – with the exception of Jäger – to popular or guild government. They invoked Aristotle and Cicero only in the course of *ad hoc* arguments for a particular cause. In a perceptive discussion of the Augsburg humanist Conrad Peutinger, Lutz says: 'the movement towards a cultural awareness of citizenship [is] clear and strong. The burgher ideology of the imperial cities, which in the *Reformatio Sigismundi* (c.1438) was bound up with a sacred fervour, was at once strengthened and secularized under the influence of humanism.' But men like Peutinger, rather than making a solid connection between the classical and contemporary city-state, adopted an essentially 'conservative' strategy on behalf of the south German cities, looking to the Emperor to defend civic liberties against princely encroachments. There was no 'development of a fighting ideology of burgher-civic politics' (Lutz n.d., 134–6). In other words, the dominant values of nation and empire stood in place of a truly civic ideology. This view is amply borne out by Jäger's career.

Jäger described the constitution of Augsburg since 1368, and of other guild towns, as 'a free estate (*status*) and a guild commonwealth' (*freie stand und zünftliche, gemaine regierung*) (82; cf. 78), as 'the free estate of guild and city' (*zünftlich und bürgerlich freie stand*) (137), and again as 'guild government by the honourable commons' (*zünftliche regierung ainer erbere gmaind*) (155). Guild rule is thus equated with free status within the Empire, with rule by the commons or community as a whole, and indeed with civic rule in general. A guild constitution means that the guilds are represented in the city council and that civic offices are open to guild members. But it also refers to a specific way of ruling that is open, enabling all citizens to participate, and based upon general consensus with fair elections to all posts, so that one achieves the basic moral ideal of 'commonalty' (*gmaind*), namely mutual respect and 'friendliness' both between classes and between rulers and ruled. As in south German practice, guild rule does not mean excluding the old patriciate from government. Jäger evinces an overriding concern for the *spirit* of the constitution; indeed, his final message was that citizens must maintain the friendly guild–civic ethos if the regime is to survive.

Jäger gave three principal reasons why 'the honourable craftsmen and community (*hantwerk und gemaind*) of this city of Augsburg' should maintain their 'stable, long-lasting, unaltered constitution, namely the free state and guild government' (78). The first was that, as an imperial city, Augsburg claims 'the liberty of the Empire', and that 'all hard-won and authentic (*erworbne und ausgeprachte*) freedoms are based upon a common citizenry' (79). The common people have shed blood for the Empire and they share all the civic 'burdens'; it would be unfair, therefore, if only those with great names or noble lineage could sit in council and direct affairs of state. 'The honourable commons' have a just claim 'to have a voice (*mitstimen*) in the honourable council and common government' (79). Secondly, just as not all preachers of the divine word and religious leaders come from the patriciate and the rich class of citizens, but rather God gives his graces to rich and poor alike, using both as overseers of his church, so too it is only just that, 'following God's ordinance in regard to vocation to civic government', all those endowed by God with 'understanding, wisdom and honesty' should be eligible for office (79–80). Thirdly, a guild regime avoids antipathy between rich and poor, of which today there are many instances, because poor as well as rich can sit in council, to which there is 'free, personal, open entry' (*ainen freien, personlichen, offnen zugang*) (80). It is the *carrière ouverte aux talents*. Because every craft-guild, from the lowest to the highest, has its representative in council, it knows its cause is heard, and consequently the common people will more readily obey the council's decisions. Rich as well as poor 'bear burdens' – i.e. there is fiscal equity – so that justice is seen to be done. Thus 'the guild regime is in itself for all men a truly fair image of evident righteousness' (*an ir selbs allermenklich der erkanten gerechtigkait gar ein lieplicher spiegel*) (80). More than any other regime, it promotes 'friendliness': when all, from the lowest to the highest, govern themselves (*selbs regieren*), there exists 'a devoted, willing, obedient, friendly community' (*ain frome, willige und gehorsame, fraintliche gmaind*) (80–1).

These arguments take us straight back to the beliefs and aspirations of the

117

early towns and the medieval guild risings. The chartered 'freedoms' of the communes, being collective, are invoked in support of popular participation. The idea of the town as community (*universitas*) entails political equality for all its members. The ideal of equal access to office, which played such a prominent part in Italian humanist thought, sprang directly from this original self-awareness of the Germanic town. Not least, Jäger made much of the guild ideal of friendship, which he invoked in particular as a remedy for class strife. Jäger's political ethic here may be summed up quite simply as respect for persons; the rich are not denounced, rather the poor (the 'honourable commons') are entitled to the same respect as they. A pious social warmth pervades his idea of commonalty and lends weight to the duty of obedience. Indeed, Jäger regarded the establishment and preservation of guild rule at Augsburg as the work of Providence (138, 144, 154), and remarked that new provision had been made for poor relief (in 1522) in order to please God (123 and n.4). Yet it is worth noting that, when theology is overtly used (in Jäger's second argument in support of guild rule), it suggests equality of opportunity rather than collective decision-making, reinforcing the value of wisdom rather than of consent. Theology is not invoked in connection with self-government as such.

Jäger's supporting arguments were derived from biblical and classical history. In order to demonstrate that 'the free state, so long as it is rightly upheld, brings all good with it' (82), he argued that a 'commonwealth' was the original constitution of all great peoples, and that they prospered so long as they maintained this; whereas, in every case, the later adoption of 'princely' rule led to decline (82–93). This also enabled him to present the guild revolution of 1368 as a return to the first principles of Augsburg's own constitution. He starts with the Jews. God always desired that he himself should be their only king and *obrister*; until the time of Samuel, they were ruled according to God's will 'only through general and particular offices, such as knights, overseers (*vorsteher*) and the elders of the people'. The Jews' troubles started when they decided to replace 'the common government given them by God' with kingship; thereafter they lost their homeland (82–4). Similarly, the Greeks were great and victorious just so long as they chose as leaders 'common persons' for their 'honesty, wisdom and understanding', rather than for their wealth. Referring tacitly to Sparta in particular, Jäger said their leader was 'like a king, but ruled the country not in pomp (*pracht*) and lordliness (*herrlichkait*), but in willing obedience'; he could only act with the consent of five ephors 'given him ... by the community'. When, due to discord, the Greeks chose 'kingly government', they lost their freedom, land, cities and strongholds (84). Carthage too prospered so long as it was ruled 'through a common government, that is through a hundred senators and councillors'; its downfall occurred when it set up '*sufices* and consuls ruling no longer as citizens but as princes' (*nicht mer wie bürgerliche regenten, sonder also fürsten gehalten).* This is 'a clear and instructive lesson for all cities of the holy empire' (85–7). These distinctions between burgher and lordly, civic and princely rule are particularly significant.

Jäger drew the same lesson from Roman history: the transition from republic to principate brought disadvantages which should be borne in mind by all guild cities (135–7). There was a clear contradiction between this argument and Jäger's own acceptance of the contemporary emperor; but he was presumably confining his argument to the internal constitution of cities. He made a lengthy and laboured comparison between the institutions of republican Rome and Augsburg (95–137), his information about Rome being taken, presumably, from Peutinger. He compared the adoption of guild rule at Augsburg in 1368 with the agreement made between the patriciate and *plebs* at Rome in 490 BC (95). In both cases, government was thereafter conducted by a combination of classes; laws at Rome were made by *senatus populusque Romanus* (103, 111–12, 129). Rome too had a guild-like character (137); the office of guild-master is analogous to the tribunate, which was established to reconcile patriciate and commons (100). In both cases, divine sanction is invoked on behalf of fairness in the council and at elections (120ff.); the educational systems are also similar (118–19).

The conclusion drawn from these historical arguments is that all those imperial cities to which God has given 'free status and a guild constitution of the city' should take the utmost pains to preserve their 'honourable, ancient guild practices, laws and ordinances'. Above all, their citizens must dwell together 'in all friendliness ... in all godliness ... with a Christian spirit' (138). His historical examples drew special attention to the dangers of civil strife, the harbinger of constitutional change and tyranny.

Guild rule, then, is presented as the constitution most appropriate for cities. Jäger's basic political values, as presented in this work, may be seen as a Protestant expression of traditional guild values. In accordance with Luther's ideal of the ruler–ruled relationship as one of mutual love, he concluded with an appeal for goodwill, friendship and obedience:

O how blessed, how supremely blessed is such a city, in which the friendly civic regime is held fast in all that is good, and subjects and citizens love their superiors, showing a willing obedience towards them in all that is good! With good reason can such a city be thankful to God the Almighty; well may the citizens call upon Almighty God from their hearts and beseech him to preserve such a liberated constitution.   (138–9)

The council is urged to consider

how friendly and loving it is that commons and council in a city should both together, in a civic, unified, friendly guild constitution, hold and direct the government, and that both together should promote and manage the common needs in all that is good; from such a celebrated constitution (*bemelter regierung*) all civic blessedness (*holdseligkait*) flows over all members of the community. (150)

The warm but slightly vague tone of Protestant spirituality is unmistakable.

It seems reasonable to conclude that during the early Reformation, from about 1520 to 1550, the social and political ethos of the Germanic guild and city was beginning to become articulate, thanks in part to the intellectual stimulus of the Renaissance. The Reformation, it goes without saying, reached the ordinary man in Germany; but, unlike the Renaissance in Italy, it had few specific constitutional norms to propose, and so enabled those that already existed to develop. It lacked the Machiavellian perception of how these values might be realized in practice; yet we may say it had an ingredient without which any social or political programme is heartless. In fact, Machiavelli and his friends achieved no greater success in saving civic institutions in the sixteenth century.

PART II

FROM THE REFORMATION TO THE FRENCH REVOLUTION

In the second part, we consider the development of the craft-guild system in various parts of Europe; it declined relatively early in England, but was thriving for much longer in Germany (ch.10). Now for the first time guilds were accorded a place in the normative theory of the social and political system (ch.11). Corporational, and to some extent guild, ideas played an important part, alongside civic ideas, in the conceptualization of the nation-state, particularly in its more representative and republican forms (ch.12). Meanwhile, liberal social and political values, and eventually theories of political economy, assumed the commanding position they have since occupied in much of western Europe. Compared with earlier expressions of the values of civil society, Hobbes emerges as a radical innovator, while Rousseau seems to have drawn the ultimate political conclusion from the ideal of personal self-determination (ch.13).

10

GUILDS AND POLITICAL CULTURE

According to a widely held myth, guilds and guild or communal values were peculiarly medieval phenomena, which have since been progressively replaced by less compact forms of association and less affective beliefs about human society. In fact, however, guilds not only survived well beyond the Middle Ages, but in some regions multiplied in number and extended their powers. While in England and Holland they declined from the mid-seventeenth century, in France and Germany the early modern period was the classic era of the craft-guild; in Bodin and Althusius, two of the founders of modern political thought, guilds were given a clearly defined position in social and political philosophy.

In France, the guild system of production was rationalized and extended by Colbert's reforms; in Spain and Prussia also, guilds became the instrument of state economic policy and formed an integral part of the mercantilist system. In Russia under Peter the Great 'attempts were made to introduce full guild organization as part of the tsar's programme of westernization' (Kellenbenz 1977, 465–8).

The 'particularized country' of south and west Germany (notably Hessen, Baden, Württemberg, Franconia, lower Bavaria) offered a different pattern of guild development, which in many ways affords the purest model of 'community' (*Gemeinschaft*) in medieval or modern history (Walker 1971, esp. 4–5). Indeed Walker suggests that when German theorists like Justus Möser and the historical Romantics described Tacitean *Germania* or medieval communalism, what they chiefly had in mind and were trying to elucidate was the guild-dominated 'home town' of early modern times; the same is partly true of Tönnies' analysis of *Gemeinschaft* (Walker 1971, 89, 105). From the Peace of Westphalia (1648) till Napoleon, the small towns of this region were enabled, by the subtle balance of central European forces, to practise virtual autonomy within economically self-sufficient districts (Walker 1971, ch.1). These towns were hot-houses of the guild system. Frequently, guilds dominated not only production and trade, but politics, social life and ethical conduct (Walker 1971, chs 2–4). The constitution and ethos of such guild towns had evolved from the twelfth-century communal movement, the fourteenth-century guild risings, and the Reformation; but in some towns the guild system was actually extended in the later seventeenth century (Walker 1971, 91). Thanks perhaps to Germany's exhaustion and depopulation from war and plague, the economy of the guild town was now more than ever localized; as economic life recovered by internal re-development, large-scale commerce hardly touched such towns, and their effectual self-government was protected by the territorial constitution of the Empire. Socially, they shrank within their own walls; marriage in particular was rigidly controlled by guilds and commune.

Only in the context of the home town is it comprehensible how the time of the notorious 'decay' of the early modern German trades guilds should have been the period probably of their greatest power to impress their values and goals upon the society of which they were components.

(Walker 1971, 76)

In this small-scale political economy – almost a communal romantic's dream – production and exchange were tightly controlled by guild monopoly. Guild and civic membership, without which one was an alien or 'ground-rabbit' (Böhnhase), was rigorously scrutinized. Informal, customary controls predominated, the roles of citizen, workman and neighbour were interlocked (Walker 1971, 137). Almost invariably, guild-masters, and often the guilds themselves, were the cornerstones of the polity (Walker 1971, 44ff.). The aim was, partly, to maintain familiarity and face-to-face reliability; this was achieved by subtle checks and marriage regulations, which produced intense 'social prudery and political stubbornness' (Walker 1971, 76, 85). The claustrophobic effects of this are evident in the case of Flegel, tinsmith of Hildesheim, who after marrying the 'wrong girl' could never get right with his guild, and was probably unable ever to practise his home craft, despite university counsel and episcopal intervention (Walker 1971, 73–7). Guild constitutions followed the earlier pattern, with the usual local variations: guild rulers were 'chosen by a process incorporating both the will of the membership and the choice of the civic authorities' (Walker 1971, 80). The attempt to remedy abuses by the imperial trades edict of 1731, which facilitated entry to trades and imposed greater state supervision, was effective only in Prussia, where it coincided with state policy; in certain towns 'no one had even heard of it' (Walker 1971, 93–7 at 97).

This 'home-town' regime, which only finally perished in the 1860s, made a profound impact on modern German political culture; the ethos of the small-townsman, not to be confused with the 'petit-bourgeois', stands as polar opposite to English and French civil society. At its core was the idea of honourableness (Ehrbarkeit), meaning 'domestic, civic and economic orderliness' (Walker 1971, 102; cf. pp.14–15 above). These guilds maintained 'a satisfactory degree of equality, by penalizing or excluding the pushy whether rich or poor, and by mutual agreements among the membership that restrained expansion and promised security' (Walker 1971, 134). It is not clear what part, if any, religion played; politically and economically, pastor and priest stood on the fringes of home-town life (Walker 1971, 129). Had Lutheranism revived, in this culture, the sacred aspect of community in lay form?

In England, on the other hand, the relation between masters and journeymen became more rigid and hierarchical, reflecting the economic power of the masters, especially when they combined the roles of producer and merchant. Usually, the great masters effectively controlled the guild organization. In London, the great 'companies' became divided into 'livery' and 'yeomanry' sections, and eventually, in many cases, masters and journeymen formed separate organizations (Unwin 1904, 41–53; cf. Clapham 1949, 253ff.). The livery companies were great privileged corporations, whose social husk survives today; their members might also be partners in merchant companies formed for overseas trade. The idea of internal democracy, however, was carried over into these companies, despite their exclusive membership, and so formed one important starting-point for political development in North America. On this point, Hobbes himself reproduced a modified version of the juristic doctrine, that in matters concerning members of a corporation as individuals all must give consent (p.24): since a merchant 'corporation' or 'society' aims not at a common good but at the individual profit of its members, 'the representation of such a body must be an assembly, where every member of the body may be present at the consultations, if he will' (152).

In France and Germany, journeymen had their own separate organizations, the *compagnonnages* and *Gesellenverbände*, going back to the late Middle Ages. Some of these developed secret rituals; the stone-dressers and carpenters claimed connection with the Templars (Coornaert 1966, 18–33, 186ff.). Their chief aim was still to uphold the status of the skilled worker, limiting numbers by initiation and secret signs as well as through carefully regulated instruction in the craft. Their ideology focused upon the moral worth of the particular profession, and upon mutual aid within an exclusive brotherhood (Coornaert 1966, 229, 310–11) – *'ma vraie patrie ... c'est la compagnonnage'* (cit. Coornaert 1966, 331); here there was unbroken continuity with the medieval guild tradition. From the fifteenth century the London printers were organized in 'chapels' with 'affinities in mock religious ritual to the French [*compagnonnages*]' (Leeson 1979, 89). Such groups tended also to nurture a general belief in human equality; 'all men are equal, made by one Maker of the like mire, the meanest beggar as the greatest prince', said the Hull bricklayers (cit. Leeson 1979, 64). The following statement by a Huguenot may well have been influenced by the same milieu: all men are made in the same form and, as it were, at the same mill, so that we should all recognize each other as comrades (*compagnons*) or rather brothers ... there can be no doubt but that we are all naturally free, because we are all comrades; and no one could imagine that Nature, when it has put us all into *compagnie*, could have put any of us into servitude.

(cit. Allen 1928, 314)

Guilds and the artisan mentality generally continued to play some part in the formation of radical political culture, although the lead was often taken by politically orientated Calvinism. The Dutch Revolt of 1565–81, the first modern war of independence which gave rise to 'the world's first parliamentary government' (Griffiths 1956, 243), took place in a country where 'the artisans, through their guilds, had a constitutional voice in the government of their towns and a long tradition of upholding it by revolutionary action' (Koenigsberger 1968, 277; Parker 1979, 245). In the English Revolution of 1640–60, the greater London guilds supported Parliament on account of favours previously shown by the Crown to 'splinter incorporations of master-craftsmen' (Ashton 1979, 92). No generalization can be made about the political allegiances of guilds, any more than about that of artisans and journeymen, in the country as a whole (Ashton 1979, 84–5). But among the lesser guilds and yeomanries of London, earlier Crown policies notwithstanding, there appears to have been significant support, first for the parliamentary cause, and then for the Leveller movement (Unwin 1938, 336–9).

Lilburne, the Levellers' leading spokesman, and also the Diggers' leader, Winstanley, were men of artisan status. Small masters and artisans were making desperate demands for the reinforcement of guild regulations, in particular the restriction of the right to practise a craft to guild members. Parliament, however, while it tolerated monopolies in foreign trade, was less favourable to domestic monopolies, from which the Crown derived considerable benefits (Ashton 1979, 86ff.). The Levellers, on the other hand, drew an implicit distinction between the domestic monopolies of the great merchants, which they condemned, and craft-guild regulations, which they were prepared to retain, essential as these were to the livelihood of the small producer (Zagorin 1954, 39–40). Their proposal to extend the franchise to all men except 'servants' appears to have favoured, among others, all those craftsmen and journeymen who could claim economic independence by ownership of their own home and loom or other equipment (Ashton 1979, 308–9).

Democratic ideas met with an immediate response in certain guilds. In London, the Levellers' programme won considerable support from the 'rank and file of craftsmen' (Unwin 1904, 207, 210; 1938, 335–9). In particular, there was 'a widespread attempt ... to apply Lilburne's democratic principles to the internal government of companies' (Unwin 1938, 339), that is, to wrest control of the guilds from the great masters. Several London crafts petitioned Parliament to this effect. Their arguments included a remarkable combination of guild tradition and Leveller ideology. On the one hand, they demanded 'a reducement of themselves to their primitive rights and privileges' (cit. Unwin 1938, 339). On the other hand, they used the political language of the Levellers in order to restate the long-standing guild principles of equality among members, self-government by general consent, and universal participation in guild elections. Lilburne had proclaimed in 1646 that 'The only and sole legislative law-making power is originally inherent in the people, and derivatively in their commissions chosen by themselves by common consent, and no other. In which the poorest that lives hath as true a right to give a vote as well as the richest and greatest' (cit. Hill and Dell 332). This idea, together with the newly current notion of 'mutual contract' between governors and governed, was taken up in a plea to the House of Commons made by the commonalty of the Weavers for equal status within the company.

> All Legal Jurisdiction over a number of people or society of men must either be primitive or derivative. Now primitive Jurisdiction is undoubtedly in the whole body and not in one or more members, all men being by nature equal to other and all Jurisdictive power over them, being founded by a compact and agreement with them, is invested in one or more persons who represent the whole and by the consent of the whole are impowered to govern by such rules of equality towards all as that both governors and governed may know certainly what the one may command and the other must obey, without the performance of which mutual contract all obligations are cancelled and that Jurisdictive power returns unto its first spring – the people from whom it was conveighed. And doubtless whatever power our governors of the Corporation of Weavers may pretend and plead for, if they have any rationally, they had it at first from the whole body. ... So that it is clear that this Grant was not to so many particular men but to the whole society and what power soever any person or persons were afterwards invested withall must of necessity be by the consent, election and approbation of the whole body.
>
> (cit. Unwin 1904, 204–5)

Parliament acceded to their request. We may say that Leveller influence made possible a new, more self-conscious and more general statement of guild ideology.

It was during this period that small masters in certain industries were able to reorganize themselves outside the great guilds dominated by the big merchants. They had won support from Charles I; the Commonwealth, however, preferred separate yeomanries within the parent company (Ashton

1979, 93; Unwin 1904, 53, 69, 200–4; 1938, 329ff.). As Unwin puts it, thanks to the contemporary development of democratic ideas, both in these cases and in cases where the commonalty regained some control over the old guild, the small craftsman's position in 'the industrial organization of which he was nominally a member might be discussed, not as a matter of vested interests, but as a question of high abstract principle' (1904, 204–5). These new groups of small masters provided one of the main links, in England, between the organizational and ethical milieu of the guilds and the early trade unions of the eighteenth century, although the filiation was complex enough (Unwin 1904, 204–5, 210; see p.173).

During the sixteenth and seventeenth centuries, guilds were generally accepted components of the political economy. In Huguenot views on political organization, there was 'a corporate element, including a variety of group or institutional privileges. ... Guilds, professions, offices and other institutions all had their specially defined and jealously guarded "liberties" which even the government could not violate with impunity' (Kelley 1981, 316). Bodin and Althusius now worked out for the first time what one may call a philosophy of the guild (see ch.11). But when, in the eighteenth century, new ideas developed about a natural economic order, guilds were subjected to increasingly critical scrutiny (see pp.159–61). Only in Germany, as learned and theoretical minds focused upon economic policy (*Polizeisachen*), were they now able to hold their own. Guild towns had a place in the Cameralists' view of political harmony, since they accepted communities as part of natural social diversity; the state was concerned only if they became infected by oligarchical corruption (Walker 1971, 146–7). J.J. Becher (1635–82) thought guilds 'the right instruments for controlling greed' (Walker 1971, 149). Christian Thomasius (1655–1728) described economic activity 'not as production but as occupations of men' (Walker 1971, 174); Christian Wolff (1675–1754) defined the driving forces of community as 'power, work and example' (Walker 1971, 148). Similarly, Justus Möser (1720–94) 'conceived economy to be a social aspect of personality' (Walker 1971, 180). Not unlike guildsmen themselves, he saw 'honour', not ambition or wealth, as 'the great mainspring of human affairs' (cit. Walker 1971, 178). Devoted as he was to an ideal of Germanic community implicitly focused upon the small guild town, he decried entrepreneurial commercialism, the putting-out system and large-scale manufacture (Walker 1971, 179–80). The implied rejection of the prescriptive power of economics as an autonomous science was to become a feature of nineteenth-century German thought, Marx included: personality and social life – 'ethics' – defined what economics was about.

11

THE PHILOSOPHY OF THE GUILD: BODIN AND ALTHUSIUS

We have seen that the Middle Ages – apart from Marsiglio's discussion of 'parts' of the state – produced no theory of the nature of guilds or their place in human society and polity. Such a theory was first developed by Bodin and, following on from him, Althusius and a succession of German writers, above all Justus Möser.

Jean Bodin (1529/30–96) introduced his reflections on guilds as part of a general discussion of the affective roots of human society (*Republic*, in French 1576, in Latin 1586, bk III, ch. vii; cf. Baudrillart 1853, 324–39; Petit-Dutaillis 1970, 202–8). Above all, he isolated the notion of *friendship* in its specifically guild-related sense. Johannes Althusius or Althaus (d.1638) brought the guild and, still more, the city, to the forefront of political theory; in his system he wove together guild and market values in a unique way. That the philosophy of the guild took wing at this particular time was due to the more systematic study of politics – a fruit of the northern Renaissance – upon which both Bodin and Althusius were engaged, and to their comprehensive concern with social phenomena, including much of what would later become 'political economy'. Although in constitutional theory they stood at opposite poles, thus providing a nice symmetry with Innocent IV and Marsiglio, Althusius' reflections about guilds were a direct development of Bodin's.

In his chapter on '*corps, collèges, états* (estates of the realm), *communautés* (towns)', Bodin looked at human society, as Aristotle had done, from the viewpoint of its component parts. These are, first, families and, secondly, colleges. A college is 'a legitimate association (*consociatio*) of three or more persons of the same status (*conditio*)'; while a *corpus* (body) is 'a grouping (*coniunctio*) of several colleges' (327). It becomes evident that 'colleges' here include associations for social, religious or professional purposes, or simply for mutual protection; in contemporary terms, Bodin's discussion referred in particular to craft-guilds, religious confraternities, academic bodies and collegiate magistracies (such as the *parlements*). Bodin identified colleges as one of four types of 'human associations bound together by law' (*hominum coetus iure sociati*), the others being families,

129

towns and states (bk I, ch. iii, 14). The family is the 'natural society' from which all 'civil societies' derive, and which they all imitate (bk III, ch. vii, 328). The family alone is strictly indispensable to human survival; men can live without states, but states cannot exist without families (328).

Briefly outlining the development of society and government, Bodin found that from the beginning the threat of brigandage (*latrocinandi licentia*) had led men to form 'friendships and associations' (*amicitias et societates*), as in the case of the ancient Greeks who created *sodalitia* and village communities for all those using the same well. This made life 'safer and more commodious' (329). Bodin is particularly concerned with the affective nature of these various simple human relationships, which he categorizes as follows: filial duty (*pietas*) between parents and children, affection (*caritas*) between siblings, friendship (*amicitia*) and benevolence between more distant relatives and neighbours. These groups marked the transition from natural to civil society: for purely natural affections 'would have grown cold, had not societies and sodalities been constituted out of *corpora* and *collegia*, in mutual sharing of legal right (*mutua iuris communione*)' (329). They are cemented by communal feasting, of which he finds examples in the ancient classical world, in the Old Testament, in the early church, and in contemporary Venice and Switzerland (330). (In fact, the early medieval mutual-protection guilds, which played a part in the development of villages and urban communes, would also fit Bodin's analysis.) Bodin concluded that such colleges were virtually essential to human society, and also that 'with such societies men have preserved their communities intact for very long periods without a state (*respublica*)', as in the case of the ancient Jews (329).

Even after states were formed, their wise founders, such as Numa and Lycurgus, fostered these sodalities; for 'they judged that there was no more stable foundation for states than the maintenance of societies and sodalities' (329). In particular, these knit society together on an affectual basis and minimize the need for legal process: 'not only were quarrels and disputes obviated without the need for magistrates, but also friendships were consolidated on a very deep basis.' Indeed, 'friendship (*amicitia*, *amitié*) was a more potent force for stabilizing and maintaining human groups and societies than justice itself.' This is because, while law courts may bring about a formal resolution of conflicts, they are powerless to remove hatred; friendship, on the other hand, achieves both purposes, and enables citizens to be reconciled with each other and with the state 'in the utmost tranquillity and benevolence' (329–30). He cites the example of craft-guilds (*opificum collegia*) in Switzerland, in which quarrels are settled informally, 'on tables with chalk rather than with ink and paper' (330). Bodin's analysis of social relationships were thus diametrically opposite to that later formulated by Hobbes, who argued that neither morality nor society could function without law and sovereign power.

In considering the position of guilds and other colleges in a modern state, Bodin insisted that they depended upon 'the sovereign's approval and concession' (331). Their head has authority only over individual members, not over the college as a whole (331). While guilds of doctors and craftsmen, and religious confraternities, do not have jurisdiction in the proper sense, they may nevertheless exercise 'moderate coercion' over their members, by means of fines, flogging or imprisonment (333). In considering whether they are 'useful to the state' today, he drew a distinction between different forms of government. In general, while it is true that colleges may be abused for seditious purposes, especially in the context of the present religious controversies, to abolish them altogether would be to root out the good with the bad (343–5). They are an excellent support for popular governments, and are admirably equipped to get rid of tyranny (345). Monarchical and aristocratic regimes, on the other hand, 'neither approve all colleges, nor think all should be abolished; they keep those they deem necessary to the state, regulating their function with excellent laws' (345). As for the royal government which Bodin advocated for France, 'royal power moderated with the best laws and institutions cannot be better supported than by *corpora* and *collegia*' (346). In this context he once again affirmed the importance of affective relationships. Empires themselves depend upon 'friendship and men's mutual charity among themselves' as well as upon justice; and justice in turn 'could in no way exist without associations' (342).

The importance of Bodin was that he was the first thinker to assign to colleges a clearly defined and integral role, alongside families, in society. He was also the first to assign to friendship, in the traditional guild sense as a specific social quality peculiar to colleges and sodalities, an irreplaceable function in the social order.

According to Petit-Dutaillis, Bodin 'dreams of a France where all subjects of the king, whether artisans, officials, clergy or nobles, are gathered into *corps* and *collèges*; he presents us with, as it were, a syndicalized kingdom' (1970, 202). This assimilates Bodin too closely with modern corporatism. It is clear, nevertheless, that Bodin saw colleges as essential partners to royal government in securing peace and social order, and that, like Innocent IV, he did not regard monarchy as a political principle to be applied systematically to every human group. Rather, he appears to have wanted to balance the concentration of legal authority at the centre with a wide diffusion of associational life. There is a stark contrast with early modern England, where Parliament was strong and guilds weak.

Johannes Althusius' *Systematic Analysis of Politics* (*Politica Methodice Digesta*), first printed in 1603 with a second edition of twice the length in 1610 (Friedrich 1932, xl), provides us with perhaps the most substantial exposition of guild ideas ever known. At the same time, principles of exchange were most subtly interwoven with those of solidarity to give a tautly balanced picture of society. His *Politics* is a comprehensive, schematized survey of the subject, in which every aspect of human social life and organization finds its place; in this respect his inspiration was both Aristotelian – in spirit and scope he was perhaps the closest modern Europe has come to full discipleship of Aristotle's political thought – and Ramist, for he focuses upon a single organizing concept (Friedrich 1932, lxi–lxiii). His emphasis upon the second half of the *Decalogue* as the goal of political action and life, and upon mutual charity and affection as the proper social bonds, establish him as one of the most deeply Christian political and social theorists.

In terms of historical context, it is apt that such a synthesis was generated by a German Calvinist who spent his later life as syndic of the small city of Emden, close to the Netherlands. Gierke (1966) regarded Althusius as the great exponent of the political culture of the Germanic Fellowship. Mesnard (1936, 567–616), wryly remarking how thus 'the forgotten man became the climax of millenial development ... by administrative dispatch', agrees that Althusius' notion of democracy reflected 'the co-ownership of the Germanic fellowships' (568, 612). Friedrich, on the other hand, sees him as 'the theorist of the developed Germanic city states'; from his familiarity with the cities of western and southern Germany, he developed 'the principles upon which the organization of these city-states rested' (1932, xix, lxxiv). Althusius' biblical, philosophical and, above all, juristic erudition was massive. In particular, he was engaged in constant dialogue with the ghost of Bodin, citing him about two hundred times (Mesnard 1936, 613–14). His thought is more consistently organic and more community-orientated than that of any medieval writer. His doctrine of the mixed constitution, of checks upon royal power and of ultimate popular sovereignty bind him closely to medieval tradition, fortified by Calvinism of the French school and inspired by recent developments in the Netherlands (Friedrich 1932, xvii; cf. Mesnard 1936, 614–15; Winters 1963). He combined the 'medieval' ideas of a collegiate, organic polity federated under the rule of law, with the 'modern' emphasis upon contract, power, reduction to first principles, systematic theory and sociological realism: 'he does not regard [the state] as organized once and for all but as being continuously occupied in staying organized' (Friedrich 1932, xc). He is the true intermediary between medieval and modern political thought. As it turned out, his book soon ceased to be widely read; Rousseau, however, knew his work (Friedrich 1932, xviii, xx n.).

The central and founding concept of Althusius' politics is *consociatio*, to which he often adds the adjective *symbiotica* – association based on living together (cf. Friedrich 1932, lxvi–lxvii; Mesnard 1936, 608, 611).

Althusius starts by discussing the two 'private associations': the family or *consociatio domestica*, which is the only 'natural association' (chs ii–iii), and the college or *consociatio collegarum* (ch. iv). He then proceeds to the various types of public *consociatio*: the city (chs v–vi), the province (chs vii–viii), and finally the kingdom or *universalis consociatio* (chs ix–xxxix), of which the empire provides a supreme example. The basic tenets of Althusius' social and political thought are to be found in the definition of *consociatio*, with which the book begins.

> Politics is the art of associating (*consociandi*) persons with a view to establishing, nourishing and preserving social life together. Hence they are called *sumbiotike* (cohabiters). The first proposition of politics, therefore, is *consociatio*; in this the cohabiters (*symbiotici*), by an explicit or tacit pact, undertake mutual obligation to one another to communicate to each other those things that are useful and necessary for the maintenance and sharing of social life. ... These *symbiotici* are, therefore, mutual helpers who, joined and associated together by a contractual bond, share those of their resources which are helpful for the commodious conduct of the life of the spirit and body; they are sharers, participants in a communion. (*Proposita igitur Politicae est consociatio, qua pacto expresso vel tacito symbiotici inter se invicem ad communicationem mutuam eorum, quae ad vitae socialis usum et consortium sunt utilia et necessaria se obligant. ... Symbiotici igitur hic sunt* sumboethoi, *qui vinculo pacti coniuncti et consociati communicant de suis, quae ad animi et corporis vitam commode degendam expediunt, et vicissim* koinonetoi, *communionis sunt participes.*) (15–16)

This is no mere repetition of the communal values of medieval thought. Rather, it is a calculated statement of how mutual need leads to exchange (*communicatio*), and exchange to solidarity (*consortium, communio*). Contract played an important part in Althusius' theory of political legitimacy (Hoepfl and Thompson 1979, 935–6), precisely because he regarded it as part of the basis for all forms of association. While, as will become clear, human need and economic exchange play a central role in Althusius' view of the origin of society, this did not mean that for him men are essentially competitive; rather the term *communicatio* (a rendering of the Greek *koinonia*: sharing, communion)* indicated that reciprocity was inherent in the process of exchange. (The function of gifts in simple societies perfectly illustrates Althusius' point.) Unlike medieval theorists, on the other hand, he does not see solidarity as simply given, instinctive, implanted in human nature; it arises out of the process of exchange. The social bonds

---

* In Aristotle, *Politics* (I, 1. 1), *koinonia* was translated *communicatio* by Moerbeke, *societas* by Bruni (I thank James Bennett for this information), and 'partnership' by Rackham.

thus generated are, none the less, durable and morally significant. As in Hegel, community is based upon deliberate choice. Althusius' point of emphasis is, in fact, not far removed from the concept of *mutual aid*.

All this becomes clearer as Althusius goes on to describe the development of the commonwealth or state (*respublica*):

> God has distributed his gifts in diverse ways among men. He did not give one person everything, but different things to different people, so that I should need what you have, and you should need what I have; thus arose the necessity, as it were, of sharing (*communicandorum*) what was needful and useful, and this intercourse (*communicatio*) could only take place in socio-political life (*politica vita sociali*). Therefore God willed that one person should need the labour and aid of another, so that friendship (*amicitia*) might overwhelm each and all. ... For if one person did not require another's aid, what society, reverence, order, reason, humanity would there be? ... These were the reasons why villages were built, cities constructed, academies founded, and why many farmers, craftsmen, smiths, architects, soldiers, merchants, the educated and the uneducated, were joined together (*copularunt*) through their diversity in civil unity and society, as so many members of the same body; so that, as people supplied each other's needs, and took from others what they required, all alike should be gathered together into a kind of public body – which we call a commonwealth (*respublica*) – and by mutual aid (*mutuis auxiliis*) should attend to the general good and safety of that body. (18)

The state, then, arises out of the God-given diversity of human abilities, specialization and the division of labour; the age-old value of mutual aid, which was fundamental to medieval guild sentiment, is here transposed and, being based on mutual need rather than the common interests of fellow-craftsmen or guild members, becomes a central value for civil or market society itself. There was nothing peculiarly Calvinist here; the idea of inbuilt professional diversity – and also the combination of exchange and solidarity – appeared in Marsiglio. The idea that friendship develops out of mutual need anticipates, to some degree, Hegel's view of the relation between the morality of 'the state' and the selfish goals of 'civil society'. As regards the relation between the state and the division of labour, Marx too would have found this passage significant.

This pattern of relationships recurs in Althusius' description of each particular *consociatio*. At each level of association, mutual need gives rise to mutual aid; solidarity is based on exchange. Society is at once 'instrumental' and 'affective'. Throughout Althusius' social and political thought, there is equal emphasis upon communal values and voluntary contract. A 'contractual bond' (*vinculum pacti*) is present in the formation of each particular *consociatio*; it is not only not incompatible with affective personal ties but plays a vital role in their creation. This will sound surprising only to those accustomed to Lockian individualism and to hearing about contract primarily in the context of the relation between government and the individual.

The 'bond' of the family is 'the communication of mutual aid, counsel and right, and faith given and accepted on either side' (22). In colleges and guilds, '*communicatio* arises when colleagues support and aid one another in their life's work (*propositum vitae*), according to agreements (*pacta conventa*)'; it relates to 'things or tasks or some mutual right or benevolence' (34). Here *communicatio* has a particular affective quality, mentioned in Scripture: 'mutual and reciprocal benevolence is the affection and love (*affectus et caritas*) of an individual member for his colleague ... by which colleagues desire and shun the same things for the general good, without discord' (I Cor. 1:10–11; Rom. 12:16; Gal. 5). Benevolence is 'nurtured, cherished and maintained by public meals, banquets and love-feasts' (37). In this context, then, mutual aid appears in its usual guild form, relating to collective security rather than exchange of goods.

When we come to the city, the principle of exchange is thoroughly integrated into that of solidarity, as it was in the general definition of *consociatio*.

> The reciprocal intercourse (*communicatio*) of citizens of the same town (*universitas*) with each other is one of things, tasks, law and mutual concord. ... The communication of tasks between citizens of the same town means that services and assistance (*ministeria et subsidia*), necessary and useful for the citizens' mutual life together (*sumbiosin ... convictum*), are performed by one citizen for the benefit of another who needs or wants them, so that through the duties of charity love may be effective.
>
> (53, 55: he goes on to cite I Cor. 12; cf. Marsiglio, p.94 above)

Christian charity is fostered by the necessary relationship of reciprocity. In particular, the city is characterized by exchange between those engaged in different *forms* of labour.

> Productive labour (*opificia*), for example the various manufacturing trades (*mechanica*), rural life, agriculture and commerce, is a private concern, relating principally to the utility of the administrators and consequently to the public utility of the city and all its inhabitants ... In order to perform mutual tasks for the conservation of each, these economic pursuits (*opificia*) have to be joined together. ... The rural worker needs the smith.   (56)

The maintenance of *amicitia* and *caritas* among citizens also requires the speedy settlement of disputes and *aequabilitas*, in the Roman sense of recognition of each person's honour in relation to his status (59).

135

The *consociatio* of the kingdom consists in the mutual provision (*communicatio*) of goods and services by the cities and provinces to each other (88). Its 'bond' is the consent and mutual faithfulness (*fides*) of the component cities and provinces, ' a tacit or explicit promise concerning the communication of goods, mutual services, aid, counsel and the same common laws'. This 'aid' includes 'the provision of prompt assistance for a needy labouring member of this universal association, by communication of goods and services' (119). In this context he deals more explicitly with *commercia*, in which the characteristics of social intercourse discussed above are fully deployed and topped off with the organic analogy.

> Such commerce is the means by which we are able to obtain what we need from others by just title and cause, and to exchange (*permutare*) with others what we have in plenty. ... Without commerce, therefore, we cannot conveniently live this social life. For there are many things which we need, and without which no one can conveniently live, many things which we cannot well, or without great inconvenience, do without; and, just as the human body cannot be healthy without its members' mutual communication of functions (*mutua officiorum communicatione*), so too the body of the commonwealth cannot be healthy without commerce. Therefore, necessity and utility of life discovered a means and measure of exchange (*permutationum modum et rationem*), by which you may give and communicate to another what he needs and cannot, any more than you, conveniently do without, and by which you, on the other hand, can receive what is useful and necessary to you. (99)

Throughout, the exchange of goods and services is understood as a moral as well as an 'economic' transaction; an essential human activity, it forms an integral part of social and political life.

It is clear that, as Gierke (1966) pointed out, Althusius made a less sharply categorical distinction than others between the state and other associations. As groupings of solidarity and exchange, they were all of the same kind. Lesser communities, professional and territorial, attain unique importance in his scheme. While individual persons make up families and colleges, it is not individuals but 'the various private associations of families, households and colleges (*coniugum, familiarum et collegiorum*)' which make up the city as its 'members' (39); and the state or universal association in turn is formed by 'the various cities, provinces and regions' as its members (88). Thus, as Gierke aptly put it, 'in this ascending series of groups, each higher stage always proceeds from the one below; and thus it is associations, and not individuals, which are the contracting parties in the formation of the higher and larger groups', so that there is 'a series of concentrically arranged groups, intervening between the individual and the general community' (1958, 71–2).

The college itself is defined as

A civil association (*civilis consociatio*) in which three or more persons involved in the same craft, mode of production, life-work and profession (*artis, opificii, vitae studii et professionis*) are associated together, with a view to having something common among themselves (*ad commune quid inter se ... simul habendum*) in respect of that function, form of life or craft which they profess. (33)

Colleges include craft-guilds, religious and learned associations, and estates of the realm (possibly also collegiate courts). A college is formed when 'persons, brought together solely by their own decision and will, establish one body, for the sake of their common utility and need in human life; that is, they agree among themselves by common consent upon a method of ruling and obeying' (33). What distinguishes the college from the other 'private association', the family, is that

this society is by its nature divisible and temporary, it does not last as long as a person's life, but saving honour and good grace may be dissolved if the contracting parties agree to separate (*mutuo contrahentium dissensu*), although in general it is necessary and useful for social life. Wherefore it is called a spontaneous and purely voluntary society, although it too may be said to have been produced by a certain necessity. (33)

Thus, *pace* Gierke (1958, 71–2), the college is precisely not a natural but a 'civil' association, formed, like all civil associations, by human will and design in response to human need and utility. Collegiate membership is the first step towards citizenship: when a man goes outside his family circle, 'then assuredly he abandons the title of *paterfamilias* and lord, to conduct himself as partner and citizen (*socium ac civem*), and in a sense departs from the family that he may enter the *civitas*' (33; cf. Bodin bk I, ch.vi, 45). In his definition of the college and its relation to the family, Althusius closely followed what Bodin had said in bk III, ch.vii of *The Republic*.

Colleges have as their general purpose 'the promotion of the functions (*officia*), business and convenience of the craft, profession or calling and the removal of hindrances to these'. The craftsmen's and workmen's colleges also provide entry to the craft for apprentices by means of formal examination leading to a certificate (*testimonium suis discipulis, examinatione solemni habita*) (35).

Althusius' whole conception of *consociatio symbiotica* led to a distinctive and, in the context of contemporary theory, revolutionary view of the constitutional position of guilds and colleges: here he differed from Bodin *toto coelo*. There is simply no question of their depending for their legitimacy on higher authority or a sovereign legal system: this is not even discussed. They are created by their members 'common consent' (33;

137

cf. Innocent IV, p.21 above). In this respect, Althusius was the only thinker who explicitly put colleges on the same *juridical* footing as the family (cf. Gierke 1958, 70–7). On the internal constitution of colleges, Althusius was content for the most part to follow medieval juristic opinion, using in particular the convenient summary in Nicolaus Losaeus' *Treatise on Corporation Law (De Iure Universitatum Tractatus)*, published at Turin in 1601 (cf. Friedrich 1932, liv–lvi; Mesnard 1936, 611). The ruler of the college (*princeps collegii*) is 'elected by the common consent of the colleagues': on this point Althusius referred to a whole cluster of New Testament texts (33). The ruler has 'power and coercion over individuals, but not over all his colleagues' (33–4). As regards legislation, 'colleges can make statutes among themselves, which they are obliged to observe, on matters concerning the administration of their goods, the craft, profession or private business' (35). The city can also legislate on these matters (58). Collegiate procedure follows the pattern prescribed by Tudeschi and the medieval civil jurists: an assembly is to be called and a two-thirds majority is required (36–7). Althusius' belief in the role of contract in the formation of civil associations led him to lay greater emphasis than his predecessors upon the rule of law within colleges. All collegiate intercourse (*communicatio*) takes place 'according to agreed pacts' (he cites Bartolus on *Digest* 47.22.4); 'these pacts and laws of the colleagues are written down in the guild books, which we call *Zunftbücher*' (34).

Althusius' other radical proposition about the constitutional role of colleges was to make them, alongside families, the constituent elements of the city: a city is 'an association of many spouses, families and colleges dwelling in one place, formed by certain laws' (39). In some cities, the senators and consuls are elected by the craft colleges (46); and in the kingdom, ephors (popular magistrates who ensure that the king governs constitutionally: cf. Skinner 1978, ii 230–3, 314–16) are elected 'by the votes of the whole people ... assembled by centuries, tribes or colleges' (145). Bodin had made families the constituent elements of the republic (bk I, ch. i, 1–3); and Althusius also gave the family a certain priority, calling it, as Bodin had done, the 'seed-bed' (*seminarium*) of public association (31–2; Bodin bk I, ch. ii, 8). But Bodin did not regard colleges as component parts, in a constitutional sense, of any political association. Althusius, in making colleges as well as families the 'members' of the city, was the only thinker apart from Marsiglio to acknowledge the political functions they actually had. He mapped out the subtle balance of differing consociations that would constitute the German empire from 1648 to 1806, and would enable guild-dominated 'home town' communities to flourish as never before, with endless local varieties of tacit self-government (Walker 1971).

Nevertheless, the kingdom or 'universal association' is, in important respects, unique. It alone possesses sovereignty (*ius maiestatis*) (91) and a 'supreme magistrate' (ch. xix). Althusius devoted by far the greatest part of his book to the commonwealth or state; he discussed at length its social composition and scope of activity, which included economic policy (ch. xxxii), as well as its political constitution. Law and its execution are principally the commonwealth's concern (chs x and xxix). Althusius was particularly concerned with the 'maintenance of concord' in the state (ch. xxxi); he discussed at some length 'the nature and affection of the people', and the importance of moral bonds between people and rulers and between all members of the community (chs xxiii–xxiv, esp. 203–5), and he stressed the need for 'mutual consensus, peace and benevolence' between people and magistrate (291).

In the commonwealth, the twin features of community and contract, which characterize all associations, achieve their fullest *constitutional* expression. First, the organic unity of the realm is affirmed in Althusius' celebrated statement of the sovereignty of the people:

> This right of the kingdom or of sovereignty (*ius maiestatis*) belongs not to the individual members [sc. cities and provinces] but to all of them collectively (*coniunctim*) and to the whole body of the association of the kingdom. ... It is not these individual [members] that hold supreme power, but all of them together acknowledge its unity in the consent and accord of the associated bodies. (91–2)

In the second place, Althusius, in one of the classic statements of the contract of government, argued that this corporate sovereignty of the realm followed from the contractual relationship between people and ruler.

> In the establishment of the supreme magistrate the members of the kingdom oblige themselves to obey him, as he takes up the authority and executive power of the kingdom offered to him by the body of the universal association. That is, the people and the supreme magistrate make an agreement between themselves, by certain laws and conditions, as to the form and method of subjection and authority. There is no doubt but that this pact or contract of commission (*contractum mandati*) entered into with the supreme magistrate obliges each of the contracting parties, so that neither magistrate nor subjects may revoke or violate it. ... But, in this reciprocal contract between the supreme magistrate as recipient of the mandate and promiser (*mandatarium seu promittentem*), and the universal association mandating him, the obligation of the magistrate, by which he binds himself to the body of the universal association, takes precedence, as is usual in a contract of commission.... From this contract of commission between people and magistrate, it is clear that the people or kingdom is complete lord (*dominum plenum*) of all authority and power, the wholly free disposition, ownership and enjoyment whereof belongs to the associated body, the united people. ...

From this contract, then, it is clear that the right given by the people to the supreme magistrate is less than the right of the people, and is not properly his. Therefore the prince does not have equal power with the people or kingdom in this [right], but a far less and inferior power. (160; cf. 5)

Government is a *commission* (cf. Rousseau, *Du contrat social* III. i).

One particularly important practical conclusion follows from Althusius' application of his theory of association by contract to the state: if the supreme magistrate fails to observe his contract, in addition to a right of resistance which may be invoked by the ephors (ch.xxxix), the commonwealth may be dissolved into its component parts. For in a kingdom 'the fundamental law is nothing other than certain *pacta*, under which several cities and provinces have come together and agreed to have and defend one and the same commonwealth with common labour, counsel and aid'; so that 'when by common consent these conditions and pacts are abandoned, the commonwealth ceases to exist' (169). This means that the cities and provinces, or perhaps just certain cities and provinces, may agree to disassociate themselves. Althusius did not labour the point, but his argument could be taken as sanctioning unilateral secession, such as had recently been achieved by the Dutch and much earlier by the Swiss. Certainly such action could have been supported by the general tenor of his argument. Althusius did not countenance any such disassociation taking place within the province, city or family. The college, however, may, like the commonwealth, 'be dissolved by the mutual dissent of the contracting parties, saving honour and good grace' (33).

Althusius held a theory of ultimate popular sovereignty, but not of popular government. The truth, he believed, was that every state, however it is described, is actually a mixture of rule by one, by the best and by the people. In kingdoms such as France and the German Empire, the democratic element is represented by the assemblies of the realm (*comitia regni*), the aristocratic by the 'intermediate magistrates' (404–5). Althusius had a low opinion of the common people's political prudence (203–5), and, in general, emphasized the subjects' duty of obedience as much as the ruler's duty to rule responsibly (chs xxiii–xxv, esp. 229; ch.xxxi). For present purposes, the main point is that he employed contract and solidarity side by side in making his case, against Bodin in particular, for ultimate popular sovereignty.

Althusius' conception of social relationships clearly owed a great deal to the Christian idea of love; indeed, in the last resort, mutual love may be said to be the pattern that emerges as he weaves together the various strands of solidarity and exchange. It has been argued that Althusius' use of Scripture was merely ornamental (Bartels, cit. Friedrich 1932, xviii; Mesnard 1936, 614–15). It is certainly true that he insisted that the study of politics was a discipline *sui generis*, and that he often used Scripture, as did the scholastics, to corroborate conclusions arrived at by other means. He rejected the view that one could deduce the normative pattern of social and political life from Scripture alone. The data of politics are provided by observation of human life as we experience it or read about it; the discipline closest to politics is jurisprudence (4). But the picture that finally emerges is inspired, as he explicitly asserts, by those parts of the *Decalogue* which relate to social conduct, interpreted, in the New Testament manner, in terms of the overriding precept of love. In other words, Christianity provides the 'form' and goal of politics, not its material nor its method. Discussing the vexed question whether the *Decalogue* should be interpreted in a political sense and applied to politics, he insisted that it should; indeed it provides the 'essence' of politics. 'All and each of the *Decalogue*'s precepts are political and associational (*symbiotica*) ... the content of the *Decalogue* is innate, essential and proper to politics (*politicae genuinia, essentialis et propria*)' (198–9). The *Decalogue*, summarized as 'the conservation of one's neighbour's life, the protection of one's neighbour, through friendship and the other duties of charity, with food, clothing and sustenance', provides the basic legal norm (193, 143). The 'administration' of the civil law is defined as a function in which

> the magistrate correctly and faithfully looks after the secular affairs (*negotia secularia*) of the second table of the *Decalogue*, which relate to the establishment and preservation of order, legality, self-sufficiency (*eutaxian, eunomian, autarkeian*) and external discipline in the state, or to the promotion of what protects and is commodious for this life, and the removal and prevention of what is incommodious. (274)

Again, for the province, he defined 'civil affairs' as 'the duties of love (*officia dilectionis*), by which a person gives each his own and does not do to a fellow-inhabitant what he would not wish done to himself, but loves him as himself' (61).

In Althusius, then, the guild values of friendship and mutual aid are given a wider social meaning in terms of exchange and reciprocity. But their meaning is not radically changed, and as applied to the guild itself they retain their old sense. Though Gierke did not quite see things this way, his estimation of Althusius was largely correct: in him Germanic Christianity achieved its truest and finest philosophical expression in social and political thought.

Althusius has been called a theorist of 'the corporatist state', or of 'corporative democracy' (Friedrich 1932, lxxxvi; Mesnard 1936, 567). He surely ranks as one of the few great theorists of corporatism. This was partly because, not unlike Marsiglio and Hegel, he was concerned with every aspect of social life as he observed it. It was also partly because, like Marsiglio and Durkheim, he attached special significance to the division of

141

labour as a dynamic factor in social life (cf. 37, 56). Althusius, however, like most other great corporate theorists, regarded the economic corporation or professional group as only one among several morally significant sub-groups in the state; the province is no less important, the family and city more important. We find, in fact, that most of the major theorists of corporatism saw mutuality and exchange not as opposites but as com-plementary. Professional groups played such a prominent role in Althusius' theory because he saw them, not – as we tend to – as mere instruments of convenience, but as essential components of human society.

12

CITY, CORPORATION AND NATION

During the early modern period, the idea of the state, and of the nation-state in particular, became firmly established in philosophy and (at least in some countries) in popular sentiment. Among philosophers, this meant above all the conception and delimitation of a unique sphere of human interaction in which the artifices of written law, officialdom and sovereignty overlaid the natural course of personal relationships (cf. Cheyette 1978). The state as a distinctive category now became the principal topic of political philosophy. Thinkers such as Hobbes, Locke and Rousseau might draw very different constitutional conclusions, but they at least agreed that the state was a human contrivance requiring specifically rational justification. Among ordinary people, nation or race was increasingly regarded as the primary human community (other than the family). What concerns us here is the manner in which concepts and values deriving from the city-state and, above all, the corporation were woven into the idea of the state and of the constitution appropriate to it. First, however, we must briefly consider the survival of the commune itself in this period.

In many parts of Europe, including those in which the nation-state first developed into maturity, there was either a decline in the independence and political culture of the city-state as such, or else an alliance between oligarchical city governments and the national authorities. On the one hand, the territorial communities of village and town remained, as before, basic units in the economic and political system of Europe. In certain areas, notably Switzerland and upper Germany, the 'medieval' village, with its reserves of common land and elected village leaders, survived into the nineteenth century (Bader 1957, 1962). Restoration of common land and of common access to pasture, forests and rivers formed part of the demands of the French peasantry in 1789 (Cobban 1961, 158), as it had of the German peasantry in 1525. Such demands formed a connection between nineteenth-century communist or anarchist programmes and the traditional mentality of agriculturalists over much of Europe.

City-states, on the other hand, suffered a catastrophic political decline in the sixteenth century. The discovery of the New World and the opening-up of shipping routes to India and the Far East transformed the commercial map, shifting the fulcrum of economic power and enterprise from the

Mediterranean to the Atlantic. Nuremberg and Venice lost out to Amsterdam and Bristol. Furthermore, many new industries, both in England and on the Continent, were located in the countryside on account of the proximity of water and raw materials, and also to evade guild regulations (Pollard 1981, 62–3). The relative decline of the political importance of cities was also related to the fact that, with the market economy assuming global proportions, economic policy was increasingly conducted on a national rather than a local basis. The national community assumed increasing importance. In the process, just as mercantilism 'represents measures copied, in part, from urban economic politics' (Weber 1958, 188), so too civic values were transferred to nation and state.

In Italy, the remaining independent city-states of Lucca, Genoa and Venice were governed by entrenched oligarchies, against whom the last popular uprising, organized by parishes and guilds, took place as late as 1746 in Genoa (Venturi 1971, 38–40). In the centralized states of Spain and France, the development of royal absolutism diminished the political role of the cities. The aspirations of the Castilian towns were crushed after the unsuccessful revolt of the Comuñeros in 1520–1 (Maravall 1963). In France, mayors were appointed by the Crown, and 'in the milieu of the eighteenth century few people knew what a *commune* was' (Petit-Dutaillis 1970, 218–19, 233). Where parliamentarism succeeded, cities retained greater autonomy. In the Netherlands, the towns emerged from the struggle for independence with enhanced prestige and powers (Parker 1979, 146); while in England the Restoration of 1660 introduced a 'localist millenium' (Ashton 1979, 351).

The homeland of communal civic culture was now Germany. While the remaining city-states, such as Lübeck and Augsburg, were oligarchical, the numerous small towns of the south and west took up the mantle of participatory democracy; there the medieval commune and guild town persisted, accentuating its communitarian features. Mack Walker has given a superb account of their political culture, with its 'institutional eccentricity and close social integrity' (1971, 35). It comprises a whole distinct chapter in the history of *mentalités*. Such towns were able to expand their local rights 'in the direction of effective autonomy' because the infinite diversity of their regimes afforded 'no general handles (concepts)' for territorial state or Empire to grasp (Walker 1971, 20, 193). Far from such towns having succumbed to oligarchy and absolutism, governments only intervened when the citizenry appealed against corruption and encroaching oligarchy; and 'reforms' by territorial states were usually 'in a *bürgerlich* direction', restoring the balance between council and community. Here the citizens showed no 'petty, spineless, submissive bearing' (as Rörig alleges: 1967, 186), but rather insisted that councils remain accountable (Friedrichs 1978; Walker 1971, 59–72). Their tacit legislative powers rested upon the age-old authority of local popular custom (*Willkür*: cf. p.55 above): 'town law breaks state law' (Walker 1971, 38–41). The interlocking powers of lesser (inner) and greater (outer) councils reveal continuity with the medieval past; the distinction between full political citizenship and legal residence was perhaps more conservatively upheld, with strict social veto upon membership in the crucial *Bürgerrecht* (Walker 1971, 137–40). Their political art lay in the communal smothering of friction; this 'was very effective indeed, and the internal key to the preservation of the community's individuality and autonomy' (Walker 1971, 55). It would appear that the majority of households supported a full citizen. This 'home town communarchy' (Walker 1971, 60) was perhaps the closest Europe has come to Aristotle's middle-class 'polity'.

> The civic constitutions and the rights of membership they embodied were instruments of a democracy among members no less fraudulent than those which many polities with more democratic affectations have had. But hometown equality and hometown democracy meant the subjugation of everybody in the community to everybody, to limits set by the whole community. (Walker 1971, 134)

Turning now to relations between the city or commune and the state, there were, in the first place, attempts to integrate the two on a confederal basis. Town governments played an important part in the French religious wars, and the general idea of a federalized kingdom was to be found among both the Huguenots and the Catholic League. The Huguenots numbered towns among the 'inferior magistrates' ordained by God which might legitimately resist tyranny (Skinner 1978, ii 204–5, 213–15, 324). Both they and the League asserted the towns' right to elect their own jurors and magistrates; the League supported Paris's claim to greater autonomy (Allen 1928, 331, 346; Mesnard 1936, 379, 384; Skinner 1978, ii 330). During the Dutch Revolt, the possibility of a confederation on the Swiss model was considered; eventually, the eighteen 'voting towns' retained considerable autonomy within the United Provinces (Parker 1979, 146, 194, 245–7). The different conclusion to events in France and the Netherlands was reflected in the contrasting doctrines of Bodin, who rejected any concession to confederalism, and of Althusius, who conceived cities and provinces as 'public associations' in their own right, with their own proper sphere of 'communication', and as the component 'members' of the commonwealth (chs 5–9). Above all, Althusius' doctrine reflected the position and aspirations of the towns of western Germany, of whose affairs he had first-hand experience. In France too, nevertheless, a strand of learned opinion continued to envisage towns as 'intermediary bodies' with their own particular place under the monarchy (Petit-Dutaillis 1970, 219–22; Venturi 1971, 74–5). Montesquieu saw towns, *parlements* and nobility as '*pouvoirs intermédiaires, subordonnées et dépendants'* which help determine 'the nature of the government' since they are 'mediating channels through which power flows' (bk II, ch. iv). For him this was one of the essential differences between monarchy and despotism: in a royal state such bodies balance and check monarchical power; 'monarchies become corrupt when corporate prerogatives and the privileges of towns are little by little taken away' (bk VIII, ch.vi; bk III, ch.x). In the mid-eighteenth century the *parlements* adopted a similar view about their own position (Cobban 1961, i 129).

It was above all in Germany, and in the context of the guild towns still thriving there, that thinkers formulated communal ideas in coherent opposition to the extension of state power. They did so by developing a notion of 'true community' and 'communal existence' (*gemein Wesen*) as a distinctive but essential category of social life, which was to be found pre-eminently where men 'arranged their affairs so as mutually to live from one another by the *bürgerliche Nahrung*' (burgher livelihood: Walker 1971, 149, summarizing Becher writing in the 1660s) – that is, in the guild town. This gave self-governing towns a legitimate *raison d'être*. Justus Möser was the most explicit exponent of this view: 'the familiar social community as primary organizer of political, economic and moral life' (as Walker puts it: 1971, 175) constitutes a group *sui generis* in between the individual and society (*Gesellschaft*) at large. Such communities are based upon honour, experience and propriety (*Ehre, Erfahrung, Eigentum*), and embody natural human diversity; their particular, unwritten norms should be kept immune from infiltration by 'academic theories and a general plan' (cit. Walker 1971, 176–7).

It was also held that a distinctive mode of government is appropriate to towns: authority is the 'servant of the community ... for the community is not there for authority's sake, but authority for the sake of the community' (Becher, cit. Walker 1971, 149). Thomasius classified guild government as 'democracy' (Walker 1971, 100). Even Justi, who advocated the integration of towns into the state *Polizei*, and regarded them, not unlike the French, as 'intermediate mechanisms to transmit harmony and order between individuals and the common weal' (Walker 1971, 168), insisted that, in the interests of such a policy, 'Major town decisions should be put before the citizenry; the state should preserve the political rights of the *Bürger*, and intervene to prevent the emergence of patrician oligarchy' (Walker 1971, 165).

Quite apart from these quasi-confederal views of the relation between city or commune and state, there were more dramatic moves to assimilate the nation-state directly to the city-state or, alternatively, to the corporation. Civic concepts and values were applied to the nation in two ways: by regarding the nation-state as the natural political environment of man, and by applying to the nation-state constitutional models taken from ancient or contemporary city-states. The process started in the Netherlands, where the term *commune* was applied to the *patria* during the Dutch Revolt (Griffiths 1968, 437). It took off during the religious and political upheavals in England from 1640 to 1660. The change wrought in the conception of the nation-state in revolutionary England, by the revival there of the civic republicanism earlier developed at Florence, has been brilliantly analysed by Pocock (1975, chs 11–12, esp. 383–402). The values of civic humanism, toughened by Machiavelli's ideal of the *popolo armato*, were now transferred from the city-state to the nation. The Calvinist idea of the 'elect nation' and neo-Calvinist views on the structure of a covenanted congregation had already begun to prise loose the ideology of kingship (Haller 1963; Pocock 1975, 337). Indeed the radical neo-Calvinists tended on the whole to be more democratic than the neo-classical writers.

Pocock perceives this great transformation of political thought, which he encapsulates as 'the Machiavellian moment', as moving from seventeenth-century England to North America in her revolutionary period (1975, ch.15). Yet it was surely in France after 1791 that the neo-classical idea of the nation as *civitas* was developed in its purest modern form; for the final apotheosis of the Machiavellian moment we should perhaps look to the Napoleonic conception of power and the state. Thereafter, the idea of the nation as the new *polis* surged around Europe; Hegel and Nietzsche were among its heirs. In Germany, a neo-Machiavellian theory of state autonomy was accepted in the later nineteenth century. There was, on the other hand, a very different small-town component in German national sentiment: the 'home-town' ethos of the warm, enclosed, regulated community of informal togetherness, became identified with perceived national tradition, partly thanks to Justus Möser's *Patriotic Phantasies* (c.1760–80: Walker 1971, 174–84). Needless to say, as democracy, folk-state, civilization and empire were welded into an integral set of supreme values, the problem of international order was posed in an acute form.

Internally, the reading-off of nation-state against the template of city-state legitimized the concept of commonwealth or republic, in which all full citizens had a stake and a voice. In England and America, Harrington's version of republicanism suggested, among other things, a distribution of power between senate and popular assembly (Pocock 1975, 382ff.). Contemporary cities vied with Athens and Rome as models of working republics, with elected and rotating officials supervised by public assemblies (Venturi 1971, 18ff.). Now at last parliament could become the full beneficiary of the prodigious authority bestowed by European peoples from early times upon the corporate community.

Rousseau pursued the opposite course. One could learn more from peasants meeting under ancestral oaks than from learned academies. While others were seeking to re-kindle the ancient civic morality in the contemporary nation and state, Rousseau proclaimed the unique and inalienable virtues of the miniature original. The small city-republic or rural district had unique moral assets; liberty diminishes with size (*Du contrat social* III. i; II. ix). Freedom as self-determination is only attainable in a state when the assembled people impose laws upon themselves: 'all things considered, I do not see how it will be possible from now on for the sovereign to retain the exercise of his rights among us, if the city is not very small' (III. xv; cf. Grimsley 1973, 112). The solution to the problem of political justice in the modern world was not, therefore, to model the large state upon the small, but rather to nurture and strengthen existing small states, and to reform large states by decentralization and subdivision. The problem of military strength would have to be met by confederation (III. xiii and xv).

At first sight, it might appear plausible to say that Rousseau was a latter-day spokesman of that communal tradition which, from the twelfth century, was indigenous to Europe. His '*acte d'association*' might be interpreted as a schematic development of the communal oath, his '*volonté générale*' as an explanation of what citizens had understood long ago as the basis of legitimate corporate acts (cf. pp.52–3). Did he not look to Geneva itself as a model and possible location for the realization of his ideal republic (Venturi 1971, 83–5)? An objective reading of *Du contrat social* dispels this hypothesis. Doubtless his central political ideas owed much to neo-classicism (Shklar 1969). But, above all, they leap from the page as the formulations of an original mind, as he himself claimed they were. The idea of the sovereign citizenry as created by 'the total alienation of each associate with all his rights to the community', so that 'each one, in uniting himself to all, none the less obeys no one but himself and remains as free as before' (I. vi) bore no relation to the mentality of the early medieval communes or the guilds. It established a new political ideal, which awoke a response in many hearts, but not because men were already attuned to it by anything other than the aspirations of human nature. His belief that Geneva might come to resemble his ideal if, as seemed just possible in the patrician–bourgeois struggles of the 1760s, she returned to her first principles (Venturi 1971, 77, 83–5), and his analogies with Sparta and Rome, were inspired by a re-reading of history in the light of philosophy, a process which was to be adopted on a large scale by the Romantic movement. Rousseau's desire to eliminate corporations (II. iii) represented a final thrust of the neo-classical ideal of the *civitas*, and it leaves us in no doubt as to how he viewed the guild mentality.

It was a supreme irony that many of the republicans who, a generation later, assumed leadership of the French Revolution, should have believed themselves to be the heirs of Rousseau (cf. Cobban 1964). Rousseau was dedicated upon the altar of centralism, and then of empire. In this respect, it was primitivists, romantics, anarchists and communists, men like Gierke,

Proudhon and Marx, with their ideals of Fellowship, *mutualité* and 'the associated producers', who more truly grasped the meaning of this most original thinker.

But the city-state was not the only model available for the nation-state. The idea of the corporation (*universitas, collegium*) and the language of corporation theory also helped to articulate the idea of the nation as an entity which could act of itself and express a corporate will, and to justify consent, representation and election as constitutional norms. Here in particular, we need to align the perspectives of Gierke and Pocock. In one respect, civic and corporational assumptions and ideals cannot even be treated as separate: for the borough or commune itself was a sub-species of the corporation *genus*. Whether one spoke of a town or city as corporation or *polis* depended on the context of debate: the former category was appropriate to law and constitutional traditionalism, the latter to neo-classical humanism.

In a wide sense, the corporation *genus* was virtually all-embracing, subsuming all categories of society from empire to guild. Since the twelfth century, it had included kingdom and nation. The language of *universitas regni* (corporation of the realm) had been especially invoked, in England, by those pressing the claims of Parliament, and of royal government by consent, representation and deliberation. The importance of this concept was that it provided a ready and respectable means of conceptualizing the kingdom or nation-state as an entity *without* immediate reference to royal authority. Since corporations were so very diverse in structure, it would make no sense to say that, for the corporation of the realm to hang together, it must be governed by a king. Moreover, the corporation idea drew attention to the totality of the membership, so that it was possible to say, in a manner also consonant with tribal tradition and with Aristotle, that any ruler was 'greater than each, less than all'.

But corporation also had a more specialized meaning, as a group formed and entered upon voluntarily, in particular by local members of the same profession, such as a guild or university. For these institutions, government by general consent and election of office-bearers were the norm. From this source, ideas related to the guild tradition played a formative part in early modern political thought. The constitutional implications of guild norms when applied to a large association, in which representation was necessary, had been charted for all to see in the pope–council disputes of the fifteenth century. Juan de Segovia, in particular, modelled the pattern of authority in the Catholic church upon the *collegium* (Black 1979, esp. 162–74). The result had been a republican theory of church government. During the French religious wars, this exercise was repeated by the Huguenots: the monarch was head of a corporation, dependent upon its consent for his authority. In a dispute between king and estates, it could reasonably be said that the latter represented the corporation as a whole, and therefore had the last word. Philippe de Mornay, for example, applied to the nation-kingdom the collegiate principle that a ruler is 'less than all, greater than each', so that 'the entire people is above the king when taken as a body' (cit. Skinner 1978, ii 334; cf. Skinner 1978, ii 268, 310, 323). During the English civil war, corporation theory was used in a similar way by some defenders of Parliament (Black 1979, 195–9; Tierney 1982, 97–102). We have noted how guild ideas on voluntary association, consent and election could be subsumed into the parliamentarian case, which the London guilds themselves strongly supported (see p.127).

In seventeenth-century English and North American political thought, we find that the principle of free association was widely invoked on behalf of territorial communities. The main inspiration here was the neo-Calvinist doctrine of the covenanted people of God as able to form a congregation on their own initiative; but the language used was that of corporation theory. The movement of thought is clear in an English separatist as early as 1613–16. 'A visible church of Christ under the Gospel' is 'a spiritual body politike ... the people also having power of free consent'; it is formed 'by a free mutuall consent of Believers joyning and covenanting to live as members of a holy society. ... By such free mutuall consent also all Civill perfect Corporations did first beginne' (cit. Hoepfl and Thompson 1979, 938).

The idea took root particularly in North America, where early political sentiment was reminiscent of the European communal movement some 500 years earlier. In 1647 the Rhode Island colonists, having noted that they had been given ('by our noble lords and honoured governors' of the Rhode Island and Providence company and 'by virtue of an ordinance of the Parliament of England') 'a free and absolute charter of civill incorporation', went on: 'Wee do jointly agree to incorporate ourselves and soe to remain a Body politicke by authority thereof, and ... do declare to own ourselves and one another to be Members of the same body, and to have right to the Freedom and privileges thereof' (Bartlett 156).

To this was added the belief that the form of government may legitimately be decided upon by general agreement amongst the original associates. This form of government often turned out to be based upon the age-old guild and communal values of consent, election and majority rule. In 1641 the Rhode Islanders said that it had been 'unanimously agreed upon' to form 'a Democracie, or popular government'. By this they meant: 'It is in the power of the body of Freemen orderly assembled, or the major part of them, to make or constitute just laws, by which they will be regulated, and to depute from among themselves such ministers as shall see them faithfully executed between man and man' (Bartlett 112, 156; Gooch 1967, 70–4; cf. Miller 1939, 408, 416, 429). It seems obvious that the Protestant emphasis upon the individual's act of faith, and the specifically Calvinist doctrine of the covenanted community, gave the impetus to this new application of an old concept of association. But the political language, and also the procedural values of consent and majority rule, were taken from the corporational milieu, and perhaps particularly from the English borough. Election was common to both sources. This was one way in which the model of lesser associations was applied to states.

This language and these values were also adopted by John Locke, though not before he had given further reasons for individual consent in his discussion of property and the state of nature. Locke's account of the way 'political society' is formed reads, from one point of view, like a general application of corporation theory, which he knew well from Grotius and Pufendorf (Laslett 1967, 74), to the state:

> When any number of men have so consented to make one community or government, they are thereby presently incorporated, and make one body politick, wherein the majority have a right to act and conclude the rest. For when any number of men have, by the consent of every individual, made a community, they have thereby made that community one body, with a power to act as one body, which is only by the will and determination of the majority. (viii. 349)

> That which makes the community, and brings men out of the loose state of nature, into one politick society, is the agreement which every one has with the rest to incorporate, and act as one body, and so be one distinct commonwealth. (xix. 424)

The corporational model was an efficacious argument for legislation by a representative assembly. It could legitimize either elective magistracy or parliamentary monarchy, depending on whether the model was applied in pure or adulterated form. In the normal corporation, the assembly dealt with major matters and appointed officials to oversee day-to-day management and enforcement of rules. This pattern emerged in Locke, who then adulterated the model in order to reconcile it with the peculiar constitution of England (x. 372).

The other possible miniature model for states was the joint-stock company, the roots of which go back to the sixteenth century; it also had historical links with the guilds, some of which had made joint-stock purchases (Clapham 1949, 262). The joint-stock company was 'anticipated in the Italian *societates*' (Clapham 1949, 262), and we have seen how Salamonio used the mercantile *societas* as a general political model (see p.85). Merchant companies based in England were chartered as territorial administrations in India and the New World. But in actual fact this model appears never to have been used explicitly, except by Peter Cornelius, a Dutchman who visited England during the Commonwealth. He suggested that for purposes of government 'individuals were to form joint-stock associations in which they lived together, but in which they might retain control of their property ... They were to elect a governor from among themselves for a year, and might re-elect him if they chose' (Gooch 1967, 177–8). It can be seen that this model would have suggested a democracy of property-owners, which could already be regarded as a legitimate deduction from the English parliamentarian and common law tradition.

This latter was probably uppermost in the mind of Locke when he discussed the relationship between property ownership and political authority, although the merchant company should not be altogether discounted; he was secretary to the Associated Proprietors of the Colony of Carolina from 1666 to 1672 (Laslett 1967, 26). Locke's repeated assertion that all legislative and executive power must be limited to the known 'end' for which it has been set up, namely 'the enjoyment of [men's] properties in peace and safety' (xi. 373, 378–9; cf. ix. 371; xiii. 385; xix. 431) is also quite compatible with his having used, not necessarily consciously, this model. When he defines the legislative and executive bodies as 'fiduciary' powers occupying a position of 'trust' in relation to the people (xi. 381; xiii. 385), Barker suggests that he was employing the notion of a legal 'trust' which, according to Maitland, was the closest equivalent in English law to the civil law corporation (Gierke 1958, 299n.; cf. Macpherson 1962, 251).

Thus social-contract theory – that essential seventeenth-century device for legitimizing the artifice of sovereignty – leaned, occasionally at least, on the corporational model of voluntary association. It was thanks to corporation theory, as well as to civic culture, that the political community itself, and in particular the nation, became the primary focus of allegiance, and that royal power became adjectival or even redundant (so that in the American Revolution 'patriots' were those who defied the king). The model of the corporation generated just that mixture of oligarchy and democracy which is characteristic of modern European 'democracy': election and consent, not participation, are the overriding norms.

13

CIVIL SOCIETY AND THE STATE

If the period c.1550–1640 saw guild theory brought to its highest point of development in Bodin and Althusius, the period c.1640–1789 was above all characterized by the development of the values of civil society. It hardly needs to be emphasized that the two successful political revolutions of early modern Europe, the Dutch Revolt of 1565–81 and the Revolution of 1688–9 in Great Britain, took place in Protestant countries which either were or were to become leaders in overseas commerce and sea power. Constitutional government, which had earlier flourished in the Italian and German cities, followed the path of trade and empire. It would appear, furthermore, that the values of civil society were first generally diffused among trading populations which were beginning to adopt a more tolerant view of what one might say in public (cf. Parker 1979, 269), and even of religious matters. The values which became dominant here were in the main those whose much earlier development in the European cities has already been noted: property rights, personal liberty and equality under the rule of law. As popular ideals, these were deeply rooted in Germanic–European Christianity, and they had been spelled out by theorists of civil society from the thirteenth century onwards (see ch.3). In the medieval towns, furthermore, belief in these ideals had already contributed to recurrent demands for wider political participation, just as it did in seventeenth-century England. On the other hand, during the later seventeenth and eighteenth centuries, the ideals of civil society were becoming ever more widely diffused in north-western Europe and France. They were acquiring a firmer and more convincing basis in theology and philosophy. And there were new developments. This was the heyday of the theory of natural rights (Tuck 1979, 143ff., chs 7–8). There was 'a new belief in the value and rights of the individual' (Macpherson 1962, 2), which may fairly be ascribed to Protestant influence. At the same time as this rise in individualism, the practical utility and moral legitimacy of corporations, whether towns or guilds, was increasingly questioned. New conceptions of man and the state relegated them to the shadows. 'Political society' or the sovereign state was thrust to the fore as the immediate expression of man's social nature, as the one and only adequate answer to his social needs, and as the sole morally meaningful human group other than the family.

In a seminal study, C.B. Macpherson has summarized the new features of the political theory arising out of civil society in seventeenth-century England:

> Society consists of relations of exchange between proprietors. Political society becomes a calculated device for the protection of this property and for the maintenance of orderly relation of exchange. .... Political society is a human contrivance for the protection of the individual's property in his person and goods, and for the maintenance of orderly relations of exchange between individuals regarded as proprietors.   (1962, 3, 264)

The emphasis began to fall on the instrumental rather than moral character of law and polity; and the purpose they are designed to serve is the protection and promotion of the system of exchange. Macpherson distinguishes between 'simple market society', in which the authoritative allocation of work is replaced by the authoritative enforcement of contracts and individuals pursue the rational maximization of gain, and 'possessive market society', in which land and labour become exchangeable commodities and inequality in enterprise, skill and resources is explicitly sanctioned (1962, 51–4). He argues that in seventeenth-century England, political theory was for the first time orientated towards the latter, and tacitly promoted the interests of a rising class of manufacturers and entrepreneurs. The crucial point, in Macpherson's view, was that it had to be agreed that the market might treat persons *unequally*. This, he believes, is the historical origin of the problems of philosophical coherence and credibility which face liberal theory today (1962, 1–4). The original premise of the great innovators in seventeenth-century English political theory, such as Hobbes, the Levellers, Harrington and Locke, was that all men are free and equal and have imprescriptible rights of person and property. But they worked out the application of these ideals to actual political structures in accordance with the requirements of 'possessive market society', accepting and legitimizing inequalities in property ownership, and making political rights dependent upon ownership of property. The result was a society in which all were formally free and equal, but in which in practice there was inequality and a new kind of dependence of man upon man, in particular of the wage-labourer upon the capitalist. Modern liberal theory requires a new language if it is to avoid these self-contradictions and realize in practice the values of liberty and equality in which it professes to believe (Macpherson 1962, 271ff.).

The ideals of 'simple market society' were certainly not new; nor, in fact, was trade in land (Macfarlane 1978, 107ff.). Furthermore, Renaissance political thought had been characterized by this very combination of legal liberty with inequality in wealth and talent, a pattern neatly encapsulated by Cicero himself (see p.40). What was new was the way that labour itself was coming to be regarded as 'a commodity exchangeable for benefit' (Hobbes 161; cf. Macpherson 1962, 59), as a form of property (Locke 305–6; cf. Macpherson 1962, 220–1) and as that which 'puts the difference of value upon every thing' (Locke 314). This brought labour out of the guild system of solidarity and into the system of exchange; it replaced work or calling as a fixed status, inherited or acquired, with its own 'honour', by occupational mobility and a free market in labour. It legitimized the transition from a guild-based and mercantilist economy to a free-market economy in the full sense; and it enabled the future science of political economy to disregard any rights of labour that were not justifiable in terms of exchange value. The precise point of innovation in this period was best grasped by Marx, who remarked how, prior to the full development of an economy based on capital, the guilds had prevented labour being treated as a commodity (1976, 284–5).

During the period c.1640–1789, two ideas relating to the process of exchange among proprietors merit special consideration: contract and personal independence. Both were rooted in earlier aspirations towards civil society, but were now given much greater scope and produced a radically different political perspective.

We have seen that contract is a distinctive type of exchange between persons, and from very early times stood high in the European scale of values. Contractual relationships of one kind or another played an important part in early Germanic society, in Christian theology, in feudal society and in the market economy. It being held no honour to exclude the king from human society, he too like any other man was bound by his contracts and promises: contractual obligation in this ordinary, private sense was well established in late medieval jurisprudence, as a feature of the ruler–ruled relationship. This view was adopted by the 'absolutist' Bodin, on the good ground that the sovereign could only be 'the avenger of mutual trust between private persons' if he himself was trustworthy; he was therefore 'obliged by pacts agreed with foreigners or citizens, just like a private person' (bk I, ch.viii, 86, 99; cf. Skinner 1978, ii 295). Moving closer to the pivot of the political system, contract had been widely used to solemnize and confirm for the future agreements reached between princes and parliaments; Marongiu suggests that 'the deep-rooted belief in the contractual nature of agreements between sovereigns and their peoples or estates' was one reason why some European parliaments survived during the age of absolutism (1968, 233). The traditional theory and practice of the contractual oath was invoked in 1581 by the United Provinces of the Netherlands as a justification for their resistance to the Spanish Crown and their declaration of de jure independence (Griffiths·1968, 511). The point about either oath or contract was that it established a relation of reciprocity between the parties on the matter in question; contract, in particular, gave rise to defined claims which could be pursued in law, failing which other means might be used (cf. Skinner 1978, ii 336; Stein and Shand 1974, 231).

But it was a considerable step from saying that there were contracts between princes and peoples to saying that the ruler–ruled relationship was in essence contractual. This step was first taken – perhaps not surprisingly, given the religious significance of oaths – by a theologian in a discussion of ecclesiastical authority. Johann Wessel Gansfort, a Netherlander (c.1418–89; cf. Skinner 1978, ii 22–3), declared that the relationship between a priest and his flock is like that between doctor and patient: the extent of his authority is defined by his competence and willingness to perform a mutually agreed service, and subordination is 'voluntary and spontaneous'. This has constitutional implications: for such a relationship can only be entered into by prior 'deliberation', and therefore 'it is almost in the nature of this obligation that subjects elect their superior'. Gansfort applied this principle to relationships between rulers and subjects in general:

> It should be the same with kings. Hence in every well-appointed commonwealth the supreme magistrate is restrained from insolence, either by the duration or by the extent of his authority, by annual tenure or by the votes of those consenting. For what does election mean but freedom of deliberation? (752, 765)

In this passage, the crucial transition has been made, so far as the ruler is concerned, from 'status' to 'contract'. It is already clear that the effect of applying the Germano-Christian idea of contract to rulership was to be the implantation of election and consent as constitutional norms, not only for corporations and cities, but for kingdoms and all states.

To this was added, in the later sixteenth century, the 'magical ring' that 'the word "covenant" had ... in Calvinist ears' (Hoepfl and Thompson 1979, 936). It was in the Huguenot movement in France, in the Dutch Revolt, in Scotland and among the English sectarians that contract or covenant finally became established as the dominant principle governing the relationship between rulers and peoples, and that the 'contract of government' was articulated (Allen 1928, 306; Hoepfl and Thompson 1979, 931, 937–8; Skinner 1978, ii 313–14, 325–6, 336, 342–3). Johannes Althusius, himself a Calvinist, was the first philosopher systematically to incorporate contract into political theory. He saw all associations, from the family to the state, as structured around mutual agreements for the exchange of goods, services and, in the case of political groups, legal right (see pp.135, 139). In this way contract entered into the formation of *society* as well as of government. He did not believe that family or city were dissoluble through breach of contract; but the kingdom or commonwealth, being a federation, was. The 'fundamental law' of a commonwealth is 'nothing other than certain pacts, under which several cities and provinces have come together and consented to maintain and defend a single commonwealth with common labour, counsel and aid': its very existence, therefore, depends upon continuous adherence to these 'conditions and pacts' (169, 404; cf. Hoepfl and Thompson 1979, 935–6).

This contractual view of society and government played a part in one of the greatest upheavals in man's view of himself and the world. Up till now, the great majority of philosophers, and so far as one knows of other people too, had believed that men were fundamentally sociable, and that the order of society established by God or nature was inherently harmonious. This corresponded to a belief in cosmic harmony; it is impossible to say whether one shaped the other. Possibly this was one reason why Manichaeanism was so shocking: it was a rejection of the establishment's creed which threatened far more than the creed of this particular establishment. It implicitly undermined one's whole view of the triumph of good over evil and of the ultimate unity of life; it was one way the oppressed could really wound their oppressors. The belief in cosmic and social harmony was of course far older than Europe and may go back to the beginnings of human consciousness; one finds it in religions and philosophies that have developed quite independently in different cultures and civilizations. To be sure, a Heracleitus might proclaim the rule of strife; but, so far as future generations were concerned, the reply of Plato had been decisive, that the One is supreme. Christianity had introduced a profound modification, which took account of contradictory experience: sin, suffering and death were significant powers, and the devil was to be feared (though not much by philosophers). The political implication was that, discord being due to sin, the right institutions were those which would reflect and implement concord by removing greed and corruption.

The perspective of Thomas Hobbes (1588–1679) was not altogether without precedent: in some ways, his account of human nature was Augustinian. Hobbes, like St Augustine, described man as inherently selfish and, for this reason, power-seeking and inexorably prone to conflict with other men. Augustine's state, like Hobbes's, could succeed in repressing conflict between men; but this was not the real solution for Augustine. Rather, it was the return of the soul to God through the inner appeal of Christ's love to his desperate self-awareness. For Hobbes, it was the social and political covenant. Hobbes's covenant is 'artificial': it does not change man's inner drives but his social context; man's moral conduct remains dependent upon the existence of a 'common power'. Man achieves peace in society by a rational calculation of his long-term interest.

Hobbes, then, used the social and governmental contract in an entirely new way. Man's basic motives are the continuation of life, the avoidance of death and pain, 'indolency of body'; to attain these and secure them for the future, he must seek power over other men (64); hence the 'condition of war

157

of every one against every one' (85). There is another, psychological reason why men are inherently competitive: 'man, whose joy consisteth in comparing himself with other men, can relish nothing but what is eminent', so that 'men are continually in competition for honour and dignity' (111). But man is also rational, and calculates that he can never attain his desires unless he can change the condition of conflict for one of peace. This he can achieve through a covenant with other men (87–93, 112–13). But, man being what he is, there is no guarantee that he will observe this covenant, or any moral principle, unless it is clear to him that it is in his interests to do so; and this will only be clear if there is 'some coercive power, to compel men equally to the performance of their covenants by the terror of some punishment, greater than the benefit they expect by the breach of their covenant' (94, cf.109–13). It was thus by means of the covenant that Hobbes was able to reconcile a view of man as competitive, power-seeking and aggressive with the prospect of social order and civilized life. It played a far more crucial role in his theory than in that of any of his predecessors. The idea of contract did not in itself imply a Hobbesian view of society; but, if one posited disharmony, contract could explain how harmony might be created.

Hobbes's analysis of the structure of human action owed much to Machiavelli's distillation of social and political experience. But his philosophical revolution was by no means confined to politics and society; it extended to human nature itself. Man's psychological drives lead to competitive conflict and never to social harmony or brotherhood; harmony is achieved by rational use of the covenant, but it never extends to men's inner attitudes towards one another in any context other than that provided by the covenant and the 'civil power'.

The extent of Hobbes's revolution now becomes clear. Social order and friendliness are artificial and imposed, based on reason not instinct; there is no inner harmony between men except that reached by calculation of individual interest. Love, brotherhood and mutual aid are secondary considerations. The values of civil society, above all security (see pp. 38–40) and equality, become absolutes. This was the final alternative to the organic view of society, the philosophy of friendship and the whole theory of corporations. It epitomizes an ultimate divide in political philosophy, and was intimately tied in with Hobbes's exclusion of theological premises, teleology and holism, and his use of empirical data and deductive analysis as the sole basis for political argument. It was only much later that a similar view was taken of organic nature as a whole, by Darwin.

The competitive view of man and society has become much more widespread since Hobbes, but it has not altogether replaced the organic view, least of all in popular thought. Hobbes's view of man, and of labour as a commodity, became a premise of capitalist economic theory and analysis. The early Political Economists implicitly followed Hobbes in seeing the reconciliation of human interests as the product of rational calculation of individual benefits. Rational maximization promotes economic growth and plenty; although men compete, their long-term interests need not conflict. Hegel, on the other hand, subsumed conflict, to which he gave as extensive a role as it had in traditional Christian thought, into an overall harmonious view, by means of the dialectic. Marx saw conflict as inevitable only in alienated class society. It reached its climax in capitalist society, when philosophers and economists falsely represented it as a general truth; but it was eventually to be resolved in communism. And in general the organic view of society and politics survived, in popular thought and philosophy, alongside the Hobbesian view; it had a great revival in the nineteenth century, and was once again commonly linked to a theory of corporations. It survives in myriad forms today; the new British Social Democrat Party is perhaps one example.

It was in England that the doctrine of freedom of trade and production – the antithesis of guild doctrine – developed earliest and, compared with the rest of Europe, remained strongest in modern times. The contrast here between England and the Continent was probably related to the way in which the legal and political legacy of the Middle Ages developed under the Tudors and Stuarts. Guilds could become an instrument for state control and royal exploitation of industry and commerce; Parliament was setting its face against Crown monopolies as an alternative method of raising royal revenues. The peculiarities of English social *moeurs* (Macfarlane 1978) should also not be discounted. Sir Edward Coke (1552–1634), chief justice from 1606 to 1616, who after 1640 became '*the* legal authority' (Hill 1962, 28), regarded guild privileges as no better than other forms of monopoly. In several judgments, he ruled against guild privilege, on the ground that it was a breach of 'the liberty of the subject', even appealing to *Magna Carta* (Hill 1965, 233–7; Wagner 1935). This became standard parliamentarist doctrine from the Civil War onwards (cf. Hill and Dell, *The Good Old Cause*, 425–6; Macpherson 1962, 143). In 1702 the House of Commons declared that 'trade ought to be free and not restrained'; in 1753 it informed the framework knitters that restrictions upon entry to their trade were 'injurious and vexatious ... contrary to the liberty of the subject' (cit. Leeson 1979, 79).

To what extent this was a continuation of an earlier tendency in English common law is uncertain; it is quite possible that both Continental mercantilism and the English free-trade ideology were the result of emphasizing different aspects of earlier practice and opinion, which was nothing like so consistently favourable to guilds as used to be supposed. On the other hand, Coke's 'unspoken assumption that men have a right to do what they will with their own person and skill' (Hill 1965, 236) looked forward to Locke and Adam Smith. Coke's decisions and Parliament's attitude helped to prise loose state control of trade and industry, which, by contrast, became much greater in France during the same period.

It was (aptly enough) Hobbes who first enunciated the peculiarly modern-capitalist potential of such a view, when he stated that 'a man's labour also, is a Commodity exchangeable for benefit, as well as any other thing' (161; cf. Macpherson 1962, 62, 148). The idea that labour itself could be bought and sold was, as Marx perceived (1976, 479–80), an essential feature of the development of industrial capitalism out of the guild economy.

In the eighteenth century the Physiocrats and the classical Political Economists took these principles as reflections of the order of nature, and built them as basic assumptions into their economic theories. The Physio-crats regarded the privileges of guilds and urban communes as 'contrary to the order of nature and the rights of the nation'; corporations of merchants or artisans 'disturb order by their rivalries and jealousies' and 'form jealous little republics, which disregard the general interest of the kingdom' (cit. Petit-Dutaillis 1970, 262–3). The argument from natural economic order reached its climax in Adam Smith's *The Wealth of Nations* (1776). The existing guild system, almost universal in Europe, led to inefficient deployment of both labour and stock; corporate privileges, restrictions on entry to a craft and on the number of apprentices kept prices, wages and profits unduly high. 'The exclusive privileges of corporations ... keep up the market price of particular commodites above the natural price, and maintain both the wages of labour and the profits of stock employed about them somewhat above their natural rate' (164). The guild system fails to ensure good workmanship and 'has no tendency to form young people for industry'; 'the real and effectual discipline which is exercised over a workman is not that of his corporatioñ, but that of his customers'. Guild restrictions injured the ordinary labourer: 'The patrimony of a poor man lies in the strength and dexterity of his hands; and to hinder him from employing this strength and dexterity in what manner he thinks proper without injury to his neighbour is a plain violation of this most sacred property'. Smith reiterated the age-old accusation against guilds, that 'people of the same trade seldom meet together, even for merriment and diversion, but the conversation ends in a conspiracy against the public, or in some contrivance to raise prices' (bk I, ch.10, pt 2, esp. 222, 225, 232–3). These arguments would soon be turned against the nascent trade unions.

Smith, like other Enlightenment thinkers, placed no value on the corporation and appealed over it to individual rights. The demands of solidarity were being subordinated to those of exchange, productive work to the laws of the market. But it was not a purely 'economic' argument. Part of the strength of his case rested on his appeal to a particular notion of justice. He reiterated the traditional concern for the public at large and for personal liberty; in addition, he invoked the individual worker's right freely to use his 'property', 'the strength and dexterity of his hands'. This stood in the place of the guild notion of justice as meaning secure employment and livelihood. The ensuing growth of trade unions and business corporations suggests that, as an analysis of the real world, Smith's thesis was highly programmatic and prescriptive.

Even in Germany similar ideas were being expressed. Becher saw 'maximum consumption of material goods' as an interest common to merchant, artisan and peasant (Walker 1971, 150). Johann Justi (1705?–71) formulated an alliance, which dominated later German political debate, between individual liberty and state power: since 'ambition to rise and the wish for material comfort' are the mainsprings of human action, and since material plenty 'would benefit individuals and through them the whole, which was the sum of individuals', 'It was therefore the place of government to *introduce* the *natural* free conditions in which all would work together spontaneously' (Walker 1971, 164, 169). The rationale of this alliance, Walker points out, was precisely the communitarian guild town, from whose smothering tutelage the individual could only be released through state action. Similarly, German jurists of this period tended to advocate greater state supervision of the guild system (Gierke 1958, 162–94).

A basic postulate of civil society was that men confront one another on equal terms in the market-place and before the law; legal freedom and legal equality are the minimum requirements. The corresponding moral ideal is autonomy. The real-life problem was that in existing society men were unequal in wealth and contracted all kinds of relations of dependence upon one another. Most ideologists of civil society were content to let matters ride and do the best they could in an imperfect world. Besides, the most immediate problem was to realize the postulates of civil society for those *not* already burdened with extreme poverty or personal dependence, to secure political rights for all those who could reasonably be expected to exercise them autonomously. But Protestantism had reinforced the notion of men's radical spiritual equality and independence. It had done so by emphasizing the sovereignty of God upon Whom *all* men are unconditionally dependent. As Dunn puts it, discussing Locke: 'In his relationship with God every man was prised loose from the tangle of seventeenth-century deference' (1969, 260).

Jean-Jacques Rousseau (1712–78), in his attempt to construct a political authority under which men could be free and a society in which self-interest coincided with duty, took a similarly radical view of equality and independence as *political* ideals. In the *Discourse on Inequality* (1755), he had argued that existing inequalities between master and slave, powerful and weak, rich and poor have no moral foundation (Grimsley 1973, 34–40). In *The Social Contract* (1762), he argued that if each citizen was to make his own contribution to the articulation of the general will – as liberty and justice required that he should – there must not only be equality of legal status and of political access, but an approximate equality of wealth: 'No citizen must be wealthy enough to be able to buy another, and none poor enough to be forced to sell himself' (II.xi). Otherwise, some citizens would be beholden to others and so incapable of political autonomy. Men must enter the legislative assembly as independent agents. In real life, then, approximate economic equality is a condition of personal independence.

It is the social contract or 'pact' itself which, by giving men civil liberty in place of natural liberty and elevating 'instinct' into 'Justice' (I.viii; II.vii), creates the condition of personal independence. It does so by replacing the dependence of one man upon another by the dependence of each upon all: 'each one, giving himself to all, gives himself to nobody' (I.vi). This same pact creates the 'city' or 'body politic' (I.vi). The condition of citizenship sets men free from personal dependence and arbitrary domination, thus fulfilling an age-old aspiration of civil society (see pp.38–9), and it does so by subjecting them to the sovereignty of the general will, with which their better selves will always agree (I.vii). Spelling this out, Rousseau says that the *relation* or *rapport* of citizens with each other must be 'as small as possible', but their relations with 'the whole body' must be 'as great as possible, in such a way that each citizen is in perfect independence of all the others, and in very great dependence upon the City ... for it is only the power of the State which creates the liberty of its members' (II.xii).

In the first place, then, legal and political equality – the age-old aspirations of civil society – are written into the terms of the social contract; they are not merely desirable goals but the necessary conditions of true policy. *La condition est égale pour tous* (I.vi; cf. II.iv). But, in the second place, this final clinching of the principles of civil society requires a deeper union among men as citizens than even earlier corporate theory had ever envisaged. The state is a 'moral and political body' (I.vii; II.iv) in the new sense of an association which alone makes morality possible. This leads to a situation which, from the viewpoint of civil society, is intolerable:

> So that the social pact may not be an empty formula, it tacitly includes this understanding, *which alone gives force to the rest*, that whoever refuses to obey the general will, will be constrained to do so by the whole body. This will mean nothing else but that one will be forced to be free; for such is the condition which, giving each citizen to the Fatherland, safeguards him from all personal dependence. (I.vii, my italics)

This is no longer civil society in its previously recognized form. On the other hand, by safeguarding the independence of the small producer in this way, Rousseau's perspective would achieve one of the basic aims of craft-guilds. This poses the question whether, in the real world, guild and civil society are in the long term compatible, and also whether civil society, when its principles are seriously applied, does not become something else. Marx would have more to say about that.

PART III

FROM THE
FRENCH REVOLUTION
TO THE PRESENT

In the third part, we shall be concerned with ideas relating to the nearest modern equivalents to the craft-guild, namely trade unions, co-operatives and corporations. It will be useful here to distinguish between the *ethos* of the trade union movement (ch.14), the *ideology* of specific programmes such as the co-operative movement (ch.15) and corporatism, and the *philosophy* of corporation and community (for these distinctions, see pp.246–8); this last took the argument back to the first principles of human association. The German Romantics introduced a new idea of community (ch.16). Hegel sought to replace the guild by the nationwide corporation, which was to subsume and transcend guild functions and values, and to which he assigned a crucial moral role in his vision of the modern state (ch.17). Gierke extended the idea of real group personality to all kinds of association, including communities of labour – of which he gave the medieval craft-guild and the modern producers' co-operative as prime examples. Tönnies, on the other hand, treated Community (*Gemeinschaft*), into which he incorporated certain guild values, as an analytical concept for sociological research (ch.18). Finally, corporatism attempted to integrate vocationally defined groups of workers into a theory of the modern state; Durkheim argued the case for occupational groups on the basis of sociological theory (ch.19).

14

GUILDS AND TRADE UNIONS: THE ETHOS OF MUTUAL AID

The industrial revolution, beginning in Britain in the mid-eighteenth century and making its full impact on Germany only a century later, combined with the French Revolution of 1789 and the Napoleonic era to alter beyond recognition the organizational and theoretical landscapes charted thus far. Britain, France and Germany were out of phase. Major differences, emerging from Britain's immunity to political revolution and the disjointed impact of industrialization, have done much to shape modern Europe. They have reached far beyond, as the USA took ideological cues from Britain, and Russia (largely via Marx) from Germany.

The English guilds, never a serious political force, had been in decline well before 1750, under the twin pressures of legal liberalism and parliamentary aristocracy. This facilitated the rapid and ruthless growth of industrial capitalism, after which the fate of guilds as economic powers was sealed anyway; they were legally abolished in 1835, though the tramping system, a tattered remnant of the crafts, survived longer (Leeson 1979, 100ff., 139, 169ff.). In France, the still intact guild system was abolished by law in 1791, as part of the revolutionary republican attack on corporations and separate jurisdictions. The less visible *compagnonnages*, however, survived as effective workmen's organizations well into the nineteenth century; as miniature freemasonries, some survive today (Coornaert 1966, 6). But in both countries, as the traditional artisans' and journeymen's organizations disappeared, their place was taken by new organizations of industrial workers, which took over many of their functions, organizational techniques and ethos. The French *compagnonnages*, and also the German *Gesellenverbände* (journeymen's associations) made an important contribution to radical working-class politics (Coornaert 1966, 333ff.; Hobsbawm 1971, 162ff.; Sewell 1980); the British connection will be considered below.

Only in Germany did guilds themselves play a significant role in the nineteenth century, thus making for a distinctive political culture and social philosophy. As before, their fate was bound up with the small 'home town', though they functioned in large cities too. Their position in the German milieu was related both to late industrialization and to the Napoleonic experience. It was also bound up with the continuing German debate about the location of *Gemeinschaft* (community) between individual and state, and the peculiarly German constellation of forces, in which individual liberty was ranged alongside state power against guild and commune.

In Germany, the values of civil society were only beginning to re-develop in juristic and philosophical thought when French conquest and hegemony attempted to impose them by force. Eighteenth-century German bureaucrats had been designing to reform and weaken the guild system under state supervision by easing the admission of newcomers, and by facilitating the movement of population and the development of wealth, the freedom of trade and of industrial innovation. For a brief period they joined forces with the agencies of Napoleonic power: the economic control of guilds was either suspended or curtailed in the south and west, and brought into line with state policy in Prussia and the north (Hamerow 1958, 21–30; Walker 1971, ch.6). But the guild towns proved impenetrable by reformers' edicts; this 'people' had little desire for the individualist tenets of popular sovereignty *à la française*. Bavaria was already abandoning the administrative struggle against her 9800 guilds, when, in the words of the Bremen shoemakers, the 'World Court' (of history) decided in favour of 'the return of our honorable, centuries-old associations' (cit.Walker 1971, 248). Napoleon's defeat led to a massive reinstatement of guild and town privileges (Walker 1971, ch.8). In the early nineteenth century, 'A greater proportion of the German population lived in small towns ... than at any other time' (Walker 1971, 332). In the 1810s, and again in the 1830s, after another interlude of bureaucratic encroachment, guild regulation of the artisan economy was re-established (Walker 1971, chs 9–10). Culturally, the Biedermeier 1830s and 1840s were dominated by a 'hometown style' of 'provincial homeliness and quiet social familiarity' – *Gemütlichkeit* (Walker 1971, 307, 328). Guilds lasted longest where, since the mid-seventeenth century, they had been toughest, meshed into the polity of small independent towns, conservative organisms in a familiar world about to change beyond recognition. The opposition, meanwhile, had decided that the only way round the problem was economic liberalization – *Manchestertum* (Walker 1971, 213–14).

In the run-up to 1848, the guilds' position became locked into the 'social question' of poverty and 'the propertyless or proletariat', as the Social Catholic Franz Bader put it in 1835 (McLellan 1972, 19–22; Walker 1971, 352). A large section of educated opinion and, increasingly, state governments looked to economic liberalism as the means of promoting national wealth. The alternative was to give town communities responsibility for finding a home and subsistence, if not a craft livelihood, for those unable to set up on their own or find regular employment (Walker 1971, 336ff.). Corporatism was already in the air. The depression and crop failures of the 1840s made threatened artisans all the more determined to cling to their traditional privileges (Hamerow 1958, 102ff.); while journeymen and ordinary labourers, in the wake of the Silesian weavers' rising of 1844, demanded a broader corporate system that would recognize their right to work. In the revolution of 1848, liberalism and guild corporatism met head-on, while state governments salvaged their position by concessions to the guilds, and Prussia watched.

> The liberals gave the Revolution its leadership, but the artisans provided it with defenders and martyrs. Everywhere during the spring uprising hungry guildsmen fought for a restoration of the guild system and the victory of man over wealth. (Hamerow 1958, 102)

The small-town guildsmen 'were nationalist along with nearly everybody else' because to them 'the *Volk* meant the people, in contrast with the states', which had repeatedly attempted to undermine guild and communal autonomies (Walker 1971, 364).

The Frankfurt parliament, of which barely 3 per cent were guildsmen, sweetened the pill of Reich citizenship for all and full occupational and residential freedom, with a pledge of local self-government (Walker 1971, 366–85). Meanwhile a national artisan congress assembled at Frankfurt in July, and presented a 'solemn protest against economic freedom', demanding limits on factory output and the restriction of the practice of crafts to persons approved by guilds. It recommended representation of guilds at all levels, culminating in a national craft assembly to formulate economic legislation (Hamerow 1958, 143–5). The journeymen, on the other hand, whose representatives also met at Frankfurt as the 'General German Labour Congress', presented their own very different programme: easier entry to guilds, manhood suffrage, a minimum wage and a shorter working day (Hamerow 1958, 147). This anticipated the programme which the German Social Democrats, in common with labour movements elsewhere, would soon adopt. To these the liberal parliament replied: 'Are we then to recreate the prosperity of our cities by putting together again the ruins of corporate control, by introducing once more the Middle Ages within the demolished walls, by turning basic social and economic laws upside down?' (cit. Hamerow 1958, 153). The conviction that 'capital and factories had to be free to spread through the country to where labor was, and labor had to be free to go and meet them ... determined the [Frankfurt parliament's] majority that there had to be freedom of movement, of settlement, and to acquire, accumulate and invest property' (Walker 1971, 374). Thus 1848 witnessed the first and last attempt by guilds and journeymen to create a national organization.

Most German states, including Prussia, supported the guilds, thus outflanking the Frankfurt parliament and, it was hoped, restoring order and native *moeurs* (Hamerow 1958, 179, 230; Walker 1971, 385ff.). As Bismarck put it,

Handicraftsmen ... constitute the backbone of the burgher class ... whose survival is essential to the healthy national life. ... I believe that the inexpensive garments of the clothing shop may after all lie uneasily on our backs, when those who make them despair of earning their daily bread honestly. (cit. Hamerow 1958, 229)

Prussia, supporting some 4600 guilds in the 1850s, thus moved into line with the south and west (Hamerow 1958, 179). In this process 'hometown society was clearly ranged against democracy' (Walker 1971, 393). But Bismarck soon discovered that the guild system meant 'excessive prices for manufactured articles, indifference to customers ... protracted lunch hours' (cit. Hamerow 1958, 250). During the 1860s, restrictions on occupational freedom and factory production were lifted in one state after another, culminating in a decree of the Prussian-dominated North German Federation (1868) which effectively ended guild control; in 1869 this was made law under the Second Reich (Hamerow 1958, 252; Walker 1971, 411ff.). Industrialization finally destroyed the German guilds and, with them, the guild-town communities (Walker 1971, 408).

The guilds' role as protectors of productive workers against the uncertainties of free markets was, however, promptly taken over by the German Social Democratic Party, which held its first congress at Eisenach in the very year the guilds were finally disbanded, and there adopted a quasi-Marxist programme. Minimum wages, shorter working hours and governmental supervision of welfare were a projection of traditional journeymen's demands into the new era. Already in 1848 Stephan Born, a printer-journeyman, had founded 'The Fraternity of German Labour' which called for producers' and consumers' co-operatives (Grebing 1969, 29–30). One way or another, guild ideals were being melted down and recast in the mould of modern socialism.

In the early nineteenth century, as in the eleventh and twelfth centuries, Europe seethed with peasant, artisan and industrial organizations, secret or open, mystical or pragmatic, revolutionary or moderate. Only there was less cultural or geographical space for them to move in: many lived a shadowy existence on the fringes of civilized society. In particular – and again reminiscent of an earlier period – there was a wide diffusion of secret fraternities and artificial kinship, especially in southern Europe, some of which have lasted into the twentieth century; the Mafia is an outstanding example (Hobsbawm 1971, 35, 47, 54–5, 97–9). The chief opening available to them (mischief apart) was mutual insurance and collective self-help among people living under the threat of poverty and insecurity, whether peasants, artisans or industrial workers, and, in particular, the corporate organization of the new and hitherto largely formless industrial working class. Some brotherhoods and, later in the century, trade unions assumed a political function by articulating the interests and aspirations of disadvantaged groups, of which there were many. Hobsbawm goes so far as to claim that, during the period 1789 to 1848, 'the secret revolutionary brotherhood was by far the most important organization for changing society in Western Europe' (1971, 162). By means of oaths, secrecy and close mutual ties, such groups kept alive and transmitted the more radical ideas generated by the French Revolution; ritual, sometimes borrowed from the Freemasons, played an important part in sustaining their sense of corporate identity (Hobsbawm 1971, 150–74, esp. 164, 172). One such group was the Irish Republican Brotherhood, dating from the 1850s. On the Continent 'the great age of the brotherhoods as a single, at least theoretically united, family probably ended with the 1830 revolutions' (Hobsbawm 1971, 166–7). The distinctly secular ideas of anarchism and Marxism assisted the transition from ritual brotherhood to political party (cf. Hobsbawm 1971, 169, 172).

The modern industrial society of Europe has no institutional equivalent to the craft-guild. The sphere of operation and economic function of the typical craft-guild were contingent upon its members being manual craftsmen separately owning their own equipment and workshop and managing their own business. (Such people exist today, notably in the building and repairing trades, but without guilds.) As a dominant form of economic organization the guild inevitably belongs to an age and culture in which handicraft production accounts for the greatest proportion of manufactured goods. In industrial society, employers' organizations are generally loose confederations, organized nationally rather than locally, and are little concerned with limiting the number of businesses, monopolizing local trade, maintaining standards of production or drawing up rules for apprentices. The last two functions are sometimes fulfilled by certain professional associations, such as the British Medical Association, the Law Society and the Institute of Chartered Accountants. On the other hand, journeymen's societies and *compagnonnages*, which evolved within or out of guilds and modelled their organization upon them, do have an approximate equivalent in the industrial trade union. This is because in both cases the members are wage-earners, whose primary concerns are minimum wages, decent working conditions and continuity of employment (cf. K. Hawkins, 1981, 15–16). The first recorded strikes to achieve these ends occurred in the Flemish cloth industry during the thirteenth century. Furthermore, trade unions have often had a moral ethos in some ways comparable with that of the guilds themselves (see p.176; Sewell 1980); with the guilds, as well as the *compagnonnages*, they share certain beliefs about the right of association, constitutional norms and practices, and the tactic of collective bargaining.

In Britain, quasi-trade unions among skilled workers date back to the seventeenth century (Court 1962, 133–4; Dobson 1980; Rule 1981). They survived the legal ban imposed by the Combination Acts of 1799–1800, which were repealed in 1824–5, to expand in the 1830s and again in the 1850s (Court 1962, 248; Pelling 1976, 24ff.). The first Trades Union Congress met in 1868. Their legal status was clarified and made more secure by legislation in 1871–5, and again in 1906. From the 1870s their growth was much more rapid, leading to the 'New Unionism' among unskilled workers following the successful London dock strike of 1889 (Court 1962, 249, 288–9; Pelling 1976, 89ff.). In France, where the ban on associations issued in 1791 was reinforced by article 1781 of the Napoleonic *Code Civil* and a further law of 1834, the *compagnonnages* of skilled workers remained the chief labour organizations until the 1860s. Legal restrictions on workers' associations were finally lifted in 1864 and 1868, and thereafter trade unions appeared on the scene; their legal position was further secured in 1884 (Clapham 1948, 77–81, 269). In Germany, where guilds disappeared only in the 1860s, the first organizations of industrial workers were more political in nature, beginning with Lassalle's General German Labour Union in 1863 and the Social Democratic Workers' Party, founded in 1869 under Marxist influence; these two merged in 1875 (Clapham 1948, 327–8; Grebing 1969, 32ff.). Trade unions only developed in any real strength after 1901 (Clapham 1948, 329ff.).

The early decline of guilds and the precocious development of trade unions in Great Britain were to some extent connected: both phenomena were certainly related to industrialization, and probably to the relative freedom of British society (cf. Unwin 1904, 227). (This precocity and long history may be a factor in the relative strength and independence of trade unions in Britain today.) It also seems likely that trade unions, along with other working-class associations, filled a gap left by the guilds. Most historians of British trade unionism have, until very recently, argued that there was little or no continuity with the craft-guilds (Pelling 1976, 9; S. and B. Webb 1920, 4, 12ff.). But it now looks as if this underestimates the complex variety of craft-guild organizations, shading off into journeymen's societies, in the later seventeenth and eighteenth centuries, and their capacity for survival and revival in altered form to meet new needs. The word 'union' itself was as old as the craft-guilds (see p.13); in 1796 the London cordwainers advocated 'a lasting union among journeymen of any trade' in order to maintain bargaining power (Leeson 1979, 95).

Long ago, Unwin suggested that the yeomanry or 'commonalty' of small masters and journeymen within guilds dominated by great merchant-producers, new splinter-guilds formed by small masters, and the diffusion of guild habits and beliefs by small craftsmen reduced to wage-labourers among the new industrial working-classes, played an important part in the formation of trade unions or similar bodies from as early as the late seventeenth century. Activities among labourers in the building trades around 1670 reveal, he argued,

> a combination of workers endeavouring to appropriate the small masters' method of incorporation to the protection of their own status as wage-earners. ... By its failure along these traditional lines, the wage-earning class was driven into secret combinations, from the obscurity of which the trade union did not emerge till the nineteenth century. At this point, then, it may be said that the latest phase of the transformed gild and the earliest phase of the trade union meet and blend. (1904, 213, cf. 200, 221)

The small master reduced to journeyman status was led

> to furnish, by virtue of his traditions and of his capacity for social action, the nucleus of a new form of organization ... the labour troubles of the eighteenth century, which marked the beginnings of trades-unionism, were mostly due to the efforts of this class of reduced small masters to organize themselves along with the journeymen on a common footing as wage-earners. (Unwin 1904, 204, 225–6)

'It is exceedingly probable', Unwin went on, 'that patient local research would reveal many similar antecedents of trades-unionism in the records of the country cloth trade' (1904, 226). This prediction is now in the process of being confirmed (Dobson, 1980; Leeson 1979; Rule 1981, 189–90; cf. Clapham 1949, 260–1).

What we have, then, is in part cultural diffusion, 'the spirit of imitation ... the transmission of the capacity for collective action' (Unwin 1904, 226). Unwin's summary of the situation as he saw it may still be taken as a fair estimate of the significance of the guild tradition in this context.

> The uncritical attempts that have sometimes been made to bring these two widely different forms of industrial organization [sc. craft-guilds and trade unions] into some sort of historical connexion have had a sound instinct behind them ... a dim recognition of the truth that a social institution needs to be explained by a reference to antecedents of its own kind. Economic conditions will not of themselves produce a trade union, nor religious convictions a church. ... [Social character] to a large extent is transmitted through conscious imitation of the older generation by the younger, of the class which has already achieved organization by that which has not. ... In this sense the Gild is to be regarded – not indeed as the parent but – as the ancestor of the Trade Union, as it was also the ancestor of the modern Employers' Association, and of many other existing forms of social organization ... a connexion undoubtedly exists which is real, significant and vital, but it needs to be traced through intermediate links. (1904, 8–9)

Others, on the contrary, have argued that some form of 'labour conscious-ness' and workers' organization is liable to arise more or less spontaneously under adverse conditions; as with the development of towns (see p.62), it is a question of how much – particularly with regard to the forms of organization adopted – one ascribes to human instinct and how much to cultural tradition.

As Leeson has recently pointed out, in some cases these links suggested by Unwin were 'not only traditional and imitative, but also organizational' (1979, 275). In addition to those already mentioned, one such link was the tramping system (Leeson 1979, 18, 103, 110–21, 259–76). Yet another was the Friendly Societies, whose rise coincided almost exactly with the guilds' decline around 1700. Not unlike the protection-guilds of the Dark Ages, they provided their members with insurance against sickness, poverty and bereavement, and met the expenses of a decent funeral; and they held ceremonial occasions and annual 'outings' (Godsden 1961; Thompson 1968, 460). In the late eighteenth and early nineteenth centuries, Friendly Societies afforded a cover for trade union activity, and some actually evolved into trade unions (K. Hawkins 1981, 18–19; Thompson 1968, 459). They continued to flourish throughout the nineteenth century, registering 4 million members in 1875.

In Germany and France the journeymen's organizations, the *Gesellenver-bände* and *compagnonnages*, dovetailed with the early trade union move-ment; they 'took over certain trade-union functions in the early industrial period before giving way to the more up-to-date trade-union pattern', for which they themselves provided a prototype (Hobsbawm 1971, 109; Coornaert 1966, 283, 303). For the most part, the old journeymen's organizations had lasted longer than in Britain, and their members swelled the ranks of the first trade unions. The emigrant German labourers in Paris and London who formed the League of Outlaws and the League of the Just, which 'in turn, under Marx and Engels, became the League of the Communists for which the famous manifesto was written', were also steeped in the tradition of the *Gesellenverbände* (Hobsbawm 1971, 168–9; Lichtheim 1968, 166–7). And, just as earlier in England the decline of guilds had been followed by the rise of Friendly Societies and trade unions, so the final demise of the guilds in Germany was followed, yet more rapidly, by the rise of a new workers' organization: for 'the law of 1869 [against the guilds], the final consecration of individualism, coincided precisely with the foundation at the Eisenach Congress, by Liebknecht and Bebel, of the Social-Democratic Labour Party' (Clapham 1948, 325). One important aspect of continuity here was belief in a regulated economic order and opposition to economic liberalism, the guild ethos thus providing a framework for the adoption of socialism.

Trade unions, Friendly and Co-operative societies and the like, tended to adopt a democratic mode of organization broadly similar to that of the craft-guilds themselves. Rules and rule books, in some cases taken over in amended form from earlier craft-guilds, were strictly adhered to (Leeson 1979, 275; Thompson 1968, 457–9). Office-bearers were elected and accountable. General meetings of members approved the rules and the constitution, and elected the officials. When increased numbers necessitated a representative assembly, there was a tendency for representatives to be mandated delegates, more accountable to the membership than, for example, British Members of Parliament are to their constituents. Today, British trade unions are more likely to consult the entire membership on matters of supreme importance than is Parliament; this amounts to a return to the first principles of the tradition out of which they partly evolved. Modern labour organizations – at least those that have arisen spontaneously – tend to be more democratic than modern states. The present dispute in the British Labour Party over the relation between Labour Members of Parliament and the Labour Party as a whole is – among other things – evidence of an inclination to replicate these features of direct democracy in the national political system.

This form of self-government, this 'code (sometimes in the form of model rules) which was extended to ever-wider sections of working people' (Thompson 1968, 458) was at least in part the inheritance of earlier craft or journeymen's societies (cf. Unwin 1904, 200, 213, 226). In Britain, it was reinforced by the tradition of sober constitutionalism among Nonconformist churches, such as the Independents, Congregationalists and Baptists. Among these, Beatrice Webb says with slight exaggeration, 'Each man and woman voted on equal terms for the elders or deacons – a committee of management – to whom they entrusted the common purse, and frequently the choice of minister'; she rightly observes that 'It is difficult to overestimate the debt which the English democracy owed to the magnificent training given by Protestant Dissent in the art of self-government' (1930, 36–7).

Workers' organizations believed implicitly in the right of association, essential as it was to their success. Despite the Combination Acts, the liberal temper of British society meant that freedom of association was in fact less threatened in early nineteenth-century Britain than on the Continent. Appeal was made to national tradition; in 1760 a tailors' society argued that 'it has been an ancient custom in the kingdom of Great Britain for divers Artists to meet together and unite themselves in societies' (cit. S and B. Webb 1920, 24n.; cf. Ludlow 1869, 391–2, 406). Once again, Nonconformist tradition reinforced a belief which itself went back to very early times in Europe (B. Webb 1930, 36). Early craft unions, like their forbears, had a strong sense of the honour, or what the Manchester smallware weavers in the 1750s called 'the Rights and Privileges', of their trade

(Leeson 1979, 275; Thompson 1968, 457, 464–6). This remains a factor in industrial disputes today.

The guild values of fraternity, friendship and mutual aid were inherited by friendly societies, trade unions and other organizations of the new industrial working class, including some radical political groups. It is here that we must look for the continuation of the earlier guild ethos. It is no doubt true of the early trade unions, as of the medieval guilds, that 'the printed constitutions of working-class associations represent rather the aspirations than the everyday actions of their members' (S. and B. Webb, cit. K. Hawkins, 1981, 18). Nevertheless, themes contained in persistently repeated slogans and mottoes tell us something about the social beliefs of those involved. The banners, tramping cards and drinking pots of Friendly Societies and early unions bore mottoes such as 'Industry and Benevolence unite us in Friendship', 'We assist each other in time of need', 'May you be united in love' (*amore sitis uniti*), and 'Unity is strength' (cit. Leeson 1979, endpapers, illustrations between pp.96–7, 128–9, 240–1). Early nineteenth-century working-men's associations proclaimed 'brotherhood', 'love and unity with self-protection' and the aspiration for 'a sure, lasting and loving society ... to promote friendship and true Christian charity' (cit. Thompson 1968, 460–2; S. and B. Webb 1920, 24n.). 'Brothers' was the title claimed by the Sicilian *Fasci*; the slogan 'All men are brothers' was adopted by the League of the Just (Hobsbawm 1971, 99; Lichtheim 1968, 167). 'The Fraternity of German Labour' was the name of a German workers' association formed in 1848, whose newspaper declared that 'the basis of fraternization is mutuality and solidarity' (cit. Grebing 1969, 29–30). Thompson sees the working-class communities of early industrial Britain as permeated by 'the rituals of mutuality' and 'the workaday ethos of mutual aid' (1968, 456, 462). It would appear that the ethic of mutual aid was, indeed, as prominent in workers' organizations in late eighteenth- and early nineteenth-century Britain as it had been in the medieval crafts (cf. Thompson 1968, 457, 460–4, 869). This could give rise to simple expressions of political philosophy which, except perhaps for the absence of reference to the deity, could have come straight from the Middle Ages:

> We, the members of this society, taking it into our serious consideration, that man is formed a social being ... in continual need of mutual assistance and support; and having interwoven in our constitutions those human and sympathetic affections which we always feel at the distress of any of our fellow creatures. ...
>
> (*The Sociable Society*, Newcastle 1812: cit. Thompson 1968, 461)

It has recently been argued that a similar ethos was passed on from the guilds and *compagnonnages* to the early industrial labour movement in France (Sewell 1980). In Britain, there is evidence of Protestant Christian influence, especially in the concept of brotherhood; the Warrington Co-operative Society prefixed its rules with the scriptural sentiment 'They helped every one his brother, and every one said to his brother "Be of good cheer"' (cit. S. and B. Webb 1920, 46). In this particular context, the kind of influence exerted by Christianity in medieval and modern times appears to have been broadly similar (cf. Thompson 1968, 40–53, 385–440, 917ff.). The ideal of fraternal harmony found a home in working-class culture at the very time when the doctrine of self-adjusting competition was winning adherents in other quarters.

In later nineteenth-century France, the term *solidarité* was increasingly preferred to *fraternité* (Hayward 1960, 17; cf. Grebing 1969, 30). It had perhaps a more secular and even scientific ring, suggesting that men not only ought to be but properly speaking were group creatures; it was also related to holistic notions of society current among the first generation of sociologists. This feature was brought out in the social philosophy of Duguit, Durkheim and Paul-Boncour (Hayward 1960, 195, 197). During the Paris Commune of 1871, it was said that 'The great idea of solidarity and mutual equality (*La grande idée de solidarité et d'égalité mutuelle*) among all peoples and all men will save us'; and again that 'Non-solidarity of interests has created general ruin. ... We must look to liberty, equality and solidarity to secure new bases for order, and to re-organize labour' (cit. Rihs 1971, 42, 224). Like fraternity during the revolution of 1789, solidarity was thus extended beyond the confines of the small group or neighbourhood, to embrace all men. It was a modern expression of the Stoic–Christian ideal. It is not inappropriate that the term *Solidarność* should have been adopted by the Polish free trade union movement of 1980, to convey the message proclaimed by *fraternitas* in similar movements in earlier epochs.

The doctrine of 'self-help', so ingrained in the spirit and practice of early trade unionism and the co-operative movement (Godsden 1973, 180; K. Hawkins 1981, 13), was neither new nor inherently opposed to fraternity: it meant that people tried to cope for themselves, both as individuals and as groups (cf. Thompson 1968, 869). What was new and subversive of the fraternal ethic was the more specific doctrine, occasionally but increasingly taken over from educated society, that the ultimate sanction of co-operative effort was that it served the interests of individuals. The 'radical culture', stemming from the Enlightenment, which Thompson finds spreading among artisans and some skilled workers around 1800, was less affective in tone, proclaiming, in the spirit of the new political philosophy of the time, that 'GENERAL UTILITY is the sole and ultimate object of society', or, as Robert Owne put it, 'the construction of a great social and moral machine, calculated to produce wealth, knowledge, and happiness, with unprecedented precision and rapidity' (cit. Thompson 1968, 866). The minute-book of the successful consumers' co-operative venture, founded by the Rochdale Pioneers in the 1840s, stated that 'the present cooperative movement [intends] ... by a common bond, namely that of self-interest, to join together the means, the energies, and talents of all for the common benefit of each' (cit. Godsden 1973, 184). The precise formulae of Utilitarianism, by explicitly reducing collaboration to a means to individual well-being, all too lightly cut off the impetus of fraternity, and perhaps also helped engender the sanitized uniformity of comfortable modern Anglo-Saxon workers the world over.

Thompson's argument that these and other features coalesced, under the impact of industrialization, into a recognizable 'working-class culture' (1968, 460ff., 781–915, esp. 888) – an important point for the validation of the Marxist theory of class consciousness – has given rise to heated debate (cf. Thompson 1968, 915ff. for his response to this debate). The evidence and argument presented in this book underline the long history of many features of this 'culture' in pre-industrial Europe. This runs counter to the claim that it was peculiar to the new industrial working class, though Thompson himself recognizes the 'long traditions of mutuality' (1968, 869). While new features were added and others, such as sworn association, fell away, the recurrence of the specific notions of fraternity, friendship and mutual aid indicates, so far as 'mutuality' is concerned, continuity rather than novelty. On the other hand, evidence presented here supports the view that, in medieval as in modern times, manual workers held certain specific social values that were less current among other groups. (Is what passes for 'the history of ideas' largely an account of the mental pastimes of the leisured?) Manual workers retained similar ideals, probably for their own good reasons, over broad tracts of historical time.

Some recent interpretations of the working-class ethos in Britain around 1800 fall into the same error as Gierke's interpretation of the medieval town and guild. From professions of belief in fraternity and mutual aid and in the unique advantages of 'union', it has been deduced that 'collectivist values [were] consciously held and propagated in political theory, trade-union ceremonial, moral rhetoric' (Thompson 1968, 463); and – worse – that 'what is properly meant by "working-class culture" ... is the basic collective idea, and the institutions, manners, habits of thought and intentions which proceed from this' (Raymond Williams, cit. Thompson 1968, 462). While it is true that workers professed an affective attitude towards their associations, and did not regard them solely as a means either to individual well-being or to the 'improvement' of living standards, this does not indicate that their attitude was 'collectivist' as this term is generally understood today. For, like medieval guildsmen, they believed no less devoutly in individual rights and liberties, to secure which was one reason why they acted in unison: there is no evidence that the subordination of the individual to the community was part of their programme.

The values of fraternity, friendship and mutual aid, which even during the Middle Ages were less in evidence in learned thought than in popular consciousness, received little attention in modern learned thought. Perhaps this was because they were considered too bound up with emotion: after Kant and Bentham spontaneous human feeling was thought an unsafe guide in moral questions. Perhaps it was because the classes which produced most of the philosophers felt no need of them. It is particularly surprising that the German Romantics, with their attachment to spirituality, warm community, societal unity and medievalism, seldom invoked fraternity and the like. One may say that they do appear in Hegel, but under very different names. The most powerful and influential formulator of socialist philosophy, Karl Marx, explicitly eschewed them. Perhaps, again, it was related to the fact that Christianity had lost ground among intellectuals. Where we do come across clusters of literary references to these values is on the fringes between learned and popular thought, when a learned man (such as Herzen or Gierke) sought contact with popular tradition, or when a working man (almost always a craftsman – Proudhon for instance) turned philosopher; or, again, among Christian socialists (cf. Vidler 1974, 97; 1966, 271–2), or among those attached to anarchism (in most cases, professed atheists).

Pierre-Joseph Proudhon (1809–65), formerly an apprenticed printer and *compagnon*, was the great apostle of 'mutuality' in the nineteenth century. He was also, among modern political thinkers, the outstanding exponent of a theory of human society which saw *mutualité* and exchange as entirely complementary; in this respect he was a successor to Althusius. 'The social contract is the supreme act by which each citizen pledges to society his love, his intelligence, his labor, his services, his products and his goods in exchange for the affection, ideas, works, products, services and goods of his fellow citizens' (97; cf. pp. 133–6 above). Lichtheim summarizes Proudhon's position as follows:

> Reciprocity is 'the principle of social reality, the formula of justice'. It is a presupposition of life itself.... In the social order there is a 'natural' economy based on work and equal sharing. It is realized by mutual exchange among the associated producers. ... The ideal social order is one in which individual producers freely exchange their products in accordance with the principle that labor creates value ... it is plain enough why Proudhon felt able on occasion to say that socialism was simply the application of Christian principles.... The producers ... require credit, which they will obtain from a central bank ... but in a sense they will provide their own credit by rendering each other mutual support, i.e. by exchanging their goods and accepting token money ... as a symbol of their mutual interdependence. This is the *système mutuelliste*

179

to which Proudhon looked for the gradual emergence of a new and better
social order.   (1970, 89, 97)

By taking account of what might be supposed to be the opposite principle –
related to 'civil society' – namely exchange, Proudhon's link between
mutuality and exchange, his conception of exchange precisely as mutuality,
gave his system resilience and made it more widely attractive.

Alexander Herzen (1812–70), usually regarded as the founder of Russian
socialism, represents the other kind of convergence between popular and
learned thought, namely the attempt by an intellectual to draw upon
popular tradition and form it into a complete social philosophy. He saw this
as the fertilization by 'the mighty thought of the West' of 'the seeds
slumbering in the patriarchal mode of life of the Slavs' (cit. Lichtheim 1970,
112). Like Proudhon, he combined an emphasis upon fraternity with a plea for
small, self-governing local units of workers, which he regarded as the great
future potential of the traditional communal village of peasant Russia, the
mir, which was to develop as a commune (*obshchina*) (Malia 1955, 198, 205).

But it was above all in anarchist theory that mutual aid was explicitly
advocated as the principle on which all society should be based. Anarchists
are united in their rejection of the state and all forms of coercive authority,
including compulsory economic organization – remnants of feudalism,
modern industrial capitalism, and, since 1919, the Bolshevik version of
communism. The schemes proposed by modern anarchists range from
extreme individualism to voluntary collectivism; but on the whole modern
anarchism stresses individual self-determination more than did earlier
comparable radical theories (Woodcock 1963, esp. 19, 40, 49). Peter
Kropotkin (1842–1921), the gentle anarchist and secular saint, made
mutual aid the pivot of a whole social philosophy. He had the breadth of
vision to realize that this meant taking on Darwinism, which was by now
coming to be regarded as an intellectual basis for the view of man as an
inherently competitive creature. (In a similar vein, the Christian Socialist
F.D. Maurice (1805–72) wrote: 'Competition is put forth as the law of the
universe. That is a lie. The time is come for us to declare that it is a lie by
word and deed' (cit. Vidler 1974, 96).) In his *Mutual Aid*, published serially
from 1890 and in book form in 1902, Kropotkin attempted, by discursive
argument and selective observation, to show that mutual aid was 'a factor
of evolution' alongside 'self-assertion of the individual', and that it was in
fact more favourable to evolutionary progress than was competition. 'The
animal species, in which individual struggle has been reduced to its
narrowest limits, and the practice of mutual aid has attained the greatest
development, are invariably the most numerous, the most prosperous and
the most open to further progress' (293, 295; cf. chs 1–2). Mutual aid has
been the most progressive factor in human societies, 'among savages' (ch.3),
'among the barbarians' (ch.4), 'in the medieval city' (chs 5–6), and 'among

ourselves' (chs 7–8). The recent development of 'the all-absorbing authority of the State' is an isolated aberration (224ff.); and 'despite all that has been done in modern States for the destruction of the village community, the life of the peasants remains honeycombed with habits and customs of mutual aid and support' (262). He drew evidence from French farming co-operatives, the survival of communal forests in Germany, and above all from his native Russia (246ff.). In industrial society, mutual aid is practised among the poor, especially among women (284ff.): 'the need of mutual aid and support which had lately taken refuge in the narrow circle of the family, or the slum neighbours, in the village or the secret union of workers, re-asserts itself again ... [as] the chief leader towards further progress' (292). His thesis was derided by natural scientists and won little support among political philosophers; but, like so many apparent oddities, it contains grains of truth (cf. 'Clan life remains strictly for birds' in *The Times*, 21 July 1982, p.2).

Lastly, perhaps we should see conflicts between trade unions and government as in part reflecting a tension between the values of guild and of civil society. The fellowship and security of workers confronts the univer-salistic legal norms of the state: two concepts of justice are involved.

15

THE IDEAL OF CO-OPERATIVE PRODUCTION

Craft-guilds had, in general, striven to promote security of employment, a decent income and socio-economic independence for the small producer. How could these goals, the last especially, be attained under modern industrial conditions? One answer was, and still is, producers' co-operatives.

During the nineteenth and early twentieth centuries the most successful producers' co-operatives were developed among small peasants in Germany and France; these never involved joint ownership of land. In France, where 'the old agriculture of the common fields' was no distant memory, the last decades of the nineteenth century saw a rapid expansion of agricultural *syndicats* (Clapham 1948, 183–9). These made collective purchases of seeds etc. and later of machinery, which was then hired out; they provided banking and insurance facilities; they facilitated co-operative marketing of wine and milk. They were especially effective at the communal (i.e. local) level, and in regions specializing in fruit, vegetables and wine, where 'the local bond and the trade interest coincided' (Clapham 1948, 187). As the British co-operative movement was inspired by the ideal of brotherhood, so this development of producers' co-operatives in France was inspired by 'the belief that the syndicates would further "social solidarity", that catchword of late nineteenth-century France.... All country folk should learn that they were members one of another' (Clapham 1948, 189).

In Germany the co-operative movement centred upon peasant banks. Initiated by Friedrich Wilhelm Raiffeisen after the famine of 1846–7, it had a strong Christian tone (Clapham 1948, 221ff.). At about the same time, some co-operative credit and purchasing associations among handi-craftsmen were set up by Schulze-Delitzsch, a liberal (Clapham 1948, 326–7; Grebing 1969, 42–3). From the 1870s, the co-operative peasant banks began to undertake the collective purchase of feed and fertilizers; they were especially effective during the difficult years facing European agriculture in the late nineteenth century, when, it has been said, they did 'more than all the agrarian and protective laws together' (Dawson, cit. Clapham 1948, 224). These were examples of the *Genossenschaft* beloved of Gierke (see pp.210, 212): from the 1890s, co-operative dairies (*Molkereigenossen-*

schaften) were also developed. Co-operatives of this kind have subsequently proved beneficial to small agricultural producers in many parts of the world.

Producers' co-operatives in industry face far more intractable problems: the scale and complexity of production, marketing and management, the rapid and unpredictable shifts of technological development and the world market, not to mention competition from firms run in the well-tried pattern of traditional, hierarchical management (cf. Clayre 1981). In the nineteenth century there was a multiplicity of schemes but very little practical success. Today, 'workers' participation' or 'co-determination' (*Mitbestimmung*), profit-sharing and ventures in which the capital resources themselves are jointly owned by the workers, are all related to the goal of *self-determination* in economic life, as well as being inspired by ideals of mutuality. Boardroom participation by workers' representatives, established by law in West Germany, exists in a variety of firms in several European countries; it generally brings a notable improvement in industrial relations, it sometimes improves productivity, and has certainly proved compatible with industrial efficiency. But it often gives the workers only the appearance of power, particularly in strategic decisions. There have been hardly any examples of successful joint *ownership* in the west; one outstanding exception is Mondragon, near Bilbao, a fully co-operative enterprise, employing some 10,000 workers and now one of 'the largest producers of refrigerators in Spain, and among the largest producers of machine tools'. It was founded by a Catholic priest, Fr. Jose Maria Arizmendi, in the mid-1950s (R. Oakeshott in Vanek 1975, 290–6, and in Clayre 1981, 46–54; cf. Clayre 1981, 185ff.).

Various forms of workers' participation have been tried from time to time in communist countries. By far the most far-reaching and successful attempt is in Yugoslavia, where under the principle of 'self-management' representative workers' councils elect and supervise the management of all industrial enterprises. Whether the system is economically efficient is very much a matter of debate (Pateman 1970, 88–102; Sirc in Clayre 1981, 161–70); and it is difficult to know whether it is the workers or the state that really 'own' the capital resources. But it has been one of the most original practical developments in democracy in the twentieth century; it includes, for example, the old Athenian practice of rotation in office (Pateman 1970, 88, 100).

In nineteenth- and twentieth-century political thought too, schemes for producers' co-operatives or 'associations of producers' have varied from the provision of joint facilities such as credit, equipment, marketing – favoured by individualists like Proudhon – to profit-sharing and common ownership of land or industrial plant, and of capital itself – the distinguishing feature of socialists, communists and some anarchists. The ideal itself was not new:

183

it was the long-standing inheritance of milleniarism and utopianism, and, in its milder form, had something in common with communal agricultural systems reaching back beyond historical time, and possibly even with the practices of pastoralists and hunter-gatherers. But in the nineteenth century it acquired new urgency from the revolutionary doctrines of 1789 – in particular, radical notions of equality and fraternity (cf. Lichtheim 1968, 17ff., 61ff.) – and from the pace of economic development in the industrial revolution.

To a considerable extent the theory of co-operative production may be seen as a response to the plight of the *artisan* when handicraft production and the guild system collapsed before the onset of industrialization. And in fact a considerable number of those advocating such schemes, as well as of their supporters, were men reared in the artisan tradition. Others, including Marx, had their consciences fired by what they saw going on around them. Writing of the Radical component in 'the making of the working-class consciousness' in Britain, Thompson says that the outlook of William Cobbett ('who *created* this Radical intellectual culture ... in the sense that he found the tone, the style, and arguments which could bring the weaver, the schoolmaster, and the shipwright into a common discourse') 'approximated most closely to the ideology of *small producers*' (1968, 820, 834, last italics mine). The independent craftsman was a manual worker whose trade stimulated intellectual awareness of his social environment. He was accustomed to economic independence; he was also likely to have travelled widely in the course of his training. These were the very people most threatened by the large-scale capitalist factory; and they were the least likely to react submissively. As Hobsbawm puts it:

> Hostile to capitalism, [artisans] were unique in elaborating ideologies which did not simply seek to return to an idealized tradition, but envisaged a just society which would also be technically progressive. Above all, they represented the ideal of *freedom and independence* in an age when everything conspired to degrade labour.
>
> (cit. Lichtheim 1970, 36, my italics)

Thus, 'the democratic upsurge around 1800 on both sides of the Atlantic ... in so far as it was urban ... was largely sustained by *independent artisans*, whose position was being undermined by the growth of industrial capitalism' (Lichtheim 1968, 101–2, my italics). In 1821 a group of London printers formed an Economical and Co-operative Society to promote 'a village of Unity and Mutual Co-operation, combining agriculture, manufacture, and trade upon the plan projected by Mr Owen, of New Lanark' (cit. Lichtheim 1968, 122). Proudhon, the great champion of the small producer whether peasant or craftsman, was by origin an apprenticed printer and *compagnon* from the Jura. His theory, combining a strong belief in the radical independence of the individual producer with an ethic of *mutualité*, bears the mark of guild and *compagnonnage* tradition. He had enormous influence on the French working-class movement in the mid-nineteenth century, his followers being 'the single largest group' in the Paris Commune of 1871 (Edwards 1969, 14, 24, 31; Woodcock 1963, 98). One of the last old-fashioned 'utopian religious' communists, who, according to Lichtheim, 'reproduced the spirit of the old millenarian fraternities' before being eclipsed by Marx, was Wilhelm Weitling, an apprenticed tailor who had led the life of an itinerant artisan (Lichtheim 1968, 168–9). But artisans made their most distinctive ideological contribution in the development and diffusion of anarchist ideas, which perhaps, among the existing ideological possibilities, most accurately represented their peculiar temper and tradition. Among the leaders of anarchism, apart from a handful of aristocrats, 'members of the artisan class of traditional handicraftsmen have been perhaps the most important: anarchist militants include an astonishing proportion of shoemakers and printers' (Woodcock 1963, 24). When, in the early 1870s, anarchism caught on in the Jura villages, Bakunin found there 'faithful adherents' among the village watchmakers (Woodcock 1963, 156, 181).

Producers' associations or co-operatives were advocated in the nineteenth century by an astonishing variety of movements, political leaders and theorists. Pride of place, in historical terms, must go to Charles Fourier (1772–1837) with his slightly fantastic project of *phalanstères* (Lichtheim 1968, 30–8); and to Robert Owen (1771–1858), a British industrialist who founded the famous controlled co-operative factory community at New Lanark in 1801, and, after this had failed, numerous other similar projects (Lichtheim 1968, 113–23). Between them, these two men represented the two great traditions of the later eighteenth century. Fourier was 'a true Rousseauist [who] thought in terms of the small agricultural community' (Lichtheim 1968, 34); Owen was a son of the Enlightenment and 'represented the industrial middle class of his age, not least in his boundless optimism, his faith in science, and his conviction that machinery, from being a curse, could be turned into a blessing for mankind' (Lichtheim 1968, 115). Owen later helped inspire the British trade union movement of the 1830s, planning a Grand National Union which 'was to transform itself simultaneously into a country-wide cooperative society, so as to provide the actual economic framework for the new socialist order' (Lichtheim 1968, 116), his followers being called 'socialists or communionists' (Lichtheim 1970, 37).

In the mid-century the ideological mix became richer still. In Britain, there were the Co-operative movement, which however soon confined its efforts to consumer co-operatives, the Christian socialists and, in the early twentieth century, the guild socialists. The Co-operators proclaimed that in their true nature men are co-operative rather than, as the world of commerce and capitalism pretended, competitors. The Christian socialists reintroduced the ideal of brotherhood; as the quasi-hegelian Edward Vansittart Neale (who from 1873 to 1892 was highly successful as general secretary of the Co-operative Union) put it:

> Theoretically, the idea we endeavoured to spread was the conception of workers as brethren – of work as coming from a brotherhood of men associated for their common benefit – who therefore rejected any notion of competition with each other as inconsistent with the true form of society, and, without formally preaching communism, sought to form industrial establishments communistic in feeling, of which it should be the aim, while paying ordinary wages and interest ... to apply the profits of business in ways conducive to the common advantage of the body whose work produced them.
>
> (cit. B. Webb 1930, 118; cf. Backstrom 1974, 30, 55, 108)

In France, producers' associations were advocated by the conspiratorial revolutionary Blanqui (Lichtheim 1968, 66), by the Christian socialist Buchez, a founder of the French co-operative movement (Lichtheim 1968, 75), and by Louis Blanc (1811–82), a democratic constitutionalist. Blanc's *L'Organisation du travail*, published in 1839, advocated self-governing workshops 'with capital advanced by the government through a central bank, but with the workers electing the directors themselves [after a brief trial period with state appointees] and thereafter keeping a control through periodic re-election' (Lichtheim 1968, 81). This formed the model for the *ateliers nationaux* briefly and unsuccessfully set up by the revolutionary government in Paris in 1848, chiefly to relieve unemployment (Lichtheim 1968, 80).

In Germany, the ideal of production by associations of workers appealed to an even wider political spectrum. In 1848 the group called 'The Fraternity of German Labour' called for producers' and consumers' co-operatives (Grebing 1969, 30), while the German General Workers' Association formed under Lassalle in 1863 stood for state-aided producers' co-operatives (Grebing 1969, 32, 37, 43). But practical arrangements for co-operative credit etc. among handicraftsmen were initiated by Schulze-Delitsch, a liberal (Grebing 1969, 42), and producers' co-operatives were strongly supported by the youthful Gierke, who may be described as a liberal nationalist (see pp.212–14).

Throughout Europe, producers' associations of one kind or another formed the ultimate goal of the great socialist, communist and anarchist visionaries, Proudhon, Marx, Bakunin and Kropotkin. Among the foremost exponents of liberalism, on the other hand, de Tocqueville appears to have implied, and J.S. Mill stated most emphatically, that producers' associations were essential to the integrity of the human person under modern industrial conditions. All these schools of thought saw co-operatives as a way of achieving human dignity through self-determination; in this respect, and also in the democratic internal structures recommended, they were to some extent a modern counterpart to the medieval craft-guild.

These advocates differed in their approach to producers' associations principally in three areas: their relationship to society as a whole, the role of the individual in the group, and the means by which they should be introduced. Liberal advocates believed that producers' co-operatives ought to be inserted into modern political society, along with other reforms making for greater individual and associational liberty. De Tocqueville suggested that, as technological progress made production on an individual basis impracticable, the role of associations, rather than of the state, should be expanded in agriculture and industry, as in other areas of life (vol. II, bk 2, ch.5, pp.116–17 and bk 4, ch.7, p.342). J.S. Mill, in his *Principles of Political Economy* (1852), reflected that, if 'mankind is to continue to improve', the dominant form of industrial organization must be 'not that which can exist between a capitalist as chief, and workpeople without a voice in the management, but *the association of the labourers* themselves on terms of equality, collectively owning the capital with which they carry on their operations, and working under managers elected and removable by themselves' (775, my italics). For Mill, producers' co-operatives were a means of reawakening the spirit of self-help and personal endeavour among those blighted by poverty and oppressive working conditions. They were to be voluntary bodies, though government and others ought to help set them up, arrange credit and offer them legal protection. Capitalism, however, should not be outlawed; it would eventually prove less attractive. Co-operative production was to be introduced by trial and error and gradual effort from the grass-roots. Its development was entirely compatible with constitutional government, parliamentary democracy and the rule of law; indeed, it was a logical application of liberal values to the new problems of the machine age and industrial capitalism.

Socialists and anarchists, on the other hand, saw producers' associations as a, or *the*, basic constituent of a new social order. They were an end in themselves, to which other values like the rule of law were subsidiary. They wanted to re-structure the whole of society on the principle of free collective association; experience led many to believe that this was, in any case, the only way producers' associations themselves could develop. Proudhon said that small groups of associated producers should 'bind themselves together under a common law in a common interest' into larger groupings, on the basis of 'a real contract in which, instead of being absorbed into the central majesty ... the individual sovereignty of the contracting parties acts as a positive guarantee of the liberty of States, communes and individuals' (113,

116; cf. Lichtheim 1968, 83–98; Woodcock 1963, 98–133). In a somewhat similar way, Kropotkin advocated what has been described as 'a voluntary association that unites all social interests, represented by groups of individuals directly concerned with them', so that 'by union with other communes it produces a network of cooperation that replaces the state'. This was his 'anarchist vision of a Russia based on the federal union of free communes, cities and regions' (Woodcock 1963, 187, 204). For Proudhon and Kropotkin, the individual remained the basis of the system.

In his view of the future condition of mankind under communism, Marx attempted to combine Enlightenment individualism and something of the German romantic idea of community. In *The German Ideology* (1845), he and Engels drew a sharp distinction between the 'surrogate' or 'illusory' communities of class and state, in which individuals are artificially brought together into dominant collectivities and only the ruling classes (*herrschende Klasse*) possess freedom, and the 'true community' (*Gemeinschaft*), in which 'individuals achieve their freedom at one and the same time in and through their association (*Association*)'. The oppressive character of the former type of community was due to the 'independence' of socioeconomic conditions from human control. Individuals, separated in reality by the division of labour, were brought into artificial unity in 'a group alien to them'. But, 'for the community of the revolutionary proletariat, on the other hand, who bring under their control their own conditions of existence and those of all members of society, it is exactly the reverse: in it individuals take part as individuals' (*Werke* iii 74–5). As Marx put it in the third volume of *Capital* (published posthumously), 'Freedom in this area can consist only in socialized man, the associated producers (*der vergesellschäftete Mensch, die assoziirten Produzenten*) regulating their exchange with nature rationally and bringing it under their common control' (*Werke* xxv 828). It was through control of economic processes both by the individual and by the community, that human autonomy was to be achieved in the modern world. Marx's theory of historical development demonstrated with peculiar force why it was impossible for the independent producer and his guild to survive in the modern world.

But Marx's 'associated producers' referred not so much to the small-scale, Rousseauistic 'associations of producers' envisaged by Proudhon and others, as to society, indeed mankind, as a whole. Harmonious, non-coercive organization was posited on the basis of most men's conscious perception of a real community of interests under communism. Thus, as in German nationalism, the ideal of the guild and the self-governing city was being writ large – this time for all mankind. It was Marx's visionary belief in the transformation of human nature that made it possible for Soviet Marxism to conceive the state as an enormous guild. But Marx was aware that his kind of communism included producers' co-operatives in the ordinary sense; he congratulated the Paris Commune on its confederal scheme (in fact, a Proudhonist plan), and many Marxists, including some governments, have done a great deal to promote co-operative production.

For some socialists, however, the collective association itself began to acquire a higher moral value to which the members might legitimately be required to subordinate their individual aims. Nevertheless, in the great divide between state socialists, of whom Saint-Simon was the earliest representative, and more 'libertarian' socialists, the latter at least always had in mind a relatively *small* association. Fourier suggested groups of about 1600 in which 'property in things of common enjoyment is held in common by the phalanx, all trade is done by the community as a whole' (cit. Soltau 1931, 154). Herzen's tone was more explicitly anti-individualist: on the banner of the coming epoch is written, he said, 'not the individual, but the commune (*obshchina*), not liberty but fraternity, not abstract equality, but the organic division of labour' (cit. Malia 1955, 198). This, however, is evidence of a specifically Russian mode of thought: Bakunin, though an anarchist, was even more overtly collectivist (Woodcock 1963, 152).

The most severe differences of opinion revolved around the means by which producers' co-operatives were to be set up, and the urgency of the task. Obviously one great divide between liberals and moderate socialists, on the one hand, and most anarchists and extreme socialists, on the other, was that the latter believed that violent revolution was necessary to the implementation of their programme. This, in turn, was related to different personal and social experiences, and to different analyses of contemporary society, which led to different views of how serious the workers' plight was under existing conditions. This was further related to the question whether producers' co-operatives should become the dominant or sole form of economic organization, or merely remain a licit alternative. The position taken on these questions tends to indicate the place producers' associations occupied in one's scale of values. He who wills the end wills also the means: scant concern for the means suggests a low priority. The point to be made here is simply that support for producers' associations covered a much wider spectrum of opinion than might be thought. (This is probably still true today.) It was not confined to any one school of thought; it cannot, in that sense, be 'labelled', nor can it easily be dismissed as utopian, fanatical or doctrinaire.

In Proudhon, Marx, Herzen and Kropotkin, the producers' association became indistinguishable from the territorial 'commune'. As used by modern thinkers, this term was principally of French origin, and it was in the Paris Commune of 1871 that Proudhon's ideas in particular had their practical test. It was here, as Petit-Dutaillis argues, that the term *commune* was restored to something like its eleventh- and twelfth-century meaning, with 'the force of a call to union among fellow-citizens against oppressors'

189

(1970, 278; cf. Rihs 1971, 98). At the same time it acquired its modern sense of co-operative or communist economic organization, as well as political self-determination. With regard to the inherent value of the small territorial unit, there was a certain convergence between liberal and anarchist ideas. Both de Tocqueville and Proudhon accorded it 'natural' status:

> The village or township is the only association which is so perfectly natural that, wherever a number of men are collected, it seems to constitute itself. (de Tocqueville vol. I, ch. 5, p. 62)

> Wherever men, together with their wives and children, gather together in one place, dwell together and cultivate their land in common, developing between them various industries, establishing relations of neighbourliness, and, whether they like it or not, making themselves mutually dependent, they form what I call a natural group. (Proudhon 118)

One of the primary aims of the Paris Commune was, indeed, simply to re-establish the communal autonomy (*les franchises municipales*) of Paris itself (Rihs 1971, 26, 56–7, 62, 101, 179, 182). A manifesto of the committee of the twenty *arrondissements*, signed also by leaders of the various revolutionary clubs, proclaimed that:

> Our country ... is taking up the tradition of the old communes and of the Revolution ... [which has been] pursued throughout the centuries with such self-denial and heroism by the artisans of the Middle Ages, by the citizens (*bourgeois*) of the Renaissance, by the fighters of 1789.... The commune is the foundation of every political constitution (*état politique*), just as the family is the embryo of societies. It ought to be autonomous, that is to say it ought to govern and administer itself according to its particular spirit, traditions and needs; to exist as a moral person preserving, in the political, national and federal grouping, its entire liberty, its own character, its complete sovereignty, like the individual within the city.... It is the communal idea (*l'idée communale*), striven for since the twelfth century, affirmed by morality, law and science, which has triumphed on the 18th March 1871.
> (cit. Rihs 1971, 219; cf. 287–8)

Petit-Dutaillis notes that all that was lacking for a complete medieval revival was 'the oath of mutual aid' (1970, 277–8; cf. pp.56–7 above). For the Proudhonists and many socialists, this ideal of the commune involved restructuring the whole of France as an association of federated communes. The bourgeois today, it was alleged, as in the twelfth century, stop short with the acquisition of 'civil [i.e. legal] liberty'; what is needed is, in addition, 'political liberty', that is the replacement of centralizing absolutism by self-governing communes. We must, the official journal went on, look to 'the Germanic countries' for 'a truly popular, truly national tradition' drawn from 'the origins of our history' (cit. Rihs 1971, 290; cf. 287–8). Similarly Engels, writing about the Paris Commune to Bebel, said, 'Let us replace the word State with the word *Gemeinde* [local community], an excellent old German word corresponding to the French word *commune*' (cit. Rihs 1971, 250–1).

This ideal of re-structuring society in small territorial units of self-governing workers proved explosive. During *la belle époque*, in the closing decades of the great European peace, it captured the hearts and minds of great sections of workers, rural and urban, as syndicalism in France, and as anarchism in Spain, and, briefly, Italy (cf. Lichtheim 1970, 213–23; Woodcock 1963, 331–5, 338–52). According to Lichtheim, 'the first preview of the syndicalist Utopia' was given when Flora Tristan

> discovered the ancient craft unions of the French working class, the *compagnonnages*, then just about to transform themselves into modern labour unions, and it was the poems and pamphlets of the *compagnons* that launched her on the road to her most influential piece of writing, *L'Union Ouvrière* (1843) ... a project for 'constituting the working class by means of a compact, solid, indissoluble Union' into a self-governing corporation. (1968, 69)

The French delegates to the anarcho-syndicalist conference in Amsterdam (1907) stated: 'The workers' union (*syndicat*) is not just an instrument of combat, it is the living germ of the future society, and the society of the future will be what we have made of the *syndicat*' (cit. Lichtheim 1970, 222). This was one of the leading aspirations of the great wave of revolutions that swept through Europe at the close of the 1914–18 war. During the early stages of the Russian Revolution, the *soviets* (councils) were widely regarded not just as the means by which power was to be seized and society reorganized by the workers and peasants, but as the basic form this reorganization should take. Lenin invoked the Paris Commune, as interpreted by Marx and Engels, as the model for the future workers' government. During the uprising in Germany during 1918–19, similar councils of workers, soldiers and sailors were more or less spontaneously set up, although it was only the left wing of the Social Democrats, soon to become the core of the Communist Party, which regarded them as the permanent political embodiment of a new regime. Similar events occurred in Hungary and, a year or two later, in Italy. With the rise of Bolshevism and moderate Social Democracy, autonomous peasants' and workers' communes became the distinctive ideal of the anarchists, who, during the Spanish civil war, organized self-government in factories and in the army, especially in Catalonia and its capital, Barcelona (Woodcock 1963, 353–73). It has remained to haunt the European conscience, in the anti-Soviet uprisings in Hungary and Poland in 1956, in Czechoslovakia in 1968, and again in Poland in 1980; and in the western anti-capitalist movements of 1968, and nowadays time and again when a plant is threatened with closure. The tradition of the Paris Commune played a part in Mao's reorganization of China, under which 'the township governments and the communes should become one', comprising about 2000 peasant households (Lui 1972, 151–2, 155). Thus there was at least an element of indirect continuity with the European town and village communes of the eleventh and twelfth centuries. The breaks in this tradition are no doubt too great to suggest that this was more than a historical legitimation of a creed which had already been adopted on philosophical grounds. The question remains: why did this creed meet with such enthusiastic support among workers and peasants in Europe and elsewhere?

It was and is central to the co-operative communal ideal that all workers should *participate* in the management and government of the economic polity, discussing and authorizing policy and undertaking executive functions in rotation. The Enlightenment bequeathed the tradition of civic humanism, according to which polity was man's natural and proper milieu, and active citizenship was essential to human development, to the nineteenth-century radicals and socialists. From an early stage the basic ideals of civic humanism struck roots in working-class consciousness (Thompson 1968, 816; Hobsbawm 1971, 168 – 'civic virtue' was a ritual password of the emigrant German workers' League of Outlaws). Theorists of the commune were quick to discover the ethos of self-administration in their own national histories. According to Herzen, in the traditional Slav commune 'each individual who was of age was an active citizen' (cit. Malia 1955, 201). Gierke put forward the same claim on behalf of the early Germanic *Genossenschaft* (Fellowship); not a little of his study of European history concerned the fortunes of participatory citizenship, which, he concluded, must today be recovered and implemented partly by means of producers' associations (see pp.212–13). Similarly today, in Tanzania, village co-operatives have been developed as an expression of the traditional principle of *Ujaama* or family fellowship.

In modern western political philosophy, the ideal of participation is based primarily on the rights of the human person. The argument was best presented by J.S. Mill, who adopted Aristotle's view of the ethical function of political activity, and brilliantly combined the priorities of Romanticism with the spirit of liberalism. The ultimate aim of all political procedures is to enable the human personality to develop its moral and intellectual qualities to the full. Essential to this is 'the cultivation of the active faculties by exercise, diffused through the whole community' (*Principles of Political Economy* 943), 'the participation of the private citizen, if even rarely, in public functions' (*Representative Government* 412), and 'a course of education for the people in the art of accomplishing great objects by individual energy and voluntary cooperation' (*Principles* 971). In the industrial sector, this can be achieved only under management by 'the association of labourers' (*Principles* 775; cf. *On Liberty* 305). The philosophical core of British guild socialism was the demand for participatory workers' democracy in industry, or, as G.D.H. Cole put it, 'the conscious and continuous exercise of the art of citizenship' (cit. Glass 1966, 62; cf. 32, 34). R.H. Tawney, in *The Acquisitive Society* (1921), put it another way:

> ultimately, if by slow degrees, power follows the ability to wield it; authority goes with function. The workers cannot have it both ways. They must choose whether to assume the responsibility for industrial discipline and become free, or to repudiate it and continue to be serfs.
>
> (cit. Glass 1966, 68)

Today, 'self-management' is the central ideal of libertarian socialism in the west, and of workers' democracy in Yugoslavia (cf. Vanek 1975).

The ideal of co-operative production fused the principle of group solidarity with that of personal independence: it was only by co-operating that men could be economically autonomous – a reminiscence of Rousseau (see p.162). It thus brought together elements of the traditions *both* of the guild *and* of civil society. As a practical programme, it has often suffered from political polarization – partly due to unrelated factors – between supporters and opponents. But no one can dismiss it without placing themselves beyond the pale of European and 'western' tradition, properly understood.

In the twentieth century, political thinkers of several schools have ascribed special value to small groups and voluntary associations. This is partly because they provide a milieu in which participation by all members is immediately practicable; thus a postulate of civic humanism can be realized through the liberal tenet of freedom of association. A multiplicity of freely formed associations has become an integral part of the political system of northern and western Europe, the USA and the white commonwealth – that is, of precisely those nations which might be expected, on ethnic and cultural grounds, to be heirs to the guild tradition. Such a system has come to be regarded as a necessary feature of a 'free society'. The constitutions of these private associations resemble those of the medieval guilds: the annual general meeting decides policy and elects strictly accountable office-bearers. Some such groups, for example political parties and labour unions, play a part, formally or informally, in the process of government – a tendency known as 'pluralism', that is

> a system of interest representation in which the constituent units are organized into an unspecified number of multiple, voluntary, competitive,

non-hierarchically ordered and self-determined (as to type or scope of
interest) categories which are not specially licensed ... by the state and
which do not exercise a monopoly of representational activity within
their respective categories.   (Schmitter 1974, 96)

De Tocqueville argued with brilliance that the freedom and the habit of
association were essential if variety, personal originality and civil liberty
were to survive in an age of democratic equality. Associations are necessary
to the moral growth of the individual and to the maintenance of civic virtue
in society at large; in other words, they realize goals once ascribed to the
polis.

> Feelings and opinions are recruited, the heart is enlarged and the human
> mind is developed only by the reciprocal influence of men upon one
> another. I have shown that these influences are almost null in democratic
> countries; they must therefore be artificially created, and this can only be
> accomplished by associations.... In democratic countries the science of
> association is the mother of science; the progress of all the rest depends
> upon the progress it has made. Among the laws that rule human societies
> there is one which seems to be more precise and clear than all others. If
> men are to remain civilized or to become so, the art of associating
> together must grow and improve in the same ratio in which the equality
> of conditions is increased.
>
>   (vol. II, bk 2, ch.5, pp.117–18; cf. Jouvenel, *Sovereignty*, p.229)

De Tocqueville regarded associations 'for political, commercial, or manufacturing purposes, or even for those of science and literature' as the only
means of checking the power of government, once 'equality of conditions'
had swept away privileged estates and corporations: 'governments of our
time look upon associations of this kind just as sovereigns in the Middle
Ages regarded the great vassals' (vol. II, bk 2, ch.7, p.126; cf. bk 4, ch.7, p.
342). Here the nascent theory of 'countervailing powers' took up where the
earlier theory of 'intermediate bodies' had left off (see pp.145–6). Proudhon
took freedom of association a stage further: central government has no
powers other than those given by local groups, and these may be withdrawn
at will. For a pure anarchist like Kropotkin, harmony between associations
can be achieved without government of any kind. In the mid-twentieth
century, pluralism has been hailed as a legitimate adaptation to modern
conditions of the liberal–egalitarian model of market society. As McWilliams puts it, in the North American context,

> Liberal realism fell back on a still earlier design, the self-regulating
> mechanism which would achieve the desired results in spite of the defects
> of men. Redefined in terms of 'groups', the market mechanism became
> once again the master concept of political thought; and, for political

194

science if not for all political men, what Theodore Lowi calls 'interest group liberalism' became 'a public philosophy'.

(1973, 558; cf. 556–9, 669)

Producers' associations had many advocates, but, when all is said and done, there was relatively little detailed discussion about them among political theorists, many of whom, like Mill, seem to have been content simply to announce their importance. Proudhon and, as we shall see, Gierke (see pp.212–14) analysed their significance and their role at somewhat greater length. Gierke's developmental theory of history culminated logically in a survey and analysis of modern producers' associations. Perhaps more attention will be paid to them now that they exist and have become a subject of empirical study. Professional corporations, on the other hand, which are often – more often than producers' associations – regarded as the modern analogue of the guilds (although the resemblance is far from complete) have received more detailed consideration by some political philosophers.

16

THE ROMANTIC PHILOSOPHY OF
COMMUNITY

Two very different views of guilds and corporations emerged in nineteenth-
and early twentieth-century Europe. The one, deriving from the Enlightenment, classical Political Economy, and to some extent Rousseau, saw them
as combinations of pettifogging sectional self-interest, subversive of liberty
and the public good. The other, deriving from German Romanticism and
Hegel, saw them as legitimate and necessary associations of producers and
merchants, to promote their common interests, secure justice for the
producer and – Hegel's contribution – develop his sense of moral
responsibility. This second view was the philosophical core and origin of
modern corporatism.

In the German Romantics and their successors, the ideal of community
assumed a new form and a cosmic meaning. There was both continuity
with, and innovation upon, earlier notions of affective community. Affective community was now expressed as an integral part of a general
philosophy of man in which historical interpretation and prescription for
the future were deliberately combined. In the following chapters, we shall
see how this opened up a new epoch of guild theory. This drew much of its
sap from the German guild tradition, and in turn exercised considerable
influence upon some contemporary political movements and their ideology.

In the first place, we must observe that, in nineteenth- and twentieth-
century Germany, more explicitly than at any other time or place, ideas of
guild, corporation and community (*Gemeinschaft*) were constructed into a
national ideology. Eventually a tragic, nay savage, destiny lay in wait for
this particular development of the tradition we have been attempting to
portray. The ideology of the guild town, when its original habitat was
destroyed by economic liberalism, was projected onto the nation, to become
the ideology of the *Volksgemeinschaft*. Mack Walker, who in a sense is
rescuing the 'home town' from Nazism, feels compelled to admit that,

> In the Third Reich ... the longings of intellectuals for national community
> and hometownsmen's parochial values, came together.... In a narrow
> political sense it really was a solution to the German problem: resolving
> the conflicting themes of national unity and [small-scale] community by

196

translating hometown values into national organization.

(1971, 427, 429; cf. 417)

Yet the question remains: was this a fate brought upon the guild tradition by its own intrinsic nature, or one that befell it only in this particular instance owing to peculiar circumstances of German history? I am certain the latter is true: for the two sides of the equation simply don't add up. Guilds and guild towns neither massacred intruders nor undertook world conquest; the Nazis favoured neither guilds nor corporations. (The aged Tönnies was himself campaigning for the Social Democrats in 1933: Cahnman 1973, 284–90.) Was it not that Nazism exploited this tradition, as it exploited primeval Germanic fellowship and Christian fear of Bolshevism, for its own quite different strategy? It is legitimate to distinguish between *Gemeinschaft* (or *Genossenschaft*) in the rich legacy of nineteenth-century German social philosophy, and in Nazi ideology; just as Thomas Mann insisted that the peculiar German mode that runs from Luther to Nietzsche should not be wiped out because the Nazis claimed to appropriate it.

The Romantics' idea of community was a result of their attempt to define German national tradition in contradistinction to the philosophy of Napoleonic France, and in terms acceptable to post-Enlightenment learning. In so doing it may be that they once again re-drew 'the boundaries between the sacred and the profane' (cf. p.62 above); in any case secular community now assumed the proportions of a religious ideal, and enormous intellectual energy was released thereby. To begin with, the French Revolution, with its ideals of individual liberty, republican government and popular nation-hood, evoked a sympathetic response in Germany. The diffusion of the values of civil society, 'catastrophic in its suddenness' in France, also began in Germany (Cobban 1961, i 135; Reiss 1970, 7). Kant implanted the ideals of civil society in the heart of moral philosophy with his notions of autonomy of the will and 'the universal law of freedom': he defined the rights of citizens precisely as freedom, legal equality and personal independence (133; Reiss 1970, 26). The young Fichte adopted an unrestricted individualism. But the Terror of 1793 and, still more, Germany's experience under Napoleon induced reactions that made Romantic political thought veer in the opposite direction. From now on, many would regard 'Caesarism' as the inevitable outcome of 'atomistic' popular sovereignty and 'vulgar' notions of liberty and equality. Besides, monarchs, statesmen and bureaucrats would be interested to know how to develop in Germany a non-revolutionary popular state, for which subjects were prepared to fight and die. The Romantics looked to the German past for an ideal of community that would measure up, in popular appeal and participatory politics, to the lofty expectations of the time.

Changes in the understanding of history, in the theory of knowledge, and above all in the perception of the self, which derived from Herder, Rousseau, Kant and Fichte, underlay the changes now wrought in social and political philosophy. Behind all empirical knowledge and scientific interpretation lie the rational intuitions of the self-conscious person. Morality comes neither from natural law nor from divine revelation, but from an inner voice of conscience and duty. The human personality is not a product of nature, not something we know through the observation of behaviour, but is rooted in self-consciousness, personal experience and the life of Spirit (Taylor 1975, 6ff.). It is to be 'posited' because without it our own inner life, of which we have direct experience, would make no sense. It is possible, therefore, to ascribe personality or 'subjectivity' not only to individuals but also to groups, in so far as these share a common language, convictions, folklore and historical experience. This theory was applied above all to the nation, but, as we shall see, it also radically transformed the theory of corporations.

Since the basis of moral thinking is the 'positing' and recognition of the 'other', morality – even knowledge itself – stands in a vital relationship to community: the two are essentially interdependent. Man is a social being, not only in the sense that his needs and aspirations require him to associate with others (as Stoic and Aristotelian philosophy maintained), but in the further sense that without communion with others he would lack all truly human character. This is true especially for compatriots, who share a historical identity, but also for mankind at large. Such a view gave rise to the doctrine that *freedom* and community can only be realized together:

> The point of departure of German law is the free, but morally bound, the *moral free will*, thus a *unified* conception of will, that reciprocally includes the marks of freedom and confinement, the being-for-itself and the being-for-others, of the individual and the communal.
>
> (Lotheissen, cit. Walker 1971, 258)

As Savigny said, 'That which binds [the people] into one whole is the common conviction of the people, the kindred consciousness of an inward necessity' (204–5).

The historical thesis was that a special kind of community, incorporating these philosophical ideas, was innate to the Germans and could therefore most readily be developed in Germany. Tacitus' description of the freedom of the early Germans had been a patriotic commonplace since the Renaissance. To this was now added an informal, heartfelt community life, a model owing much to the home towns that were so stoutly resisting Napoleon's enlightened despotism. This was generally ascribed to medieval *Germania*: Novalis described medieval Christendom as 'an enormous guild (*Zunft*)' (127ff.). Karl Friedrich Eichhorn, whose *German Politics and Law* was written in 1808–23, as an exponent of 'the primal nature of community', 'knew when he began writing that he would find something like the home town at the historic heart of German society' (Walker 1971, 249–58, at 250, 252). In one respect at least, Eichhorn's historical idea of freedom is, in fact, analogous to medieval guild and civic experience: freedom is achieved, not by a former master's say-so, but by entering 'a fellowship of rights within a people's community (*Volksgemeinde*)' (cit. Walker 1971, 257). In other words, freedom depends upon a particular type of association: this idea would reappear in Marx (see p.188). Continuing a guild theme, Jakob Grimm believed that 'the basis of real societies is love, and the more societies like that there were, the better; universities recognized that in their *gemütliche Gemeinschaften* ... and trades guilds were another place to look for it' (Walker 1971, 258–9).

The crucial step taken by the Romantics was to apply this ideal of close-knit community to the vastly wider context of the entire nation. As Walker puts it, guild moralism was 'tied into the sense of nationality'; they tried to transfer 'the communal freedom of Möser and the home town, which was specifically and necessarily localized within the sphere of familiarity, into a national communal freedom' (Walker 1971, 259). Thus the Romantics combined the ideal of reverence for authority with that of spontaneous allegiance and geniality (*Gemütlichkeit*); since all are fellow-members, the strength of the whole and the freedom of the individual go side by side. Novalis said that we must combine 'the ancients' love of the glorious state family (*Staatsfamilie*)' with 'the delightful feeling of freedom ... informal contact with all fellow citizens (*Staatsgenossen*), pride in man's universality, joy in personal rights and in the property of the whole, and strong civic sense (*das kraftvolle Bürgergefühl*)' (139; 150–1). The bonds between people and government are affective. As a Württemberg deputy, referring to the home towns themselves, put it in the 1830s: 'Community itself is the goal and not the instrument of the state' (cit. Walker 1971, 314). This was the fateful heritage which, though of itself far too general a conception to 'lead to' Nazism, was fed into that ideology, contributing signally both to its mass appeal and to its intellectual credibility. Gierke himself saw fellowship groups of all sizes as *eiusdem generis*. Given the problem of national unity, it was very difficult to confine the *Gemeinschaft* ideal to the small community, whence it had sprung and where alone it could retain its truly affective character among familiars.

It was this idea of state and nation as community which led to the Romantics' notion of their 'wholeness' (*Ganzheit, Totalität*). In their philosophy of individual and community, the organic analogy assumed a much stronger meaning than ever before: the state is a unity of the same order as the individual, since its parts cannot be separated without ceasing to be themselves. The state is a 'moral person' in quite a new sense (cf. Kluckhorn 1925, 85–6; Taylor 1975, 23). Law and government both ought to be, and in the nature of things intrinsically are, expressions of *Volksgeist*, 'objects of popular belief' (*Volksglaube*), 'the common consciousness of the nation' (Savigny 204–5). In the modern state, as opposed to earlier small states, 'The people must have grasped the idea of popular unity, so that the people live in a feeling of unity, and this is the first principle of its life' (Schleiermacher 195–7). As Müller put it in 1808–9:

> The state is ... the intimate association of all physical and spiritual needs, of the whole physical and spiritual wealth, of the total internal and external life of a nation into a great, energetic, infinitely active and living whole. ... The state is the totality of human affairs ... [the] expression of divine order in human form. ... The individual now ... sees that he himself is *nothing*, but ... he is *everything* in the great whole of which he is a member ... and he can participate in its immortality.
>
> (146, 150, 157, 163)

Here indeed was a socio-political philosophy that soared like a Gothic cathedral, quite unlike anything compounded by medieval thinkers stooping over their refined glosses.

The Romantics' views on economic relationships also reflected guild norms. Already in 1800, Fichte, in a work significantly entitled *The Closed Commercial State* (*Der geschlossene Handelstaat*), was advocating a kind of planned economy. As Reiss summarizes him, 'the state has the obligation to ensure that everyone can live by his work', and therefore has the right to assign to each person 'a definite sphere of economic activity ... every individual has to enter a trade and must publicly declare his vocation' (1955, 16; cf. Bowen 1947, 26ff.). But this was planning not primarily in the interests of wealth but of social order and personal fulfilment. In 1802 Bader was already criticizing Adam Smith's system of 'so-called freedom or passive state economy' (cit. Kluckhorn 1925, 92; cf. Müller 149). The Romantics looked favourably on the guild system itself. Their ethical concern and their whole conception of community and state led them to reject, along with individualism and contractarianism in general, both the primacy of the profit motive in economics and the application of market values to political exchange. The state is based on faith and mutual trust, not on calculations of expedience, of personal loss and gain (Müller 145; Novalis 140–1; Reiss 1955, 25–6); economic relationships are based on moral or even, in Müller's view, theological criteria. State regulation must prevent excessive inequalities (Schleiermacher: Reiss 1955, 36). Their opposition to industrial capitalism anticipated the later course of artisan and socialist sentiment. Nineteenth-century corporatism, which leant heavily on Romantic assumptions, was a transposition of the guild system to the national economy.

The generation of thinkers which experienced Germany's humiliation by

Napoleon and then her eventual liberation created a new political language, stamped with historicism, holism and organicism. They influenced both popular and learned ideology; their hold over the nascent science of sociology was only exorcized by Weber's cool mind, as was their tendency to conflate 'value' and 'fact'. The historical precedent for their ideas appears to have been Justus Möser and the German home town (Walker 1971, 248ff.). There was certainly nothing in medieval theory or practice that could be said to point towards the Romantic idea of community any more than to modern individualism; medieval history has subsequently been obscured by the Romantic myth. Seldom has such a small band of men exercised such prodigious influence over their future compatriots; that they did so was due not least to their affiliation with the values of the guild towns.

17

THE PHILOSOPHY OF THE
CORPORATION: HEGEL

Hegel's view of corporations was the first explicit attempt by a modern philosopher to give guild values and aspirations a central place in political theory. Durkheim followed him in this field, and their achievements have not been significantly improved upon since. Hegel still presents a unique challenge to received views on the function and significance of vocational and economic groups.

The political philosophy of Hegel, while in many respects it moved in the direction charted by the Romantics and subsumed their priorities, was also, and perhaps for the most part, his own creation, rooted in his philosophy as a whole (for this and what follows see especially Taylor 1975, 365–461). As in Aristotle, the state was given a singularly important place in a conception of the human cosmos arrived at through logical thought, and soaring beyond mere politics. The state is not self-authorizing, but attains its focal position because it is the environment in which the universal, objective good is realized, Spirit actualized, the real made rational. In Hegel's doctrine, 'morality reaches its completion in a community' (Taylor 1975, 377); for the true ethical life (*Sittlichkeit*) displaces the centre of gravity ... from the individual onto the community, which is seen as the locus of a life or subjectivity, of which the individuals are phases. The community is an embodiment of *Geist* (Spirit), and a fuller, more substantial embodiment than the individual' (Taylor 1975, 378). The state is the supreme community, the 'mature totality which ... constitutes *one* Being, the spirit of *one* People' (Hegel, *Philosophy of History*, 52). In *The Philosophy of Right* (PR) (published in 1821), Hegel designed a constitution for the modern state. This was intended to give practical expression to the state's essential features, realize human potential to the full, and locate the endowments of the human spirit in a practical setting, which is itself a part of cosmic order and necessary to the fulfilment of Spirit. Composed in the years immediately following the liberation of Germany, this was also a version, albeit entirely *sui generis*, of the restoration strategy. Hegel showed, in more powerful detail than any of his contemporaries, how the various institutions of existing Germanic states might articulate the postulates of Spirit; more than the Romantics, he insisted that the people themselves, organized in appropriate sub-groups, were also the subjective and particular bearers of Spirit.

The state is made up of family and civil society (bürgerliche Gesellschaft). The process of socialization begins in the family, to whose norms the individual adapts himself instinctively and spontaneously. In civil society, men pursue their own individual ends under a system of law which upholds their 'abstract' rights. As members of the state, they are once again taken up into a wider community; here the ethical life reaches its culmination, as they at last pursue the general good as coterminous with their own particular needs and aims, recognizing themselves in 'the other' (cf. Taylor 1975, 433– 4). Here men become truly self-conscious, rational, moral beings; the practical world is ordered as it should be. Since it is the real and the rational which are here brought into alignment, Hegel is concerned throughout to show how each of these various 'moments' of the state, which had recognizable counterparts in contemporary Europe, might play its part in the development of men as rational, moral and political beings.

All men are not capable of playing an equal part in each moment. While all are members of a family, a class and the state itself, they are divided into three broad classes (Stände), the agricultural, the commercial, and the 'universal class' of civil servants, corresponding to a necessary division of tasks; and the special role of each man depends upon which class he belongs to. This division is based both on the needs of the whole and on the particular preferences and abilities of individuals.

A man actualizes himself only in becoming something definite, i.e. something specifically particularized; this means restricting himself exclusively to one of the particular spheres of need. In this class-system, the ethical frame of mind therefore is rectitude and esprit de corps, i.e. the disposition to make oneself a member of one of the moments of civil society by one's own act, through one's energy, industry, and skill, to maintain oneself in this position, and to fend for oneself only through this process of mediating oneself with the universal, while in this way gaining recognition both in one's own eyes and in the eyes of others.   (PR 133)

Whereas in ancient societies 'the allotment of individuals to classes was left to the ruling class ... or to the accident of birth', in the modern western state 'the essential and final determining factors are subjective opinion and the individual's arbitrary will, which win in this sphere their right, their merit, and their dignity' (PR 132–3). You can achieve the universal only through the particular.

At this point we encounter Hegel's ideas on the moral role of the 'corporation' (Korporation). This was a new departure in 'guild' theory, to be taken up by a great number of modern thinkers, pre-eminently by

Durkheim. Whereas the ethical life of the family is especially developed in the agricultural class, and that of the state by the class of civil servants, the ethics of civil society are especially developed in the business class. 'The class between them, the business class, is essentially concentrated on the particular, and hence it is to it that Corporations are specially appropriate' (*PR* 152). This is because in the world of production and trade, people are primarily concerned with pursuit of their own 'particular', selfish aims; conscious pursuit of the 'universal' good is largely unconscious, contingent, 'abstract' and therefore peculiarly weak. By producing and trading, businessmen contribute to the overall welfare of society, but it is not their immediate intention to do so. Therefore this class stands in special need of moral socialization. This is achieved by their membership of corporations, consisting of those engaged in the same craft or line of business, i.e. of occupational groups.

> The labour organization of civil society is split, in accordance with the nature of its particulars, into different branches. The implicit likeness of such particulars to one another becomes really existent in an association, as something common to its members. ... A member of civil society is in virtue of his own particular skill a member of a Corporation, whose universal purpose is thus wholly concrete and no wider in scope than the purpose involved in business, its proper task and interest.   (*PR* 152)

Membership of a corporation gives the tradesman 'evidence of his skill and his regular income and subsistence, i.e. evidence that he is somebody'; it gives him a sense of identity. But at the same time, the corporation is concerned to pursue the well-being of *all* those involved in a given profession; in this way the businessman also becomes directly involved in the pursuit of the good of others, and more aware of the relation between his own work and society at large. 'It is also recognized that he belongs to a whole which is itself an organ of the entire society, and that he is actively concerned in promoting the comparatively disinterested end of this whole' (*PR* 153).

The corporation thus plays a vital role in the moral development of the individual:

> As the family was the first, so the Corporation is the second ethical root of the state, the one planted in civil society. The former contains the moment of subjective particularity and objective universality in a substantial unity. But these moments are sundered in civil society to begin with; on the one side there is the particularity of need and satisfaction, reflected into itself, and on the other side the universality of abstract rights. In the Corporation these moments are united in an inward fashion, so that in this union particular welfare is present as a right and is actualized. The sanctity of marriage and the dignity of Corporation membership are the

two fixed points round which the unorganized atoms of civil society revolve.   (*PR* 154)

The single person attains his actual and living destiny for universality only when he becomes a member of a Corporation, a society etc.
(*PR* 201; cf. Heiman 1970, 133; Avineri 1972, 165; Althusius p.138 above)

It is a 'second family for its members' (*PR* 153).

Corporations mediate between the individual and society at large, the state; they overlap the private and public spheres. They socialize individuals, but they are also integrally related to the state authorities; they play a role in the organization of production and trade, and also in the moral formation of society as a whole. (Like Aristotle, Hegel saw economic regulation as a sub-political function.) He appears to have accepted the Roman law view of their legal status: 'it is only by being authorized that an association becomes a corporation' (*PR* 153, 290; Heiman 1970, 125).

The internal or economic functions of the Corporation are as follows: A Corporation has the right, under the surveillance of the public authority, (a) to look after its own interests within its own sphere, (b) to co-opt members, qualified objectively by the requisite skill and rectitude, to a number fixed by the general structure of society, (c) to protect its members against particular contingencies, (d) to provide the education requisite to fit others to become members.   (*PR* 152–3)

These correspond closely to the traditional functions of the guild. But Hegel gives two further moral twists to the welfare function. First, businessmen have a right to make money; wealth and poverty are in general the legitimate rewards of good work or laziness. But, if he were an isolated member of society, the businessman would feel the need to acquire and display wealth in order to 'gain recognition for himself by giving external proofs of success in business, and to these proofs no limits can be set' ('conspicuous consumption' as Veblen called it). In the corporation, however, he acquires 'duties to [his] fellow associates', such as the corporate provision of welfare. This leads on to a second point: poverty may be caused by factors outside the craftsman's control, such as 'the increasing mechanization of production', and so a further benefit of the corporation is that 'the help which poverty receives loses its accidental character and the humiliation wrongfully associated with it'. The result is that 'riches cease to inspire either pride or envy', and that 'rectitude obtains its proper recognition and respect' (*PR* 153–4). This is a good example of Hegel's perception of the interaction of conscious and unconscious, morally significant and morally indifferent, factors in society. The institution, by its very existence, transforms relationships, both by mitigating the bad effects of the laws of the market and by giving human relationships a moral context, which would have been lacking if there were no formal ties between individuals.

Next, the corporation has legal functions; while insisting on overall supervision by the state, Hegel implicitly regards these as still belonging to the private or economic sphere. These are 'to manage the private property and interests' of 'particular spheres', by which he appears to mean the general regulation of economic affairs and the administration of justice in economic matters, that is to say in matters which traditionally had come within the scope of guild and municipal courts (prices, wages, conditions of work, weights and measures, quality of goods). In these areas, Hegel (vaguely but characteristically) combines authorization from below and from above.

> It is the business of these officials to manage the private property and interests of these particular spheres and, from that point of view, their authority rests on the confidence of their commonalties and professional equals. On the other hand, however, these circles of particular interests must be subordinated to the higher interests of the state, and hence the filling of positions of responsibility in Corporations etc., will generally be effected by a mixture of popular election by those interested with appointment and ratification by higher authority.
>
> (PR 189; cf. *Political Writings* 160; Taylor 1975, 435–6, 441)

This faithfully reflected the variety of earlier practice (see pp.7, 18, 23–7).

In defining the relation between corporations and the state (the latter refers to both government and society at large), Hegel took up two ideas which had precedents in earlier theory and practice, but to which he gave a new edge by incorporating them in his general view of the state. First, the individual only participates in the political life of the state *through groups*, including corporations, which alone, properly speaking, are the state's members. In civil society

> the individual is in evidence only as a member of a general group. The state, however, is essentially an organization each of whose members is in itself a group of this kind, and hence no one of its moments should appear as an unorganized aggregate. ... The circles of association in civil society are already communities. (PR 198; cf. Althusius p.136 above)

The legislature is composed of three elements: the monarchy, the executive (ministers and civil servants), and the Estates. The Estates are divided into two houses, one representing the agricultural, the other the business class (PR 193–201). The electoral units of this second house are the corporations and similar groups.

> [society] makes the appointment as a society, articulated into associ-

ations, communities and Corporations, which although constituted already for other purposes, acquire in this way a connection with politics. ... The concrete state is the whole, articulated into its particular groups. The member of the state is a member of such a group, i.e. of a social class, and it is only as characterized in this objective way that he comes under consideration when we are dealing with the state. ... Owing to the nature of civil society, its deputies are the deputies of the various Corporations. (PR 200, 202)

This then is the principle of articulation or organic differentiation (*Gegliederung*: Taylor 1975, 451): to attain political status, individuals have to be organized into groups, while the state requires a diversity of such members in order to realize and embody the diversity of human life and the Spirit. Thus families, occupational groups and municipal communes had an authentic role to perform in socializing people in an orderly discipline, articulating their needs and integrating them into the whole body of the state. (One might perhaps call this hierarchical federalism.) As we have seen, Althusius similarly made families and guilds the constituent parts of the city, and cities and provinces the constituent parts of the 'universal association'. Hegel, however, also saw this as a means to truly effective participation by the masses in politics: 'It is of the utmost importance that the masses should be organized, because only so do they become mighty and powerful. Otherwise they are nothing but a heap, an aggregate of atomic units' (*PR* 290). In other words, this was one way by which he attempted to incorporate a popular voice, muzzled perhaps, into his system of government, thus (he hoped) taking account of advances made under the banner of popular sovereignty. It would appear that, like Aristotle and Machiavelli, he saw such political participation as conducive to civic virtue. This, then, was a 'functional' theory of representation of the kind which appeared in many subsequent corporatist programmes.

Secondly, Hegel (like de Tocqueville after him) took up the pre-Revolutionary notion of corporations as popular checks upon the arbitrary power of central government – *corps intermédiaires*.

The security of the state and its subjects against the misuse of power by ministers and their officials lies directly in their hierarchical organization and their answerability; but it lies too in the authority given to societies and Corporations, because in itself this is a barrier against the intrusion of subjective caprice into the power entrusted to a civil servant, and it completes from below the state control which does not reach down as far as the conduct of individuals. (PR 192)

The proper strength of the state lies in these associations [sc. Corporations and municipal governments]. In them the executive meets with legitimate interests which it must respect, and ... the individual finds protection in the exercise of his rights, and so links his private interest with the maintenance of the whole. (PR 290)

At the time when Hegel was writing, there was divergence of opinion in Germany as to whether the powers of the guilds should be restored or not (see p.168). It seems clear that on this as on other questions Hegel attempted to take account of both sides of the argument, allowing the tradesman liberty within a general framework designed to promote justice. He adhered to his general orientation, that progress lay in the moralization and rational improvement of traditional institutions. He wanted to restore professional organizations, but not in their old form. As he said, in his comments on the proceedings of the Estates Assembly in Württemberg, after observing that medieval guilds became too powerful because of the weakness of central government:

> After the development of the supreme powers of the state had been completed in recent times, these subordinate communities and guilds were dissolved or at least deprived of their political role and their relation to internal constitutional law. Now, however, it would surely be time, after concentrating hitherto mainly on introducing organization into the circles of higher state authority, to bring the lower spheres back again into respect and political significance, and, purged of privileges and wrongs, to incorporate them as organic structures in the state.
>
> (*Political Writings* 263; cf. *PR* 290)

He avoided the term 'guild' (*Zunft*), using instead *Korporation* or fellowship (*Genossenschaft*) (Heiman 1970, 125 and n.). His 'functional' notion of political representation via corporations was a systematization of the role guilds had often played in city government.

Hegel's major contribution to the theory of the corporation was his analysis of its moral role; this derived from his profound and original understanding of the interaction between economic and moral forces. It was in the context of the corporation that he attempted to come to terms with the whole question of morality and the market. On the other hand, it is perhaps surprising that in this respect he made no distinction between commerce and handicraft. He also left the journeyman or day-labourer in a decidedly inferior position, declaring him unfit for corporation membership (*PR* 153) (though the other 'societies' he mentioned may have included the journeymen's *Gesellenverbände*). It is difficult, moreover, to see how in practice restricted entry to a profession, to be determined by 'the general structure of society', can be reconciled with choice of vocation according to 'the individual's arbitrary will' (*PR* 153, 132–3). Hegel's view of the relation between corporation and state was a development from earlier practice and (implicitly) from the views of Marsiglio and Althusius: here his major innovation lay in his conception of the state. His statements on the authority of the state over corporations, and on the demarcation of spheres between them, are an attempt to tread the line between corporate independence and subordination – between what today is sometimes called liberal and state corporatism. Taylor, indeed, admires Hegel for having seen that 'modern society needs ... a ground for differentiation, meaningful to the people concerned, but which at the same time does not set partial communities against each other, but rather knits them together in a larger whole' (1975, 415–16). It is surely right that, as Hegel indicates, producers and merchants should have a measure of autonomy in regulating their affairs, but that this should function within perimeters set by the long-term needs of the wider community. Only one should perhaps acknowledge that those engaged in production and commerce, who have to work out the details and apply them in real life, have a task every bit as formidable as that of statesman or philosopher.

18

FELLOWSHIP AND COMMUNITY: GIERKE AND TÖNNIES

The contribution of Otto Gierke (1841–1921) to modern guild theory was his application of the new idea of the real personality of the group – itself a radical extension of earlier organic thought – to producers' associations. Orphaned at 14, by the age of 40 he had completed three volumes of *Das deutsche Genossenschaftsrecht* (*DGR*) (*The German Law of Fellowship*), as well as his masterpiece on Althusius, fathered six children, and fought in the wars of 1866 and 1870, being awarded the Iron Cross in the latter (J.D. Lewis 1935, 22–3; Stutz 1922, 9ff.). Superficially he looks the archetype of 'Teutonic scholarship' – more footnotes than text. But the first volume of *Das deutsche Genossenschaftsrecht*, published when he was twenty-seven, was a work of passionate youthful conviction; poise and punch carry it along as a great national epic.

Gierke inherited, ultimately from Herder and the Romantics and proximately from Georg Beseler, the conviction that law, like language, is the expression of a people's spirit; a nation has its own social values imprinted on its customs and institutions. He set out to expound the unique principles of German *Recht*, and to recommend them to the modern world; in particular he saw Fellowship (*Genossenschaft*)* as the solution to the problem of individual and society, of liberty and authority. He defined Fellowship by historical exegesis of supposed type-cases, such as the *comitatus* of warrior-adventurers and the medieval guild, as well as by formal terms of jurisprudence: indeed, like other Romantic historicists, he believed that the ideal type already lay in history's womb. The truly distinctive mark of a Fellowship is that it is a group with a 'collective personality' as real as that of an individual organism. There is no division between leaders and followers because both are subsumed into the group's

* An untranslatable word. Dictionary definitions include: co-operative society (economic), fellowship or brotherhood such as guild (historical), solidarity in general (religious). It can be used both as an abstract noun ('comradeship'), and for particular groups. It is also modern German for the early Germanic *comitatus*. In Remarque's *All Quiet on the Western Front*, when the soldiers realize the hollowness of the ideals they had been brought up with at school etc., the one thing left to them is *Genossenschaft*.

210

personality. This does not dominate the individual members; rather, they commit themselves willingly to the group, and participate in its actions *at least* by giving genuine internal assent. Group personality takes care of the problem of sovereignty because the ruler is not a distinct 'person', commanding or representing the rest, but rather the 'organ' through which 'the invisible collective person appears as a perceptive, deliberating, willing and active unity' (*Wesen* 153; cf. 143–9; J.D. Lewis 1935, 55–61). It is not simply the purpose of the group that binds it together, but its unity as a spiritual being.

The origins of this theory of real group personality, and of Gierke's historicism, lay in German Romanticism. Kant had refuted Humean empiricism by developing Rousseau's notion of the general will as 'a pure act of the understanding which reasons, in the silence of the passions' (cit. Grimsley 1973, 103), to say that we know ourselves as moral beings by direct inner intuition. The Romantics had proclaimed that we know the reality of community in the same way. On the other hand, Herder had applied his 'expressivist anthropology' to whole peoples, each of which 'has its own way of being human' (Taylor 1975, 15); and Hegel had said that 'each particular national genius is to be treated as only one individual in the process of universal history' (*Philosophy of History* 53). Gierke's was a radical development of this theme. He applied the notion of personality as the hidden reality underlying particular manifestations to *all human groups*: shared feelings and convictions tell us that the group to which we belong is a real thing with its own subjectivity, a collective personality (*Gesammtpersönlichkeit*). Hegel, in effect, applied this only to the state; Gierke parted company completely from Hegel at this point, and applied it no less to other groups. This was a line of thought which had been particularly developed in Germany, and which would find a characteristically perverse dénouement in Nazism, since when less has been heard of it. The immediate future, in social science and jurisprudence, appears to have belonged to nominalism, to Weber and Kelsen; the development of structuralism may now indicate otherwise.

One of the most important consequences of this theory was that all groups, from nation to guild, are seen as *eiusdem generis*, since all are Fellowships. Gierke believed that the autonomy of associations was to be Germany's unique and crowning contribution to the theory and practice of liberty: 'these lesser communities and companies ... alone offer the opportunity of combining the large, inclusive, unified state with active civil freedom and self-government' (*DGR* i 1–4 at 3).

Let us first see what he had to say about guilds and their modern equivalent. Gierke believed that the medieval craft-guild was a supreme example of Fellowship in practice. It was a 'chosen' (as opposed to natural) 'union', springing from a spirit of collective 'self-help'. It generated moral awareness, a sense of both duty and rights. Above all, it was 'in public as in private law a collective personality (*Gesammtpersönlichkeit*) ... an invisible unity ... a subject of Right ... for which the visible assembly was but the body and the guild officials the organs' (*DGR* i 358–408 at 405–6; cf. 221–6). But in early modern times craft-guilds had degenerated into enclaves of selfish privilege (*DGR* i 643–6). A fresh start had to be made.

In true historicist manner, Gierke saw a new movement towards a higher moral type of occupational association burgeoning in the world around him. Since *c.*1800, the 'modern association movement', welling up 'from within the people', is combining 'the two moments of [group] personality and free choice' in a 'higher development of the same principle' as that of the guilds of old (*DGR* i 903–4; cf. 652–3). Modern associations are the beneficiaries of liberalism: they have more specific purposes, do not embrace the whole man and so leave the individual more free (*DGR* i 653–5, 882, 904–5). But – again like the Romantics – he saw the movement towards freedom as defective until a specifically German feature is added, namely that of the group itself as a free personality.

In the closing section of the first volume of *Das deutsche Genossenschaftsrecht*, Gierke turned his attention to modern industrial society. His concern here was to identify the 'comradely' (*genossenschaftlich*) elements in modern industrial organization, and to explore how the 'free Fellowship for economic ends' could be further developed (*DGR* i 907–1111). (He nowhere considers the resuscitation of craft-guilds, which were finally abolished in the same year in which this volume was published.) Having noted the growing proliferation of labour unions, trusts and business corporations, Gierke turned to the joint-stock company: is it a *Genossenschaft*? While it is recognized as such in law (*DGR* i 1005), he found difficulty in saying much in its favour, and concluded that 'it is only organized capital', liable to be dominated by selfish considerations, and accompanied by 'the danger of atrophy of free human personality among those without capital' (*DGR* i 1023, 1029). This is because association is here centred upon property rather than persons.

He now turns to the 'personal Fellowship for economic ends' (*DGR* i 1030–111). Whereas earlier economic fellowships existed 'only for the possessing classes (*Stände*)', the fact that today 'non-propertied classes' stand in need of capital and depend upon it, has given rise to 'a system of wholly new fellowship life for economic and industrial ends, which contains the first beginnings of inexhaustible wealth and unforeseeable range'. Thus 'in our century initiative here too ... has gone back to the people'; 'the development of special forms of fellowship among the labouring classes has created new organizations rich in future potential' (*DGR* i 1029–30). The examples he gives are insurance societies, societies providing banking and credit facilities, and consumers' and producers' co-operatives (*DGR* i

1034). Since 1848 there had indeed been a striking development in Germany, unique for the time, of co-operative peasant banks and of attempts to arrange co-operative credit facilities for craftsmen (see p.182). Gierke noted with approval the growth of trade unions in England, in particular their democratic method of organizing strikes through committees, and of co-operatives and political movements to obtain universal suffrage, among workers in both France and England (*DGR* i 1042–3).

From Gierke's point of view, the advantage of co-operatives over joint-stock companies is that in them capital serves the ends of the human person and not vice versa. Members put in a given sum or their whole belongings 'solidarisch', and are debtors on their own account: thus 'personal economic powers [are] bound together into a collective force' (*DGR* i 1034). But, rather than hiring propertyless persons to work for them, they work in person, and 'the right of the partners (*Genossenrecht*) is non-transferable'. Thus there is no separation between person and capital, which consequently does not become an end in itself (*Objekt*): 'the capitalist moment is interwoven with the organism'. Indeed, the rules of the association must ensure an 'organic binding between the Fellowship and its capital'. Above all, '[human] personality is the basis and aim of the Fellowship' (*DGR* i 1030–4). Such a *Genossenschaft* is, like the guilds of old, a 'school of ethical life' (*Sittlichkeit*) (*DGR* i 1048). For these associations, while characterized by the principle of self-help, bring an 'ethical moment' into the pursuit of economic gain; this is because, as against the egoism of capitalist organizations, the workers are not working solely for themselves as individuals, but, since they are partners in a co-operative enterprise, their operations are based upon a 'common mind' (*Gemeinsinn*) (*DGR* i 1035).

The highest type of such personal economic Fellowship is the producers' co-operative which Gierke analysed in a prophetic vein in his closing pages (*DGR* i 1088–111). Here 'productive labour itself forms the association' (*die produktive Arbeit selbst associirt*) (*DGR* i 1035). This 'associated labour' directs the productive enterprise, either on its own or alongside capital: the co-operative can start either as a group of workers who acquire capital, or as a group of capitalists who incorporate workers into full membership of their enterprise (*DGR* i 1089–90) (he cites recent developments in company law in Britain, France and Germany: *DGR* i 1094ff.). The producers' co-operative will give social and cultural assistance to its members, and exercise a supervisory role in moral as well as economic affairs; an 'ethical economic community', it does more than any other economic Fellowship to develop 'the ethical moment of the personal Fellowship' (*DGR* i 1094). Its structure will include a general assembly; a representative 'organ' of directors will be elected from among the 'comrades', but with strictly defined powers and removable 'at any moment'.

213

Such a *Genossenschaft*, Gierke concluded, possessed a 'collective personality' (*Gesammtpersönlichkeit*) *vis-à-vis* both its own members and the outside world (*DGR* i 1109–10).

Gierke included in his discussion of economic associations a remarkable analysis and moral condemnation of capitalism, reminiscent of Marx. The supremacy (*Übermacht*) of modern capital has an inherent tendency to render more and more people, especially small farmers and artisans, propertyless; the existing gap 'between propertied and propertyless is being widened to infinity'. Secondly, the unity of the capitalist firm is constituted by a 'lordship group': 'the representative of capital or the capital body itself [sc. the shareholders] is the absolute economic lord (*Herr*)'. The organization is directed solely by the intelligence of the capitalist head of the firm; the workers are not living members of the firm. As in earlier lordship groups, there is no constitution, so that 'labour is without rights' (*Die Arbeit ist rechtlos*). As 'the impersonal power of capital' grows ever 'more steely', 'the economic existence of the serving members is wholly absorbed', and is determined 'through an alien power (*eine fremde Macht*), in the life of which [the workers] have not the smallest share. ... The free human personality is more and more stunted, until only its name and its abstract right remain' (*DGR* i 1036–8). There is a grave danger that this will lead either to a new caste system or else to social revolution. Such a fate can only be avoided by developing the power of economic association. This alone can enable the working classes to escape servile labour (*Lohnarbeit*), and to achieve economic independence (*DGR* i 1039–40). Gierke rejected socialism and communism because they fail to take account of the principle of Fellowship; they are, rather, an expression of authoritarian Roman ideas, 'another organization from above' (*DGR* i 1039). There can, none the less, be co-operation between the state and economic Fellowships, for example in industrial legislation to shorten the working day (*DGR* i 1039–40).

Gierke, then, in this early work saw economic co-operatives, and producers' co-operatives in particular, as the appropriate application of the Germanic principle of Fellowship to modern industrial society. His was one of the most notable contributions to the theory of producers' associations in the nineteenth century. As associations which render possible a development of ethical life, and at the same time maintain or restore the independence of the worker, such co-operatives are for him a modern counterpart to the medieval craft-guild. The peculiar characteristic of Gierke's theory of the co-operative is the interweaving of freedom and community which characterized his view of the Fellowship in general. A sense of outrage at the dispossession of the independent craftsman and small farmer in the wake of industrial capitalism dominates these pages.

By means of his theory of the Fellowship, Gierke built the principle of participation by all full members into the Romantic notion of the community as mystical totality. His historical exegesis of the Fellowship as a perennial feature of German political culture enabled him to combine the drive for participation with conservative nationalism.

The similarity with Marx, both in Gierke's brief analysis of capitalism and in his notion of workers' self-organization, is obvious. But, although the first volume of *Capital* was published in 1867, there is no reason to suppose that he knew of Marx's work; Gierke was not one to omit references, and he did refer to Lassalle (*DGR* i 1039). The convergence between these two thinkers, so very different in other respects, is explicable in other ways. Both Marx and Gierke inherited certain priorities, a moral language, from the German Romantics (cf. Levin 1974; McLellan 1972, 50–66, 243–4). Both saw the development of the human personality as the ultimate norm; and they were both aware of the supreme importance of an appropriate institutional framework to achieve this end. There was a long-standing tradition in German thought which regarded economics as the handmaid of ethics. Indeed, opposition to 'capitalism' was more or less endemic, as it was not, for example, in Great Britain. The situation in Germany at this time was more fluid and unstable than elsewhere, and hence more open to radical proposals, due to the late but rapid advent of industrialization, which undermined long-standing and deeply-held convictions about economic organization. Indeed, Gierke's political ideas had been anticipated by the Prussian Popular Union when, in 1861, it made a bid for artisan support:

> Freedom through the participation of the subject in legislation and through the autonomy and self-government of corporations and communities. ... No turn to bureaucratic absolutism and social servitude ... no imitations of the political and social institutions which have led France to Caesarism. (cit. Hamerow 1958, 246)

Knowledge of Gierke's work, on the other hand, reminds us how much Marx owed, in his general orientation, to the existing structure of social belief; it was, after all, in Germany that Marxism first became a popular movement. What distinguished Gierke from Marx, on the other hand, was the former's greater emphasis upon freedom, and upon the personal independence of the worker as one goal of co-operation.

But the nation-state too is a Fellowship. Gierke's view of the relationship between the state and other associations rests upon the premise that in Germany the Fellowship principle is so deeply ingrained in popular consciousness that an increase in the power and authority of the nation-state can but promote the further development of free-floating lesser groups. It is a fundamental principle of German law that all groups are legitimate expressions of human social impulses and already possess a moral personality of their own; the state has no choice but to recognize this existing social fact as already constituting corporate personality in the legal sense. Groups, like individuals, must be allowed to lead their own internal life in freedom. Further, the state differs from other Fellowships only in external sovereignty: this does not put it in a category separate or superior to that of other groups; the state, like all modern associations, does not embrace the whole of human life but exists only for certain specific purposes ('Grundbegriffe', 173). All kinds of groups – territorial, vocational, religious and social – are as significant as the state itself for the life of man, and have as much right to exist. In the first volume of *Das deutsche Genossenschaftsrecht*, Gierke said that the idea of the modern German state consists in 'the identity of state and people' and in 'the constitutional state' (*Rechtstaat*). He went on:

> Such a state is not generically different from the lesser communities of public law – the local communities (*Gemeinde*) and corporations (*Körperschaften*) – but stands in relation to them only as the more perfect to the less perfect stage of development. It is the product of the same power.... It is therefore homogeneous with the local communities and Fellowships.
>
> (*DGR* i 832–3, trans. J.D. Lewis 1935, 63; cf. *Wesen* 173, 182)

This was a plea for the maintenance of town and guild autonomy along the lines established in the aftermath of 1848. It was the doctrine for which Maitland, Figgis and the British guild socialists most admired Gierke.

But, at least from 1870, the Second Reich became for Gierke the Fellowship *par excellence*. This was partly based on a mystical experience:

> There are hours in which the community spirit manifests itself with primitive force in almost tangible form and so fills and dominates our inner being that we are scarcely conscious of our single existence as such. Such a sacred hour I experienced here in Berlin's *Unter den Linden* on 15 July 1870 [the date of Bismarck's publication of the Ems telegram which sparked off the Franco-Prussian war].   (*Wesen* 150)

Consequently, while continuing to uphold freedom of association in principle, he in practice identified group personality and Fellowship above all with the fortunes of the German nation-state. 'Prusso-German to the bone' (Stutz 1922, 43), he was borne along on the nationalist tide, then shattered by the defeat of 1918. His response was to join the ultra-conservative German National Party and advocate a 'folk-state ... to win a broader basis and a deeper anchorage in the consciousness of all classes of the Folk than it had before' (cit. J.D. Lewis 1935, 68). Nazism, had he lived to know it, might have seemed the obvious solution. He disowned the Weimar constitution, though one of his pupils, Hugo Preuss, helped to draft its articles on associations and believed the concept of state sovereignty to be redundant (Bowen 1947, 69; Emerson 1928, 130, 142ff.). Of Gierke and others it has been shrewdly observed that, 'The trick was to assume that a communal true Germany of the past would unfold naturally into a national true Germany of the present and future' (Walker 1971, 424).

Gierke's ambivalent work, so bold in aspiration yet cloudy in execution, the youthful prophet declining into dogmatic old age, bears the mark of the modern German tragedy. Indeed, the model of the relationship between leader and followers in the Fellowship, when applied to the nation-state, becomes remarkably like Hitler's *Führer* principle. The homology between small community and state was absurd. Human familiarity can only be extended to a certain point, beyond which it has to be tempered by the norms of civil society. As de Jouvenel puts it, 'The small society, as the milieu in which man is first found, retains for him an infinite attraction ... he undoubtedly goes to it to renew his strength; but ... any attempt to graft the same features on a large society is utopian and leads to tyranny' (pp. 135–6). Must we then conclude that the ultimate horror endured by Europe was, among other things, the state as guild?

Ferdinand Tönnies (1885–1933) wrote his book *Community and Association* (*Gemeinschaft und Gesellschaft*) during the years 1876–87. His basic categories owed much to Gierke (Cahnman 1973, 34–5; cf. Tönnies 68–70, 248). Whereas Gierke had analysed Fellowship (*Genossenschaft*) by means of history, Tönnies explored Community (*Gemeinschaft*) from the viewpoint of its psychological character (the modes of thought cognate to it), and of its sociological structure (the types of human relationship involved, and the types of social organization in which it might be found). One difference between Gierke's Fellowship and Tönnies' Community was that the former focused upon the warrior band (*comitatus*), the latter upon the family, as prototype. But there was considerable overlap in the kind of relationships indicated, and in the other groups cited as manifestations (for example, guild and town). In both writers, the romantic distillation of the Germanic folk tradition of borough, commons or small town (*Gemeinde, gemein Wesen*) was a decisive starting-point (Walker 1971, 355–6, 424–5).

As Gierke had contrasted the felt community and real personality of the German Fellowship with the artificial association of Roman law, so Tönnies contrasted the 'spontaneous will' (*Wesenwille*) of the organic Community, in which members feel themselves part of the same affective group, with the 'deliberate will' (*Kürwille*) of the Association (*Gesellschaft*), in which the members regard the group primarily as an instrument for achieving their separate personal ends (87–9). 'Community should be understood as a living organism, Association as a mechanical aggregate and artifact' (39). Time and again Tönnies ascribes artificial personality to the Association (e.g. 78, 86, 205) – hence his interest in Hobbes.

Tönnies's intention was to expound Community and Association as analytical bases for the scientific study of society, and in particular of movements intrinsic to modern society. Yet he seems impelled by the very nature of his models to describe Community in sympathetic terms, as a warm and caring relationship, and Association in rather unsympathetic terms, as a conglomeration of men grouped together by cold rational calculation. The gulf between feeling and thought – that is, both between personal conviction and scientific method, and between the affective and the rational generally – which Hegel and the Romantics had sought to transcend, reappears in his work, as he certainly believed it did in the contemporary world. He was far less optimistic than Gierke about the possibilities for achieving organic community in the modern world; less gullible, he also saw National Socialism for what it was.

In some ways, Tönnies' Community coincides with what I have called the guild, and his Association with what I have been calling civil society. It goes without saying that his concepts are more far-reaching, and also more abstract, than anything attempted here. He distinguished three types of Community, based on blood, locality and mind; these produce relationships of, respectively, kinship, neighbourhood and *friendship*. Logically and (he implies) historically, kinship or family provides the prototype. But the highest form of Community is that of the mind, issuing in friendship: and this turns out to be a community based pre-eminently upon 'common *work or calling* and thus on common beliefs' (223, my italics). Thus the idea of community based on vocation, which is closely related to what has been discussed here in terms of guilds, appears at the centre of Tönnies' thought. Friendship arises from 'similarity of work and intellectual attitude':

> It comes most easily into existence when callings or crafts are of the same or similar character. Such a tie, however, must be made and maintained through easy and frequent meetings, which are most likely to take place in a town. (49)

He even says that town, village, tribe or people 'can be conceived as a special kind of guild or religious community' (57). Moreover, a typical town is likely to be 'a community of guilds, which, through mutual co-operation, provides the houses of the burghers and thus itself with useful and beautiful things' (63). A central value of Community, finally, is *mutual aid* (46,50). He thought that co-operative production, 'if and when it is able to protect itself against relapsing into mere business' (228), was the only way of reinstating Community in the modern economy, a hope he shared with the young Gierke and Herbert Spencer (p.xxvin.). On the other hand, Community was not confined to small, face-to-face societies: a tribe, people or nation (*Volks-Gemeinde*) qualifies as Community, so long as there exists 'a common state of mind which in its higher forms – common customs and common beliefs – penetrates to the members of the *Volk*' (56; cf. 52). But although he clearly had contemporary phenomena in mind, his writing here seems analytical and not intended as an endorsement of nationalism.

Tönnies is an outstanding example of the tendency to regard Community as the primitive and natural type of human group, and Association as the peculiar product of modern rationalism. We may wish to say, rather, that man has always been a roaming creature, open, when opportunity offered, to far-flung exchange with other regions and tribes. The settled agricultural community and the 'home town' are not human norms. Families quarrel; exchange is no more artificial than speech. We can certainly say that Tönnies got his time-scale wrong: rationalistic Association in Europe goes back to the twelfth century.

19

DURKHEIM AND MODERN CORPORATISM

Corporatism was one European response to the ethical and organizational problems of *laissez-faire* industrialization. It was a distinctive programme for political economy. Whether consciously or not, it followed a similar prescriptive pattern to that laid down by Hegel for the corporation itself; but it gave the state less authority over corporations than Hegel had apparently envisaged. In turn, the movement contributed to a new theoretical formulation of the social function of occupational groups, in Durkheim. Whereas socialists often ascribed moral worth to working-class groups, corporatists wanted trade unions to merge with employers' associations, so as to form an organization based not on status or class but on the profession or field of production. They favoured economic regulation by the corporations themselves, with assistance from government only when necessary; in general, they were as much opposed to state control as to *laissez-faire*. Some, however, envisaged more extensive co-operation, and even symbiosis, between corporations and the state.

Corporatism began in Germany, in direct continuity with the guild tradition, and soon struck root in France and Belgium; it was taken up somewhat later in southern Europe and South America (Bowen 1947; Elbow 1953; Schmitter 1974; Vidler 1964, 144–5; Walker 1971, 294). In the nineteenth century, corporatist theory took hold most easily in countries with a strong guild and mercantilist background: 'In continental Europe the notion of the privileged corporation has ... been carried straight over into modern thought from the guild system' (Shonfield 1965, 162). In the period 1870–1940 corporations received more attention from ideologues than guilds had ever done; the profusion of corporatist theories was spectacular. The leading minor theorists were, in Germany, Karl Marlo (1810–65) and Albert Schäffle (1831–1903) (Bowen 1947, 53–8, 124–37); and in France Albert de Mun (1841–1914) (Elbow 1953, 85ff.; Vidler 1964, 119–23), Léon Duguit who taught law at Bordeaux from 1886 to 1928, and Joseph Paul-Boncour, whose popularization of Durkheim's ideas in *Le fédéralisme économique* (1900) made a considerable impact (Hayward 1960, 185–97). In 1934 the Rumanian Mihail Manoilesco published *Le siècle de cor-*

poratisme, regarded by some as the classic of corporatism (Schmitter 1974, 117–27). While corporatism proved especially attractive to some Catholics, partly because it offered a *via media* between capitalism and socialism, partly because of its moral tone and appeal to tradition, its leading theorists, with the exception of de Mun, were Protestant or non-Christian (Schmitter 1974, 90; cf. Vidler 1964, 144–5).

Craft-guilds themselves were invoked with nostalgia in Catholic circles, finding honourable mention in Pius XI's social encyclical *Quadragesimo Anno* (1931) (Camp 1969, 38–9), just as they were by Ruskin and William Morris. Guild socialism, an English adaptation of corporatism and the only modern movement to adopt the term 'guild', drew its immediate inspiration from A. J. Penty's *The Restoration of the Guild System* (1906) and S.G. Hobson's *National Guilds* (1914) (Glass 1966, 17–8, 32). But in general corporatists were careful to distinguish their programme from the guild system which, in those parts of Europe where it had lasted longest, was still associated with exclusive privilege and tenacious conservatism.

The chief tenets of corporatism were, first, that each profession or sector of industry should have an organization embracing all those engaged in it; and, secondly, that these corporations should be given responsibility for deciding pay, working conditions and the like, for settling industrial disputes by means of special tribunals, and for determining industrial and economic policy in conjunction with or in place of state agencies. Naturally there were many variants of these proposals. Generally speaking, the first aim was to gain full legal recognition for existing producers' associations, and then to amalgamate employers' and employees' associations on a craft basis or the nearest possible equivalent.

These proposals were advocated on both moral and practical grounds: justice and stability were the criteria most often appealed to. By including both workers and managers in a single body, and giving this ultimate responsibility for overall management, though not actual ownership of capital, it was hoped to eliminate class conflict. The corporation, usually in conjunction with the state, would ensure continuity of employment and a decent livelihood; workers would be given some say in the management of industry. Such an increase in social justice would eliminate poverty, disruption by strikes, and the threat of violent revolution. But corporatists also emphasized *esprit de corps* and the moralizing effects of corporate fellowship. Workers would be given a sense of identity, of the worth of their occupation, of professional honour and duty – here there was certainly continuity with the craft-guild tradition.

To us today, the most interesting feature of corporatist thought is the idea that shared membership of a profession creates a genuine community. The corporatists' whole conception of community marks them off from other schools of thought. On the one hand, they repudiated any notion that

221

individuals can be conceived of outside society or that society is an association of individuals for merely utilitarian ends. On the other hand, they rejected collectivism and the Romantic elevation of the state. Men are inherently and *ex hypothesi* social beings, but social life can take a multiplicity of forms; it is normal to belong simultaneously to several different kinds of association – a family, a corporation, a club, a locality, a church, a nation-state and so on – and to be deeply committed to and dependent upon each of these for a different sphere of life. Each is a genuine community, answering real human needs and aspirations and binding persons together in its own unique way. Their special plea was that the professional group be acknowledged as one distinctive category of association, arising from human nature, fundamental to human needs and personal development in the sphere of work, and therefore fully deserving recognition as a legal and moral entity, just like family, church or state. The essential role of earlier guilds in their argument was that they indicated that modern society had deviated from the norm; evidence from European and non-European history, and from other contemporary cultures, suggested that the individual-state dichotomy quite failed to grasp the real complexity of human society.

The corporation was not simply a group one entered for convenience; like the family it had a moral and spiritual dimension. In this respect, their social theory was in the Romantic mould, affective rather than instrumental. Some corporatists would go so far as to say that the difference between corporation and state was only one of degree. This was the new meaning they gave to the organic view of society; the whole is made up of self-subsistent parts into which individuals are already integrated. As Paul-Boncour put it:

> There is more genuine solidarity between the members of the same profession than between the inhabitants of the same neighbourhood. ... A professional community creates between its members an interdependence, a real and positive solidarity, analogous to that engendered by a territorial community.   (cit. Hayward 1960, 197)

'Solidarity' was indeed a key word for corporatists. The state, then, cannot exist without families and corporations any more than they without the state. No single association can claim to represent the individual exhaustively in the public sphere. As the British guild socialist G.D.H. Cole put it in 1917:

> We now see such associations as natural expressions and instruments of the purposes which certain groups of individuals have in common, just as we see the State ... as the natural expression of other purposes which the same individuals have in common when they are grouped in another way.
> (*Self-government in Industry* 129; cf. *Quadragesimo Anno*, cit. Camp 1966, 126–7)

Such a view of professional groups led to the proposal by many corporatists that 'functional' representation should, in whole or in part, supplant territorial representation in local and national government. This aspect of corporatism, relating however to labour unions (*syndicats*), was advocated by the international socialist minority in the Paris Commune, as 'the organic basis of rational representation', with a historical reference to the medieval crafts in Italy (cit. Rihs 1971, 242; cf. 241, 248). It would indeed involve a return to medieval urban practice, and to the political ideas of Marsiglio and Althusius. Schäffle argued that, to the existing parliament, there should be added 'a body of representatives from the great public and popular groupings' (cit. Bowen 1947, 136). Functional representation was one of the most distinctive doctrines of British guild socialism. Cole argued that the population should be represented both as producers and as consumers: in communes, regions and state there would be two chambers, one elected by the guilds, the other by territorial constituencies. 'I conceive that the various Guilds will be unified in a central Guild Congress, which will be the supreme industrial body, standing to the people as producers in the same relation as Parliament will stand to the people as consumers' (Cole 134; cf. Glass 1966, 19, 45). The scheme was fully worked out in his *Guild Socialism Re-stated* (1920: Glass 1966, 45). Following Gierke, guild socialism rejected the traditional notion of state sovereignty and advocated 'the co-sovereignty of the Guilds and the State' (Cole 6; cf. Olson 1965, 114–16).

By far the most intellectually satisfying exposition of corporatism is that of Emile Durkheim (1858–1917), who first expounded his views on professional associations in his *Leçons de sociologie* (*Lessons in Sociology*), a series of public lectures delivered in 1896–1900 at Bordeaux (cf. Lukes 1973, 137), but not published till 1950 (the English translation is best avoided). These made an immediate public impact in France, partly through the popularization by Paul-Boncour (Lukes 1973, 541n.). The message was repeated and refined in the preface to the second edition of *De la division du travail social* (*Division of Labour in Society*: 1902). Durkheim's contribution to the theory of professional groups was sociological: his argument derived its peculiar force from its being a coherent extension and practical application of the whole theory of society expounded in *Division of Labour* (first published in 1893) and *Suicide* (1897).

Durkheim held that human society is *sui generis*, a plane of being conceptually distinct from that of the individual, moving according to its own collective dynamic, the understanding and scientific investigation of which is the task of sociology (cf. Lukes 1973, 9ff., 20–1). His 'central interest was in the ways in which social and cultural factors influence, indeed largely constitute, individuals' (Lukes 1973, 13). It is possible to know the complexion and movement of society as a whole. In practice, this involved for Durkheim a combination of bold hunches based on reflection and detailed study of such key social phenomena as law, religion and morality – a characteristically later nineteenth-century undertaking, partly philosophical, partly empirical. Individuals are essentially formed by society; they depend upon it for their sense of who they are and how they should behave; it gives them a moral language. Society is the 'necessary condition' of the moral world: ' man is a moral being only because he lives in society, since morality consists in being solidary with a group and varies with this solidarity' (*De la division du travail social* (*DTS*) 394; cf. Lukes 1973, 416). In this way he gave a quasi-scientific meaning to the notion of 'solidarity' popular in France at the time (see p.177; Lukes 1973, 138–40). Among his major works, *Division of Labour* examined the different forms such social solidarity could take, and *Suicide* examined the results of breakdown in social solidarity. In both works, he was using sociology to throw light on contemporary problems, with a view to opening the way for remedies.

In his first published article, in 1885, Durkheim reviewed Schäffle's *Structure and Life of the Social Body*, a classic of organic corporatism, and in 1886–7 he won a scholarship to visit Germany. The 'German contribution to the nascent science of sociology', especially 'what he called the new organic conception of society' (Lukes 1973, 88) did much to form his notion of social holism. There was thus, for him too, a clear link with German Romanticism (cf. Lukes 1973, 79–85, 124). On his return from Germany, Durkheim wrote that 'The individual is an integral part of the society into which he is born; the latter pervades him from all sides; for him to isolate and abstract himself from it is to diminish himself' (cit. Lukes 1973, 88); and, later, 'Personally, I owe much to the Germans. It is in part from their school that I acquired the sense of social reality, of its organic complexity and development' (cit. Lukes 1973, 92). In *Division of Labour*, he was to say that 'the form of the whole determines that of the parts. Society does not find the bases on which it rests already formed in men's consciences; it creates them for herself' (*DTS* 342).

In *Division of Labour*, Durkheim's most ambitiously schematic work in which he undertook to analyse the general evolution of society, he distinguished two main types of society depending on whether solidarity was 'mechanical' or 'organic'. Primitive society was divided into 'segments', such as clans, analogous to the cells of early organic life, each self-sufficient and identical in structure. Here morality was determined most of all by *la conscience commune* or *collective* ('the set of beliefs and sentiments common to the average members of a single society': cit. Lukes 1973, 151), which impresses upon each individual a more or less identical sense of duty. This was 'mechanical solidarity'. Modern society, on the other hand, is far less homogeneous, being divided, like the higher forms of organic life, into specialized 'organs'. This is due to the division of labour, the principal significance of which is, not so much that it has facilitated economic development, but that it has given rise to a wholly new configuration of morality. As social functions became specialized, people became less and less members of a single undifferentiated society, and more and more grouped into occupational categories as merchants, lawyers, various kinds of craftsmen and so on. As a result, the common conscience has gradually lost its hold: 'It is the division of labour which, more and more, fills the role previously filled by the common conscience. It is the principal bond of social aggregates of the higher type' (DTS 148; cf. 26, 79ff., 267). This produces 'organic solidarity'. Durkheim's central argument was that the division of labour is neither, as Political Economy suggested, a merely utilitarian device for increasing wealth and happiness, nor, as Marxism proclaimed, a necessary evil to be transcended in due time. Rather, it has a profound moral significance; it 'becomes the pre-eminent source of social solidarity', and 'by the same token, the basis of the moral order' (DTS 396). The result is that 'The categorical imperative of the moral conscience is in the process of assuming the following form: *Enable yourself to fulfil a determinate function usefully*' (DTS 6). This gives rise to a different and indeed more advanced and superior type of morality: 'What characterizes the morality of organized societies, compared with that of segmentary societies, is that it has something more human, and thus more rational, about it' (DTS 404). It can be the means to the further moral development of the human personality (DTS 211ff., 398ff.). Durkheim identified the principal cause of this change in social rather than economic factors, the growth of population interacting with new moral ideas to produce in society a greater 'dynamic or moral density' (Lukes 1973, 168).

This new moral complexion of society has two aspects: first, an enhanced value attached to the individual as such. 'As all other beliefs and practices take on a less and less religious character, the individual becomes the object of a sort of religion. We regard the dignity of the person as an object of worship' (DTS 147; cf. 208, 395ff.). This is partly because, in the process of the division of labour, the individual becomes more detached from his native milieu, has to take more choices upon himself, notably with regard to his occupation, and so becomes more aware of himself as a separate entity. This need not, as some believe, lead to alienation from his fellows or the moral disintegration of society; rather , a more complex but no less effective kind of social solidarity can develop. It is in the very nature of a society in which division of labour operates that individuals are more, not less, dependent upon one another economically, and the correlative of this is that men can develop an increased awareness of the intrinsic value of all fellow-members of society as persons. In the second place, the various occupations

225

into which society is divided become the basis for social solidarity; as the duties common to all members of society alike decrease in number and importance, the duties common to members of a profession increase, and ethics revolve to a greater extent around one's occupational status.

The task of citizen and statesman today is to develop this moral aspect of the division of labour and bring organic solidarity to full fruition. The transition from mechanical to organic solidarity, and the occurrence of 'abnormal' or 'pathological' forms of the division of labour (cf. Lukes 1973, 28–30), are responsible for the serious dislocation felt throughout contemporary society. Old loyalties and certainties are breaking down, while new ones are imperfectly developed. This is why so many people suffer from *anomie*, lack of moral structure, a feeling of aimlessness in life; and it is the ultimate cause of commercial crises and the apparent antagonism between labour and capital (*DTS* 344–60). The most pressing problem of contemporary society is that, just as society is becoming 'essentially industrial', the whole of economic life and relationships is in a condition of 'juridical and moral *anomie*', being unregulated by law or morality (*DTS* ii, xxxvi; *Leçons* 48–9; Filloux 1977, 345). There is no moral structure, no set of norms or agreed rules, no framework within which disputes may be resolved; employers and unions confront one another like separate states, 'there are no regular contacts between them'. Hence the conflict endemic in economic life today; any agreements that are reached reflect only the distribution of power at a particular moment, 'they consecrate facts, they cannot create rights' (*ils consacrent un état de fait, ils ne sauraient en faire un état de droit*) (*DTS* vii–viii). 'It is the law of the strongest which rules, and there is inevitably a chronic state of war, latent or acute'; this contradicts the very purpose for which society itself exists (*DTS* iii). Since one's occupation takes up an increasing area of one's life, and this is unregulated by morality, there exists the danger of 'general demoralization' (*DTS* iv).

What we require is not a new common conscience (that was to be the strategy of twentieth-century totalitarianism). Rather, first, we need to become aware that certain moral beliefs, notably the sanctity of the person, are shared and sanctioned by society at large. Secondly, and most urgently, we need to develop professional ethics; and this, given Durkheim's view of morality in general, means developing an appropriate social organization of the professions. Moral duties arise out of one's membership of a society and so vary in relation to the type of society. One has specific duties as member of a family and state, and civic duties vary from one state to another. But, in societies with organic solidarity,

> individuals are grouped no longer according to their inherited relationships, but according to the particular nature of the social activity to which they devote themselves. Their natural and necessary milieu is no longer that of their birth, but that of their profession. (*DTS* 157–8)

226

Social identity rests increasingly on occupation; people see themselves in terms of their life activity, of what they do, rather than of their background, who they were born as. Indeed, it is possible to foresee that one day 'all our social and political organization will be based exclusively, or almost exclusively, on professions' (*DTS* 167). Compared with segmentary society and the common conscience, those rules 'which together constitute professional ethics (*la morale professionnelle*)' have 'a much more marked diversity', depending upon whether one is a teacher, soldier, industrialist and so on. Thus 'there are as many moralities (*morales*) as there are different professions, and, since as a rule each individual practises only one profession, the result is that these different moralities apply to altogether distinct groups of individuals' (*Leçons* 43–4).

This was why Durkheim saw the answer to the *anomie* of modern commercial and industrial life in the reconstitution of economic groups. It is not simply that people engaged in production and exchange have the wrong moral standards, nor that they are failing to live up to moral standards they already have. What is lacking is a structure or 'language' in which claims can be meaningfully asserted and settlements can command more than merely external assent. This can only be provided by professional groups. This was how Durkheim applied his general sociology of ethics to the problem.

> Ethics are always the work of a group, and they cannot operate if this group does not protect them with its authority. (*Leçons* 46)

> The only moral personality which stands above individual personalities is that formed by the collectivity. It alone, furthermore, has that continuity and indeed perpetuity which is necessary to constitute a norm. (*DTS* v)

Further, no society can function without 'moral discipline':

> If, in the occupations which take up nearly all our time, we follow no other rule than that of enlightened self-interest, how can we develop the taste for impartiality, self-forgetfulness and sacrifice? ... There must be rules which tell each fellow-labourer his rights and duties, not only in a general and vague way, but precisely and in detail, having regard to the principal circumstances arising in the course of ordinary life. ... But an ethic cannot be improvised. It is the work of the very group to which it must be applied. (*Leçons* 50–2; cf. *Suicide* 378ff.)

The only solution is the formation of professional groups, of 'special groups in society whose concern it is to elaborate [professional ethics] and which will ensure that they are respected' (*Leçons* 46).

> In order that this professional ethic may establish itself in the economic order, the professional group, which is almost entirely lacking in this area

of social life, must constitute or reconstitute itself. (*Leçons* 55)

The only group which answers to these, necessarily diverse, conditions is one that would be formed by all those taking part in the same industry, united and organized in a single body ... in one word, a public institution. (*DTS* vi, viii)

The aim of these reconstituted corporations is not, primarily, to impose any particular set of rules, but above all to ensure that 'economic activity is penetrated with other ideas and other needs than those of individuals, that it become socialized', and that 'the professions may become moral milieux' (*Leçons* 67). What is needed is 'a moral force capable of containing the egoism of individuals, of sustaining in the workers' hearts a more lively sentiment of their common solidarity, of preventing the law of the strongest from applying itself so brutally to industrial and commercial relations' (*DTS* xi-xii). This cannot be undertaken by society as a whole or the state because the 'public conscience' is little concerned with professional ethics 'precisely because they are not common to all members of society' (*Leçons* 45–6). In general, economic affairs are too specialized to admit of effective regulation by the state (*DTS* vi, 348ff.).

All this has a somewhat Hobbesian ring: there is a 'state of war', and the very foundations of the moral universe depend upon a structural adaptation. Only it is not, as Hobbes would have it, 'a common power' but rather group life itself which is required. Durkheim was here, despite himself, re-applying Rousseau's notion of the radical moral transformation made possible in man by the creation of society. Again, while Marx thought that division of labour was one of the causes of present misery, Durkheim was advocating the normalization of the division of labour through the introduction of a group life appropriate to it. Such a *régime corporatif* is necessary not so much for economic as for moral reasons: it alone can enable economic life to be 'moralized' (*Leçons* 67). The professional group is to play a socializing role analogous to that of the family (*DTS* viii; *Leçons* 18, 64); while it may be less important than the family, its significance for the individual increases as professions become increasingly differentiated (*DTS* xix).

Such professional groups will make men happier by giving them a sense of their solidarity with others. Reversing Adam Smith's jibe against corporations, Durkheim says that, when people with common interests associate, it is not simply in order to protect those interests, but also 'for the delight of only being one among several ... of living in communion', of being 'able to lead one and the same moral life together' (*Leçons* 63). Group life does not so much impose moral authority upon people from without as kindle within them a moral sense of their own. The group is 'a source of life *sui generis*', from which comes 'a warmth which reanimates men's hearts, opens them to

228

sympathy and destroys egoism' (*DTS* xxx). Here Durkheim seems to have ascribed to professional groups something of that power for moral transformation which Rousseau had applied to the state.

But what about the liberty of the individual? Must we not fear that the professional group, as the 'organ' which replaces the earlier 'segment', may not be just as oppressive as the common conscience of old, and that 'the corporate and professional spirit' may not 'replace the parochial spirit'? Durkheim's own answer lay in the very nature of organic solidarity. First, corporations only affect people in their professional lives; in other respects, they will continue to enjoy the increased liberty acquired by the breakdown of mechanical solidarity. Secondly, the same individualist pressures which have 'lightened the collective yoke' in society at large, will 'produce their liberating effect inside the corporation as well as outside it' (*DTS* 289–90; cf. M.J. Hawkins 1980, 40). Compulsory membership in corporations need be no more oppressive than in territorial units like the commune, which we take for granted (*Leçons* 76). Durkheim countered the objections of liberals by insisting that 'economic independence' is essential if liberty is to be 'other than nominal'; and experience has shown 'what complex regulation' is needed to secure such independence for individuals (*DTS* iii–iv). There is an analogy with the classical argument of liberal political theory, that individual liberty depends upon the very existence of law and government. Durkheim does not, however, meet the argument that, by increasing the power of the producers, corporations might act in their own collective self-interest against the interests of consumers.

Durkheim appealed to Roman and medieval history as evidence that professional corporations 'respond to some profound and lasting need' in man (*Leçons* 56–61 at 58; 69–74; *DTS* viii–xi, xxi–xxvi), and that they are able to 'constitute a moral milieu' (*Leçons* 62; *DTS* xii–xvi). He discounted prejudice against the corporations of the *ancien régime* as due to their having been in a state of degeneration (*Leçons* 56); his special admiration for the craft colleges of ancient Rome was perhaps intended to suggest that corporations are compatible with republicanism (*DTS* viii–xi). Any social institution can become atrophied; this does not mean it should be abolished, but rather reformed (*DTS* xvi, 197). His intention was not to restore the earlier guilds in their original form, but to 'constitute or reconstitute' them in a form appropriate to 'the actual conditions of our collective life' today (*Leçons* 55, 69). Market exchange used to operate primarily within an urban area, but has now become 'national and international'; so too the corporation must be extended into a national institution (*DTS* xxvii–xxviii; *Leçons* 74). This will enable it to avoid the *immobilisme* of earlier guilds, and to correspond harmoniously with 'the mobile equilibrium of needs and ideas' (*DTS* xxix–xxx). But he does not indicate how corporations can cope with the international market.

Durkheim, then, is asking for 'restored and renewed corporations' (*Leçons* 78). The practical functions of the corporation are to regulate contracts of employment, working conditions, pay, industrial health and welfare, and relations between employers and employees (*DTS* xxxv; *Leçons* 74, 77). Like other corporatists, he saw corporations as a means of overcoming class conflict; this would follow from their more positive function of developing social solidarity and professional ethics. The existing separate organizations of workers and employers need to be fused into single corporations for each section of industry (*DTS* vii; Filloux 1977, 348). Industrial disputes will require 'special tribunals which, in order to be able to give completely independent judgment, have rights as varied as the forms of industry' (*Leçons* 77). Durkheim shared the general view of corporatists, that corporations must not only be given legal status, but must have authority to settle disputes with legal sanctions (*DTS* vii). Like Hegel, he suggested that welfare would best be administered within the professional group, where there is 'a certain mental and moral homogeneity' (*DTS* xxx). Corporations could also provide educational and recreational facilities, as labour unions sometimes did in his own day (and as they do in communist countries now) (*DTS* xxxi). They are to be governed by their own democratically elected 'administrative council, a sort of miniature parliament'. The distribution of electoral power between employers and employees should correspond to 'the relative importance given by opinion to these two factors of production' (*Leçons* 74; Filloux 1977, 344).

Durkheim was at one with other corporatists in rejecting both *laissez-faire*, the disastrous consequences of which were plain to him, and state control. There is some dispute as to whether or not Durkheim should be called a 'socialist' (Filloux 1977, 351–2; Lukes 1973, 265, 546): it depends on one's definition of socialism. He rejected government ownership or management of industry. The corporation must operate alongside the state 'without being absorbed by it, that is to say, while remaining a secondary group, relatively autonomous, it must become national' (*Leçons* 74). Only by remaining independent of government can corporations respond flexibly enough to changing conditions and the diversity of industrial development. By means of corporations, 'economic life can be self-regulating and self-determining without losing its diversity. ... It is this diversity which constitutes the proper task of the corporation' (*DTS* xxviii–xxix). But he appears to have been sensitive to the socialist objection that, having removed the workers' organizational independence and right to strike, corporations would leave the relationship between capitalist, manager and worker basically unchanged. It was clear to him that any considerable inequality in the distribution of capital or income would prevent the development of a shared professional ethic. He therefore recommended a radical reduction in economic inequality by imposing strict limits on the amount of heritable wealth. Further, he suggested that the corporation itself might take over from the family the ownership, management and transmission of industrial and commercial property (*DTS* xxxv–xxxvi). This would in effect be a step towards co-operative production.

Durkheim suggested, like many others at the time, that corporations should also play a political role, with 'functional' representation by professions replacing geographical electoral units.

> There is even reason to suppose that the corporation is called to become the essential base, or one of the essential bases, of our political organization ... Everything points to the possibility that, if progress continues in the same direction as now, it will have to assume an ever more central and dominant place in society. (*DTS* xxxi)

In this way, 'political assemblies will more accurately reflect the diversity of social interests' (*DTS* xxxi). This would reproduce in the modern nation-state the relation between government and guilds in some earlier cities (cf. *DTS* xxi ff.). Professions should form the primary subdivisions of the nation: 'the organized profession or corporation should be the essential organ of public life'; 'society ... will become a vast system of national corporations' (*DTS* xxxi–xxxii). Echoing Hegel, he re-formulated the earlier French notion of *corps intermédiaires*: 'a nation cannot survive unless a whole series of secondary groups, close enough to individuals to attract them strongly into their sphere of action and so involve them in the general stream of social life, inserts itself between the individual and the state' (*DTS* xxxiii).

Durkheim provided corporatism with an intellectual foundation in the new discipline of sociology. This provided a new range of arguments for corporatists, who avidly used his ideas. Apart from his Bordeaux colleague, the law professor Duguit (Lukes 1973, 103), his most distinguished disciple was Manoilescu (Filloux 1977, 346; Schmitter 1974, 117ff.). He however ended up supporting fascism, and the fascist adaptation of corporatism did much to discredit Durkheim. It is doubtless (Filloux 1977, 336ff., 348) quite unfair to assimilate Durkheim to fascism. There was, however, a problem which Durkheim shared with all corporatists: how are corporations to be set up? Durkheim insisted that the corporative regime 'cannot be set up by a professor at his desk, nor by a statesman'; it can only be 'the work of the groups concerned' (*Leçons* 69). But what if the groups concerned don't act? It is the same problem faced by Marxists with regard to the proletarian revolution. Durkheim suggested that initiative should be taken by the state, and that 'once [the group] is formed and so able to start living, it would develop of itself, and nothing would be able to anticipate or arrest this development' (*Leçons* 78). By 1902 his tone was more urgent: juridical reform in economic matters cannot be contemplated 'unless one begins by creating the organ necessary to the establishment of new law [namely corporations]' (*DTS* xxxvi). This could leave the way open to the kind of state-sponsored corporations introduced under fascism. In general, however, it would appear that Durkheim's view of corporations was closely aligned with his belief in secular democratic republicanism. Corporations are to govern themselves by democratic means (cf. Filloux 1977, 351–2).

What of Durkheim's central argument, that corporations are essential for the development of law and morality in business life and industrial production? This has suffered in esteem because of criticisms of Durkheim's whole approach to sociology in which, it is said, prior assumptions, however intelligent in themselves, played so great a part as to render the resulting generalizations unscientific. Durkheim's belief that morals spring from society seems to have blinded him to the possibility of *corporate egoism*. It is often true that people are prepared to give special consideration to fellow-members of a club or union; but, as Adam Smith pointed out, this may be prejudicial to outsiders. It is not only virtues that can acquire collective force. Durkheim's belief in the cure-all effects of corporations was backed up by no scientific study of corporations, for the good reason that none existed; the conclusions he drew at second hand from ancient and medieval history appear on the whole as little more than wishful half-truths.

But, as has been pointed out by Fox and Flanders (1969) and as few contemporary observers would perhaps deny, Durkheim's particular understanding and interpretation of the problems of industrial capitalism continue to be relevant today precisely because there is a lack of any normative order within which collective bargaining or legal arbitration can operate effectively, with that degree of consent from those concerned which is necessary to any legal system. Whether or not the remedy is to establish corporations is another matter. In a country like Britain that moral space is already occupied by unions. Durkheim would certainly have wished 'the two sides of industry' to come closer together, as a *pis aller*. But he would have pointed out – rightly, I think – that they can only do so if they speak the same language; and this can only occur if they have a perceived identity of interests. In fact, co-operative production is a no less realistic alternative than corporatism; and probably some move towards workers' shareholding, workers' control and the like is the only way in which a perceived identity of interests can be established.

Durkheim is the most recent philosopher of the corporation. He has some things in common with earlier theorists, and is in some ways *sui generis*. He gave quasi-scientific meaning to the age-old value of guild solidarity. Throughout history, philosophical theories of the guild have been linked to the organic conception of society; Durkheim, however, gave the organic analogy new meaning, as pre-eminently applicable to modern societies

232

characterized by an advanced division of labour. Marsiglio, Althusius and Hegel had, each in their own way, linked the case for corporate organization to an awareness of the importance of the division of labour in society. Althusius ascribed hardly less significance to the division of labour than Durkheim did, and he too saw it as a profoundly moral phenomenon. What differentiates Durkheim here is his historicist view of the progression of the division of labour. The idea that corporations are a means of moralizing individuals engaged in business and production originated in Hegel. But Durkheim, perhaps because he attached importance to empirical data, perhaps because he was a good modern individualist, showed less disdain for the economic activity about which he was preaching.

When all was said and done, corporatism had been devised by concerned intellectuals; it was not a grass-roots movement, did not represent the ideology of any specific group, and therefore lacked the kind of popular support which could have carried it to power under its own impetus. A kind of 'state corporatism' (Schmitter 1974, 99–104) was introduced by the Italian fascists, by Salazar in Portugal, by Franco in Spain, and by the Vichy regime in France (it has also been adopted in some South American countries). State corporatism has thus tended to become part of a right-wing package, a radical alternative to socialism. In such cases the corporations tend to be state-inspired and state-orientated, and far more subordinate to government than any corporatist theorist would have wished. As for Nazi Germany, 'The actual political and economic organization of the Third Reich did not even roughly correspond to the specifications laid down by any of the main schools of corporatist theory' (Bowen 1947, 12).

On the other hand, certain other features of the corporatist programme have been adopted by some of the most stable European democracies, beginning with Norway, Sweden and Switzerland between the wars, and since 1945 by the Netherlands, Austria and West Germany (Schmitter 1974, 99–107). In these cases, independent economic interest groups, that is, labour unions and employers' organizations, have been voluntarily co-opted into the economic decision-making process of government, for fixed periods or on an open-ended basis. In the words of one author, they thus acquire 'quasi-legal status and a prescriptive right to speak for their segments of the population. They influence the process of government directly, bypassing [parliament]. They are agents of authority. They deputize for the state in whole sectors of public life' (Huntford cit. Schmitter 1974, 99). A similar development has occurred informally in Britain, notably in the Wilson era, and tends to be favourably regarded by centre groups, including the new Social Democratic Party. This is a development of pressure-group pluralism; as Shonfield noted in 1965, 'The British, for all their anti-corporatist tradition, allow effective power to slide into the hands of the corporations without subjecting them to public control – for national doctrine insists that they are no more than free associations of individuals' (1965, 162–3; cf. Beer 1969, 395, 419).

In these cases, labour unions and employers' groups participate officially in the management of the national economy. The chief purpose is to control the business cycle, ensure regular economic growth and maintain social stability (Lehmbruch 1979, 54). In other words, free enterprise has found it necessary not only to recognize occupational groups but to give them an integral role in economic policy. Some see this as a necessary feature of complex, highly developed economies, others as 'a powerful influence for reinforcing class dominance' (Panitch 1979, 139; cf. Lehmbruch 1979, 59; Schmitter 1974, 105–7). This has been called 'liberal' or 'societal' corporatism. But this would appear to be an abuse of language: while such arrangements produce some of the effects of corporatism, there are to begin with no true corporations, in the sense intended by modern corporatist theory, namely craft- or industry-based organizations, but rather representatives of workers on one side and management on the other. It is, rather, the consultation or politicization of economic interest groups. The entire moral dimension of the 'corporation' is lacking (cf. Fox and Flanders 1969). Indeed, it may be doubted whether either 'state' or 'liberal' corporatism is worthy of the name.

On the other hand, there are some similarities with the role of guilds in earlier times. The craft-guilds could either be used as instruments of state economic policy, as in France, or, as in the guild towns, achieve a place in government. (State and liberal corporatism correspond roughly to the Roman and Germanic views of lesser associations respectively.) If we see 'liberal corporatism' as a kind of power-sharing, there is some analogy with the way in which, in some medieval towns, political movements of craft workers formed new oligarchies, with relatively little redistribution of wealth, but more accountable to certain groups of workers, notably those in the key industries of a region. Under favourable conditions, chiefly in towns of middling size, some guilds were probably more successful – their leading members being men of substance and managerial experience – in implementing economic policies which suited them, than modern labour unions have been so far. And some medieval cities probably approximated more closely to the nineteenth-century corporatist model than any modern state yet has.

One has the impression that, since the demise of modern corporatist theory in the fascist era, political theory has lagged behind political practice. This is especially true in the case of the new and relatively silent advance of liberal corporatism. As Anderson says, 'Corporatist practices exist in all modern polities, but we have no coherent theory of corporatist construction' (p. 281). There are of course very many empirical studies of the role of interest groups of all kinds in political life; recognition of their significance has given rise to the 'pluralist' approach adopted by many political scientists. And indeed among political theorists groups other than the state, whether based on occupation, locality or political affiliation – labour unions, pressure groups, parties – have been hailed as beneficial 'countervailing powers' (McWilliams 1973, 556–9; Anderson, 'Political design', pp.279–84). But the moral dimension of such groups, their subjective meaning and place in human existence, have tended to disappear from sight, especially in the Anglo-Saxon world. Political theorists have been occupied with other questions. Corporations tend to be dismissed as tainted with fascism, or the fad of a bygone era. They are of little concern to most socialists (what did Marx says about them?). But the chief reason, among mainstream 'western' political philosophers, is surely the dominance of liberal, utilitarian and Enlightenment values and preconceptions. Corporations either elude the net or are contemned by classical liberalism. Michael Oakeshott, one of the most original thinkers of our time, is implicitly anti-corporatist. He insists that 'civil association' and 'enterprise groups' be kept quite distinct, in theory and practice; the latter have no significance whatever for moral life (*On Human Conduct* chs 2–3).

Anderson attempts to fill the gap in the following way. The relation of industrial groups to each other and to the state should be regarded as 'that of the structured adversary procedure ... based on the models of collective bargaining and judicial process. ... Affected interests appear in the role of litigants before an independent tribunal whose decisions are justified on the basis of explicit criteria of regulatory law'. Among these criteria will be 'the public interest', defined not only as 'the consumer's interest', but also as the general welfare and 'orderly development' of industry. There will thus be

> a combination of bargaining between peak interest associations with a specific conception of public macroeconomic management ... full employment, an active manpower policy, equal pay for equal work, and a capitalist system of industrial decision-making in which productive efficiency is measured in terms of international competitiveness.
>
> ('Political design', 292–7)

This is better than nothing, but it entirely overlooks any moral dynamic within the 'corporation' itself, and the need, perhaps most imperative of all, 'to fashion agreed normative codes ... compatible with the rapidity of technological and social change in our time', the need 'for the reconstruction of normative order' in the economic sphere (Fox and Flanders 1969, 173–80). Keynes summed up the matter rather better in 1926:

> I believe that in many cases the ideal size for the unit of control and organization lies somewhere between the individual and the modern state. I suggest, therefore, that progress lies in the growth and recognition of semi-autonomous bodies within the state – bodies whose criterion of

action within their own field is solely *the public good as they understand it*, and from whose deliberations motives of private advantage are excluded ... bodies which in the ordinary course of affairs are mainly autonomous within their prescribed limitations, but are subject in the last resort to the sovereignty of democracy expressed through parliament. I propose a return, it may be said, towards the medieval conception of separate autonomies.   (cit. Schmitter 1974, 110, my italics)

Such a system would not, he believed, be 'seriously incompatible' with capitalism (Schmitter 1974, 108ff.). This encapsulated something of what Hegel, Gierke and Durkheim had been trying to say.

This would appear to be the final stage reached hitherto by theorists of the community of labour, and it may actually turn out to mark the end of the tradition explored in this book. The growth points of modern industry hardly seem to lend themselves to ideas based on mutual aid and the protection of producers' interests. Occupations themselves may become less, rather than (as Durkheim thought) more, important in many people's lives.

CONCLUSION TO THE
TRANSACTION EDITION

In Europe, liberal values and the corporate organisation of labour developed simultaneously and in the same milieu from the twelfth to the seventeenth centuries. Both thrived in towns (to which corporate labour organisation was usually confined), and both affected the ideology of the European commune and city-state in specific and discernible ways. Guilds and civil society were distinctive features of European society precisely from the time when this became most markedly different from other societies in the world. Between them, guilds and civil society produced the spiritual atmosphere in which the modern economy and political society gestated. Self-governing labour organisations and civil freedom developed side by side as coherent practices. The values of mutual aid and craft honour on the one hand, and of personal freedom and legal equality on the other, formed the moral infrastructure of our civilisation. It was not a question of 'either...or.' Rather, these different principles balanced, harmonised, and even cross-fertilised one another (freedom of association, for example).

Political theory and the world of learning, however, from the start emphasised liberal values as the chief element in social and political justice. Only a very few philosophers (though among them some of the most adventurous) thought that solidarity and exchange—the poles around which the values of guild and civil society, respectively, rotate—are not opposites but complementary, and attempted to weave these together into a texture as tough and complex as that of urban society itself. Marsiglio, Althusius, and Hegel, each drawing inspiration from Aristotle, were outstanding examples of this. Similarly, Aristotle had worked out for Greek city-states a middle way that combined elements of democracy and oligarchy.

The Enlightenment and industrialisation led to the exaltation of liberal values and an attack on corporate solidarities. Guilds disappeared and were only in part replaced by trade unions. The values of market exchange have been in the ascendant ever since. The values of corporate labour organisation continued to be upheld for a while among industrial workers, and were placed at the centre of political theory by some disciples of the Romantic movement; they became a focus for co-operators, socialists, and corporatists. Some forms of socialism sought to combine once again the social and political norms of civil society with those of fraternity (for example, Eduard Bernstein's 'evolutionary socialism'). The more dogmatic versions of liberalism and socialism wrenched apart the ideals of freedom and of workers' rights and so contributed to the confrontation between the 'free world' and 'Communism.'

Today, principles of the free market have come to pervade economic theory, popular consciousness, and political ideology. To be liberal and not illiberal is a precondition for respectability in moral discourse. It is held legitimate and beneficial to put one's own interest as an individual first, provided others are free to do the same. At this very moment the values of what I have called civil society are being vigorously championed by Western politicians and employed in partisan debate on the national and the international arenas. This is presented as the pure political truth and the essence of Western civilization.

Hegel, Durkheim, and recently liberal corporatism, on the contrary, maintained the possibility of *symbiosis* between corporate and liberal values. What has occurred in the longer term in modern *European* states is somewhat different but it too may be seen as a kind of symbiosis. At the very moment when guilds were finally abolished in Germany, Bismarck began to champion an idea of the state as a large-scale mutual-insurance society (above, p. 170). This went well with nationalism (you should love your own people) and was funded by imperialism. It was taken up in Britain as 'neo-liberalism' (Mark I) or 'positive liberty' as expounded by T.H. Green and applied by the Liberal government of 1905-11. From now on the modern European state would take on the role of protection association not only in the minimal Nozickian sense of prevention of force and fraud but also in the guild mode of social insurance and providing—or trying to provide—full employment for its citizen-members. Totalitarian regimes came to power as extreme versions of this. A distinctively German idea of the nation-state as a guild-like community, protecting its members at all costs (but in a completely fanatical way), came to a cataclysmic end.

After 1945 this symbiosis of the ideals of liberty and social-economic security was renamed Social Democracy, and was adopted by most West-European governments. Workers' rights and social insurance, alongside liberalisation of trade, were prominent in the public policies of the European Union. This, broadly speaking, is what has become identified as the European model of capitalism. Some West-European governments went further, taking up the ideal of co-operation (above, pp. 184-86), and giving employees the right to participate in certain managerial decisions within the firm: notably, the West-German co-determination law (Boswell 1990).

The Thatcher-Reagan model, on the other hand, championed liberal values to the exclusion of workers' rights and, to varying degrees, of social insurance. Sometimes described as neo-liberalism (Mark II), this has been identified as the American (or, if speaking French, Anglo-Saxon) way of doing capitalism. In business corporations, it gives 'all power to the soviets' (as Lenin would have said)—of investors. Despite this, in some respects the USA under George W. Bush and especially since September 11 looks like a 300-million-strong guild designed to protect and privilege its voting citizen-members—of which the 30 percent hike in steel tariffs might be symptomatic.

Some might say that the concepts of the state as, on the one hand, a super-guild—a generalised protection and mutual-assurance society—and, on the other hand, the champion of civil liberties, remain the two contenders for support today. But the attempt to unite aspects of both of these concepts in a single practice—which we have seen happening in city-states and advocated by some major theorists—is still on the agenda. This is surely what is meant by the 'third way' advocated by President Clinton and by New Labour under Tony Blair (see also 'The Middle Way': Macmillan 1938/1966). So often dismissed as trivial or meaningless, that term really does embody a combination of the values of guild and civil society. Contrary to a belief widely held today, it has proved possible and advantageous, in various historical circumstances, to combine these in both theory and practice. Hayek too at least gave voluntary associations a role in liberal capitalist order (as 'the independent sector': Hayek 1982: iii 49-51). It is not a case of 'Under which king, Bezonian? Speak or die.'

The decline of guild values is one reason why liberalism has failed to achieve the liberation of man/woman as producer. The labour process is not meaningful to the majority of workers. There is a parallel in politics: representative government and legal equality comprise the essence of 'Western democracy,' with political participation in practice a luxury for the few.

Yet, the work or enterprise group, whether it be a team of hunters, an industrial unit, a labor union, or 'the scientific community,' has specific moral worth. It is a unique type of human society. Western political theory has forgotten about it, and gives instead exclusive moral worth to the family and the nation-state. These are commonly regarded by Westerners as the only proper forms of group identity, the only proper objects of collective loyalty.

But, if we are asked which groups we feel we belong to and attach moral importance to, if we consider from which social sources we derive our personal values—in short, which communities have meaning for us—most of us will come up with different and complex answers. Peer groups, school, work mates, church, fellow-scientists, regiment, drinking companions—not everyone would back state or nation against all of these. In some cases moral and cultural values *are* coterminous with a national community; but in many others, perhaps especially in the Middle East and less developed countries, they are not (Reicher and Hopkins 2001). In all cases, moral and cultural values in practice owe a great deal to family, school, peer group, occupational community, church, and to religious or cultural entities such as 'the West' or Islam (or, in the twentieth century, Communism) (see Black 1988a). It is when these other ties are weak that people attach too much importance to the nation. A state without lesser associations is a monstrosity.

Part of the problem is that those groups which in real life bind people together in so many ways are regarded as merely optional, based on taste or convenience. Belief in any kind of solidarity of labour has declined increasingly over the past century. This has led to the impoverishment of our social being and consciousness, which Marx called 'alienation' and Durkheim 'anomie'—the sad privatisation of modern 'civilised' man and woman.

It does not help that the 'great tradition' of Western political thought, in for example Aristotle, Hobbes, Rousseau, and Oakeshott, credits the state with unique qualities which in real life are much more widely diffused among a multiplicity of groups. (Only Aristotle offered a clear argument of why, in terms of the underlying goals of human existence, the state should be regarded as the supreme association; and much of what he said was true only of the Greek *polis*.) We should revise this and say that state and nation do command respect, but for the same mixture of prudential and moral reasons as numerous other groups. They may be legally sovereign, but they are not morally unique.

This whole arena of associational life, of which I have here attempted to trace the history in popular attitudes and political theory, is one which Western political thought desperately needs to re-occupy, and to synthesise with its often fanatical concentration on the values of civil society (see Hirst: 1994). Something like guild theory might fill at least some of the gaps left by liberalism, of which we are painfully aware.

But here ideology itself presents a barrier. Today, not only are the values of liberalism so dominant in Western Europe and America that they have become virtually synonymous with what is called (with geographical inaccuracy) 'Western' political thought; they are also widely regarded as incompatible with the values of the guild, that is, with any kind of serious solidarity other than family or nation-state. Today, generally speaking, the values of social solidarity in a variety of groups are championed by non-'Western' political societies. (The practical results, it has to be said, are not encouraging.)

No sane person would dispute that liberty and human rights are precious assets; indeed, perhaps the most urgent task facing us is to extend the values of civil society to the international arena by according to other cultures and peoples the same respect and tolerance that we claim within our own society for each individual and his or her beliefs.

The history of ideas, however, clearly demonstrates that these liberal values of civil society are *only one half* of Europe's political tradition, and that in several cultural milieux and in several social philosophies they have coexisted with, and thrived alongside, the values of fellowship and mutual aid. In any case the values of civil society cannot stand alone. The attempt to elevate them above all other values is of course driven partly by the interests of those already possessing wealth and power, and their propaganda needs.

It is not merely that liberal values always operate within a given social context and cannot be wrenched from other organs of sentiment and practice within their society. The truth is, rather, that the rights and liberty of the individual are *only one way* of articulating the Golden Rule; they do not stand in isolation at the summit of the scale of human values. If these norms of civil society are separated from the living texture of social life, where they always intermingle and cross-fertilise with other values, and if they are made into absolutes, they actually wither. If, for example, there are no limits to what some may acquire and others may lose in the marketplace, then in practice many become deprived of both personal independence and legal equality. In real life, exchange between persons is not opposed to or separable from social solidarity. Exchange itself, whether of gifts or of commodities, can and should be a means to the formation of social bonds. We need market freedom *and* workers' rights if we are to have a society in which people have enough to eat *and* feel fulfilled as human beings.

But the conceptual and moral dominance of individual interests has led to all associations being regarded as mere instruments for the pursuit of individual ends. Even the family is sometimes reduced to this. The problem is not that lesser associations are frowned upon or find it difficult to attract members (see Putnam 2000). It is, rather, that little intrinsic worth is ascribed to them. In Western political science, for example, they are sometimes defined simply as means for the 'aggregation' and 'articulation' of 'interests.'

Lesser associations, and in particular occupational groups, *are* particular interest groups; they are not always beneficial to outsiders or the public interest (Olson 1982). But, like the family, they have an intrinsic value, both as a *necessary means* to other goals and as an *end in themselves*, as part of the ultimate good of human experience. Community of labour *is* instrumental as a means of achieving other goods; in this it is no different from the family: it achieves what cannot be done by individuals in isolation.

Again, intermediate groups may act as countervailing powers against the dominance of the state or other large groups (which invariably means the dominance of a few individuals). They can, as Durkheim said, play a vital role in developing public morality. But, once such groups are seen as merely instrumental in *any* of these ways, they tend to atrophy.

I would argue that we need to recognise that the community of labour—the idea of the guild—also has, like the family, a deeper dimension (which Durkheim would call a moral dimension). It is imprinted upon the human psyche, no doubt from the time when we first ganged together to hunt wild animals (which some say also stimulated the development of speech and the brain). It is implanted in our experience as a species.

That is to say, community of labour and the groups that go with it cannot be reduced to any or all of the specific functions they may fulfil; they are social units with human meaning. Working together or sharing a craft creates a specific type of relationship. It forges bonds of a unique kind, less intense and pervasive than those of personal love or friendship, but truly human bonds none the less. *The guild, therefore, is an end in itself.* This does not mean that the work group is an absolute, any more than the nation-state: it can go wrong. But, as a category of social life, it is irreplaceable in human affairs.

In the past twenty or so years since the first issue of this book, the world of labour has moved further than ever away from the values of corporate solidarity explored here. Never in human history, or at least since the time of the Pharaohs (if then), have production, manufacture, and commerce been further removed from concerns about human solidarity. Justice in the present system and its institutions means the rights of investors and consumers. The rights of workers or producers (as every author has cause to know) are defined by the market, that is (at best) the sum of consumers' desires and shareholders' interests. With an irony deeper than I can bear, the heir to the corporations discussed in this book is the modern American or European multi-national corporation (Calise 1994 and 2002).

Yet the past twenty years have also seen an outpouring of writings on 'community' (Sandel 1998, Etzioni 1995, Putnam 2000). The importance of the small territorial group—the old commune or today's neighbourhood—for a healthy democracy and even for psychological well being has been reasserted. The principle of subsidiarity—that different kinds of decisions need to be taken at different levels of political society, from international community to neighbourhood, and that they should be taken at the level closest to those affected, that is, generally speaking the 'lowest' level possible—has found much support in the European Union, and especially in Germany (Blickle et al. 2002, Norr and Oppermann 1997).

Again, the virtues of 'pluralism' are preached, particularly in favour of religious and cultural groups. 'Multiculturalism' has succeeded distributive justice as the moral guiding star. This can be expressed in terms of 'sphere sovereignty': human nature requires a variety of mutually independent and collaborating spheres of activity (Chaplin 1993 and 1995, Dooyeweerd 1997, Skillen and McCarthy 1991). But, as applied to the world of work, this has been entirely top-down: business corporations have indeed acquired more independence—and partly *at the expense of* workers' groups. Can a man or woman find a happiness in their sect (where they spend perhaps two hours per week) which they cannot find in their work (where they may spend up to sixty hours per week)?

This is of course part of globalisation: to put things simply, there seems no alternative to global capitalism. Communism, which was morally both worse (in practice) and better (in theory), has proved unviable anyway. The 'twin towers' indicates that at least one alternative to global capitalism is very much worse. The question, therefore, is what form global capitalism will take. I see few grounds for optimism. Is it possible that freedom for the investor and security for the worker can be balanced globally, as within the economic system of a single state? For the moment global capitalism shows little sign of reforming itself in this direction.

One value prominent in the ancient and pre-modern world but absent from ours is honour. Of course, people today have self-respect, and may still kill or be killed for sex or territory. But 'I could not love thee, dear, so much loved I not honour more'? The precise mix of ethics and self-awareness that led Romans to suicide and Christians to martyrdom is not prominent in our scale of values. The honour of the artist or craftsman (Eric Newby was lent a shirt in wartime Italy which had been made before the French revolution) is available to a much smaller proportion of the population today than even twenty years ago.

And yet in the academic community, and so conceivably in other communities defined by people's life-work, there is perhaps some sense of collegiality based on a common enterprise. This is not a guild in the historical sense; it is more the sense of spiritual solidarity which, in the old days, a British miner could feel with a Russian miner (Toennies, above, p. 218). It was best captured by Joseph Conrad in *Lord Jim* when he spoke of 'the fellowship' and 'solidarity' of the craft. Jim ought to 'squirm for the honour of his craft.' One's fellow seamen were 'an obscure body of men held together by a community of inglorious toil and by fidelity to a certain standard of conduct... We aren't an organised body of men, and the only thing that holds us together is the name for that kind of decency.' That was 1900.

APPENDIX: A NOTE ON METHOD

The history of moral and political ideas* has developed from pseudo-philosophy into a scientific field of study, with its own criteria of evidence and proof. (To be sure, choice of subject and literary tone still usually tell us something about a scholar's personal values – if they did not, the ghosts of the past would perhaps remain quite bloodless.) The history of ideas as grandly signifying over-arching movements of thought and society, often believed to demonstrate progress towards an enlightened present, has given way to a less pretentious pursuit of popular and learned mentalities (Le Goff 1974), of moral and political universes of discourse, 'languages' (Pocock 1971) or 'ideologies' (Skinner 1978). This may be undertaken as a field of study either distinct from, or interacting with, social and political history; Pocock (1975) favours the former, Skinner and the French school the latter approach.

Pocock has shown how the historian can, by meticulous reading, lay bare the mental structure of a school or tradition; once-famous doctrines emerge from his scalpel as parts of a complex (or paradigm) of ideas, in which they cohere and their function can be rationally understood. Skinner (1969) indicates how such universes of discourse evolve and operate in relation to a specific set of practical problems encountered at a particular time. The success of these approaches obviously depends upon the sensitivity with which they are employed. For the Pocockian there remains the danger of reading something into the sources, or creating an artificial paradigm by being too selective, or of adding one's own flourishes. Skinner tends to concentrate on the purely *political* context; it may be equally and sometimes more helpful to look (as I have attempted to do here) at the *socio-economic* circumstances in which people wrote. Furthermore, it is not enough just to ask what immediate practical needs give rise to a particular emphasis in political theory or moral language. It is better first to survey moral language and practical environment separately and *in toto*; then one can record not only where the two coincide, but where (as we have sometimes seen happen) they simply shoot past each other. Why was it that certain matters of

*By 'ideas' is meant here everything from ordinary people's tacit assumptions, the coded practices and cultural genes transmitted through learning, to ideals, dreams and philosophy.

contemporary importance, such as the socio-economic and political role of guilds, received little attention, and why was it that writers so often urged in vain the adoption of alternative standards or practices? One finds that political ideas do not necessarily reflect a current situation; rather, they very often cry out for what is absent. Men dream of what they do not have: there were enormous differences between ancient Rome and Renaissance Florence, and the great age of corporatist theory came, not when guilds were flourishing, but in the heyday of economic liberalism.

Then there is the danger of accepting the myth of coherence. This is a survival from the idealist view of history, according to which not only are ideas the principal motor of historical change, but any set of social phenomena can best be understood in relation to a *single* basic 'idea' pervading them all. Ullmann, for example, follows Gierke in seeing history as an epochal conflict between rival ideas; only he has replaced 'lordship' and 'fellowship' with the 'descending' and 'ascending' notions of government (1961, 197, 219). It is quite common to try to deduce from practice and selected utterances a coherent set of values, supposed to have existed at some point in time. Yet this whole notion of a *coherent* community ethic or set of attitudes is a pure invention. It derives from Herder and Hegel; it leads to frequent use of words like *Weltanschauung* and 'ideology'. Why should we suppose that a whole group of people, large or small, held a single set of convictions, each of which meshed in with the rest, or was derived from a central core of principles? In reality, if we consider any individual we know well, or ourselves, while we will occasionally find surprising connections between what is thought about one thing and about some other apparently disconnected topic, we will also find that quite different mentalities jostle together within the same living human soul. There is no reason why we should believe all a person's thoughts to be reducible to a single set of related convictions, let alone that these should be discernible and describable by someone else. One moment I may want to be a family man, another I may want to go off with a group of friends or visit a mistress. One moment I may want to maximize my gains on the stock exchange or in a supermarket, another moment I contribute to a charity. These pieces of conduct simply do not fit together into any neat pattern. Consistency may or may not be admirable, but it is not generally practised. When we really want to know what people are like, perhaps we should call in not Weber or Durkheim but Dostoevsky and Nietzsche.

The same is true for groups. In medieval and Renaissance towns and guilds, we find liberal-bourgeois convictions jostling beside communal ones. On certain occasions modern trade unionists gather collective muscle, on others they behave as rational individualistic consumers. The most liberal state does not apply the principles of *laissez-faire* in time of war. The unverified opinion that rational explanation applies to collectivities but not to individuals is a pure invention of nineteenth-century sociology in its attempts to become a rational science. It is often most vigorously upheld for those very cases where there is practically no evidence: early man, primitive society and the like. Whenever you tap this hypothesis, it cracks, bends and breaks. This also cautions one against too ready a use of the concept of 'paradigm'. As we have seen in Jäger's case, historical truth often does not come up to our expectations, nor even comply with good taste.

Much intellectual history used to be written with the implication that 'it is, after all, [a] world outlook which in the final analysis effectively shapes social reality' (Ullmann 1961, 291). Nowadays there is an inclination to bow to the materialist prejudice that social and political ideas are in the last analysis, when interpreted so as to reveal their true character, 'ideological' justifications of a partisan position which had already been adopted in response to some threat. This is an unwarranted presupposition, the result of mere prejudice. Rather, as we approach the sources, we should keep an open mind on this matter. Social and political writings *are* often vehicles for certain interests, but they are not *necessarily* so: the extent to which they are, must be weighed in every instance. Ideas form part of a situation which has to be elucidated without prejudging which factors are causally most important.

Bearing this question in mind, let us consider the heuristic problems which arise when we enquire into states of mind of the past or in cultures other than our own. We are severely limited by our sources. It may be argued that we can only know what either ordinary people or leaders really thought from intimate documents, such as diaries or personal letters, which, for wide tracts of the past, are handed down to us only in the case of a few exceptional individuals. But certain tactics may legitimately be used to get round this problem. In the first place, there can be inference from practice to mentality. A good description of what this involves has been given by Arthur Hibbert (speaking of the policies of medieval towns in relation to their economic beliefs):

It is reasonable to use another type of evidence – indirect evidence. This consists of the elements of regularity and consistency in urban economic practice. Where there are such regular trends the policy of a town may be considered as more or less 'conscious', but policy it is so long as the regularities are genuine and can be referred to probable motives. Medieval townsfolk did not always expound the aims and ideas which underlay their activities – they did not trouble, they would not, they could not; when they did their words may have been lost. Common sense suggests that hidden motives may properly be deduced from known practice.   (1963, 157; cf. Strauss 1966, 76)

It was partly with this in mind that Weber recommended the use of 'ideal

246

types', possible points of view coherently defined: one can then judge by their actions how far people were possessed of a Protestant ethic or a medieval-urban economic viewpoint.

In the second place, public documents such as charters, diplomatic letters, speeches, legal reports, may, if properly analysed, tell us at least something about the underlying mentality of those concerned. One must enter here the obvious caveat that what people write down for public consumption is not always an accurate reflection of what they really think; even in conversation it may be socially unacceptable to say certain things (Lukacs 1978, 171ff.). Numerous official pronouncements are written with the deliberate intention of legitimizing a course of action, persuading an adversary, placating a foe, or impressing the populace: their 'rhetoric' is intended to appeal to a specific audience. Yet for this very reason, it is likely to tell us something about the mentality of that audience. To quote Hibbert on medieval towns again:

> There is abundant evidence in the preambles to municipal statutes, in the reports of chroniclers, in the arguments used by interested bodies in economic disputes, that principles informed practice. Sometimes the aims and ideas made public were those which really gave coherence to economic activity, sometimes they were a dishonest façade hiding a shabby structure of selfishness and opportunism. Yet the most disingenuous statements of policy have their value; they argue a need to indulge popular belief that certain patterns and principles of economic behaviour were good and useful. (1963, 157)

The casual use of certain words, sentiments, arguments in public documents may thus be revealing, both for the mentality of the authors and for that of their audience. One can read between the lines in order to ascertain the general opinions and assumptions of leaders and people. Ullmann and others have justifiably looked for 'Weberian slips'. Even so, we must not lightly generalize from what one ruler or body proclaimed to the mentality of the whole group, let alone of society at large. Obviously, it is only by such means that we can measure the influence of ideas, in either the short or the long term, upon actual events and trends. We must stop talking about what people thought when we do not have adequate means of verification. Only when we have verified how people thought can we measure the part their ideas played in forming their life and conduct; only then can popular or official consciousness, as we have interpreted it, become a potential explanatory factor.

The ideas that are found to have existed by this method may also be causally relevant, in that what cannot be defended in terms of a rhetoric may not be done (as in the current dispute in Northern Ireland, on both sides). On the other hand, the sentiments expressed may be sincerely meant, but not so sincerely as to be acted upon with regularity. Finally, one must not discount the possibility that certain aspects of conduct may remain almost entirely unaffected by the prevailing moral language (for example, the taking of bribes may be generally accepted and go unmentioned). One cannot, therefore, take current political language as an accurate guide to what is actually happening, even in people's minds, but only to the mental world that is presently articulated. Obviously, however, when other evidence is lacking, the preoccupations of authors and intellectuals may be our only clue as to what is actually going on.

At this point, it is useful to distinguish different levels of self-awareness, rationality and originality of thought. The need to distinguish learned doctrine from popular consciousness has been generally recognized (cf. Gierke 1873, 2–3 and 1881, 2–4; Calasso 1954a, 267ff.; Kern 1939, 152–3; Imbart de la Tour 1948, 547–51 and 1944, 330ff.; Herde 1973, 83n.). There are many gradations between raw sentiment and systematic philosophy. It is convenient to distinguish between (1) ethos, (2) ideology, (3) philosophy; and, within the last, between (a) rational and (b) 'poetic' philosophizing.

First, then, there is popular consciousness, the existing social ethos of everyday life (for example the idea of mutual aid in guilds and trade unions). This includes local, tribal or national *moeurs*, civic, patriarchal, imperial or meritocratic presuppositions; they are the substratum of morality and law, and invariably outlive 'the death of political thought'. They influence action at all levels of society. In advanced societies, they are partly religious, partly philosophical; in all societies, they include a large amount of custom. Custom is the interaction of group sentiment and the environment, the outcome of experience. It differs by group and region; but a particular, differentiated custom can, like a biological mutation, become generalized and diffused over wider and wider regions and peoples. Nor must we rule out the possibility of 'human universals' in conduct and belief. Such popular consciousness is, like the geographical and technical environment in Braudel's view, usually subject to slow, long-term change. Rapid 'paradigmatic' changes are more common in learned doctrine, but these too may filter down to all levels of society, and in certain cases (e.g. the Reformation) this process may also be fast. This is likely to have been, in the first instance, a change not directly in 'political thought', but in the underlying orientation of belief, often religious in character. This affects popular belief in the long term, and perhaps in a more enduring way than it affects learned doctrine.

Secondly, a more thoughtful and systematic rationalization of existing procedures or customary thought patterns – which I will call 'ideology' – often emerges when power is being contested, corruption is perceived, or current beliefs challenged. Then the need for conscious orientation arises. The first step towards theory is the elucidation of the core of a practice, of its 'true' nature and its bearing on a particular problem that has arisen.

Already, to articulate is to specify, and so perhaps subtly to begin to modify, the assumptions of ordinary living. There may be an appeal to 'reform', to reapply existing norms to a suspected disease. A spokesman or leader may develop or exploit an existing ethos for a special occasion. Or he may outline existing *moeurs* in abstract, idealized form so as to smooth out anomalies and apply the given model more systematically. A whole series of writings, such as the city chronicles and *The Shepherd's Eye*, are examples of this. Then there is abstraction, from familiar behaviour patterns, codes and institutions, of a model which, while claiming truth on the basis of what all are supposed already to believe, is in existing circumstances actually revolutionary. Here political thought arises from subjectively perceived ideal forms of community life. Such is the milleniarist and utopian mode. The conservative counterpart is rationalization of what already exists, as being, if we did but look closely, already in harmony with the ideal, or the best possible approximation to it 'things being as they are' (*rebus stantibus ut nunc*) (cf. Mannheim 1936). In both cases, we perceive now the beginnings of 'ideology' – a set of claims on behalf of some scheme or institution, claiming support from general truths.

In this category we may usually place the transmission of ideas from an external source, whether an earlier culture or a different contemporary one. It is possible for the discursive, 'ideological' treatment of an institution or movement in one society to influence, through written transmission, people at a different time or place, as occurred with Ciceronian political values. The Renaissance is a type case of this whole procedure. The adoption of such 'alien' ideas being generally the work of a few highly cultured people, if an attempt is made to impose them on the whole population, the result is likely to be an increase in *Obrigkeit*, however beneficial the ideas in themselves may otherwise be. In the main, they can be assimilated only through education of a rather advanced nature, and are therefore liable to remain the prerogative of a few; such has largely been the fate of classical ideals in modern Europe. As Kern puts it, 'the developed technique of modern civilized life has created a schism between learned, educated culture and popular thought, which has never got beyond medieval or semi-medieval notions' (1939, 199).

The very fact that any of these kinds of 'ideological' activity takes place has some effect upon the situation or culture in question. They heighten awareness, they make people question, they bestow confidence. If, on the other hand, a movement, such as the medieval crafts or the modern trade unions, arises within a society but is unable to gain a footing in the normative language of that society, it is at an enormous disadvantage: this is what Gramsci called the problem of cultural 'hegemony'.

Thirdly, there is political *philosophy*. At first sight, it might appear that popular preconceptions have far more social and historical influence than philosophical teachings. But here we must distinguish between two different kinds of 'philosophy'. First, there is the systematic construction of a rationally argued theory about what is going on in the world and how we ought to conduct ourselves; in politics, this means working out anew for oneself a general conception of social and political life, coherent, logical, based on first principles. This is a peculiarly western kind of philosophy, deriving from Plato, and it is uncertain to what extent if at all it has existed elsewhere. Such political philosophy clearly only arises in conjunction with a generally philosophical turn of mind, and is extremely rare. The other 'poetic' kind of philosophy is similar in intention but does not proceed by systematic, rational, coherent or logical argument, but rather by myth, poetry and challenge: it is epigrammatic and anecdotal. This type is far more widespread, and seems to have developed in many of the major civilizations, in China, India, Greece and Judaism. It still exists in western civilization, among those with something to say who are prepared to operate knowingly outside the established philosophical tradition, for example the early Marx and Nietzsche. What the two types of philosophy have in common is that they both have a fundamentally original view of life, morals, politics, but they proceed by different methods and often address different audiences. They are both more pioneering than ideology, and less closely related to an existing tradition; both are trying to express a fresh view of things, and both demand extensive reorientation. The first 'Platonic' approach leads to the systematic analysis of political concepts and values, and to descriptive, empirical political science. The second, 'poetic' approach is more easily accessible to great numbers of people, and is often aimed at a wider, even a mass audience.

The importance of this distinction here is that the two kinds are related to practice in quite different ways; while the former has seldom been widely influential, the latter very often has. The teachings of Confucius, Jesus, Rousseau and Marx have actually become popular preconceptions (although the relation between the original message and the later received tradition is notoriously problematic). Both kinds are innovative and reflective, they both detach themselves from tradition and call directly from soul to soul. But the first kind is suited only to people with a high degree of education, and is influential, if at all, only in the long term. Plato was influential in the long term, for example in inculcating 'rationalism in politics'. Aristotle seems only to have influenced other political philosophers and scientists. Hobbes has affected the way a large number of people, particularly in responsible positions, look at society and politics. Philosophy in the 'poetic' sense (Confucianism, Christianity, Marxism), on the other hand, has deeply affected the way great numbers of people, indeed whole cultures, view society and politics, and has in some cases done so relatively quickly. But the influence of either kind of philosophy is not as a rule straightforwardly political; rather, philosophy affects the 'paradigms' through which we think about society and politics. Few would dispute that 'ideas' in the sense of the second kind of philosophy have had a considerable effect upon social and political history. This is not to suggest they were operative 'in themselves'; they always required certain vehicles of transmission; and different ideas appealed to different peoples at different times.

The difference between the natural sciences and normative political thought is, of course, that for the latter there is no generally accepted test of the validity of a particular theory or viewpoint. The result is that, while there may be 'paradigmatic breakthroughs', these are not necessarily decisive and do not necessarily ever command general assent; they may merely add to the existing stock of possible ways of viewing politics. Thus we have today neo-Thomist, Hobbesian, Lockian, Marxist and other paradigms, all co-existing in the world, even within a particular cultural unity (such as 'the west'), and even within a particular country. In some cases, these may become the stuff of party politics; how much radical tension of this kind a society can survive is of course a crucial, and very debatable, question.

The historian as such is not concerned with the objective truth of philosophies of either of the kinds mentioned above. Further, he can only judge whether a thinker has *tried* to be objective, or has merely been cloaking a particular interest in 'ideological' garb, with the utmost care: to suppose that all philosophy has a sinister interest is the wildest of prejudices. We must not rule out *a priori* the possibility that someone may be enquiring into the nature and value of social and political phenomena with as sincere an attempt at objectivity as the natural scientist. The philosopher may or may not be moved to write on social and political questions by a problem immediately facing him and his society; it would not appear that this was Aristotle's or Aquinas' *primary* intention. He may be intending to communicate not so much with his immediate circle, or even with men of his own time, but with mankind at large and the future, distant if need be. He should be taken seriously, unless the contrary can be reasonably shown. Such a person believes his undertaking to be just as 'practical' as that of the reformer, because he believes that only a fundamental reorientation of current belief will solve a problem: so it was with Plato and Marx.

Instead of adopting either idealist or materialist prejudices, it would seem closer to the truth to say that ideas are an essential part of any human society. They are not something tacked on, that comes afterwards and 'reflects' an already accomplished situation. Without mental life, man is not man. Concepts of society are as old as self-awareness itself. This affects the way one studies both the history of ideas and history in general: '"past actualities" ... cannot be rightly understood apart from their conceptual environment' (Chrimes, intro. to Kern 1939, xv–xvi), 'a social classification exists, in the last analysis, only by virtue of the ideas which men form of it' (Bloch 1961, 268). Moral language itself is an inextricable part of social phenomena, which, given a different language, might themselves be different. We must deny from the outset that a political language is necessarily the creature of the movement with which it is associated. We must once and for all rid ourselves of Marxist and other conventions, according to which all conscious activity 'springs out of' or 'is an expression of' some other real 'base'.

In intimate relationships between persons, for example, words used to express love or devotion are part of the relationship, which cannot properly be understood or described without reference to such words. The 'language' employed is part of the social action. Tender or not so tender words affect the bonds of mutual attraction, which without vocalization might not have been as in fact they were. The same is true of social and political language generally, as employed (for example) in relationships between a commander and his men, an employer and his employees, a worker and his colleagues, two businessmen doing a deal. Morale depends as much on underlying beliefs and on what is said, as it does upon looks, gestures and even, within certain very plastic limits, the disposition of material forces. In economic activity, trust between those exchanging goods and co-operation among those engaged in production are not mere afterthoughts; and if they are treated as merely instrumental, they lose their efficacy. Oaths are an outstanding example. Verbal pledges, whether between man and woman or between members of socio-economic groups, however informally expressed, may crucially affect future attitudes and conduct. Guilds and other associations bound themselves together by oath: was not language here an essential part of what was going on? It is true that language *may* reflect an existing practice. But it may also change an existing situation by articulating various viewpoints, and, as in oaths, it may itself be a form of social action.

Language may also, as Skinner suggests (1978, i xii–xiii), impose limits upon what is considered feasible, or considered at all; it may inhibit divergences from existing norms, as when market practices are suppressed in the Soviet Union in the name of 'communism', or the power of trade unions curtailed in Britain in the name of 'liberty' and 'democracy'. On the other hand, the 'normative vocabulary available at a given time' (Skinner 1978, i xi) may *lag behind* and be unable to deal with aspects of what is actually going on, with newly developing social relations, as in the case of merchant-capitalist ascendancy in Renaissance Florence and the political role of multi-national business firms today. Neologisms have to be coined to describe new phenomena; these may or may not successfully establish themselves in current usage. The political language of a society is often a vehicle for continuity; legal language especially, inasmuch as it relies upon precedent, is a conservative force. A society poor in a certain area of social language, as is English in terms to describe group life, may nevertheless be rich in those things which cannot yet adequately be articulated. But, unless normative language can be adapted, this wealth may prove fragile.

BIBLIOGRAPHY

Primary sources

Acciaiuoli, Donato, *In Aristotelis Libros Octo Politicorum Commentarii*, Venice, 1566.

Accursius, *Glossa Ordinaria Super Digesto*, Lyon, 1539.

Albert the Great, *Commentary on Aristotle's Politics* in S. Borgnet (ed.), *Alberti Magni Opera Omnia*, vol. 8, Paris, 1891.

Albert the Great, *Commentary on the Sentences*, in S. Borgnet (ed.), *Alberti Magni Opera Omnia*, vol. 29, Paris, 1894.

Althusius (Althaus), Johannes, *Politica Methodice Digesta*, intro. by C.J. Friedrich, Cambridge, Mass., 1932.

Altmann, W. and Bernheim, E. (eds), *Ausgewälte Urkunden zur Erläuterung der Verfassungsgeschichte Deutschlands im Mittelalter*, 5th edn, Berlin, 1920.

Anderson, C., 'Political design and the representation of interests', in P. Schmitter and G. Lehmbruch (eds), *Trends towards Corporatist Intermediation*, Beverly Hills and London, 1979, pp. 271–97.

Antonino, St, of Florence, *De Usuris*, in *Tractatus Illustrium Iurisconsultorum*, vol. 7, Venice, 1584, fols 78v–113r.

Antonino, St, of Florence, *Summa Theologica*, 4 vols, Verona, 1740 (repr. Graz, 1959).

Aquinas, St Thomas, *De Regimine Principum (On Princely Government)*, bk I, in A.P. d'Entrèves (ed.), Aquinas, *Selected Political Writings*, Oxford, 1954, pp.2–83.

Aquinas, St Thomas, *In Libros Politicorum Aristotelis Expositio (On the Politics)*, ed. R.M. Spiazzi, Turin, 1951.

Aquinas, St Thomas, *Selected Political Writings*, ed. A.P. d'Entrèves, Oxford, 1954.

Aquinas, St Thomas, *Summa Theologiae*, ed. T. Gilby and P. Meagher, 60 vols, London and New York, 1964–75.

Aristotle, *Politica*, ed. W.D. Ross, Oxford, 1957 (*Politics*, trans. H. Rackham, *Loeb Classical Library*, Cambridge, Mass. and London, 1950).

Baldus de Ubaldis de Perusio, *Commentaries on the Codex*, Venice, 1615.

Baldus de Ubaldis de Perusio, *Commentaries on the Digest*, Venice, 1616.

Baldus de Ubaldis de Perusio, *De Constituto*, in *Tractatus Universi Iuris*, vol. 5, Lyon, 1549, fols 105r–105v.

Baldus de Ubaldis de Perusio, *De Statutis*, in *Tractatus Illustrium Iurisconsultorum*, vol. 5, Lyon, 1549, fols 86r–154v.

Bartlett, J. (ed.), *Records of the Colony of Rhode Island and Providence Plantations*, vol. 1 (1636–63), Providence, Rhode Island, 1856 and New York, 1968.

Bartolus of Sassoferrato, *Commentaries on the Codex*, Turin, 1577.

Bartolus of Sassoferrato, *Commentaries on the Digest*, Turin, 1577.

Bartolus of Sassoferrato, *Tractatus de Regimine Civitatis* (*On City Government*), ed. D. Quaglioni, *Pensiero Politico* 9 (1976), pp.70–93.

Belleperche, Pierre de, *Questiones*, Lyon, 1517.

Bodin, Jean, *De Republica Libri Sex* (*On the Republic*), Paris, 1586.

Bracton, Henry de, *De Legibus et Consuetudinibus Angliae*, ed. G.E. Woodbine, 4 vols, New Haven, Conn., 1915.

Brandolinus, Aurelius, *De Comparatione Reipublicae et Regni ad Laurentium Medicem Libri Tres*, ed. Abel Jenö in *Irodalomtörteneti Emlekek*, vol. 2: *Plaszorszagi XV Szazadbeli Iroknak*, Budapest, 1890, pp. 79–183.

Bruni, Leonardo, of Arezzo, *Funeral Speech for Nanno Strozzi*, in S. Baluze, *Miscellanea*, vol. 3, Paris, 1680, pp. 226–48.

Bruni, Leonardo, of Arezzo, *Laudatio Florentinae Urbis* (*Eulogy of Florence*), ed. H. Baron, *From Petrarch to Leonardo Bruni*, Chicago, 1968, pp. 232–63.

Bucer, Martin, *De Regno Christi*, ed. W. Pauck, *Melanchthon and Bucer* (*Library of Christian Classics*, vol. 19), London, 1969, pp. 174–394.

Buchanan, George, *De Iure Regni apud Scotos*, in *Opera Omnia*, vol. 1, Edinburgh, 1715.

Buridan, John, *Questiones Super Octo Libris Politicorum*, Oxford, 1640.

Butrio, Antonius de, *Commentary on the Decretals*, Lyon, 1532.

Calvin, John, *Institutes of the Christian Religion*, ed. J.T. McNeill, trans. F. Battles, 2 vols (*Library of Christian Classics*, vols 20–1), London, 1961.

Castro, Paulus de, *Commentary on the Codex*, Venice, 1593.

Castro, Paulus de, *Commentary on the Digest*, Venice, 1593.

Castro, Paulus de, *Consilia*, pt 1, Lyon, 1532.

Chroniken der deutschen Städte, ed. Historische Kommission der bayerische Akademie der Wissenschaften, Leipzig–Stuttgart, 1862–1931 (repr. Göttingen, 1961).

Cicero, *De Officiis*, ed. C. Atzert, Leipzig, 1958 (trans. W. Miller, *Loeb Classical Library*, Cambridge, Mass. and London, 1975).

Cicero, *De Republica*, ed. K. Ziegler, Leipzig, 1964 (trans. C. W. Keyes, *Loeb Classical Library*, Cambridge, Mass. and London, 1951).

Cino, *see* Pistoia.

Codex Diplomaticus Lubecensis: Lübeckisches Urkundenbuch, 1 Abt.: *Urkundenbuch der Stadt Lübeck*, pt 8, Lübeck, 1889.

Codex Iustinianus, ed. P. Krüger, Berlin, 1963.

Cole, G.D.H., *Self-Government in Industry*, London, 1971 (repr. 1972).

Decretalium Collectiones (Decretals), ed. A. Friedberg, 2nd edn, Graz, 1959.

Decretum Gratiani, ed. A. Friedberg, 2nd edn, Graz, 1959.

Digesta, ed. T. Mommsen and P. Krüger, Dublin–Zurich, 1966.

Durkheim, E., *De la division du travail social (DTS)*, Paris, 1973. (*The Division of Labour in Society*, trans. G. Simpson, New York, 1933.)

Durkheim, E., *Leçons de sociologie: physique des moeurs et du droit*, 2nd edn, Paris, 1969. (*Professional Ethics and Civic Morals*, trans. C. Brookfield, London, 1957.)

Durkheim, E., *Suicide*, trans. J. Spaulding and G. Simpson, London, 1952.

Eberlin von Günzberg, Johann, (*A New Organization of the Secular State*), trans. J. S. Schapiro, *Social Reform and the Reformation* (*Columbia University Studies in History, Economics and Public Law*, 34), New York and London, 1909, pp. 118–25.

Eixemines, Francesc, *Regiment de la cosa publica*, ed. P. Daniel de Molino de Dei, Barcelona, 1927.

Ennen, L. (ed.), *Quellen zur Geschichte der Stadt Köln*, vol. 4, Cologne, 1870 (repr. 1970).

Erasmus, Desiderius, *Institutio Principis Christiani* (*Education of a Christian Ruler*), in *Opera Omnia*, vol. 4, Lyon, 1703, pp. 560–611.

Exea, Andreas ab, *De Pactis*, in *Tractatus Illustrium Iurisconsultorum*, vol. 6, pt 2, Venice, 1584, fols 1r–29v.

Fonti e studi sulle corporazioni artigiane del medio evo, ed. R. Deputazione di Storia patria per la Toscana, vol. 1: *Statuti dell'arte della Lana di Firenze (1317–1319)*, ed. A. Agnoletti, Florence, 1940–8; vol. 2: *Statuti dell'arte dei Rigattieri e Linaiolo di Firenze (1296–1340)*, ed. F. Sartini, Florence, 1940–8.

Gansfort, John Wessel, *De Dignitate et Potestate Ecclesiastica*, in *Opera*, repr. Nieuwkoop, 1966, pp. 748–71.

Geismayr, Michael, (*A National Constitution*), trans. J.S. Schapiro, *Social Reform and the Reformation* (*Columbia University Studies in History, Economics and Public Law*, 34), New York and London, 1909, pp. 147–51.

Giannotti, Donato, *Discorso sopra il fermare il governo di Firenze*, in F. Polidori (ed.), *Opere politiche e litterarie di Donato Giannotti*, vol. 1, Florence, 1850.

Gierke, Otto von, *Das deutsche Genossenschaftsrecht (DGR)*, vol. 1, Berlin, 1868 (repr. Graz, 1954).

Gierke, Otto von, *Das Wesen der menschlichen Verbände*, trans. J.D. Lewis, *The Genossenschaft-theory of Otto von Gierke*, Madison, 1935, pp. 139–57.

Gierke, Otto von, 'Die Grundbegriffe des Staatsrechts und die neuesten Staatsrechtstheorien', trans. J.D. Lewis, *The Genossenschaft-theory of Otto von Gierke*, Madison, 1935, pp. 166–85.

Gierke, Otto von, 'German constitutional law in its relation to the American constitution', *Harvard Law Review*, 23 (1910), 273–90.

Girolami, Remigio de', *De Bono Pacis (The Benefit of Peace)*, ed. C.T. Davis, 'Remigio de' Girolami and Dante: a comparison of their conceptions of peace', *Studi Danteschi*, 36 (1959), 123–36.

Hegel, G.W.F., *The Philosophy of History*, trans. J. Sibree, New York, 1956.

Hegel, G.W.F., *The Philosophy of Right (PR)*, trans. T.M. Knox, Oxford, 1942.

Hegel, G.W.F., *Political Writings*, trans. T. M. Knox, Oxford, 1964.

Hill, C. and Dell, E. (eds), *The Good Old Cause: The English Revolution of 1640–1660*, 2nd edn, London, 1969.

Hobbes, Thomas, *Leviathan*, ed. M. Oakeshott, Oxford, n.d.

Hocsem, John of, *Chronicon (Episcoporum Leodentium)*, ed. G. Kurth, Brussels, 1927.

Hostiensis, *Commentary on the Decretals*, 2 vols, Paris, 1512.

Hostiensis, *De Syndicis*, in *Summa Aurea Super Titulis Decretalium*, Venice, 1570, fols 103v–105v.

Innocent IV, *Commentary on the Decretals*, Turin, 1581.

Institutiones, ed. P. Krüger, Dublin–Zurich, 1966.

Jäger, Clemens, *Weberchronik (Chronicle of the Weavers' Guild at Augsburg)*, ed. F. Roth and J. Hansen in *Chroniken* (see entry under *Chroniken*), vol. 34, pp. 39–295.

Jouvenel, B. de, *Sovereignty: An Inquiry into the Political Good*, Cambridge, 1957.

Kant's Political Writings, ed. H. S. Reiss, trans. H. Nisbett, Cambridge, 1970.

Keutgen, F. (ed.), *Urkunden zur städtischen Verfassungsgeschichte (Ausgewählte Urkunden zum deutschen Verfassungsgeschichte*, ed. G. von Below and F. Keutgen, vol. 1), Berlin, 1901.

Kropotkin, P., *Mutual Aid: A Factor in Evolution*, ed. P. Avrich, London, 1972.

Lasserre, D. (ed.), *Alliances confédérales 1291–1815*, Zurich, 1941.

Latini, Brunetto, *Li livres dou tresor (Treasury)*, ed. F.J. Carmody (*University of California Publications: Modern Philology*, 22), Berkeley, Ca, 1948.

Locke, John, *Two Treatises of Government*, ed. P. Laslett, 2nd edn, Cambridge, 1967.

Loesch, H. von (ed.), *Die kölner Zunfturkunden nebst anderen kölner Gewerbeurkunden bis zum Jahre 1500*, Bonn, 1907.

Machiavelli, Niccolo, *Discorsi sopra la prima Deca di Tito Livio*

(Discourses), ed. M. Bonfantini, Niccolo Machiavelli, *Opere*, Milan–Naples, n.d., pp. 87–420. (Trans. C.E. Detmold, *The Prince and the Discourses*, New York, 1950, pp. 103–540.)

Machiavelli, Niccolo, *Il principe (The Prince)*, ed. M. Bonfantini, Niccolo Machiavelli, *Opere*, Milan–Naples, n.d., pp. 3–86.

Machiavelli, Niccolo, *Ritratto delle cose della Magna (German Affairs)*, ed. M. Bonfantini, Niccolo Machiavelli, *Opere*, Milan–Naples, n.d., pp. 487–92.

Maino, Giason del, *Commentary on the Digest*, in *Opera Omnia*, vols 2–7, Lyon, 1540–2.

Marsiglio of Padua, *Defensor Pacis (The Defender of the Peace)*, ed. C. W. Previté-Orton, Cambridge, 1928.

Marx, K. and Engels, F., *Werke*, 39 vols, Berlin, 1956–68.

Mill, J.S., *Considerations on Representative Government*, ed. J. Robson, *Collected Works of John Stuart Mill*, vol. 19, Toronto, 1977, pp. 371–578.

Mill, J.S., *On Liberty*, ed. J. Robson, *Collected Works of John Stuart Mill*, vol. 18, Toronto, 1977, pp. 203–310.

Mill, J.S., *Principles of Political Economy*, ed. J. Robson, *Collected Works of John Stuart Mill*, vols 2–3, Toronto, 1977.

Mirandola, Pico della, *Oratio de Hominis Dignitate*, ed. E. Garin, *Prosatori Latini del Quattrocento*, Florence, 1942, pp. 102–65.

Montesquieu, *De l'esprit des lois*, in *Oeuvres complets*, Paris, 1964, pp. 527–795.

Müller, Adam, (Selections from *The Elements of Politics*), trans. H.S. Reiss, *The Political Thought of the German Romantics*, Oxford, 1955, pp. 143–71.

Novalis, *Die Christenheit oder Europa*, ed. R. Taylor, *The Romantic Tradition in Germany*, London, 1970, pp. 136–52. (Trans. H.S. Reiss, *The Political Thought of the German Romantics*, Oxford, 1955, pp. 126–41.)

Oakeshott, M., *On Human Conduct*, Oxford, 1975.

Oculus Pastoralis Sive Libellus Erudiens Futurum Rectorem Populorum (The Shepherd's Eye), ed. L. Muratori, *Antiquitates Italicae medii aevi*, vol. 4, Milan, 1741, pp. 95–128.

Patrizi, Francesco, *De Institutione Reipublicae (Republic)*, Paris, 1534.

Patrizi, Francesco, *De Regno et Regis Institutione (On the Kingdom)*, Paris, 1578.

Philippi (ed.), *Preussisches Urkundenbuch*, vol. 1, pt 1, Lüneberg, 1882 (repr. Aalen, 1961).

Piccolomini, Aeneas Sylvius, *Descriptio Altera Basileae (Second Description of Basle)*, *Concilium Basiliense*, ed. J. Haller *et al.*, vol. 8, Basle, 1936, pp. 191–204.

Piccolomini, Aeneas Sylvius, *Germania*, ed. A. Schmidt, Cologne–Graz, 1962.

Pistoia, Cino Sighibuldi da, *Commentary on the Codex and Parts of the Digest*, Frankfurt, 1578.

Planitz, H. (ed.), *Quellenbuch der deutschen, österreichischen und schweizer Rechtsgeschichte*, Graz, 1948.

Porcari, Stefano, *Orazione (Speeches)*, ed. G. Cavalieri Giuliari, *Prose del giovane Buonaccorso da Montemagno (Scelta di curiosita litterarie inedite o raro dal seculo xiii al xvii)*, Bologna, 1874, pp. 28–65 (cf. Weinstein 1970, 58).

Porcius, Christophorus, *Commentary on the Institutes*, Venice, 1580.

Proudhon, Pierre-Joseph, *Selected Writings*, ed. S. Edwards, trans. E. Fraser, London, 1970.

Ptolemy of Lucca, *De Regimine Principum (On Princely Government)*, bks II–IV, Thomas Aquinas, *Opuscula Omnia Necnon Opera Minora*, vol. 1: *Opuscula Philosophica*, ed. J. Perrier, Paris, 1949, pp. 270–426.

Reformation of the Emperor Frederick III, trans. J.S. Schapiro, *Social Reform and the Reformation (Columbia University Studies in History, Economics and Public Law*, 34), New York and London, 1909, pp. 104–14.

Révigny, Jacques de, *Lecture on the First Part of the Codex*, MS, Caius College, Cambridge.

Rockinger, L. (ed.), *Briefsteller und Formelbücher des 11. bis 14. Jahrhunderts*, repr. Aalen, 1969.

Roffredus of Benevento, *Questiones Sabbatinae*, in *Corpus Glossatorum Iuris Civilis*, ed. Juris Italici Historiae Institutum Taurinensis Universitatis, repr. Turin, 1968.

Romano, Egidio, *De Regimine Principum (On Princely Government)*, Rome, 1556. French translation ed. S.P. Molenaer, Livres du Gouvernement des Rois: *A Thirteenth-Century French Version of Egidio Colonna's Treatise* De Regimine Principum, New York, 1899.

Rousseau, Jean-Jacques, *Du contrat social*, ed. R. Grimsley, Oxford, 1972.

Sächsische Weichbildrecht, jus municipale Saxonum, ed. A. von Daniels and Fr. von Gruben, Berlin, 1858.

Salamonio, Mario, *De Principatu (On Sovereignty)*, ed. M. d'Addio *(Pubblicazioni dell'istituto de diritto pubblico … dell'Universita di Roma*, 4), Milan, 1955, pp. 11–75.

Salamonio, Mario, *Orationes ad Priores Florentinos (Speeches)*, ed. M. d'Addio *(Pubblicazioni dell'istituto di diritto pubblico … dell'Universita di Roma*, 4), Milan, 1955, pp. 79–126.

Salisbury, John of, *Metalogicon*, ed. C. Webb, Oxford, 1929.

Salisbury, John of, *Policraticus*, ed. C. Webb, 2 vols, Oxford, 1909.

Salutati, Coluccio, *Invectivum in Antonium Luschum Vicentium*, in E.

Garin, *Prosatori latini del Quattrocento*, Florence, 1942, pp. 8–37.

Savigny, F. C. von, (Selections from *On the Vocation of Our Age for Legislation and Jurisprudence*), trans. H.S. Reiss, *The Political Thought of the German Romantics*, Oxford, 1955, pp. 203–11.

Schleiermacher, F.E.D., (Selections from *On the Concepts of Different Forms of the State*), trans. H.S. Reiss, *The Political Thought of the German Romantics*, Oxford, 1955, pp. 173–202.

Smith, Adam, *The Wealth of Nations*, bks I–III, London, 1970.

Tocqueville, Alexis de, *Democracy in America*, ed. P. Bradley, trans. H. Reeve and F. Bowen, 2 vols, New York, 1945.

Tönnies, Ferdinand, *Community and Association (Gemeinschaft und Gesellschaft)*, trans. C. P. Loomis, London, 1955.

Tudeschi, Niccolo de', *Commentary on the Decretals*, 7 vols, Venice, 1578.

Twelve Articles of the Peasants (1525), trans. B.J. Kidd, *Documents Illustrative of the Continental Reformation*, Oxford, 1911 (repr. 1967), pp. 174–9.

Versor, Johannes, *Questiones Super Octo Libris Politicorum*, Paris, 1497.

Viterbo, John of, *Liber de Regimine Civitatum (The Government of Cities)*, ed. C. Salvemini in A. Gaudentius (ed.), *Bibliotheca Juridica Medii Aevi*, vol. 3, Bologna, 1901, pp. 217–80.

Zabarella, Franciscus, *Commentary on the Decretals*, Lyon, 1517.

Secondary sources

Addio, M.d' (1954) *L'idea del contratto sociale dai sofisti alla Riforma e il 'De principatu' di Maria Salamonio*, Milan.

Albertini, R. (1955) *Das florentinische Staatsbewusstsein im Übergang von der Republik zum Prinzipat*, Bern.

Allen, J. (1928) *A History of Political Thought in the Sixteenth Century*, London.

Andreas, W. (1943) *Deutschland vor der Reformation, eine Zeitenwende*, 4th edn, Stuttgart–Berlin.

Ashton, R. (1979) *The English Civil War: Conservatism and Revolution 1603–1649*, London.

Avineri, S. (1972) *Hegel's Theory of the Modern State*, Cambridge.

Backstrom, P. (1974) *Christian Socialism and Co-operation in Victorian England: Edward Vansittart Neale and the Co-operative Movement*, London.

Bader, K. (1957) *Studien zur Rechtsgeschichte des mittelalterlichen Dorfes*, pt 1: *Das mittelalterliche Dorf als Friedens- und Rechtsbereich*, Weimar.

Bader, K. (1962) *Studien zur Rechtsgeschichte des mittelalterlichen Dorfes*, pt 2: *Dorfgenossenschaft und Dorfgemeinde*, Cologne–Graz.

Baldwin, J.W. (1970) *Masters, Princes and Merchants: The Social Views of*

Peter the Chanter and His Circle, 2 vols, Princeton, NJ.

Barber, B.R. (1974) *The Death of Communal Liberty: The History of Freedom in a Swiss Mountain Canton*, Princeton, NJ.

Baron, H. (1939) 'Calvinist republicanism and its historical roots', *Church History*, 8, 30–42.

Baron, H. (1966) *The Crisis of the Early Italian Renaissance. Civic Humanism and Republican Liberty in an Age of Classicism and Tyranny*, rev. edn, Princeton, NJ.

Baudrillart, H. (1853) *Bodin et son temps: tableau des théories politiques et des idées économiques au 16e siècle*, Paris.

Baxa, J. (1972) 'Romantik und konservative Politik', in G.-K. Kaltenbrunner (ed.), *Rekonstruktion des Konservatismus*, Freiburg, pp. 443–68.

Becker, M.B. (1967) *Florence in Transition*, vol. 1: *The Decline of the Commune*, Baltimore, Md.

Beer, S. (1969) *Modern British Politics*, London.

Black, A. (1979) *Council and Commune: The Conciliar Movement and the Fifteenth-Century Heritage*, London.

Black, A. (1980) 'Society and the individual from the Middle Ages to Rousseau: philosophy, jurisprudence and constitutional theory', *History of Political Thought*, 1, 145–66.

Blanshei, S.R. (1976) 'Perugia 1260–1340: conflict and change in a medieval Italian urban society', *Transactions of the American Philosophical Society*, 66(2), 1–128.

Blecher, M. (1975) 'Aspects of privacy in the civil law', *Tijdschrift voor Rechtsgeschiedenis*, 43, 279–96.

Bloch, M. (1961) *Feudal Society*, trans. L. Manyon, London.

Bolgar, R.R. (1958) *The Classical Heritage and Its Beneficiaries*, Cambridge.

Bowen, R.H. (1947) *German Theories of the Corporative State with Special Reference to the Period 1870–1919*, New York.

Brady, T.A. (1978a) *Ruling Class, Regime and Reformation at Strasbourg 1520–1555 (Studies in Medieval and Reformation Thought, 22)*, Leiden.

Brady, T.A. (1978b) 'Patricians, nobles, merchants: internal tensions and solidarities in south German ruling classes at the close of the Middle Ages', in M. Chrisman and O. Gruendler (eds) *Social Groups and Religious Ideas in the Sixteenth Century (Studies in Medieval Culture, 13)*, Kalamazoo, pp. 38–45.

Brandt, A. von (1954) *Geist und Politik in der Lübeckischen Geschichte*, Lübeck.

Brown, P. (1982) *Society and the Holy in Late Antiquity*, London.

Brucker, G. (1977) *The Civic World of Early Renaissance Florence*, Princeton, NJ.

Buckland, W.W. (1963) *A Text-Book of Roman Law from Augustus to*

Justinian, 3rd edn (rev. P. Stein), Cambridge.

Büttner, H. (1973) 'Die Bischofsstädte von Basel bis Mainz in der Zeit des Investiturstreits', in J. Fleckenstein (ed.) *Investiturstreit und Reichsverfassung*, Munich, pp. 351–62.

Bynum, C.W. (1980) 'Did the twelfth century discover the individual?', *Journal of Ecclesiastical History*, 31, 1–17.

Cahnman, W.J. (ed.) (1973) *Ferdinand Tönnies. A New Evaluation*, Leiden.

Calasso, F. (1954) *Medio evo del diritto*, vol. 1: *Le fonti*, Milan.

Calasso, F. (1957) *I Glossatori e la teoria della sovranita: studio di diritto comune pubblico*, 3rd edn, Milan.

Camp, R.L. (1969) *The Papal Ideology of Social Reform: A Study in Historical Development 1878–1967*, Leiden.

Canning, J. (1980) 'The corporation in the political thought of the Italian jurists of the thirteenth and fourteenth centuries', *History of Political Thought*, 1, 9–32.

Carlyle, A.J. (1941) *Political Liberty: A History of the Conception in the Middle Ages and Modern Times*, Oxford.

Carlyle, R.W. and A.J. (1903) *A History of Medieval Political Thought in the West*, vol. 1: *The Second to the Ninth Century*, Edinburgh and London.

Carlyle, R.W. and A.J. (1936) *A History of Medieval Political Thought in the West*, vol. 6: *Political Theory from 1300 to 1600*, Edinburgh and London.

Chenu, M.-D. (1968) *Nature, Man and Society in the Twelfth Century*, trans. J. Taylor and L. Little, Chicago, Ill.

Cheyette, F.L. (1978) 'The invention of the state', in B. Lackner and K. Philp (eds) *Essays on Medieval Civilization*, Austin, Texas, and London, pp. 143–78.

Clapham, J.H. (1948) *The Economic Development of France and Germany 1815–1914*, 4th edn, Cambridge.

Clapham, J.H. (1949) *A Concise Economic History of Britain from the Earliest Times to 1750*, Cambridge.

Clarke, M.V. (1926) *The Medieval City State: An Essay on Tyranny and Federation in the Later Middle Ages*, London.

Clayre, A. (ed.) (1981) *The Political Economy of Co-operation and Participation: A Third Sector*, Oxford.

Cobban, A. (1961) *A History of Modern France*, vol. 1: *1715–1799*, 2nd edn, Harmondsworth.

Cobban, A. (1964) *Rousseau and the Modern State*, 2nd edn, London.

Cohn, N. (1957) *The Pursuit of the Millennium: Revolutionary Millenarians and Mystical Anarchists in the Middle Ages*, London.

Coleman, J. (forthcoming) 'The theme of *dominium* in thirteenth- and fourteenth-century political thought', *History of Political Thought*.

Coornaert, E. (1947) 'Les ghildes médiévales (Ve–XIVe siècles): définition–évolution', *Revue Historique*, 199, 22–55, 208–43.

Coornaert, E. (1966) *Les compagnonnages en France du moyen âge à nos jours*, Paris.

Coornaert, E. (1968) *Les corporations en France avant 1789*, 2nd edn, Paris.

Court, W.H.B. (1962) *A Concise Economic History of Britain from 1750 to Recent Times*, Cambridge.

Cox, Harvey (1965) *The Secular City: Secularization and Urbanization in Theological Perspective*, New York and London.

Davis, C.T. (1960) 'An early Florentine political theorist: Remigio de' Girolami', *Proceedings of the American Philosophical Society*, 104, 662–79.

Dawson, J.P. (1960) *A History of Lay Judges*, Cambridge, Mass.

Dawson, J.P. (1968) *Oracles of the Law*, Ann Arbor, Mich.

Dickens, A.G. (1974) *The German Nation and Martin Luther*, London.

Dirr, P. (1910) 'Clemens Jäger und seine Augsburger Ehrenbücher und Zunftchroniken', *Zeitschrift des historischen Vereins für Schwaben*, 36, 1–32.

Dobson, C.R. (1980) *Masters and Journeymen: A Pre-history of Industrial Relations, 1717–1800*, London.

Dollinger, P. (1955) 'Les villes allemandes au moyen âge: les groupements sociaux', in *La Ville*, pt 2 (*Receuils de la société Jean Bodin*, 7), Brussels, pp. 371–401.

Duff, P.W. (1938) *Personality in Roman Private Law*, Cambridge.

Dunn, J. (1969) *The Political Thought of John Locke: An Historical Account of the Argument of the 'Two Treatises of Government'*, Cambridge.

Duparc, P. (1975) 'Confraternities of the Holy Spirit and village communities in the Middle Ages', in F. Cheyette (ed.) *Lordship and Community in Medieval Europe*, New York, pp. 341–56.

Edwards, S. (1969) (introduction to) *Selected Writings of Pierre-Joseph Proudhon*, London, pp. 13–36.

Elbow, M. (1953) *French Corporative Theory, 1789–1948: A Chapter in the History of Ideas*, New York.

Elliott, J.H. (1970) *Imperial Spain 1469–1716*, London.

Emerson, R. (1928) *State and Sovereignty in Modern Germany*, New Haven, Conn.

Evans, D. (1979) 'The populus in late medieval Roman law', London, Diss.

Feenstra, R. (1954) 'Les villes des Pays-Bas septentrionaux – Histoire des institutions administratives et judiciaires', in *La Ville*, pt 1 (*Receuils de la société Jean Bodin*, 6), Brussels, pp. 605–34.

Feenstra, R. (1956) 'L'histoire des fondations à propos de quelques études récentes', *Tijdschrift voor Rechtsgeschiedenis*, 24, 381–448.

Feenstra, R. (1963) 'Les *Flores utriusque legis* de Jean de Hocsem et leur édition au XVe siècle', *Tijdschrift voor Rechtsgeschiedenis*, 31, 486–519.

Feine, H.E. (1950) *Kirchliche Rechtsgeschichte*, vol. 1: *Die katholische Kirche*, Weimar.

Filloux, J.-C. (1977) *Durkheim et le socialisme*, Paris.

Fink, Z.S. (1940–1) 'Venice and English political thought in the seventeenth century', *Modern Philology*, 38, 155ff.

Fox, A. and Flanders, A. (1969) 'The reform of collective bargaining: from Donovan to Durkheim', *British Journal of Industrial Relations*, 7, 151–80.

Friedrich, C.J. (1932) (introduction to) *Johannes Althusius (Althaus), Politica Methodice Digesta*, Cambridge, Mass.

Friedrichs, C.R. (1978) 'Citizens or subjects? Urban conflict in early modern Germany', in M. Chrisman and O. Gruendler (eds) *Social Groups and Religious Ideas in the Sixteenth Century* (*Studies in Medieval Culture*, 13), Kalamazoo, pp. 46–58.

Gewirth, A. (1951) *Marsilius of Padua, the Defender of the Peace*, vol. 1: *Marsilius of Padua and Medieval Political Philosophy*, New York.

Gierke, O. von (1868) *Das deutsche Genossenschaftsrecht*, vol. 1: *Rechtsgeschichte der deutschen Genossenschaft*, Berlin.

Gierke, O. von (1873) *Das deutsche Genossenschaftsrecht*, vol. 2: *Geschichte des deutschen Körperschaftsbegriffs*, Berlin.

Gierke, O. von (1881) *Des deutsche Genossenschaftsrecht*, vol. 3: *Die Staats- und Korporationslehre des Altertums und des Mittelalters und ihre Aufnahme in Deutschland*, Berlin.

Gierke, O. von (1900) *Political Theories of the Middle Age*, trans. F. Maitland (from *Das deutsche Genossenschaftsrecht*, vol. 3, pp. 501–640), Cambridge.

Gierke, O. von (1958) *Natural Law and the Theory of Society 1500 to 1800*, trans. E. Barker (from *Das deutsche Genossenschaftsrecht*, vol. 4, pp. 276–541), Cambridge.

Gierke, O. von (1966) *The Development of Political Theory*, trans. B. Freyd (from *Johannes Althusius und die Entwicklung der naturrechtlichen Staatstheorien*), new edn, New York.

Gilbert, F. (1965) *Machiavelli and Guicciardini: Politics and History in Sixteenth-Century Florence*, Princeton, NJ.

Gilbert, F. (1968) 'The Venetian constitution in Florentine political thought', in N. Rubinstein (ed.) *Florentine Studies*, London, pp. 463–500.

Gilby, T. (1958) *Principality and Polity: Aquinas and the Rise of State Theory in the West*, London.

Gilissen, J. (1954) 'Les villes en Belgique – Histoire des institutions administratives et judiciaires des villes belges', in *La Ville*, pt 1 (*Receuil de la société Jean Bodin*, 6), Brussels, pp. 531–604.

Gillet, P. (1927) *La personnalité juridique en droit ecclésiastique spéciale-ment chez les Décrétistes et les Décrétalistes et dans le Code de Droit Canonique*, Malines.

Gilson, E. (1955) *History of Christian Philosophy in the Middle Ages*, London.

Glass, S.T. (1966) *The Responsible Society: The Ideas of Guild Socialism*, London.

Godsden, P. (1961) *The Friendly Societies in England 1815–1875*, Man-chester.

Godsden, P. (1973) *Self-Help: Voluntary Associations in Nineteenth-Century Britain*, London.

Gooch, G.P. (1967) *English Democratic Ideas in the Seventeenth Century*, 2nd edn, Cambridge.

Grebing, H. (1969) *The History of the German Labour Movement: A Survey*, trans. E. Körner, London.

Griffiths, G. (1956) 'Representative institutions in the Spanish empire: the Low Countries', *The Americas*, 12, 234–43.

Griffiths, G. (1968) *Representative Government in Western Europe in the Sixteenth Century*, Oxford.

Grimsley, R. (1973) *The Philosophy of Rousseau*, Oxford.

Grossi, P. (1958) '*Unanimitas*: alle origine del concetto della persona giuridica nel diritto canonica', *Annali di Storia del Diritto*, 2, 229–331.

Guenée, B. (1971) *L'Occident aux XIVe et XVe siècles: les états* (*Nouvelle Clio*, 22), Paris.

Haller, W. (1963) *Foxe's Book of Martyrs and the Elect Nation*, London.

Hallis, F. (1930) *Corporate Personality: A Study in Jurisprudence*, Oxford.

Hamerow, T.S. (1958) *Restoration, Revolution, Reaction: Economics and Politics in Germany, 1815–1871*, Princeton, NJ.

Harding, A. (1980) 'Political liberty in the Middle Ages', *Speculum*, 55, 423–43.

Harvey, J. (1950) *The Gothic World 1100–1600: A Survey of Architecture and Art*, London.

Hawkins, K. (1981) *Trade Unions*, London.

Hawkins, M.J. (1980) 'Traditionalism and organicism in Durkheim's earlier writings, 1885–1893', *Journal of the History of the Behavioural Sciences*, 16, 31–44.

Hayward, J.E.S. (1960) 'Solidarist syndicalism: Durkheim and Duguit', *Sociological Review*, 8, 17–36, 185–202.

Heers, J. (1973) *L'Occident aux XIVe et XVe siècles: aspects économiques et sociaux* (*Nouvelle Clio*, 23), Paris.

Heers, J. (1974) *Le clan familiale au moyen âge: étude sur les structures politiques et sociales des milieux urbains*, Paris.

Heiman, G. (1970) 'The sources and significance of Hegel's corporate doctrine', in Z. Pelczynski (ed.) *Hegel's Political Philosophy*, Cambridge, pp. 111–35.

Herde, P. (1973) 'Politische Verhaltenweisen der florentiner Oligarchie 1382–1402', in *Geschichte und Verfassungsgefüge, Frankfurter Festgabe für Walter Schlesinger (Frankfurter historische Abhandlungen, 5)*, Wiesbaden, pp. 156–249.

Hexter, J.H. (1979) 'Republic, virtue, liberty and the political universe of J.G.A. Pocock', in J.H. Hexter, *On Historians*, Cambridge, Mass., pp. 255–303.

Hibbert, A. (1963) 'The economic policies of towns', *Cambridge Economic History*, vol. 3, Cambridge, pp. 157–229.

Hill, C. (1962) *Puritanism and Revolution*, London.

Hill, C. (1965) *Intellectual Origins of the English Revolution*, Oxford.

Hobsbawm, E.F. (1971) *Primitive Rebels: Studies in Archaic Forms of Social Movement in the Nineteenth and Twentieth Centuries*, 3rd edn, London.

Hoepfl, H. (1982) *The Christian Polity of John Calvin*, Cambridge.

Hoepfl, H. and Thompson, M. (1979) 'The history of contract as a motif in political thought', *American Historical Review*, 84, 919–44.

Holmes, G. (1973) 'The emergence of an urban ideology at Florence, c.1250–1450', *Transactions of the Royal Historical Society*, 5th series, 23, 111–34.

Imbart de la Tour, P. (1944) *Les origines de la Réforme*, vol. 2, 2nd edn, Melun.

Imbart de la Tour (1948) *Les origines de la Réforme*, vol. 1, 2nd edn, Melun.

Imbart de la Tour (n.d.) *Les origines de la Réforme*, vol. 4, Melun.

Joachimsen, P. (1910) *Geschichtsauffassung und Geschichtschreibung in Deutschland unter dem Einfluss des Humanismus (Beiträge zur Kulturgeschichte des Mittelalters und der Renaissance, 6)*, Leipzig.

Jolowicz, H. and Nicholas, B. (1972) *Historical Introduction to the Study of Roman Law*, 3rd edn, Cambridge.

Jones, P. (1965) 'Communes and despots: the city-state in late medieval Italy', *Transactions of the Royal Historical Society*, 5th series, 15, 71–96.

Kellenbenz, H. (1977) 'The organization of production', *Cambridge Economic History*, vol. 5, Cambridge, pp. 462–548.

Keller, H. (1973) 'Pataria und Stadtverfassung, Stadtgemeinde und Reform: Mailand im "Investiturstreit" ', in J. Fleckenstein (ed.) *Investiturstreit und Reichsverfassung*, Munich, pp. 321–50.

Kelley, D. (1981) *The Beginning of Ideology: Consciousness and Society in the French Reformation*, Cambridge.

Kern, F. (1939) *Kingship and Law in the Middle Ages*, trans. S. Chrimes, Oxford.

Klein, J. (1967) 'Medieval Spanish gilds', *Facts and Factors in Economic History: Articles by Former Students of E.F. Gay*, repr. New York, pp. 164–88.

Kluckhorn, P. (1925) *Persönlichkeit und Gemeinschaft: Studien zur Staatsauffassung der deutschen Romantik* (Deutsche Vierteljahrschrift für Literaturwissenschaft und Geistesgeschichte, Buchreihe 5), Halle–Saale.

Koenigsberger, H.G. (1968) 'Western Europe and the power of Spain', *New Cambridge Modern History*, vol. 3, Cambridge, pp. 234–318.

Koenigsberger, H.G. and Mosse, G.L. (1968) *Europe in the Sixteenth Century*, London.

Kristeller, P.O. (1961) *Renaissance Thought: The Classic, Scholastic and Humanistic Strains*, rev. edn, New York.

Kuhn, T. (1963) *The Structure of Scientific Revolutions*, Chicago, Ill.

Lagarde, G. de (1943a) 'Individualisme et corporatisme au moyen âge', *Université de Louvain, receuil de travaux d'histoire et de philologie*, 3 (18), 4ff.

Lagarde, G. de (1943b) 'La philosophie sociale d'Henri de Gand et Godefroid de Fontaines', *Université de Louvain, receuil de travaux d'histoire et de philologie*, 3 (18), 57–134.

Lagarde, G. de (1946) *La naissance de l'esprit laique au déclin du moyen âge*, vol. 6, Paris.

Lagarde, G. de (1958) *La naissance de l'esprit laique au déclin du moyen âge*, vol. 2, 2nd edn, Louvain–Paris.

Lambert, J. (1891) *Two Thousand Years of Gild Life*, Hull.

Lane, F. (1973) *Venice, a Maritime Republic*, Baltimore, Md, and London.

Laslett, P. (1967) (introduction to) John Locke, *Two Treatises of Government*, 2nd edn, Cambridge.

Le Bras, G. (1940–1) 'Les confréries chrétiennes: problèmes et propositions', *Revue Historique du Droit Français et Étranger*, series 4, 19–20, 310–63.

Le Bras, G. (1963) 'Conceptions of economy and society', *Cambridge Economic History*, vol. 3, Cambridge, pp. 554–75.

Leeson, R. (1979) *Travelling Brothers: The Six Centuries' Road from Craft Fellowship to Trade Unionism*, London.

Le Goff, J. (1964) 'Métier et profession d'après les manuels de confesseurs au moyen âge', in P. Wilpert and W. Eckert (eds) *Beiträge zum Berufsbewusstsein des mittelalterlichen Menschen* (Miscellanea Medievalia, 3), Berlin, pp. 44–60.

Le Goff, J. (1974) 'Les mentalités', in J. Le Goff and P. Nora (eds) *Faire l'histoire*, vol. 3, Paris, pp. 76–94.

Le Goff, J. (1977) 'Métiers licites et illicites dans l'Occident medieval', in J.

Le Goff (ed.) *Pour un autre moyen âge: temps, travail et culture en Occident*, Paris.

Lehmbruch, G. (1979) 'Consociational democracy, class conflict and the new corporatism', in P. Schmitter and G. Lehmbruch (eds) *Trends towards Corporatist Intermediation*, Beverly Hills, Ca, and London, pp. 53–62.

Lentze, H. (1933) *Der Kaiser und die Zunftverfassung in den Reichsstädte bis zum Tode Karls IV*, Breslau.

Le Roy Ladurie, E. (1980) *Montaillou: Cathars and Catholics in a French Village 1294–1324*, trans. B. Bray, Harmondsworth.

Levin, M. (1974) 'Marxism and Romanticism: Marx's debt to German conservatism', *Political Studies*, 22, 400–13.

Lewis, E. (1954) *Medieval Political Ideas*, 2 vols, London.

Lewis, J.D. (1935) *The Genossenschaft-theory of Otto von Gierke: A Study in Political Thought* (*University of Wisconsin Studies in the Social Sciences and History*, 25), Madison, Wisc.

Lichtheim, G. (1968) *The Origins of Socialism*, London.

Lichtheim, G. (1970) *A Short History of Socialism*, London.

Ludlow, J. (1869) 'Old guilds and new friendly and trade societies', *Fortnightly Review*, new series, 6, 390–406.

Lui, J. (1972) 'The people's communes and the Paris Commune', *Studies in Soviet Thought*, 12, 149–65.

Lukacs, J. (1978) *1945: Year Zero*, New York.

Lukes, S. (1973) *Emile Durkheim, His Life and Work: A Historical and Critical Study*, Harmondsworth.

Lutz, H. (n.d.) *Conrad Peutinger, Beiträge zu einer politischen Biographie*, Augsburg.

Macfarlane, A. (1978) *The Origins of English Individualism: The Family, Property and Social Transition*, Oxford.

McLellan, D. (1972) *Marx before Marxism*, rev. edn, Harmondsworth.

McNeill, J.T. (1949) 'The democratic elements in Calvin's thought', *Church History*, 18, 153–71.

Macpherson, C.B. (1962) *The Political Theory of Possessive Individualism: Hobbes to Locke*, Oxford.

McWilliams, W.C. (1973) *The Idea of Fraternity in America*, Berkeley, Ca.

Maitland, F.W. (1957) 'Township and borough', in H.M. Cam (ed.) *F.W. Maitland, Selected Historical Essays*, Cambridge, pp. 3–15.

Malia, M. (1955) 'Herzen and the peasant commune', in E.J. Simmons (ed.) *Continuity and Change in Russian and Soviet Thought*, New York, pp. 197–217.

Mannheim, K. (1936) *Ideology and Utopia: An Introduction to the Sociology of Knowledge*, London.

Maravall, J.A. (1963) *Las comunidadas de Castilla*, Madrid.

Maravall, J.A. (1966) *Estudios de Historia del Pensiamento español, Edad media*, serie primera, Madrid.

Marongiu, A. (1968) *Medieval Parliaments: A Comparative Study*, trans. S.J. Woolf, London.

Martin, C. (1951) 'Some medieval commentaries on Aristotle's *Politics*', *History*, 36, 29–44.

Martines, L. (1968) *Lawyers and Statecraft in Renaissance Florence*, Princeton, NJ.

Martines, L. (1980) *Power and Imagination: City-States in Renaissance Italy*, London.

Marx, K. (1976) *Capital*, vol. 1, trans. B. Fowkes, Harmondsworth.

Marx, K. (1977) *Selected Writings*, ed. D. McLellan, Oxford.

Maschke, E. (1959) 'Verfassung und soziale Kräfte in der deutschen Stadt des späten Mittelalter, vornehmlich in Oberdeutschland', *Vierteljahrschrift für Sozial- und Wirtschaftsgeschichte*, 46, 289–349, 433–76.

Meek, C. (1978) *Lucca 1369–1400: Politics and Society in an Early Renaissance City-State*, Oxford.

Mesnard, P. (1936) *L'essor de la philosophie politique au XVIe siècle*, Paris.

Michaud-Quantin, P. (1964a) 'La conscience d'être membre d'une *universitas*', in P. Wilpert and W. Eckert (eds) *Beiträge zum Berufsbewusstsein des mittelalterlichen Menschen* (Miscellanea Medievalia, 3), Berlin, pp. 1–14.

Michaud-Quantin, P. (1964b) 'Aspects de la vie sociale chez les moralistes', in P. Wilpert and W. Eckert (eds) *Beiträge zum Berufsbewusstsein des mittelalterlichen Menschen* (Miscellanea Medievalia, 3), Berlin, pp. 30–43.

Michaud-Quantin, P. (1970) Universitas: *expressions du mouvement communautaire dans le moyen âge latin*, Paris.

Mickwitz, G. (1936) *Die Kartellfunktionen der Zünfte und ihre Bedeutung bei der Entstehung des Zunftwesens: eine Studie im spätantiker und mittelalterliche Wirtschaftsgeschichte* (Societas scientiarum Fennica: commentationes humanarum litterarum, 8 (3)), Helsinki.

Miller, P. (1939) *The New England Mind: The Seventeenth Century*, Cambridge, Mass.

Mitteis, H. (1975) *The State in the Middle Ages, a Comparative Constitutional History of Feudal Europe*, trans. H. Orton, Amsterdam.

Möller, B. (1972) *Imperial Cities and the Reformation*, trans. H. Middelfort and M. Edwards, Philadelphia, Pa.

Morris, C. (1972) *The Discovery of the Individual 1050–1200*, London.

Moulin, L. (1953) 'Les origines religieuses des techniques électorales et délibératives modernes', *Revue Internationale d'Histoire Politique et Constitutionelle*, new series, 3, 106–48.

Mulgan, R.G. (1977) *Aristotle's Political Theory: An Introduction for*

Students of Political Theory, Oxford.

Mumford, L. (1966) *The City in History: Its Origins, Its Transformations, and Its Prospects*, Harmondsworth.

Mundy, J. (1954) *Liberty and Political Power in Toulouse 1050–1230*, New York.

Mundy, J. (1973) *Europe in the High Middle Ages*, London.

Najemy, J. (1979) 'Guild republicanism in Trecento Florence: the successes and ultimate failure of corporate politics', *American Historical Review*, 84, 53–71.

Nelson, B. (1969) *The Idea of Usury: From Tribal Brotherhood to Universal Otherhood*, 2nd edn, Chicago, Ill.

Oberman, H.A. (1981) *Masters of the Reformation: The Emergence of a New Intellectual Climate in Europe*, Cambridge.

O'Brien, G. (1920) *An Essay on Medieval Economic Teaching*, London.

Olson, M. (1965) *The Logic of Collective Action: Public Goods and the Theory of Groups*, Cambridge, Mass.

Ozment, S.E. (1975) *The Reformation in the Cities: The Appeal of Protestantism to Sixteenth-Century Germany and Switzerland*, New Haven, Conn.

Pacaut, M. (1963) 'Aux origines du guelfisme: les doctrines de la ligue lombarde (1167–1183)', *Revue Historique*, 230, 73–90.

Panitch, L. (1979) 'The development of corporatism in liberal democracies', in P. Schmitter and G. Lehmbruch (eds) *Trends Towards Corporatist Intermediation*, Beverly Hills, Ca, and London, 119–46.

Parker, G. (1979) *The Dutch Revolt*, Harmondsworth.

Pateman, C. (1970) *Participation and Democratic Theory*, Cambridge.

Pelling, H. (1976) *A History of British Trade Unionism*, 3rd edn, London.

Peters, E. (1977) '*Pars parte*: Dante and an urban contribution to political thought', in H. Miskimin, D. Herlihy and A. Udovitch (eds) *The Medieval City*, New Haven, Conn., pp. 113–40.

Petit-Dutaillis, C. (1970) *Les communes françaises: caractères et évolution des origines au XVIIIe siècle*, repr. Paris.

Pfeiffer, S. (1979) *Soziales Recht ist deutsches Recht: Otto von Gierkes Theorie des soziales Recht (Züricher Studien zur Rechtsgeschichte, 2)*, Zurich.

Planitz, H. (1954) *Die deutsche Stadt im Mittelalter*, Graz–Cologne.

Pocock, J.G.A. (1971) *Politics, Language and Time: Essays on Political Thought and History*, New York.

Pocock, J.G.A. (1975) *The Machiavellian Moment: Florentine Political Thought and the Atlantic Republican Tradition*, Princeton, NJ.

Pollard, S. (1981) *Peaceful Conquest: The Industrialization of Europe 1760–1970*, Oxford.

Post, G. (1964) *Studies in Medieval Legal Thought: Public Law and the*

State, 1100–1322, Princeton, NJ.

Quillet, J. (1970) *La philosophie politique de Marsile de Padoue*, Paris.

Reiss, H.S. (1955) *The Political Thought of the German Romantics*, Oxford.

Reiss, H.S. (1970) (introduction to) *Kant's Political Writings*, Cambridge.

Rihs, C. (1971) *La Commune de Paris, sa structure et ses doctrines (1871)*, Geneva.

Robinson, I.S. (1978) *Authority and Resistance in the Investiture Contest: The Polemical Literature of the Late Eleventh Century*, Manchester.

Rörig, F. (1967) *The Medieval Town*, trans. D. Bryant, London.

Roth, F. (1926) 'Clemens Jäger, der Verfasser des Habsburgisch-österreichischen Ehrenbüches', *Zeitschrift des historisches Vereins für Schwaben*, 46, 1–75.

Roth, F. (1927) 'Clemens Jäger, nacheinander Schuster und Ratsherr, Stadtarchivar und Ratsdiener', *Zeitschrift des historisches Vereins für Schwaben*, 47, 1–105.

Rubinstein, N. (1958) 'Political ideas in Sienese art: the frescoes by Ambrogio Lorenzetti and Taddeo di Bartolo', *Journal of the Warburg and Courtauld Institutes*, 21, 179–207.

Rubinstein, N. (1965) 'Marsilius of Padua and Italian political thought in his time', in J. Hale, J. Highfield and B. Smalley (eds) *Europe in the Later Middle Ages*, London, pp. 44–75.

Rubinstein, N. (1968) 'Florentine constitutionalism and Medici ascendancy in the fifteenth century', in N. Rubinstein (ed.) *Florentine Studies*, London, pp. 442–64.

Rule, J. (1981) *The Experience of Labour in Eighteenth-Century Industry*, London.

Rupprich, H. (1935) *Humanismus und Renaissance in den deutschen Städten und an der Universitaten*, Leipzig.

Schlesinger, W. (1975) 'Lord and follower in Germanic institutional history', in F. Cheyette (ed.) *Lordship and Community in Medieval Europe*, New York, pp. 64–99.

Schmitter, P.C. (1974) 'Still the century of corporatism?', *Review of Politics*, 36, 85–131.

Schneider, J. (1954) 'Les villes allemands au moyen âge – Competence administrative et judiciaire de leurs magistrats', in *La Ville*, pt 1 (*Receuils de la société Jean Bodin*, 6), Brussels, pp. 467–516.

Seigel, J.E. (1966) '"Civic humanism" or Ciceronian rhetoric? The culture of Petrarch and Bruni', *Past and Present*, 34, 3–48.

Sewell, W.H. (1980) *Work and Revolution in France: The Language of Labor from the Old Regime to 1848*, Cambridge.

Shklar, J.N. (1969) *Men and Citizens: A Study of Rousseau's Social Theory*, Cambridge.

Shonfield, A. (1965) *Modern Capitalism: The Changing Balance of Public and Private Power*, Oxford.

Skinner, Q. (1969) 'Meaning and understanding in the history of ideas', *History and Theory*, 8, 3–51.

Skinner, Q. (1978) *The Foundations of Modern Political Thought*, 2 vols, Cambridge.

Slicher van Bath, B.H. (1977) 'Agriculture in the vital revolution', *Cambridge Economic History*, vol. 5, pp. 42–133.

Soltau, R. (1931) *French Political Thought in the Nineteenth Century*, London.

Spitz, L. (1963) *The Religious Renaissance of the German Humanists*, Cambridge, Mass.

Sprandel, R. (1968) 'Die Handwerker in den Nordwestdeutschen Städten des Spätmittelalter', *Hansische Geschichtblatter*, 86, 37–62.

Stein, P. (1973) 'Common law', *Dictionary of the History of Ideas*, vol. 2, New York, pp. 691–6.

Stein, P. and Shand, J. (1974) *Legal Values in Western Society*, Edinburgh.

Strakosch, H. (1972) 'Liberalismus und Konservatismus. Gegensatz und Möglichkeit einer Synthese', in G.-K. Kaltenbrunner (ed.) *Rekonstruktion des Konservatismus*, Freiburg, pp. 489–522.

Strauss, G. (1966) *Nuremberg in the Sixteenth Century*, New York.

Stutz, U. (1922) 'Zur Erinnerung von Otto von Gierke, Gedächtnisrede', *Zeitschrift der Savigny-Stiftung für Rechtsgeschichte, germ. Abt.*, 43, pp. vii–lxiii.

Sullivan, J. (1896–7) 'Marsiglio of Padua and William of Ockham', *American Historical Review*, 2, 409–26, 593–611.

Sullivan, J. (1905) 'The manuscripts and date of Marsiglio of Padua's *Defensor Pacis*', *English Historical Review*, 20, 293–307.

Taylor, C. (1975) *Hegel*, Cambridge.

Tellenbach, G. (1940) *Church, State and Christian Society at the Time of the Investiture Contest*, trans. R. Bennett, Oxford.

Thompson, E.P. (1968) *The Making of the English Working Class*, rev. edn, Harmondsworth.

Thrupp, S. (1963) 'The gilds', *Cambridge Economic History*, vol. 3, Cambridge, pp. 230–80.

Tierney, B. (1955) *Foundations of Conciliar Theory: The Contribution of the Medieval Canonists from Gratian to the Great Schism*, Cambridge.

Tierney, B. (1982) *Religion, Law, and the Growth of Constitutional Thought 1150–1650*, Cambridge.

Trinkaus, C. (1970) *In Our Image and Likeness: Humanity and Divinity in Italian Humanist Thought*, 2 vols, London.

Troeltsch, E. (1931) *The Social Teaching of the Christian Churches*, vol. 2, trans. O. Wyon, London.

Tuck, R. (1979) *Natural Rights Theories: Their Origin and Development*, Cambridge.

Ullmann, W. (1955) *The Growth of Papal Government in the Middle Ages. A Study in the Ideological Relation of Clerical to Lay Power*, London.

Ullmann, W. (1961) *Principles of Government and Politics in the Middle Ages*, London.

Ullmann, W. (1967) *The Individual and Society in the Middle Ages*, London.

Unwin, G. (1904) *Industrial Organization in the Sixteenth and Seventeenth Centuries*, Oxford.

Unwin, G. (1938) *The Gilds and Companies of London*, 3rd edn, London.

Vanek, J. (ed.) (1975) *Self-Management: Economic Liberation of Man*, Harmondsworth.

Venturi, F. (1971) *Utopia and Reform in the Enlightenment*, Cambridge.

Vidler, A.R. (1964) *A Century of Social Catholicism, 1820–1920*, London.

Vidler, A.R. (1966) *F.D. Maurice and Company: Nineteenth-Century Studies*, London.

Vidler, A.R. (1974) *The Church in an Age of Revolution: 1789 to the Present Day*, rev. edn, Harmondsworth.

Wagner, D. (1935) 'Coke and the rise of economic liberalism', *Economic History Review*, 6, 30–44.

Waley, D. (1969) *The Italian City-Republics*, London.

Walker, Mack (1971) *German Home Towns: Community, State and General Estate 1648–1871*, Ithaca, NY, and London.

Webb, B. (1930) *The Co-operative Movement in Great Britain*, rev. edn, London.

Webb, S. and B. (1920) *The History of Trade Unionism*, 2nd edn, London.

Weber, M. (1958) *The City*, trans. D. Martindale and G. Neuwirth, New York and London.

Weider, M. (1931) *Das Recht der deutschen Kaufmannsgilden des Mittelalters (Untersuchungen zum deutschen Staats- und Rechtsgeschichte*, 141), Breslau.

Weinstein, D. (1970) *Savonarola and Florence: Prophecy and Patriotism in the Renaissance*, Princeton, NJ.

Werveke, H. van (1963) 'The rise of the towns', *Cambridge Economic History*, vol. 3, Cambridge, pp. 3–41.

Wilda, W. (1831) *Das Gildenwesen im Mittelalter*, Halle (repr. Aalen, 1964).

Wilks, M. (1972) 'Corporation and representation in the *Defensor Pacis*', *Studia Gratiana*, 15, 251–92.

Winters, P.J. (1963) *Die 'Politik' des Johannes Althusius und ihre zeitgenossischen Quellen: zur Grundlegung der politischen Wissenschaft im 16. und im beginnenden 17. Jahrhunderts*, Freiburg-im-Breisgau.

Witt, R. (1969a) 'The "De tyranno" and Coluccio Salutati's view of politics and Roman history', *Nuova Rivista Storica*, 53, 434–74.

Witt, R. (1969b) 'Coluccio Salutati, citizen of Lucca (1370–2)', *Traditio*, 25, 191–216.

Witt, R. (1971) 'The rebirth of the concept of republican liberty in Italy', in A. Molho and J. Tedeschi (eds) *Renaissance Studies in Honor of Hans Baron*, De Kalb, Ill., pp. 175–91.

Woodcock, G. (1963) *Anarchism: A History of Libertarian Ideas and Movements*, London.

Zagorin, P. (1954) *A History of Political Thought in the English Revolution*, London.

BIBLIOGRAPHY (2002)

This is a Bibliography of works referred to in the new Introduction and Conclusion but not included in the main Bibliography.

Andress, David (1999) *French Society in Revolution, 1789-1799*, Manchester, Manchester University Press.

Black, Antony (1988a) *State, Community and Human Desire: a group-centred account of political values*, London, Wheatsheaf.

Black, Antony (1988b) 'The Individual and Society' in *The Cambridge History of Medieval Political Thought*, ed. J.H.Burns, Cambridge University Press, pp. 588-606.

Black, Antony (1990) *Community in Historical Perspective*: a translation of selections from *Das deutsche Genossenschaftsrecht (The German Law of Fellowship)* by Otto von Gierke, transl. Mary Fischer, Cambridge, Cambridge University Press.

Black, Antony (1992) *Political Thought in Europe 1250-1450*, Cambridge, Cambridge University Press.

Black, Antony (1993) 'The Juristic Origins of Social Contact Theory,' *History of Political Thought*, 14, pp. 57-76.

Black, Antony (1996) 'Individuals, Groups and States: a Comparative Overview' in ed. Janet Coleman, *The Individual in Theory & Practice* (in series *Origins of the Modern State*, eds W. Blockmans & J-P. Genet), Oxford, Clarendon Press, pp. 329-40.

Black, Antony (1997a) 'Christianity and Republicanism from St. Cyprian to Rousseau,' *American Political Science Review* 91, pp. 647-56.

Black, Antony (1997b) 'Communal Democracy and its History' in *Political Studies* 45, pp. 5-20.

Black, Antony (2001a) *The History of Islamic Political Thought from the Prophet to the Present*, Edinburgh University Press.

Black, Antony (2001b) 'Concepts of Civil Society in pre-modern Europe,' in Kaviraj and Khilnani 2001: 33-8.

Blickle, Peter (1986) 'Kommunalismus, Parlamentarismus, Republikanismus,' *Historische Zeitschrift* 242, pp. 529-56.

Blickle, Peter (1985/1992) *Communal Reformation: the Quest for Salvation in Sixteenth-century Germany*, trans. Thomas Dunlap, Boston Mass., Humanities Press.

Blickle, Peter (2000) *Kommunalismus. Skizzen einer gesellschaftlichen Organisationsform (Communalism. Sketches of a form of social organisation)*, vol. 1: *Oberdeutschland*, vol. 2: *Europa*, Munich, Oldenbourg.

Blickle, Peter, Thomas O. Hueglin and Dieter Wyduckel, eds (2002), *Subsidiaritaetsprinzip als rechtliches und politisches Ordnundsprinzip* (*Subsidiarity as a Principle of Legal and Political Order*), Berlin, Duncker and Humbolt.

Bossenga, Gail (1991) *The Politics of Privilege: the old regime and revolution in Lille,* Cambridge University Press.

Bossy, John (1985) *Christianity in the West, 1400-1700,* Oxford, Oxford University Press.

Boswell, Jonathan (1990) *Community and the Economy: the theory of public co-operation,* London, Routledge.

Brady, Thomas A. (1998) *Communities, Polities and Reformation in early modern Europe,* Leiden, Brill.

Brett, Annabel (1997) *Liberty, Right and Nature: Individual rights in later scholastic thought,* Cambridge University Press.

Bulliet, Richard W. (1994) *Islam: the View from the Edge,* New York, Columbia University Press.

Calise, Mauro (1994) 'Da sponda a sponda: la metamorfosi corporativa tra Europa e America,' *Annale ISAP,* 2, pp. 1-33.

Calise, Mauro (2002) 'Corporate Authority in a long-term comparative perspective,' in Blickle et al., eds (2002).

Chaplin, Jonathan (1993) 'Subsidiarity and Sphere Sovereignty: Catholic and Reformed Conceptions of the Role of the State,' in F. McHugh and S.M. Natale, eds, *Unfinished Agenda: Catholic Social Teaching Revisited,* Lanham, NY.

Chaplin, Jonathan (1995) 'Dooyeweerd's Notion of Societal Structural Principles,' *Philosophia Reformata* 60-1, pp. 16-36.

Dooyeweerd, Herman (1997) *Essays in Legal, Social and Political Philosophy,* ed. Alan Cameron, Lewiston-Lampeter, Edwin Meller Press.

Epstein, S.R. (2000) *Freedom and Growth: the Rise of States and Markets in Europe 1300-1750,* London, Routledge.

Etzioni, Amitai (1995) *The Spirit of Community: rights, responsibilities and the communitarian agenda,* London, Fontana.

Fiske, John (1899) *The Dutch and Quaker Colonies in America,* Boston, Houghton, Mifflin.

Friedeburg, Robert von (2001) review of Blickle (2000), *English Historical Review* 116, pp. 141-3.

Genicot, Leopold (1990) *Rural Communities in the Medieval West,* Baltimore MD, Johns Hopkins University Press.

Hamilton-Bleakley, H.M. (2002) 'Rules, Righteousness, Character and Freedom: right reason in late medieval ethical thought,' Diss. University of Cambridge.

Hirst, Paul (1994) *Associative Democracy: new forms of economic and social governance,* Cambridge, Polity.

Hayek, F.A. (1982) *Law, Legislation and Liberty,* 3 vols in 1, London, Routledge and Kegan Paul.

Inalcik, Halil (1973) *The Ottoman Empire: the Classical Age 1300-1600,* London, Weidenfeld and Nicolson.

Kaviraj, Sudipta and Khilnani, Sunil, eds (2001) *Civil Society: History and Possibilities*, Cambridge, Cambridge University Press.

Lustig, R. Jeffrey (1982) *Corporate Liberalism: the Origins of Modern American Political Theory, 1890-1920*, Berkeley CA, University of California Press.

Macmillan, Harold (1938/1966) *The Middle Way*, Basingstoke, Macmillan.

Munro, John D. (1999) 'The Symbiosis of Towns and Textiles: Urban Institutions and the Changing Fortunes of Cloth Manufacturing in the Low Countries and England, 1280-1570' in *Journal of Early Modern History: Contacts, Comparisons, Contrasts* 3, pp. 1-74.

Najemy, John (1982) *Corporatism and Consensus in Florentine Electoral Politics, 1280-1400*, Chapel Hill NC, University of North Carolina Press.

Nederman, Cary J. (1992) 'Freedom, Community and Function: Communitarian Lessons of Medieval Political Theory,' *American Political Science Review*, 86, pp. 977-86.

Nisbet, Robert (1953) *The Quest for Community*, Oxford University Press (reissued, Institute for Contemporary Studies, 1990).

Norr, K. and Oppermann, T. eds (1997) *Subsidiaritaet: Idee und Wirchlichkeit. Zur Reichweite eines Prinzips in Deutschland und Europa (Subsidiarity: Idea and Reality)*, Tuebingen, J.C.B. Moehr.

Oexle, Otto Gerhard (1988) 'Otto von Gierkes "Rechtsgeschichte der deutschen Genossenschaft"', in N. Hammerstein, ed., *Deutsche Geschichtswissenschaft um 1900*, Steiner, pp. 193-217.

Olson, Mancur (1982) *The Rise and Decline of Nations: Economic Growth, Stagflation and Social Rigidities*, New Haven, CT, Yale University Press.

Prodi, Paolo (1992) *Il Sacramento del Potere: il giuramento politico nella storia constituzionale dell' Occidente (The Sacrament of Power: the political oath in the constitutional history of the West)*, Bologna, Il Mulino.

Putnam, Robert D. (2000) *Bowling Alone: the Collapse and Revival of American Community*, London, Simon and Schuster.

Reicher, Steve and Hopkins, Nick (2001) *Self and Nation*, London, Sage.

Revel, Jacques (1987) 'Les corps et communautes' in Keith Michael Baker, ed. *The French Revolution and the Creation of Modern Political Culture*, vol. i: *The Political Culture of the Old Regime*, Oxford, Pergamon.

Reynolds, Susan (1994) *Fiefs and Vassals: the medieval evidence reinterpreted*, Oxford, Clarendon Press.

Sandel, Michael (1998) *Liberalism and the Limits of Justice*, 2nd edn Cambridge University Press.

Schilling, Heinz (1988) 'Gab es im spaeten Mittelalter und zu Beginn der Neuzeit in Deutschland einen staedtischen "Republikanismus"? (Was there a civic 'republicanism' in Germany in the late Middle Ages and the beginning of the modern period?') in H.G.Koenigsberger, ed., *Republiken und Republikanismus im Europa der Fruehen Neuzeit*, Munich, Olderbourg, pp. 101-45.

Schilling, Heinz (1992) *Religion, Political Culture and the Emergence of Early Modern Society: Essays in German and Dutch History*, Leiden, Brill.

Scott, Tom (1986) *Freiburg and the Breisgau: town-country relations in the age of the Reformation and the Peasants' War*, Oxford, The Clarendon Press.

Scribner, R.W. (1994) 'Communalism: universal category or ideological construct? A debate in the historiography of early modern Germany and Switzerland,' *Historical Journal*, 37, pp. 199-207.

Skillen, James W. and McCarthy, Rockne M., eds (1991) *Political Order and the Plural Structure of Society*, Atlanta GA, Scholars Press.

Skinner, Quentin (1998) *Liberty Before Liberalism*, Cambridge, Cambridge University Press.

Tierney, Brian (1997) *The Idea of Natural Rights: Studies on Natural Rights, Natural Law and Church Law 1150-1625*, Atlanta GA, Scholars Press.

Toennies, Ferdinand (1887/2001) *Community and Civil Society (Gemeinschaft und Gesellschaft)*, ed. Jose Harris, trans. Jose Harris and Margaret Hollis, Cambridge University Press.

Tracy, James D. (forthcoming) 'On the Dual Origins of Long-term Debt in Medieval Europe' in Karel Davids and Marc Boone, eds *The Market for Urben Renten, 1450-1750*.

Viroli, M. (1992) *From Politics to Reason of State: the acquisition and transformation of politics 1250-1600*, Cambridge University Press.

Weber, Max (1904-5/1930) *The Protestant Ethic and the Spirit of Capitalism*, trans. Talcott Parsons, London, Allen and Unwin.

Other Recent Works

On Medieval Communities in General:

Bader, Karl S. and Dilcher, Gerhard (1999) *Deutsche Rechtsgeschichte: Land und Stadt—Buerger und Bauer im Alten Europa (The History of German Law: Town and Country—Burghers and Peasants in Early Europe)*, Berlin, Springer.

Blickle, Peter, ed. (1997) *Resistance, Representation and Community*, Oxford, Clarendon Press.

Reynolds, Susan (1984) *Kingdoms and Communities in Western Europe, 900-1300*, Oxford, Clarendon Press.

On the Legal Personality of the Association (Universitas):

Reynolds, Susan (1995), 'The History of the Idea of incorporation or legal personality: a case of fallacious terminology,' in Susan Reynolds, *Ideas and Solidarities of the Medieval Laity*, Ashgate.

On Guilds:

Oexle, Otto Gerhard (1982) 'Die mittelalterliche Zunft als Forschungsproblem (The Medieval Guild as a Research Problem),' *Blaetter fuer deutsche Landesgeschichte* 118, pp. 1-44.

Oexle, Otto Gerhard (1985a) 'Conjuratio und Gilden im fruehen Mittelalter. Ein Beitrag zum Problem der sozialgeschichtlichen Kontinuitaet zwischen Antike und Mittelalter (Oath-taking and Gilds in the early Middle Ages. An essay on the problem of continuity in social history between antiquity and the Middle Ages),' in B.Schwinekoeper, ed., *Gilden und Zuenfte*, Sigmaringen, Thorbeke.

Oexle, Otto Gerhard (1985b) 'Gruppenbildung und Gruppenverhalten bei Menschen und Tieren. Beobachtungen zur Geschichte der mittelalterlichen Gilden (Group formation and group behaviour in humans and animals. Observations on the history of medieval guilds),' *Saeculum 36*.

Epstein, S.R. (1991) *Wage Labourers and Guilds in Medieval Europe*, Chapel Hill NC, University of North Carolina Press.

Prak, Maarten (1996) 'Individual, Corporation and Society: the rhetoric of Dutch guilds (18th century),' in Marc Boone and Maarten Prak, eds, *Individual, corporate and judicial status in European cities (late middle ages and early modern period)*, Ghent, Garant, pp. 255-79.

Schulz, Knut (1986), *Gesellen und Gesellen-Verbaende am Oberrhein (Journeymen and their associations on the upper Rhine)*, Sigmaringen, Thorbeke.

On Cities:

Dilcher, Gerhard (1996) *Buergerrecht und Stadtverfassung im europaeischen Mittelalter (Civic rights and city constitutions in medieval Europe)*, Cologne, Boehlau Verlag.

Jones, Philip James (1997) *The Italian City-State: from Commune to Signoria*, Oxford, Clarendon Press.

Meier, Ulrich (1994) *Mensch und Buerger: Die Stadt im Denken spaetmittelalterliche Theologen, Philosophen und Juristen (Man and Citizen: the City in the Thought of late-medieval theologians, philosophers and jurists)*, Munich, Oldenbourg.

On Medieval Political Thought:

Berman, Harold J. (1983) *Law and Revolution: the Formation of the Western Legal Tradition*, Cambridge Mass., Harvard University Press.

Canning, Joseph (1994), *The Political Thought of Baldus de Ubaldis*, Cambridge University Press.

Coleman, Janet (2000) *A History of Political Thought from the Middle Ages to the Renaissance*, Oxford, Blackwell.

Kempshall, M.S. (1999) *The Common Good in Late Medieval Political Thought*, Oxford, The Clarendon Press.

On Althusius:

Hueglin, Thomas O. (1999) *Early Modern Concepts for a Late Modern World: Althusius on Community and Federalism*, Waterloo, Ontario, Wilfrid Laurier University Press.

On Otto von Gierke:

Dilcher, Gerhard (1974-5) 'Genossenschaftstheorie und Sozialrecht: ein "Juristensozialismus" Otto v. Gierkes? (Corporation theory and social justice: was Otto von Gierke a "juristic socialist"?)' *Quaderni fiorentini per la storia del pensiero giuridico moderno*, 3-4, pp. 319-65.

John, Michael (1989) *Politics and Law in Nineteenth-century Germany: the Origins of the Civil Code*, Oxford University Press.

On Associations Today:

Gutmann, Amy (1998) *Freedom of Association*, Princeton University Press.

Hirst, Paul Q., ed. (1989) *The Pluralist Theory of the State: selected writings of G.D.H. Cole, J.N. Figgis, and H.J. Laski*, London, Routledge.

Stapleton, Julia, ed. (1995) *Group Rights: Perspectives since 1900*, Bristol, Thoemmes Press.

NAME INDEX

Figures in italic indicate key entries.

SUBJECT INDEX

Lightning Source UK Ltd.
Milton Keynes UK
UKOW04f0157171214

243266UK00002B/171/P